Managing Knowledge

CRITICAL PERSPECTIVES ON WORK AND ORGANISATIONS

Series editors:

David Knights, Department of Management, University of Keele
Paul Thompson, Department of Business Studies, University of Edinburgh
Chris Smith, School of Management, Royal Holloway, University of London
Hugh Willmott, Manchester School of Management, UMIST

This series offers a range of titles examining the broad areas of work and organisation within a national and global arena. Each book in the series is written by leading experts and covers a topic chosen to appeal to students and academics. Originating out of the International Labour Process Conference, the series will be informative, topical and leading edge.

Published:

Alan Felstead and Nick Jewson *Global Trends in Flexible Labour*

Paul Thompson and Chris Warhurst *Workplaces of the Future*

Macmillan Critical Perspectives on Work and Organisations Series
Series Standing Order ISBN 0-333-73535-8
(outside North America only)

You can receive future titles in this series as they are published by placing a standing order. Please contact your bookseller or, in case of difficulty, write to us at the address below with your name and address, the title of the series and the ISBN quoted above.

Customer Services Department, Macmillan Distribution Ltd
Houndmills, Basingstoke, Hampshire RG21 6XS, England

Managing Knowledge

Critical Investigations of Work and Learning

Edited by
Craig Prichard, Richard Hull, Mike Chumer and Hugh Willmott

First published 2000 by
MACMILLAN PRESS LTD
Houndmills, Basingstoke, Hampshire RG21 6XS
and London
Companies and representatives throughout the world

ISBN 0–333–92156–9 hardback
ISBN 0–333–92157–7 paperback

A catalogue record for this book is available from the British Library.

This book is printed on paper suitable for recycling and
made from fully managed and sustained forest sources.

10	9	8	7	6	5	4	3	2	1
09	08	07	06	05	04	03	02	01	00

Typeset by Ian Kingston Editorial Services, Nottingham, UK
Printed & bound in Great Britain by Creative Print and Design (Wales)

Published in the United States of America by
ST. MARTIN'S PRESS, INC.,
Scholarly and Reference Division,
175 Fifth Avenue, New York, N.Y. 10010

ISBN 0–312–23363–9

Contents

Preface

This book is inevitably the work of networks. To use the language of the Actor-Network theorists for a moment, the book is the work of some human and some non-human networks. It owes much to that irrepressible piece of software called TCP/IP, to telephone cables and the speed at which signals traverse this 'net'-work. Three months of intensive and virtually faultless contact between ourselves and our contributors via the Internet proves for us just how powerful this network has become in moving academic work onto the printed page. But, as many of the contributors to this volume argue, software, cable and signals do not make a network. This collection of essays on knowledge and knowing at work owes much much more to human networks: relationships built on the sometimes delicate, sometimes robust practices of debate and discussion between colleagues who engage in critical research and reflection on the constantly changing character of work and organizations. This network brings together researchers, authors, conference organizers, universities and the book's publisher, Macmillan. We would like to thank all those who make up this complex for their efforts in bringing this collection together.

Acknowledgements

Special thanks must go to the editors of the Critical Perspectives on Work and Organization series, David Knights, Chris Smith, Paul Thompson and Hugh Willmott. Their particular network links also to a series of conferences where six of the chapters in this collection were initially presented: the first Critical Management Studies Conference (Manchester, July, 1999), the annual International Labour Process Conference and the Critical Perspectives on Accounting Conference (New York, April, 1999). Our thanks to the organizers of these events. The volume's six other chapters are the work of linkages between colleagues in North America, Britain and New Zealand. In New Zealand, thanks must be extended to Deborah Jones at Victoria University in Wellington for organizing a one-day symposium in June 1999 on knowledge work and workers, where Roy Jacques, Deborah and Craig Prichard presented their work.

Thanks must also be passed to Richard Hull and his family. The Hulls provided great food, numerous pots of coffee and the kitchen of their home in Pecket Well, West Yorkshire (UK) for the crucial one-day editorial get-together in July 1999. And finally thanks to you, the reader for 'joining' us in this network. We're sure that by opening the covers of this book you will find innovative investigations and challenging discussion of 'knowledge' in work organizations – enjoy!

Notes on the Contributors

LYNNE BAXTER is a lecturer in Operations Management at Heriot-Watt University, Edinburgh, UK. She obtained an MA in Sociology from the University of Edinburgh and a PhD from Manchester Business School. Her dissertation subject area was on power relations and the implementation of technical change. She has been an investigator on two EPSRC research projects, the first investigating 'Barriers to Co-operative Supply Relationships', and the second into the 'Estimation of Software Development Time'. Publications from this research have appeared, for example, in *IEEE Transactions in Engineering Management*. Her current research interests include software development and business 'improvement'.

GEORGE CALLAGHAN is a social science Staff Tutor with the Open University. He received his PhD in labour market flexibility from the University of the West of England in 1996. His current research interests are in work organisation and the labour process, with particular reference to new forms of service sector work.

MIKE CHUMER is the Multi-Media Librarian responsible for Media and Digital Services in the John Cotton Dana Library at Rutgers University. He is also adjunct faculty for the School of Communication, Information, and Library Studies at Rutgers, where he teaches the graduate level Management Information Systems (MIS) and Database Management Systems (DBMS) courses. Mike did his undergraduate work at the United States Naval Academy, completing his Graduate work at both the Georgia Institute of Technology (Masters level) and most recently Rutgers University (PhD level). He has been in the computer technology field since 1967, having held management positions as an officer in the United States Marine Corps and as a manager within AT&T LongLines. He has lectured on Information Technology diffusion and use for the American Management Association as well as at management-oriented conferences since 1984. His present research interests include critical research on the diffusion and effectiveness of instructional information technologies at the organisational, managerial, and individual levels.

NIALL HAYES is a Lecturer in Information Management at the Management School, Lancaster University, UK. Prior to his appointment at the Management School, he was a lecturer in Business Information Systems at the University of Manchester, UK. His research interests centre on the relationship between information systems and social and organisational change. He is particularly interested in the areas of computer-supported cooperative work, knowledge working and improvization. His publications include 'Work-arounds and Boundary Crossing in a High Tech Optronics Company: The Role of Co-operative Work-flow Technologies' (forthcoming in the *Journal of Computer Supported Co-operative Work*).

DONALD HISLOP is currently working as a lecturer at Sheffield Business School's Change Management Research Centre. Prior to this he worked at Warwick Business School as a senior research fellow on a research project looking at networking and knowledge issues involved in the implementation of IT-based process innovations. Donald's PhD, on the post-Cold War transformations of the UK's military industrial base, was completed at Edinburgh University.

RICHARD HULL is Lecturer in Sociology with the Department of Human Sciences and the Centre for Research on Culture, Innovation, and Technology, both at Brunel University. He was previously Research Fellow in the Centre for Research on Innovation and Competition, Manchester, and the Centre for Research on Organisations, Management and Technical Change, Manchester School of Management, UMIST. He has conducted extensive research on the history of computing, the use of IT in organisations, and knowledge management. His current research areas are health innovations, the conduct of expert labour, and more broadly in the social theory and philosophy underpinning social studies of science and technology. He is co-editor of the forthcoming collection *Knowledge and Innovation in the New Service Economy* (Edward Elgar), and is on the Editorial Board of *New Reviews in Information Systems Research*. Recent articles have appeared in *Organisation; Economy & Society; Research Policy; Journal of Technology Transfer; Accounting, Management & Information Technologies; Ergonomics;* and *New Technology, Work & Employment*.

ROY JACQUES received his MBA (1983) and PhD (1992) degrees from the University of Massachusetts, Amherst, and has taught in the USA and New Zealand. He is presently an associate professor at the California School of Professional Psychology, Los Angeles in the Organisational Psychology doctoral. He is a past chair of the Gender and Diversity division of the Academy of Management. His research interests centre on the relationship between social identities of marginality and dominance and the changing relationships structuring so-called 'post-industrial' work realities.

DEBORAH JONES is a Senior Lecturer in Organisational Behaviour at Victoria University of Wellington. Her current passions focus on working with both feminist post-structuralist theory (often seen as excessively esoteric) with action/research (often seen as inadequately theoretical). Current research interests include: self-managing teams; issues of identity – ethnic, gender, national – in organisations; and discourses of competence. Her academic background includes a masters degree in linguistics and literature, and a doctorate in management studies. She has dropped in and out of academic life several times, and been involved in many kinds of teaching, writing and feminist activism.

DOROTHY LANDER has, since 1998, been faculty advisor to graduate students in a self-directed, practice-based distance learning program leading to a Master in Adult Education at St Francis Xavier University, Nova Scotia, Canada. *Valuing embodied consumers who can know and tell* is the unifying theme throughout her career as manager of housing and food service at St Francis Xavier (1976–1994), as a doctoral researcher at University of Nottingham (1997), and in her current research, a feminist genealogy of moral learning that focuses on the moral regulation of drinking practices re-membered across gender and generation. A description of her career may be found in Lander, D. (1999) Telling Transgression: a Bridge Between Contract and Carnival in Making Student Services Policy, *Journal of Education Policy*, 14: 6.

DARCY LEFEVRE is currently a graduate student at the University of Oklahoma where she is working on a joint MLIS/MA (Master of Library and Information Studies/Master of Arts in History of Science) program. She is a graduate assistant to the History of Science Society bibliographer.

CLAIRE MCINERNEY is an assistant professor in the School of Library and Information Studies at the University of Oklahoma. Her research is in the areas of information and knowledge management, virtual organisations, and information ethics. The book *Providing Information to the Virtual Office* is her most recent publication.

ALAN MCKINLAY has written extensively on the social history of craft labour and the application of the work of Michel Foucault to contemporary labour processes. He is currently researching work organisation in the television industry and the rebuilding of trade unionism in microelectronics.

SUE NEWELL is Professor of Innovation and Organisational Analysis at Nottingham Business School, Nottingham Trent University. She was previously a senior lecturer at Warwick Business School and a lecturer at Aston, Birmingham and Portsmouth Universities. Her main research interest centres on understanding innovation processes, focusing on the diffusion, design and appropriation of complex information and communication technologies. She has obtained funding from both the ESRC and the EPSRC for pursuing this research interest and the current chapter is based on research funded by the ESRC.

CRAIG PRICHARD recently returned to Aotearoa/New Zealand after nine years in the UK. While in Britain he held research and teaching posts at the University

of Central Lancashire, University of Nottingham and in the School of Manage-
ment at Lincoln. He now teaches communication papers in the Department of
Human Resource Management on Massey University's Turitea Campus in
Palmerston North. He has contributed chapters to other essay collections,
including *The Body and Organisation* (eds. Hassard, Holliday and Willmott) and
Men as Managers, Managers as Men (eds. Collinson and Hearn), and his own book
Making Managers in Colleges and Universities (Open University Press), based
around PhD research conducted in Britain from 1993–1997, was recently
published. A key theme in his research has been the problematics surrounding
the embodiment of performative, gendered and managerial dispositions in
professional and service work organisations.

MIRIAM SALZER-MÖRLING is Assistant Professor in the School of Business at
Stockholm University. She received her PhD in Business Administration from
Linköping University in 1994, based on a study of sense-making across borders.
Her current research centres on story-telling, artefacts, knowledge, and culture
as control in the shaping of organisational life.

HARRY SCARBROUGH is Professor of Organizational Analysis at the University of Leicester Management Centre. Harry has researched and published
extensively on knowledge and technology issues, including *The Management of
Expertise* (Macmillan, 1996) and papers in *Organization Studies* and the *Journal of
Management Studies*. His current research explores the role of social networks in
shaping innovation processes.

JACKY SWAN is a Reader in Organisational Behaviour at Warwick Business
School, University of Warwick. She completed her PhD at the University of Wales,
Cardiff. Her current research interests are in technological innovation and innovation diffusion. She is a founding member of IKON – the Innovation, Knowledge
and Organisational Networking Research Unit. Her research projects have focused
on the roles of professional associations and IT suppliers in technology diffusion
across Europe; the processes of knowledge articulation that link inter-firm diffusion
and intra-firm implementation of innovation; and networking and knowledge
creation in research teams. A new project will examine knowledge management in
project-based environments. She has published widely, including recent articles in
Organisation and *Organisation Studies*.

PAUL THOMPSON is Professor of Organisational Analysis in the Department
of Human Resource Management at the University of Strathclyde. He was
previously Professor of Management in the Department of Business Studies,
University of Edinburgh. His research and publishing interests focus on organisational analysis, the labour process and workplace innovation. Over the past
few years he has been leading an ESRC-funded project on the Manufacturing of
Workplace Innovation in the Scottish Spirits industry. Recent published work

includes *Workplaces of the Future* (edited with Chris Warhurst, Macmillan, 1998) and *Organisational Misbehaviour* (Sage, 1999, with Stephen Ackroyd). He is a co-organiser of the International Labour Process Conference and Editor for the Macmillan Series 'Management, Work and Organisations' and 'Critical Perspectives on Work and Organisations'. When not being an academic, he is also Editor of *Renewal: A Journal of New Labour Politics*.

GEOFF WALSHAM is a Research Professor of Management Studies at the Judge Institute of Management Studies, Cambridge University, UK. His teaching and research are centred on the development, management and use of computer-based information systems, and the relationship of information and communication technologies to stability and change in organisations and societies. He is particularly interested in the human consequences of computerisation in a global context, including both industrialised and developing countries. His publications include *Interpreting Information Systems in Organisations* (Wiley, 1993) and *Information Technology and Changes in Organisational Work* (edited with Orlikowski, Jones, and DeGross, Chapman & Hall, 1996).

CHRIS WARHURST lectures at the University of Strathclyde, Glasgow. His teaching, wring and research focuses on management and labour issues in the international economy, work organisation, and socialist industry. Articles have appeared in the USA, the Middle East, and Western and Eastern Europe. He has co-organised a number of the Annual International Labour Process Conferences. He is the author of *Between Market, State and Kibbutz* (Mansell, 1999)and the co-editor of *Workplaces of the Future* (Macmillan, 1998), *The Management and Organisation of Firms in the Global Context* (HAS, 1999) and *A Different Future: The Modernisers' Guide to Scotland* (Big Issue, 1999). His current interests are 'aesthetic labour'; knowledge and work; and the transfer of 'soft technologies' to host country indigenous firms via the FDI of MNCs.

HUGH WILLMOTT is Professor of Organisational Analysis in the Manchester School of Management. He is currently working on a number of projects whose common theme is the changing organisation and management of work, including projects in the ESRC Virtual Society and Future of Work programmes and an ICAEW funded study of strategic reorientation. His most recent books include *Skill and Consent* (Routledge, 1992, co-edited), *Critical Management Studies* (Sage, co-authored), *Making Quality Critical* (Routledge, 1995, co-edited) and *Managing Change, Changing Managers* (CIMA, 1995, co-authored). *Making Sense of Management: A Critical Introduction* (Sage, co-authored) was published in 1996. *Management Lives* (Sage, co-authored), *The Re-engineering Revolution* (Sage, co-edited) and *The Body and Organisations* (Sage, co-edited) are all appearing in 1999. Hugh has served on the editorial boards of a number of journals, including *Administrative Science Quarterly; Organisation; Organisation Studies* and *Accounting, Organisations and Society*.

ALI YAHKLEF received his PhD in organisation theory from the School of Business, Stockholm University, Sweden, where he now works as lecturer in management and marketing. His main research areas include knowledge formation in organisation, emerging forms of organisation, IT-based entrepreneurship and post-industrial marketing. His recent publications include 'IT Outsourcing and the Construction of Accountable Worlds', in *Organisation* (1998) and 'Mapping the Subject in Advertising', *Consumption, Market and Culture*, 3: 2 (1999).

Introduction: Situating Discussions About 'Knowledge'

Mike Chumer, Richard Hull and Craig Prichard

The last decades of the 20th century saw explosive growth in discussions about knowledge – knowledge work, knowledge management, knowledge resources, knowledge-based firms and organisations, knowledge-based economic growth, and the knowledge economy. These discussions took various forms, ranging from journalistic chat, consultants' rhetoric and economic statistics, through to national and supra-national policy prescriptions. In this book we seek to maintain some 'critical distance' (Mingers, 2000) from these discussions in order to describe in more precise detail their complex relations with the real worlds of work and organisations. On the one hand, it is clear that these discussions partly reflect some real and significant changes, such as the diffusion of new Information and Communications Technologies (ICTs) and the increasing financial importance of intellectual property rights. On the other hand, it is also the case that these discussions build upon and have been enabled by particular trends in the social sciences which have complex and sometimes contradictory political and ethical underpinnings (Hull, 2000). The contributors to this volume adopt varying forms of critical perspective on the knowledge discussions and their effects upon work and organisations, offering detailed new insights informed by their empirical and theoretical work.

In this Introduction we outline some of the background to the emergence of the 'knowledge discussions' in a variety of disciplines, and make some initial suggestions for establishing 'critical distance'. To give just a brief example, consider the field of knowledge management. Is this *really* a hot topic? A simple AltaVista Internet search in late 1999 using the term 'knowledge management' resulted in no less than 54,000 Web pages, an astonishing growth given that the term probably first appeared in 1994 (Hedlund, 1994; Bohn, 1994) and became popularised in 1996[1] following the work of Leonard-Barton (1995). Many of these Web pages are sophisticated marketing tools. The aim of these pages is to get readers close, but not too close, to the 'secrets' that consultants and the new

---

1 See, for instance, *The Economist*, 13 January, 1996, pp. 67–8. Later in this year The Economist Intelligence Unit, in collaboration with the IBM Consulting Group, published an influential report: *The Learning Organisation: Managing Knowledge for Business Success.*

raft of 'guru'/experts can offer for managing various forms of knowledge. A prominent item on this massive Web-generated list reads:

> What is Knowledge Management? by Karl Erik Sveiby. This online course by Karl Erik Sveiby, one of the founders of Knowledge Management, teaches the basics of know-ledge management in 30 easy and... (http://knowledgecreators.com/km/kes/kes1.htm, emphasis added).

Digging deeper, Sveiby's page calls out: 'Quote me'. So we do:

> Trust is the bandwidth of communication.
>
> The difference between a company's market value and book value can be directly attributed to its intangible assets.
>
> Knowledge grows when shared and grows when used; unused knowledge deteriorates.
>
> Tapping into customer and employee knowledge is one of the first steps to building a more successful organization.

Inevitably, perhaps, this Web page concludes with the promise that 'I will explain why in the next 30 minutes...'. Sveiby is one of many. The after-guard includes management 'pop stars' like Peter Drucker and Peter Senge. They have turned toward, and turned up, the 'heat' around 'knowledge'. In one article Drucker states, 'Knowledge constantly makes itself obsolete, with the result that today's advanced knowledge is tomorrow's ignorance' (Drucker *et al.*, 1997, p. 22). He suggests that as we enter the new millennium knowledge management should be the primary organizational focus. Senge, in a complimentary fashion, states that,

> Increasingly, successful organizations are building competitive advantage through less controlling and more learning – that is, through continually creating and sharing new knowledge (Drucker *et al.*, 1997, pp. 31–2).

Collectively, these popularizers have suggested a retooling of work, and indeed all aspects of existence, around 'knowledge'. Displaced are the musings over re-engineering, total quality and downsizing. It is as if the Word is again coming down from on high that in order to compete in today's world organizations must now learn how to idenitify, manage and apply knowledge in all its diverse forms.

And yet there is something terribly obvious and familiar about this. Isn't the management - identification, codification and application – of knowledge a defining feature of Taylorism? The quest to harness, monopolize and system-atize knowledge is hardly a novel application and pre-occupation of manage-ment. What is more significant about these snippets from the Web is firstly, as we have already suggested, that they all seek to establish new forms of authority and expertise about knowledge without any reflection on the relationships between power and knowledge. Secondly, they are equally unreflective about the questions of 'Why knowledge?' and 'Why now?'.

Why Knowledge? And Why Now?

If we look beyond the 'heat' and the 'hype' around 'knowledge', we discover a jumbled picture emerging in the broad field of management research and consultancy. So before we can address the questions, 'Why knowledge?' and 'Why now?', some sense needs to be made of this disjointed field. Two major influences could be said to be driving this activity around 'knowledge' in mainstream management: the word of the expert/consultant, and the research emerging and reproduced from the established academic disciplines. Within each the locus of advice, expertise and questioning underlying the term 'knowledge' produces different 'maps', which makes traversing the geography contentious at best. Let us give some examples of the malleable terrain being sketched.

Advice from Academia: Information and Library Science

In the information and library sciences the seminal work in the field concentrated on the retrieval of information. Since the early Cranfield Studies (Cleverdon, 1961, 1967), much research has been conducted on indexing and classifying information and knowledge in order to successfully retrieve objects in the form of books, journal articles and other textual materials (Brookes, 1975; Goffman and Newell, 1966; Ingwersen, 1992; Lancaster, 1969; Salton, 1968; Salton and Lesk, 1968; Saracevic *et al.*, 1968; Sparck-Jones, 1977). These works and many others produced the technology underlying the modern search engines used on the Internet. Today, with an the exponential growth in knowledge contained in electronic form, the TREC (text retrieval and evaluation conference) studies are providing insights into how to search huge volumes of text using many query constructs, including natural language queries (Harman, 1994; Harman, 1997). The present interest in forms of rich text, such as video, audio, graphics and animation, each representing digital objects housed in virtual digital libraries, provides yet another dimension of knowledge and information retrieval research (Arms *et al.*, 1997; Benton Foundation, 1997; Fox and Marchionini, 1998; Lagoze *et al.*, 1998; Levy and Marshall, 1995). Meta-data as entry points for these new forms of textual material are issues that research libraries, as well as libraries in general, are wrestling with as they attempt to identify, classify and store knowledge in addition to constructing robust information infrastructures which permit universal access and retrieval (Chilvers and Feather, 1998; Milstead and Feldman, 1999; Weibel *et al.*, 1998). The major assumption of research in the Information/Library Science field is, however, that knowledge is something that can be objectified, catalogued, classified, and therefore selectively retrieved (surrogates for objects normally form the basis of retrieval for the entire object).

Computer Science and Information Systems

This assumption, that knowledge is an object and can be codified and distributed, underpins the linked fields of computer science and information systems[2]. These fields form one of the crucial components of 'knowledge management'. Most advisors assert that managing 'knowledge' *is not* (simply) about computer infrastructures (Davenport and Prusak, 1998; Coleman, 1999; Liebowitz, 1999). Nevertheless the collaborative and information retrieval potential of Internet technologies particularly (email, groupware, discussion spaces, intranets) is at the core of many organizational initiatives labelled 'knowledge management' (see Chapters 4–7 in this volume). For the firm, the 'promise' of such technologies is twofold. There is the promise of enhancing innovation and of reducing the costs of coordination. In relation to the latter a report by consultants KPMG asserts that such technologies 'embody the dream that when one person learns something, everybody else in the company knows it' (KPMG, 1999). People's 'learning' here is assumed to be able to contribute directly or indirectly to the formation of economic value. As we note below, this assumption – underpinned by economic theories – can be easily 'over-hyped'. In terms of the technologies, however, their ability to deliver on this promise, to 'do the dream', is highly problematic. This issue is at the core of at least five of the case studies in this volume (Chapters 2–7). These chapters expose the precarious character of this 'promise', and illustrate in unambiguous ways what Davenport and Prusak (1998, p. 29) identify as the 'reality of knowledge politics': 'If knowledge is power, then the owners of knowledge have power that may dissipate if other people come to know what they know'[3].

Organizational Learning

'Learning' and 'innovation' mark a second route that writers take across this uneven terrain of 'knowledge'. Rather than investigate or recommend computer technologies and infrastructures, consultants and academics here address the social technologies and infrastructures of individuals, groups and

2   There have, however, been some significant tendencies within computer science and information systems development which make quite different assumptions about the characteristics of knowledge. These tendencies can be seen especially within the sub-disciplines of Human–Computer Interaction, Computer-Supported Co-operative Work and Soft Systems development methodologies (Hull, 1997).

3   Correction: this book discusses an example of tacit knowledge transfer between groups of tunnelling engineers in Boston, USA, and Wellington, New Zealand (Davenport and Prusak, 1998, pp. 99–100). Davenport and Prusak's anonymous firm is said to have been involved in a tunnel that linked two islands. Unfortunately this is incorrect. There is no tunneling project in New Zealand which links two islands, be they the main two islands or any others.

organizations (see, for example, Blackler, 1995; Allee, 1997; Choo, 1998; Senge, 1990 and earlier work by Argyris and Schön 1974; Argyris, 1990; Schön, 1983). Drawing on a range of concepts and frameworks, this field of work is also premised on the promise of improving the depth, spread and speed by which employees acquire and apply commercially valuable knowledge. For example, in both the consultant and academic literatures Nonaka and Takeuchi's (1995) work *The Knowledge Creating Company* is a key resource here. These authors emphasis the social, tacit and practical character of learning. They suggest various ways to enable this process in the service of product and service innovation. The essence of these are rich social interactions which they argue enable the conversion of dynamic context-specific tacit knowing into explicit distributable knowledge. As might be expected, this text is also a key resource for much of the activity in strategic management circles around 'knowledge'.

Strategic Management

The various works of Nonaka (1991, 1994) were in essence very poorly grounded in the literature on 'theories of the firm' – that is, the literature from economics and strategic management which addresses questions such as why firms exist at all, how they decide which activities to pursue within the firm and which to buy in, and how they gain and maintain competitive advantage. This literature had, however, rarely addressed questions of knowledge and the firm in such a specific manner, and Nonaka's works clearly provoked a challenge. Two significant responses were the special issue of *Strategic Management Journal* (Volume 17, Winter 1996), and the special issue of *Organization Science* (Volume 7, No. 5, 1996). In each case there is a range of responses to the challenge to integrate theories of knowledge with theories of the firm. Spender (1996), for instance, formulates what has become a fairly standard response: a 'knowledge-based theory of the firm' can yield new insights beyond those 'neo-classical' theories which focused on the balance (the 'production function') between capital and labour; and also beyond the more recent 'resource-based' theories which focused on 'capabilities' and 'core competencies'. This 'knowledge-based' theory emphasizes the dynamic aspects of the firm, in contrast to the neo-classical emphasis on static equilibrium, and it focuses on those knowledge-based processes involved in the evolution and stabilisation of new activities within the firm. An approach more informed by the sociology of knowledge is suggested by Tsoukas (1996), who argues for a focus on organisational practices, as it is they which build and sustain any organisation's knowledge system. At the other extreme, Foss (1996a,b) argues that such knowledge-based theories, while interesting, cannot ever provide sufficient explanations for the formation and thus evolution of firms, for which better explanations are found in the study of contracts and asset ownership. Here, as elsewhere in much of the management and organisation studies literature, there is a heavy reliance on work in economics.

Economics

Economics is one of the core disciplines in business schools and hence provides much of the intellectual geography for the emergent discussions of 'knowledge' within management and organisation studies. Curiously, this is the case for both mainstream economics, as for instance with the early work of Arrow (1962), and for the various *opponents* of the mainstream, whether Marxist (e.g. Wainwright, 1994; Hodgson, 1999), neo-liberal (e.g. Hayek, 1945; Machlup, 1962; Stigler, 1961), or merely liberal (e.g. Becker, 1964, Galbraith, 1967)[4]. The credit must go to Hayek for first introducing 'the problem of knowledge' into economics, and it formed a key element of his argument against central state planning in general and socialism in particular, and in favour of the maximum role for free markets. For Hayek, the increasing specialisation and complexity of knowledge are taken to invalidate the possibility of any central authority having the fullest possible knowledge of all factors relevant to purchasing decisions. By contrast, evolutionary economics, which is based on the central role of tacit knowledge within 'routine' economic behaviour, has always argued that the state must have a central role in regulating markets (Nelson and Winter, 1982). This dual focus on specialisation and complexity on the one hand, and tacit knowledge on the other, has now been augmented by a variety of observations of the effects of new ICTs. Much of the economics literature, both mainstream and heterodox, tends to take the simplistic view that ICTs have simply emerged as an external factor of the global economy, not shaped by any earlier tendencies, and that they are now simply promoting the new role of knowledge in the economy (OECD, 1996; Howitt, 1996; Edvinsson and Malone, 1997; Hodgson, 1999). A more sophisticated and persuasive view is that ICTs have emerged alongside the significant problems encountered with earlier 'Fordist' patterns in the organisations and technologies of industrial economies and societies. We are witnessing a shift from that earlier 'techno-economic paradigm' to a new one in which ICTs evolve in response to those problems and in turn create new problems (Freeman and Perez, 1988). On this account, the current focus upon knowledge and learning in economies is essentially a temporary phenomenon, an indication of the requirement to adjust to the new techno-economic paradigm, which will eventually settle down into some new set of social, economic and organisational arrangements (Freeman, 1996).

Establishing Critical Distance

As well as recommending different processes and techniques, the fields of information science, organizational behaviour, strategic management and economics

---

4   Some of the implications of this curious alliance, across the political spectrum, around questions of knowledge, are discussed in Hull (2000).

offer differing explanations for the emphasis on 'knowledge'. Information science/systems points to technological change as a key 'driver' (Sviokla, 1998); organization behaviour to complexity (Allee, 1997); strategic management to market pressure (Neef, 1998), or the scarcity of expert labour/knowledge (O'Dell and Grayson, 1998), or the inevitable counterbalance to the earlier business process re-engineering. Meanwhile, economics points to a 'new economy' where the nature of goods exchanged/produced has changed with intangible inputs increasing in value over 'hardware' (OECD, 1996); and accountancy points to the problems of valuation as these businesses and this 'new economy' comes to dominate (see Chapter 2).

Of course, there is nothing hard and fast about these divisions. There is significant 'sharing' of responses to the questions 'Why knowledge?' and 'Why now?'. But there is another reason to highlight this divergence: the commodification and sale of knowledge itself. It is a perhaps a paradox that if we assume a knowledge economy, then the research and advice that management specialisms offer is not simply commentary but itself part of this formation. Each 'field' is sourcing advice for exchange relations. Such commodification also demands some form of distinctiveness and the ability to 'lock' knowledge consumers 'in' to each formulation. So information science offers technology that optimizes query/response in searching scenarios. Information systems offers machinic learning, intranets, groupware and 'intelligent' agents underpinned by a understanding of technological progress. Strategic management offers distinctive approaches to doing business (e.g. the licensing and sale of the process as product rather than the product itself) underpinned by an understanding of competitive market relations. Accounting offers different methods of valuation; and organisation behaviour offers a suitable learning/talking 'cure' to overcome 'knowledge bottlenecks' or lack of innovation and creativity. Economics, meanwhile, collects statistics and pronounces on the 'big picture' (the rise of particular sectors, new goods and services, and the competition between nations in the knowledge economy stakes).

As a consequence we face a field of competing explanations to the questions of 'Why knowledge?' and 'Why now?'. It seems wise then to acquire some 'critical distance' from each field so that some assessment of each field's assumptions and priorities can be made. John Mingers (2000) offers some pointers to getting some 'critical distance'. He suggests initially some scepticism toward assumptions that are taken for granted. Questioning the assumptions that each field of expertise makes about the world, about what is important, and what advice should be offered is one way to adopting such a critical stance.

He suggests also some wariness toward 'ultimate authorities'. On this basis, we should be wary of what we might call 'the Moses Effect'. This means being sceptical of 'cookbook' approaches that assume that the fullness and richness of knowledge can be understood and quickly managed. The Moses Effect is the result of unchallenged, prescriptive communication viewed as infallible or uncontestable flowing from a source or sources to an audience assumed to be waiting for the 'commandments' upon which to act. The power of the Moses Effect in organisations resides in the perception by workers and managers alike that two conditions are present: source infallibility and intermediary legitimacy. In relation to knowledge management the source of the 'Word' is predominantly the cohort of shapers of managerial thought – the icons, the gurus – some of whom have been mentioned above. It is as if their text is etched in stone by the finger of God – or so the stories might go.

Mingers also suggests that getting 'critical' also means studying *the impact or effect* of some phenomena – the activity around 'knowledge' in this case. Organizations, or more correctly organizational practices, have social, environmental, historical and political effects. If firms adopt particular knowledge management practices, such as attempting to elicit previously tacit knowledge for coding into databases, this is likely to have an impact on the long-term employment opportunities of some workers. Let's face it: if a worker's tacit knowledge and know-how can be codified and tucked into databases for access by anyone at any time from any place, then what is the value of that worker to the organization? If a firm sells a particular work process to another or initiates a joint venture which distributes the work process offshore, what will be the impact on people and their environment?

Lastly, and most importantly for Mingers, 'critical distance' involves concern over the relationships between knowledge, power and interests. Of course there is a strong critical tradition in organization studies (Marsden and Townley, 1996) which can provide compelling responses to the question 'Why Knowledge, Why now?' (Thompson and Warhurst, 1998; Curry, 1997). Some of this has its roots in a 'big picture' critique provided by Karl Marx and his early and more recent supporters (Braverman, 1974; Marglin, 1976; Freeman and Perez, 1988). 'Critical distance' built on this line of debate might suggest that the answers to 'Why knowledge?' and 'Why now?' lie in the 'stage' of crisis currently afflicting parts of world capitalism. It would be tempting to argue that the 'heat' and 'hype' around 'knowledge' amounts to an ideological effort on the part of a broad alliance of interests propelled by an intensified struggle for control of labour's ability to learn and develop expertise. In other words, if knowledge, rather than the ownership of plant and machinery, is regarded as the key source of value, then workers, managers and professionals are likely to confront intensive ideological efforts – in forms of self-management for instance – designed to enrol, extract and exploit these forms of value.

An alternative form of 'big picture' analysis places the 20th century concern with expertise and knowledge in the context of emergent modes of government, or governmentality (see e.g. Barry *et al.*, 1996; Rose, 1999), rather than in the context of 'old-fashioned' Marxist structuralist analysis. Taking a 'post-structuralist' perspective on long-term changes and continuities in society, such analyses suggest that we – as populations, as members of organisations, and as individuals – are increasingly governed through forms of expertise which operate indirectly, rather than directly through the formal pronouncements and decisions of 'big government' or senior management. They operate indirectly through our own increasing awareness of those forms of expertise, such as 'budgeting', 'being accountable' and 'being good citizens and members of communities' (Rose, 1999). Taking this a stage further, it has been suggested that the specific rise of interest and concern with 'knowledge' is a reaction to perceived problems with older forms of expertise, in particular the Positivist model of scientific knowledge and technological change, and that this focus on 'knowledge as a unit of analysis' is consequently characterised by deep metaphysical and ethical contradictions (Hull, 2000; see also Chapter 4 in this volume).

But we don't necessarily need such 'big picture' analyses to get some 'critical distance' in relation to 'knowledge' work and management. We could explore how conflict over knowledge work and its management is an extension of a long-running battle for control of professional white collar work more generally. While computer programmers might seem to personify the current generation's 'professional', the control of knowledge in the professions of law, architecture, medicine, science and engineering has an equal place in this discussion. Indeed, the way in which knowledge management recasts the work of these professions as 'knowledge flows', 'stocks of knowledge' or 'codified and embodied knowledge' might be seen as yet another important chapter in a very long-running saga over the power and interests that produce professional knowledge work.

Even so, software programmers seem a much more up-to-the-minute group upon which to exploring this intersection of power and interests in relation to 'knowledge'. In this collection Lynne Baxter, for instance, shows how programmers attempt to maintain control over their labour while their employers attempt to 'tie' their expertise and learning 'in' – through electronic surveillance of project work in this case. Baxter suggests that such tensions and tussles over the control of the programmers' labour are literally written into the numerical or logical routines of computer code, and the programs themselves become 'actors' in this drama.

Of course, from the employer's point of view, knowledge management initiatives can be seen as driven by heightened vulnerability and scarcity of particular forms of labour. Expert labour is potentially both panacea and serious problem. Experts can 'walk' – join or become the opposition – or quite easily pour the intellectual equivalent of 'sand' into the corporate gearbox. From this point of departure research and advice over the nature of 'knowledge', over the work patterns and practices of knowledge workers (Blackler, 1995), and the development of 'knowledge management solutions' which attempt to extract and share valuable knowledge (see Chapter 5) can be seen – with a bit of 'critical distance – as part of the long-running battle for control over expert labour in the face of heightened uncertainty and risk.

But it is perhaps in relation to 'learning' that such a 'critical distance' is most valuable. There is a vast literature on learning – some of which offers some 'critical' distance (Apple, 1995; Freire, 1972; Giroux, 1981; Lather, 1991). In this work learning is neither simply functional for a society, an organization or an individual, nor the site of individual achievement. Learning is a political process. If work organizations, which typically have sought to reduce the cost to themselves of learning and education, now regard learning as central to their survival, then relations between power and interests at the intersection of 'knowledge' need to be explored. For instance, some teachers know from experience the link between poverty and attainment, and the need for ways of 'de-schooling' to encouraging genuine learning and education. And yet much of the knowledge management literature insists on essentially psychologistic understandings of 'the learning process', ones derived from Piaget and Polanyi, for instance, rather than, to take some counter-examples, Vygotsky or Paolo Freire.

These latter theorists ground learning in the exploration of social relations. Freire (1972), for instance, asserts that the generation of new knowledge comes from dialogue over questions of what we know, where this knowing comes from and what interests it serves. Real learning for Freire has as its goals the development of critical citizens and the rejuvenation of democracy (Wallis and Allman, 1996). Freirean 'knowledge management' – if it were possible to pose such a description – would ask how learning works to liberate human beings from oppressive social relations, inequality and exploitation.

Alongside this characterisation of learning in the strategic management and organizational behaviour fields runs a similar kind of discussion of 'creativity' and the absolute requirement for innovation. By adopting some 'critical distance' we might suggest that such discussion is engaged in attempting to translate 'creativity' and 'innovation' into more predictable and controllable processes; for example, where 'knowledge production' can be measured and assessed in the same ways that cars were counted and checked off the line. What is often conveniently forgotten is that creativity is about rebellion (or transgression, at least) and involves: 'tearing a hole in the fabric of our reality', to paraphrase D. H. Lawrence. Poets, painters and other artists know this, especially those who continue to 'scandalise' the modern sentiment. Creativity and innovation must essentially be about rebellion and resistance because they are about challenging the prevailing paradigms. Some critical distance gives us a chance to explore these meanings which do not sit happily with the *management* of knowledge. Here lurks one of the essential tensions. The disciplinary and discursive attempts to present Moses' Tablets of Knowledge, to lay down the 'laws' and prescriptions in ten easy lessons, must inevitably encounter and encourage everyday organisational practices and perspectives which run counter to those 'laws'.

The Book's Chapters

This book, then, is a collection of works that offer critical insights into the advice and attempts at managing knowledge and knowledge workers. It is by no means prescriptive and does not suggest that knowledge or its management can be taught online in 30 minutes. It invites the reader to think and reflect on the processes and practices that surround this emphasis on 'knowledge' in contemporary management. Each author investigates some aspect of the knowledge work and management phenomena. Each provides insights from a critical distance.

The first four chapters investigate the interplay between profession, practice, and the evolving discursive formation of knowledge management.

In Chapter 1, McInerny and LeFevre remind us that knowledge management is not new and has been accomplished over the past centuries by the seminal work of the documentalists. Cataloguing, indexing, storing and retrieving information and knowledge have been and are the major effort of librarians, especially those working within organisational special libraries. Current discursive demands upon these special librarians, as 'knowledge practitioners', create a place in tension between the traditional values of their practice and the new knowledge management values of the organisation. This tension is explicated in the chapter.

A key aspect of the emergence of knowledge management is the dramatic rise in recent decades of the value of 'intangible assets' relative to the 'tangible assets' of capital and labour. Before that rise in relative value the 'intangibles' were merely the remainder on the balance sheet which could not be counted, those company assets such as brand, customer loyalty, copyrights and patents that are owned by a company but have no value until traded. In Chapter 2, Yahklef and Salzer-Mörling describe and critique the emergence of techniques for counting 'Intellectual Capital', the term now employed to value those intangibles that are supposedly countable. The struggles underlying numerical representation as reality are surfaced in a way where the formation of the symbolic nature of a numerical reality is exposed under the critical microscope. Accountants as knowledge practitioners and shapers of organisational reality, in particular, are called to reflect critically on the assumptions of their profession in light of the current knowledge management discourse.

A key area for knowledge management is that of the specialised knowledge held by a limited number of experts, and a useful example of such expertise is software development. In Chapter 3, Baxter investigates how software developers maintain their position as experts. Drawing similarities between the manufacturing process and software development, she suggests that the 'encoding of embodied and embedded knowledge in manufacturing technology' occurs in software development as well. She contrasts the assumptions about software 'bugs' held by software developers with the assumptions of end users. Using Actor Network Theory (ANT), Baxter shows how the interests of software developers are mobilized around 'encultured routines', which in turn become 'encoded' within the practice of software development as knowledge.

A lesser cousin to the management of knowledge is the management of expertise, and in Chapter 4 Hull seeks to turn the tables by examining knowledge management as merely a new form of expert labour. Critiquing the dominant 'reductionist' and 'realist' theories of expert labour, he develops an alternative more reflexive perspective on the 'conduct' of expert labour which distinguishes between the 'discipline' and the everyday practices. This is then applied to knowledge management by discussing the historical emergence of its disciplinary aspects and describing case study research on Knowledge Management Practices (KMPs) within five Research and Development (R&D) settings. This reveals a stark contrast between what is actually happening with KMPs and the rhetoric of the discipline, which points to the need for 'detailed analysis of very specific KMPs' and the effects of their embeddedness within certain organisational contexts.

The role of Information and Communication Technologies (ICTs) in leveraging creativity, innovation and knowledge sharing by enhancing communication between knowledge practitioners as well as between and within knowledge management communities is the focus of the next three chapters.

Hayes and Walsham, as a result of a two and a half year empirical study, describe in Chapter 5 the political effects on organisational communities resulting from the use of groupware (Lotus Notes). The dominant knowledge management theme suggests that knowledge sharing is unproblematic. However, the perception by communities formed around the use of groupware as to their political or apolitical (safe) nature influences and problematizes the degree of actual knowledge sharing. This work directly challenges much of the 'hype' surrounding the potential of groupware to leverage knowledge sharing.

In Chapter 6, Newell, Scarbrough, Swan and Hislop research the role that knowledge plays in organisation-wide intranet diffusion scenarios. They investigate the coordination (or lack of it) within one of the largest European banks as they implement intranets. Their study, which focuses upon three specific diffusion cases, suggests that the effects of intranet implementation and use may not result in the consensual view of reality or concerted action desired by the organisation as a whole. A degree of community knowledge – 'sedimentation' – may set in which runs counter to the desired effect of sharing knowledge across the organisation.

McKinlay is concerned in Chapter 7 with the tension behind making tacit knowledge explicit by digitally capturing that knowledge and populating organisational databases with it. The new drug development process within a pharmaceutical firm is investigated against the theoretical backdrop of Foucault's Power/Knowledge construction and the effect of that construction on codifying tacit/practical knowledge. Research worker and team resistance to this codification is introduced as a problematic to which a 'softening of control' is posited as a possible solution.

The next two chapters expose the tensions surrounding service work and its relationships to knowledge work.

Chapter 8, by Thompson, Warhurst and Callaghan, surfaces discontinuities in the 'textual armour' within which knowledge economy 'pronouncements' are housed. Their case study research, which is the basis for the chapter, explores the tensions between knowledge and service work. Pronouncements surrounding the conduct of and differences between 'knowledge work and services' are exposed and critically reviewed. Policy implications resulting from the fissure are explicated and posited as a framework that should underlie both organisational and government action.

The practice-of-service-work debate is continued by Lander in her reflexive autobiographical narrative (Chapter 9). She exposes the tension between a past self which performed service work and a present self performing knowledge work from a position of the other. What makes the narrative intriguing is that both the past self and present self worked for the same organisation separated by a temporal space. In constructing her autobiography she critically exposes the assumptions surrounding the service work discourse. Her narrative also includes a reflexive analysis of her own reflexivity, resulting in suggestions that could affect managerial cognition and action.

The last two chapters explain the powerful effects that discourse has on the body engaged in knowledge management practices.

The reflexive mood is continued by Jones in Chapter 10. Drawing on field work conducted by studying EEO practitioners, she reflects upon herself as an academic engaged in knowledge management *qua* individual and in collaboration with others. She articulates the tension between self as practitioner, as knowledge worker, investigating others performing knowledge work. In that reflexive mood Jones attempts to create positions from which critique can be grounded. In so doing she confronts the inscribing force behind discourses in general on the bodies that submit to its formative control. She concludes her reflexive journey by positing a 'new canon' that frees us from the insulation of our discursive formation enabling a richer understanding of the objects of scholarly investigation.

Using as a theoretical backdrop Foucault's suggestion that the productivity of power is dependent upon the creation of a knowledgeable, consumptive, communicating body, in Chapter 11 Prichard creates a compelling case for discursive formations that coax, rather than repress. Discourses that politely invite the body to participate and subtly pull the body in its direction of choice tend to be more invasive than those which discipline the body. When the discursive formation, such as the dominant knowledge management thread, suggests innovation, creativity, communication and knowledge sharing as a tantalizing pull, the body is sure to follow. One look at the illustration in the chapter dramatically encapsulates the discursive effect upon the body of the 'knower'.

The book concludes with a lively exchange between the editors of this volume and Roy Jacques. Jacques proposes the 'Need for a knowledge theory of value'. His position is critiqued from a wide variety of perspectives. It is this wide variety, this pluralistic quality, of knowledge and its management which is so important to grasp. It is not the magic bullet to be learned in 30 minutes by an online course and then shot into the heart of a managerial discourse. To grasp the many faces and characteristics of knowledge and its management takes time and effort. That is the collective message of this book.

Bibliography

Allee, V. (1997) *The Knowledge Evolution; Expanding Organizational Intelligence*, Boston, MA: Butterworth-Heinemann.

Apple, M. (1995) *Education and Power*, New York: Routledge.

Argyris, C. (1990) *Overcoming Organizational Defenses: Facilitating Organizational Learning*, Needham, MA: Allyn Bacon.

Argysis, C. and Schön, D. (1974) *Theory in Practice*, San Francisco: Jossey-Bass.

Arms, W., Blanchi, C., and Overly, E. A. (1997) 'An Architecture for Information in Digital Libraries', *D-Lib Magazine* (February) (http://www.dlib.org/dlib/february97/cnri/02arms1.html).

Arrow, K. (1962) 'The economic implications of learning by doing' *Review of Economic Studies*, 29, 155–73.

Barry, A., Osborne, T., and Rose, N. (eds.) (1996) *Foucault and Political Reason: Liberalism, Neo-liberalism and Rationalities of Government*, London: UCL Press.

Becker, G. (1964) *Human Capital; A Theoretical and Empirical Analysis with Special Reference to Education*, Chicago: Chicago University Press.

Beckman, T. (1999) 'The Current State of Knowledge Management', in Liebowitz, J. (ed.), *The Knowledge Management Handbook*, London: CRC Press, pp. 1:1–22.

Benton Foundation (1997). 'Buildings, books and bytes: Libraries and communities in the digital age', *Library Trends*, 46: 1, 178–223.

Blackler, F. (1995) 'Knowledge, Knowledge Work and Organizations: an Overview and Interpretation', *Organization Studies*, 16, 1021–46.

Bohn, R. E. (1994) 'Measuring and Managing Technological Knowledge', *Sloan Management Review*, Fall, pp. 61–73.

Braverman, H. (1974) *Labour and Monopoly Capital*, New York: Monthly Review Press.

Brookes, B. C. (1975) 'The Fundamental Problem of Information Science', in Horsnell, V. (ed.), *Informatics 2*, London: ASLIB.

Chilvers, A. and Feather, J. (1998). 'The Management of Digital Data: A Metadata Approach', *The Electronic Library*, 16: 6, 365–72.

Choo, C. (1998) *The Knowing Organization: How Organizations Use Information to Contruct Meaning, Create Knowledge and Make Decisions*, New York: Oxford University Press.

Cleverdon, C. (1962) *Report on the Testing and Analysis of An Investigation Into the Comparative Efficiency of Indexing Systems*, Cranfield, UK: College of Aeronautics.

Cleverdon, C.(1967) 'The Cranfield Tests of Indexing Language Devices', *ASLIB Proceedings*, 19: 6, 173–94.

Coleman, S. (1998) *Knowledge Management: Linchpin of Change*, London: ASLIB.

Curry, J. (1997) 'The Dialectic of Knowledge-in-Production: Value Creation in Late Capitalism and the Rise of Knowledge-Centered Production', *Electronic Journal of Sociology*, 2, 3. Available at: http://www.icaap.org/iuicode?100.2.3.3.

Davenport, T. and Prusak, L. (1998) *Working Knowledge, How Organisations Manage What they Know*, Boston, MA: Harvard Business School Press.

Drucker, P., Dyson, E., Handy, C., Saffo, P. and Senge, P. (1997) *Looking Ahead: Implications of the Present*, Harvard Business Review.

Edvinsson, L. and Malone, M. (1997) *Intellectual Capital: Realizing Your Company's True Value by Finding its Hidden Brainpower*, New York: HarperCollins.

Foss, N. J. (1996a) 'Knowledge-based Approaches to the Theory of the Firm: Some Critical Comments', *Organization Science*, 7: 5, 470–6.

Foss, N. J. (1996b) 'More Critical Comments on Knowledge-based Theories of the Firm', *Organization Science*, 7: 5, 519–23.

Fox, E. A. and Marchionini, G. (1998) 'Toward a Worldwide Digital Library', *Communications of the ACM*, 41: 4, 29–32.

Freire, P. (1972) *Pedagogy of the Oppressed*, Harmondsworth: Penguin.

Freeman, C. (1996) 'The Two-Edged Nature of Technological Change: Employment and Unemployment', in W. Dutton (ed.), *Information and Communication Technologies: Visions and Realities*, Oxford: Oxford University Press.

Freeman, C. and Perez, C. (1988) 'Structural Crises of Adjustment: Business Cycles and Investment Behaviour', in G. Dosi *et al.* (eds.), *Technical Change and Economic Theory*, London: Pinter.

Galbraith, J. K. (1967) *The New Industrial State*, London: Hamish Hamilton.

Giroux, H. (1981) *Ideology, Culture & the Process of Schooling*, London: Falmer.

Goffman, W. and Newell, V. A. (1966) 'Methodology for Test and Evaluation of Information Retrieval Systems', *Information Storage and Retrieval*, 3: 1, 19–25.

Harman, D. (1994) *TREC-3*, SIGIR '94 Proc. New York: ACM Press.

Harman, D. (1997) *Proceedings of the Fifth Text Retrieval Conference (TREC-5)*, NIST SP500-238, Gaithersburg, MD.

Hayek, F. (1945 [1949]) 'The Use of Knowledge in Society', *American Economic Review*, 35: 4, 519–30. Reprinted in Hayek, F. (1949) *Individualism and Economic Order*, London: Routledge & Kegan Paul, Chapter 4, pp. 77–106.

Hedlund, G. (1994) 'A Model of Knowledge Management and N-form Corporation', *Strategic Management Journal*, 15 (Summer Special Issue), 73–90.

Hodgson, G. M. (1999) *Economics & Utopia: Why the Learning Economy is Not the End of History*, London: Routledge.

Howitt, P. (ed.) (1996) *The Implications of Knowledge-Based Growth for Micro-Economic Policies*, Alberta, CA: University of Calgary Press.

Hull, R. (1997) 'Governing the Conduct of Computing: computer Science, the Social Sciences and Frameworks of Computing', *Accounting, Management and Information Technologies*, 7: 4, 213–40.

Hull, R. (2000) 'Knowledge and the Economy: Some Critical Comments', *Economy and Society*, 29: 2, 315–30.

Ingwersen, P. (1996) 'Cognitive Perspectives in Information Retrieval Interaction: Elements of a Cognitive IR Theory' *J. Documentation*, 52: 1, 3–50.

KPMG (1999) 'IKON Conference Report', available at `http://kpmg.interact.nl/new/confer_IKON.html`.

Lagoze, C̄., Fielding, D. and Payette, S. (1998) 'Making Global Digital Libraries Work: Collection Services, Connectivity, Regions and Collection Views', *Proceedings of Digital Libraries*, 98, 134–44.

Lancaster, R. W. (1969) 'MEDLARS: Report on the Evaluation of its Operating Efficiency', *American Documentation*, 20: 2, 119–42.

Lather, P. (1991) *Getting Smart: Feminist Research and Pedagogy With/in the Postmodern*, New York: Routledge.

Leonard-Barton, D. (1995) *Wellsprings of Knowledge: Building and Sustaining the Sources of Innovation*, Boston: Harvard Business School Press.

Liebowitz, J. (ed.) (1999) *Knowledge Management Handbook*, London: CRC Press.

Levy, D. M. and Marshall, C. C. (1995) 'Going Digital – a Look At Assumptions Underlying Digital Libraries', *Communications of the ACM*, 38: 4, 77–84.

Machlup, F. (1962) *The Production and Distribution of Knowledge in the United States*, Princeton: Princeton University Press.

Marglin, S. (1976) 'What Do Bosses Do? The Origins and Functions of Hierarchy in Capitalist Production' in A. Gorz (ed.), *The Division of Labour and Class Struggle in Modern Capitalism*, Hassocks: Harvester Press (translated from the French).

Marsden, R. and Townley, B. (1996) 'The Owl of Minerva: Reflections on Theory in Practice', in Clegg *et al.* (eds.) *Handbook of Organization Studies*, London: Sage, pp. 659–75.

Milstead, J. and Feldman, S. (1999) *Cataloging by Any Other Name*, available at: http://www.onlineinc.com/onlinemag/OL1999/milstead1.html#projects.

Mingers, J. (2000) 'What is it to be Critical? Teaching a Critical Approach to Management Undergraduates', *Management Learning*, 31: 2 (forthcoming; previously published in 1998 as Warwick Business School Research Paper No. 284).

Neef D. (ed.) (1998) *The Knowledge Economy*, Woburn, MA: Butterworth-Heinemann.

Nelson, R. and Sidney, W. (1982) *An Evolutionary Theory of Economic Change*, Cambridge, MA: Harvard University Press.

Nonaka, I. (1991) 'The Knowledge-Creating Company', *Harvard Business Review*, 69: 6, 96–104.

Nonaka, I. (1994) 'A Dynamic Theory of Organizational Knowledge Creation', *Organization Science*, 5: 1, 14–37.

Nonaka, I. and Takeuchi, H. (1995) *The Knowledge Creating Company: How Japanese Companies Create the Dynamics of Innovation*, Oxford: Oxford University Press.

O'Dell, C. and Grayson, C. (1998) *If Only We Knew What We Know; the Transfer of Internal Knowledge and Best Practice*, New York: The Free Press.

OECD (1996) *Employment and Growth in the Knowledge-based Economy*, Paris: OECD.

Rose, N. (1999) *Powers of Freedom: Reframing Political Thought*, Cambridge: Cambridge University Press.

Salton, G. (1968). *Automatic Information Organization and Retrieval*. New York: McGraw-Hill.

Salton, G. and Lesk, M. E. (1968) 'Computer Evaluation of Indexing and Text Processing', *Journal for the Association of Computing Machinery*, 15: 1, 8–36.

Schön, D. (1983) *The Reflective Practitioner: How Professionals Think in Action*, New York: Basic Books.

Senge, P. (1990) *The Fifth Dimension: The Art and Practice of the Learning Organization*, New York: Doubleday.

Saracevic, T. *et al.* (1968) *An Inquiry Into Testing Information Retrieval Systems*. CSL: Final Report, Center for Documentation and Communication research, School of Library Science, Case Western Reserve University.

Sparck-Jones, K. (1977) *Information Retrieval Experiment*, London: Butterworth.

Spender, J.-C. (1996) 'Making Knowledge the Basis of a Dynamic Theory of the Firm', *Strategic Management Journal*, 17 (Winter Special Issue), 45–62.

Stigler, G. (1961) 'The Economics of Information', *Journal of Political Economy*, 69: 2, 213–15.

Sviokla, J. J. (1998) 'Virtual Value and the Birth of Virtual Markets', in Bradley, S. P. and Nolan, R. L. (eds.) *Sense & Respond: Capturing Value in the Network Era*, Harvard, MA: Harvard Business School Press.

Thompson, P. and Warhurst, C. (eds.) (1998) *Workplaces of the Future*, London: Macmillan.

Tsoukas, H. (1996) 'The Firm as a Distributed Knowledge System: a Constructionist Approach', *Strategic Management Journal*, 17 (Winter Special Issue), 11–25.

Wainwright, H. (1994) *Arguments for a New Left: Answering the Free-Market Right*, Oxford: Blackwell.

Wallis, J. and Allman, P. (1996) 'Adult education, the "critical" citizen and social change', in J. Wallis (ed.), *Liberal Adult Education: the End of an Era?*, Nottingham: Continuing Education Press.

Weibel, S., Kunze, J., Lagoze, C. and Wolf, M. (1998) *Dublin Core Metadata for Resource Discovery*, Request for Comments: 2413 Network Working Group, Internet Engineering Task Force (ftp://ftp.isi.edu/in-notes/rfc2413.txt).

1 Knowledge Managers: History and Challenges

Claire McInerney and Darcy LeFevre

Processing data can be performed by machine, but only the human mind can process knowledge or even information (Jesse Shera, 1983)

Introduction

The term 'knowledge management' is a slippery one. Like its cousins 'information' and 'document', there are many ways to think about knowledge management (KM). In simple language KM is an effort to capture not only explicit factual information but also the tacit information and knowledge that exists in an organisation, usually in the minds of employees in order to advance the organisation's mission (Broadbent, 1998; Davenport and Prusak, 1998). Explicit information includes reports, briefing papers, the information on certain Web sites or intranets, and other documents that are created within an organisation. Usually explicit information is owned by the firm, since it is developed internally or through sponsored projects. Some KM systems also include documents that have been gathered from external sources. Tacit knowledge exists within a person as a result of the experience and learning of employees. It is often captured in transcripts, written reports, or electronic documents. DiMattia and Oder (1997, p. 33) offer this succinct definition of knowledge management:

> KM involves blending a company's internal and external information and turning it into actionable knowledge via a technology platform.

Virtually all large firms that create knowledge management systems use information technology to organise, store and codify knowledge and make it accessible to members. In most cases the firm's knowledge resides in repositories or libraries of reports and other documents that are linked electronically with names of experts, contact information, and other tools that facilitate continual use and revision of the knowledge banks (Borghoff and Pareschi, 1998). These knowledge management systems range from fairly simple best practices databases to elaborate systems that include customized reports and interconnected expert knowledge flows and communication webs of great sophistication. Some firms use technology to help employees improve their decision making. Expert knowledge is used to make rules and guidelines that

1

inform the decisions of others, such as insurance underwriters or mortgage bankers (Ruggles, 1998).

With the proliferation of knowledge work, perhaps it was inevitable that knowledge management would emerge to become one of the top issues of an age where consultants live on the Internet and intellectual capital provides the new competitive edge (Koenig, 1996). KM did not grow up overnight, however, nor did it appear in corporations without precedent or tradition. Since the early days of the twentieth century, documentalists and special librarians[1] have been engaged in the work of acquiring and disseminating mission-critical information and knowledge for organisational employees (Buckland, 1998; Rayward, 1983, 1998a,b; Williams, 1998; Wilson, 1983).

This chapter analyses knowledge management (KM) critically from the point of view of the information professional or knowledge manager. It describes how the role of librarians, based on a tradition of documentalists, parallels the role of knowledge managers. It also shows how concepts and practices inherent in knowledge management are related to skills and abilities commonly associated with the work of information professionals. It raises ethical issues related to the professional management of an organisation's knowledge, including, trust, fairness, autonomy and privacy. It also discusses some of the issues related to selecting and using professional technology tools for ethical knowledge management.

Can Knowledge Really Be Managed?

Much of what has been touted as knowledge management sounds very much like database development or information management: collecting documents; storing them; providing directories, search mechanisms and links; creating lists of experts; etc. (Davenport, 1997). KM, however, has some distinguishing characteristics that separate it from the more traditional ways of dealing with data and information. Knowledge, higher than data or information in the intellectual 'food chain' (Barlow, 1994; Davenport and Prusak, 1998; Haeckel and Nolan, 1993), requires human experience and analysis. As Davenport and Prusak (1998, p. 5) say, 'Knowledge derives from minds at work'. The knowledge that employees have can include their 'competencies, skills, talents, thoughts, ideas, intuitions, commitments, motivations, and imaginations' (Harari, 1994, p. 57). Knowledge relates to how well people do their jobs, how they interact with customers or clients, and how they monitor and adjust methods for getting the knowledge work done in the highest quality way. There is no doubt that the knowledge management trend has been influenced by the total quality movement and other business improvement strategies. How can workers develop the shared visions proposed by Peter Senge (1990), for example, or operate consistently as learning organisations without the ability to share knowledge with each other?

Recent business practice has been to downsize and create lean organisations where fewer employees do more (DiMattia and Oder, 1997; Rifkin, 1995; Schor, 1991). Along with a legion of mergers and acquisitions and the accompanying reduction in force, firms were finding that the knowledge gained and developed through seasoned employees was walking out of the door along with their early retirement bonuses and severance packages (Davenport and Prusak, 1998). Knowledge-based organisations such as accounting firms, consulting businesses, advertising agencies and many others found that they were losing their chief asset – the organisation's intellectual capital – when employees left. The effort to create knowledge management systems has grown largely out of the fear that a company's competitive edge was fragile when dependent on the minds and learning of individual workers. Companies soon discovered that they needed a solid and ongoing system to archive these assets and to put methods in place to share the knowledge that had been developed internally over time.

It is a highly challenging task to extract expertise and learning from one person and 'transfer' it to another, but the alternative is to lose valuable knowledge gained through hard work, experience, training and teamwork. Although it may seem impossible in some sense to accomplish 'mind share' without knowledge sharing, organisations constantly reinvent projects and have no way to leverage past experience and knowledge worker expertise. In a time when many employees are working at customer sites, on the road, or from home in the virtual office, casual exchange of informal information or knowledge gained on a past project is much more difficult. In today's high-paced business climate, even workers in the same building try to save time by leaving email messages for each other instead of stopping by a colleague's office (McInerney, 1999).

Marianne Broadbent, director of the IT Executive Program for Gartner Group[2], says, '...perhaps knowledge management is an oxymoron, and it will be followed in a few years by "managing wisdom" when neither are really possible' (Broadbent, 1998, p. 23). Although Broadbent is sceptical and critical of some poor attempts to 'manage knowledge', she does say that KM, in fact, is not only possible, to a degree, but also necessary in a competitive business climate. In order to understand what is going on, she says, one must examine the data–information–knowledge spectrum. To clarify what KM is and is not, Broadbent says, 'Knowledge management is about enhancing the use of organizational knowledge through sound practices of information management and organizational learning' (1998, p. 24).

A Knowledge Management Case

To draw a clearer picture of how an organisation's knowledge management system might work, here is an example from a hypothetical company, based on research conducted in 1998 at four large global corporations in the northeastern area of the USA.[3] Compu-tronics, a high-technology company that produces hardware and software, is known for innovation in a competitive worldwide market. Sales executives, product developers, engineers, and other staff all need the latest information in order to stay current in the volatile computing field. In addition, a recent strategic decision was made to reduce real estate costs by sending 1,500 workers home to work via computer and telecommunications lines. These employees and the sales staff, who are almost always on the road, need constant information and knowledge sharing.

In order to meet the needs of company employees, the head of information services, a department composed primarily of librarians, and the head of the MIS business enterprise group act as co-leaders in the knowledge management process. The information services librarians conduct routine trend scanning to find information that they load on industry-specific Web sites. They take questions by phone and perform information research and refer employees to others in the corporation who might help with solutions and expertise. In addition they manage archives of photographs and other 'documents'. The business enterprise group, mostly MIS professionals, created software that administers a profile to each new employee to determine the kind of customized information that individuals need. The head of this department says that he is trying to 'carve out the relevancy' of information and knowledge for each employee. Reports and other electronic documents are then routed to the employees according to the results of the profile. Some of these documents are created internally, and others come from a variety of sources. The business enterprise group also manages a great store of knowledge bases, including best practices and project reports, in an electronic repository, and they also serve as standards managers for the hundreds of Web sites available from the company. Those who create Web sites consult this group to make sure that the company is maintaining its articulated standards for intranet and Internet sites. Collaboration tools are made available for downloading and are continually updated in company intranet sites.

Challenges to a completely functioning and valuable KM system for Compu-tronics (or any other organisation) include the ability to:

- understand the kind of information that each employee needs and desires
- design effective employee questionnaires and keep employee profiles current
- develop routines for project reporting
- map knowledge repositories to allow for easy navigation to documents
- establish access points (subject headings) and links to knowledge documents
- track trends and acquire current information related to the firm's mission
- evaluate the KM system to determine where improvements can be made.

Figure 1.1   The knowledge management process

Some of the processes just described might be considered routine information services, but others (for example, creating routines for company project reporting) do fall under the aegis of knowledge management. The amalgam of this coordinated and detailed attention to information and knowledge is also the kind of effort commonly referred to as knowledge management by corporate information directors and chief information officers. See Figure 1.1 for a graphic representation of a typical knowledge management system.

Who Are the Knowledge Managers?

The KM process is often undertaken by a team of individuals with various skills, often including Management Information Systems (MIS) professionals, Web developers, and others. In large companies that have well-organised information centres or special libraries, librarians are often a critical part of the knowledge management team; in fact, they may initiate the process. Librarians at the big five accounting firms all have an active and critical role in their company's KM process (DiMattia and Oder, 1997).

For special librarians, working with knowledge is a natural progression in a history of providing information in the form of documents through the twentieth century. More than a caretaker of books, the special librarian knows the organisation well and acts more like an information broker or an information guide, taking requests for information and connecting internal clients with people or resources to solve information problems, all the while keeping in mind the organisation's key goals. According to Davenport and Prusak (1998, p. 29), 'Librarians frequently act as covert knowledge brokers, suited by temperament and their roles as information guides to the task of making people-to-people as well as people-to-text connections'.

In contrast to the average public library, a special library usually has a small collection of books. Instead of extensive book stacks, the information resources usually consist of highly specialised collections of journals, journal indexes, directories, journals and reports. Librarians understand information use and the people issues in transfer of knowledge, and they know how to organise documents so that users can find what they need when they need it. Their work is often invisible[4] because they often operate behind the scenes, but the history of the field reveals that librarians do consider themselves to be in a knowledge-intensive profession.

A legacy of documentation and organisation of knowledge

Librarians have a long history of transferring knowledge. A tradition of working with an organisation's intellectual resources can be traced to the documentalists in Europe and America in the first half of the twentieth century. In Europe, Paul Otlet had a grand vision of collecting, codifying and organising the world's knowledge. In the 1890s Otlet and his colleague Henri LaFontaine formed the Brussels Institute (later the International Institute of Bibliography), devoted to bibliographic studies, and they also began the International Federation for Documentation (FID) (Rayward, 1983). Although he was an attorney by profession, and a self-made documentalist, Otlet and his followers were, in many ways, like librarians (Shera, 1983). As Rayward (1983, p. 348) points out, however,

> Otlet wanted libraries to cease being mere depositories and to become vital institutes of documentation providing special information services on all matters of interest to all members of the public who might wish to use them. He wanted to see all libraries transformed into what he called offices of documentation.

The American counterpart to the FID, the American Documentation Institute, is generally considered a precursor of today's American Society for Information Science (ASIS), an association with a substantial number of librarian members who study information organisation, retrieval and use (American Society for Information Science, 1999). Some also consider the first documentalist organisations as earlier versions of the American-based Special Libraries Association

(SLA) and the British-based Association of Special Libraries and Information Bureaus (Aslib) (Shera, 1966).

Knowledge, hypertext, the Internet and virtual reality

The documentalists were concerned with all things that contain knowledge, but Otlet and others found these documents and other items in great disarray, with few easy ways to retrieve a knowledge object (Rayward, 1998b). To them, the term 'document' could mean written papers, postcards, articles, patents, film, graphics, statistics and even objects. Otlet (1907, 1990, p. 105) said:

> ...documents consist of whatever represents or expresses an object, a fact, or an impression by means of any signs whatever (writing, picture, diagrams, symbols).... Knowledge and impressions would last for only a limited time without the help of graphic documents to capture and hold them fast because *memory* alone is insufficient for recollection... documents form the graphic memory of humanity, the physical body of knowledge.

Documentalists were the original multimedia librarians, acquiring and cataloguing all manner of documents to assist others in making sense, extracting meaning and gaining knowledge. Rayward (1983, p. 347) summarises the documentalists' mission this way:

> The problem was to find out what each contributed to the sum of knowledge, what each contained of potentially useful information, and to express and connect this flexibly, creatively to what already existed.

Elaborating on Dewey's Decimal Classification scheme, Otlet applied rigour and cascading subject categories[5] to create the Classification Decimale Universal (or UDC in English) in order to arrange logically what we would call today the literature of the social sciences (Rayward, 1998b; Otlet, 1895–96, 1990). Otlet's classification work in collaboration with many of the great scientists and scholars of Europe was applied to the collections of 25 learned societies who deposited their works in a joint collection in Brussels. Otlet and his cohorts actively sought out these works as well as information from the Library of Congress, which regularly forwarded catalogue cards to Brussels, and the British Museum, which sent its catalogue.

The European documentalists went far beyond collecting and codifying documents. They were fierce in developing networks of content producers and evangelised their desire to create a worldwide network of knowledge exchange. Otlet invented a kind of manual hypertext system, dividing documents into 'chunks' of information (pictures, newspaper reports, drawings etc.) and placing them on cards that related to each other through elaborate indexing,[6] including the same database management system listed above, the UDC (Buckland, 1998; Rayward, 1998b). The documentalists, along with Otlet, also developed navigational schemes in order to connect pieces of related information.

They are also credited with an early idea of an interconnected international network of knowledge like the Internet and a scholar's workstation with connections to phone, wireless telegraphy, television and telex (Rayward, 1998c). The idea was for scholars to call up all the communications and documents they wanted on the screen, and the machine would do the work of retrieving the needed information (Rayward, 1998b). The workstation would allow scholars to study in a virtual workspace or an online environment that could be described as a rudimentary vision of virtual reality.

As early as 1912, segments of the American library community were involved in documentation work similar to that of the European documentalists. Special librarians, at first a special interest group within the American Library Association, eventually established their own organisation, the Special Libraries Association (SLA). Although they did not adopt the terminology 'documentalists', in essence they were functioning as their European counterparts. Their information centers organised correspondence received by the employing firms and classified it as well as collecting other specialised documents for use by scientists and other professionals. In 1915 Ethel Johnson, an SLA member, said:

> Before everything else, it [the special library] is an information bureau. The main function of the general library is to make books available. The function of the special library is to make information available (Johnson, 1915, p. 174).

Some members of the library community did not embrace all of Otlet's ideas nor all of his practices. But enough did in order for French librarian Suzanne Briet, who is sometimes called 'Madame Documentation', to draw the comparison between American special librarians and European documentalists after a visit to the USA in 1954 (Williams, 1998). Buckland (1998, p. 170) summarises Briet's comments when he remarks, 'Although the term "documentation" was scarcely known in the U.S.A., its techniques were ably practiced in the form of reference service and special library service both within and separate from large general libraries'. There is some controversy among historians of librarianship about how much American librarians, even special librarians, wanted to align themselves with professional documentalists (Williams, 1998), but the fact is that special librarians had a lot in common and worked in similar ways to those who considered themselves documentalists.

Changing roles

In recent years the role of the special librarian has changed despite the consistency of purpose that has guided special librarians from their documentalist roots. Rather than a radical departure from the information provision role of times past, current professionals who staff information centres and special libraries have adopted new tools to do their work. Special librarians have embraced technology and have become experts in using commercial online information services, such as Lexis-Nexis and Dialog, in using search engines on the Internet, in designing and developing Web sites, and in transferring electronic information. In library schools, many of which have changed their names to Schools of Information Management or Information Science, aspiring information professionals continue to take courses in research, information needs, organisation of information and information use, but also courses in database development, systems and networks, and knowledge management.

When examining the literature and practices of corporate knowledge management, there are similarities, subtle though they may be, between the special librarian's role and that of the knowledge manager. Librarians merely use a different vocabulary for what they do, but they are as active in knowledge management as some of their MIS colleagues. At Microsoft Corporation, for example, the Information Services staff have initiated the 'knowledge architecture' project in order to index, organise and manage the company's organisational knowledge. Part of this project is to make a comprehensive thesaurus of knowledge contained on Web sites, and to seek alliances with others in order to have partners in knowledge acquisition (Scott and Kirby, 1999). The key technical skill for librarians is cataloguing information/knowledge. Knowledge management business articles discuss 'codification', or the 'organisation of knowledge' (Davenport and Prusak, 1998; Hansen *et al.*, 1999; Ruggles, 1998); library literature discusses 'classification', 'indexing', and 'subject headings' (Ranganathan, 1949, 1989; Rowley, 1988). See Table 1.1 for a list of terms commonly used in business to describe KM processes and comparable terms from the library or information field.

Another stock in trade for librarians is their ability to interview information users to determine their information needs. Although it may seem counterintuitive, many information seekers start their search with a very limited view of the information they actually need. Users know a problem exists, but their idea of which information/knowledge to use to solve the problem can be murky. Then there's the question of where to find it. Librarians are trained to ask questions to determine the precise information needed so that relevant material can be found. It is this ability to communicate and understand information use that makes librarians ideal partners in knowledge management efforts. In a 1997 knowledge management study of 431 American and European firms, executives stated that even though KM projects are being developed, there are still important agenda items to be addressed in the effective management of knowledge.[7] Three of those agenda items were (Ruggles, 1998, p. 4):

- mapping sources of internal expertise

- creating networks of knowledge workers

- establishing new knowledge roles

**Table 1.1   Knowledge management terms from
business and library literature**

Business literature	Library literature
Codification	Classification
Collection	Selection, collection
Dispersal	Dissemination
Access	Catalogue creation
Knowledge transfer	Document delivery
	Networking
Extraction	Abstracting
Repository	Archive
Flow of knowledge	Circulation
Profiling	User surveys
Personalisation	Selective dissemination of information
Absorption	Use
Knowledge generation	Content creation
Mapping sources	Creating pathfinders
Web site development	Web site development

Librarians have – as a basic skill – an ability to map information/knowledge sources and to provide guides and access points to these maps. Their people and interviewing skills, and, particularly for special librarians, their networking skills position them clearly in a role where they assist knowledge workers in networking with each other. Some librarians are taking a lead in managing organisational knowledge. Others could be tapped for their expertise and service orientation to do the same. The executives in the Ernst & Young study were also clear in stating that people, not technology, will make the difference in sharing knowledge if they take on new roles to manage the knowledge that exists in the organisation (Ruggles, 1998).

What Are the Professional Ethics Issues in KM?

As a profession, librarians share a fundamental concern with information ethics. This concern spans the data–information–knowledge hierarchy. Data quality, freedom of information, and fairness and trust in knowledge transfer are just some of these concerns. Because the practice of knowledge management is still developing, ethical parameters in the practice are still emerging as well. There are some ethical issues that information professionals might identify and pay attention to as KM becomes more commonplace in organisations. These ethical issues include justice or fairness, autonomy, trust and privacy.

The explicit/tacit division and ownership of knowledge

Clearly, all explicit material created on the job belongs to the organisation and its storage in knowledge repositories is appropriate. Who owns the knowledge residing within employees is another question. Several professions, such as physicians and professors, are facing ethical dilemmas regarding the ownership of knowledge. One of the hallmarks of a professional is the specialised knowledge that he or she has; however, KM is threatening to take the tacit knowledge of professionals and make it a commodity for sale by the organisation. The health care industry has made efforts to capture the tacit knowledge of physicians for large diagnostic and treatment knowledge bases (Hansen *et al.*, 1999). This would allow less qualified and less experienced individuals to give health care advice based on a doctor's knowledge and expertise. In higher education some universities want to own the work done by faculty members on course Web sites. This would allow other instructors to use the labour and knowledge of the professor who created the Web site to conduct a course over and over again without the involvement of the professor who developed the course. This exploitation of a professional's knowledge raises questions of fairness and justice. Can professionals retain their autonomy after their knowledge has been 'mined' by the organisation? In addition, we could ask why corporate presidents and vice presidents, college deans and health care CEOs are not being asked to share their knowledge.

Trust, autonomy and privacy

By all accounts, trust is a key ingredient in the management of knowledge (Davenport and Prusak, 1998). If parties do not trust each other, it is doubtful that the knowledge transfer will be complete because new knowledge from the different parties will not be valued or absorbed. Creating knowledge repositories also requires an element of trust. There is an editorial process that occurs with KM, and those who do the editing are not always those who submit reports. It is possible that sensitive or key information might be deleted, and reports may not be summarised accurately when they are abstracted. There may be slippages in content. These publishing problems depend on trust between writers and repository creators or editors.

Those who share their knowledge need to trust that it will be used for legitimate purposes. A subsequent project might fail, for example, and the knowledge made available from a named employee might be blamed for influencing the failed project. Those whose names are listed 'publicly' in knowledge bases need to trust that they will be contacted and consulted when their expertise is truly needed. In large companies where there are thousands of employees, for example, individuals responsible for legendary successful projects could potentially be inundated with questions, email messages and phone calls. Their time could quickly be taken over by colleagues in search of knowledge.

Another misuse of knowledge bases can occur when clients are fooled into thinking they have hired an expert. A trusting client might assume that, in contracting with an established firm, it will have experts working on a problem. In a consulting project, though, a new hire, depending primarily on the company's knowledge bases, presents herself as an expert, but in fact she may be inexperienced and have little first-hand knowledge of any similar situation. Making tacit expert knowledge explicit could present a false sense of expertise on the part of employees who still need training, apprenticeships and experience before presenting themselves as knowledgeable. Not only does this 'expertise gap' violate the trusting relationship between client and consulting agency, but it is also dishonest and unfair. If one party to a contract is not acting in good faith or fulfilling its part of the bargain in an honest and straightforward manner, the relationship will soon falter. In the long run both parties to the contract will suffer. The consulting firm will not procure return business and dishonest practices may endanger its reputation. The client will not receive the expert knowledge which it needed and expected from the agreement.

Autonomy is as important as trust and fairness in the management of today's knowledge organisations. Knowledge workers, by their nature, respond well when allowed to schedule their own work times, arrange their own workspace, and complete work in the manner that they choose. For knowledge work, the results are important, but how they are arrived at can be at the discretion of the worker (Hesse and Grantham, 1991). Telecommuting workers in organisations have shown managers that they really don't need to see their staff physically on the premises in order to trust their work or get good results (Gordon, 1997; Frolick *et al.*, 1993). Autonomy can be co-opted by poorly managed knowledge systems, however, when email messages are monitored, or when text documents created on computer systems are captured for public repository purposes. This type of excessive oversight and recording of an individual's work can be an oppressive invasion of privacy. The advantages to the organisation of 'knowledge capture' are likely to be overshadowed by the negative environment created when work is so scrupulously watched and documented. There must be boundaries between interior space within the individual and the 'public' space of work and production.

Ethical issues in the use of technology tools

Some ethical issues that information professionals face are related to the technology systems employed for knowledge management. According to one estimate, there are now more than 1800 software products being marketed as knowledge management tools (*Financial Times*, 1999). A study done by Ovum estimates that the knowledge management software market will increase from $285 million in 1998 to $1.6 billion in 2002 (Computergram International, 1998). These increased numbers show that KM software has become a lucrative commodity, and it presents the potential for every start-up and well-established software firm to market many products as knowledge management tools, whether or not they can really help with true knowledge management.

Executives or system administrators who choose KM software need to be mindful of the pitfalls that some products present and cautious of possible ethical problems. 'The Reflective Knowledge Manager 2.0'[8] is a product developed by a well-known international software firm. It constructs a 'group memory' by compiling email and text documents entered by users, who copy the group memory when sending email. Users can then access the data in several ways. They can go to the headings that interest them, or designate certain headings of interest and then be notified by email or on a personal Web page each time new data are added to that category. The headings are predetermined by the company's managers, or may be set up using software provided by the software company. There are also templates available for certain common areas. For this system to be useful, employees must save their work to the group memory, which can be accomplished through training, encouragement or simply executive fiat.

If workers use 'Reflective Knowledge Manager' consistently, it provides a way for them to keep abreast of what has been done in an area and what is currently under way. The problems arise with ensuring first that the workers add information to the system, and second that they retrieve the information or knowledge regularly. Then there is the matter of adding headings consistently. As librarians know, any five people will use five different subject headings to describe the same document. For example, if a document consists of a presentation to a new client about a wireless communication system for accessing email and Internet Web sites, is the correct heading for the document the client's name? Or 'wireless communication' or 'email' or 'Internet' or 'Web site' or all of these terms? An ideal document retrieval system would use all of the terms with cross-referencing to the others. Then there is the question of using the same terms for the same or similar concepts consistently. For example, Minnesota-based 3M Corporation, a possible client, might be listed in a KM system under '3M' or 'Minnesota Mining and Manufacturing' or 'MN Mining & Manufacturing' etc., and the software would file each name in a different place in an alphabetized subject/client list. Users may or may not find the documents pertaining to 3M, depending on the version of the company's name they use. In order to have a system that employees will trust and use, consistency, currency, usability and stability are critical. These quality criteria are necessary to establish a system that employees will use and consider dependable. The method for organising documents is a key factor in helping users find what they need. A high-quality system with many subject headings and cross-referencing would be time-consuming and expensive to implement and maintain, and without training it would be useless.

One solution to the problem of getting employees to add narrative information into the group memory would be to develop a system that tracked all computer usage and automatically saved information to the group memory. For example, it could keep track of Internet sites visited, documents saved etc. and add that information to the knowledge repository.

'Ever Vigilant Entity' (EVE)[9] does just that. According to the developer's Web site, it 'audits every user operation, so you know who is doing what with which documents. Even denied operations, such as trying to view or delete documents without the necessary access rights, are recorded'. This solution raises ethical questions about autonomy and privacy. When is a document first saved to the 'group memory'? Are works-in-progress going to be available for everyone to view? How are employees going to react to a system that forces them to share everything that they do? And what happens when employees leave the company to go to work for competitors, and they have had access to the most recent projects of other employees? Of course, the transfer of intellectual property from one firm to another by employees who move to a new job is not a new problem, but today the stakes are higher and temptations deeper.

According to countless reports, today's job market is the tightest it's been in memory (Lienert, 1998; Powell, 1999). The result is that employees, especially those in knowledge-intensive positions, are job-hopping in order to seek better salaries and benefits. KM systems like EVE allow works in progress to be captured and copied easily. In a rapidly changing business climate that makes its fortune through innovation and technology products, bringing a 'new' idea to a company can be money in the bank. With writable CD drives and other portable storage devices readily available, cheap and easy to use, transporting organisational knowledge to a new organisation can be done quickly and quietly. The sharing of knowledge can be beneficial, but damage can be done as well by the unscrupulous employee who practises unauthorised 'sharing'.

Some knowledge management systems are little more than best-practice databases. This kind of system stores reports of practices that a company has tried and found successful. One problem, though, is that workers are expected not only to consult the systems (a good idea), but are then also advised to replicate best practices. Replicating is often a fine way to leverage the organisation's knowledge, but it might be a way to limit innovation as well if the requirements to 'do exactly as before' are too stringent. Employees can be held accountable for not using the 'best' methods that have proven successful for other parts of the company and are now included in the company's knowledge store. With a system like EVE it is very easy to check to see which information an employee has accessed and which he or she has not. Some see this potential monitoring ability as stifling creativity by forcing employees to follow one set method for each type of project. In the long run, strict adherence to best practice might hamper the development of new ideas, and it might limit the progress of the company (Schrage, 1999).

Any kind of monitoring also eats away at organisational trust. More important, perhaps, is the effect that continual computer monitoring has on the way that people see their workplace and feel about their labour. Computer monitoring can affect individual performance by causing psychological problems, feelings of powerlessness and shame, and depression (Brown, 1996; Zuboff, 1988). Although companies may have a legal right to monitor email, database access, keystrokes and other aspects of technology use, the implications of invading privacy and limiting personal autonomy will have repercussions in illness, lost work time and health care costs.

The success of a knowledge management system is largely dependent on the employees and the corporate culture in which it is being implemented. Because the knowledge that the system is attempting to capture is the tacit knowledge of an employee, without their cooperation a KM system is not successful. Even with the cooperation of employees, capturing something more than information (i.e. knowledge) in an electronic format is difficult. Employees need training in quality reporting that captures the knowledge rather than information or data in order to make it a true KM system and not merely a database.

After the knowledge is collected, a system for reaching the employees who need it must be in place. While knowledge management software products are designed with this in mind, information professionals within the company could provide much more tailored and useful classifications, especially if they understand effective channels for access to and distribution of the knowledge. Corporate librarians as knowledge managers can use their training in cataloguing and indexing information to be extremely helpful in the codification process of the knowledge management enterprise. A corporate librarian already understands the knowledge needs of the firm, and is therefore in a position to help determine the sort of knowledge management system that would be best for the organisation.

Conclusion

Knowledge management is more than just technology or software. It is a sophisticated way for an organisation to share intellectual assets. KM is best practised in situations that are collaborative and team-oriented. Effective knowledge management calls on those who are experienced to provide the knowledge that they have gained to those who develop the firm's knowledge repositories. It is up to information specialists, then, to treat the knowledge and the people responsible for it in fair and just ways that engender trust and confidence in the systems that are established.

This chapter has argued that special librarians, influenced by the work of Otlet and other documentalists, are well-prepared to assist in organisations' knowledge management efforts. Special librarians have expertise in determining knowledge needs, in connecting experts with novices, in organising and codifying knowledge, and in evaluating technology tools for knowledge storage and retrieval. They can share the work of gathering and organising the organisation's knowledge. Librarians are often the informal knowledge brokers in large firms (Davenport and Prusak, 1998).

These information professionals also have a tradition and share a fundamental value in ethical professional practices in information and knowledge transfer. We have laid out some of the emerging ethical issues in knowledge management relating to trust, autonomy and privacy, with examples of KM software that pose potential ethical problems. These are issues of interest to information professionals as well as those who have a stake in the managing and sharing of the organisation's knowledge. Innovative practices in business or information technology usually precede the legal and organisational sanctions governing their use. Knowledge management can be accomplished fairly and ethically with some reflection on how individuals are being treated and how their work, experience, and knowledge is honoured and respected. Involving a wide spectrum of information professionals who have experience and understanding of ethical information practices is one step toward solid and effective knowledge management systems.

Acknowledgements

We are indebted to Ron Day, Visiting Assistant Professor, University of Oklahoma, who read this chapter and gave us helpful comments and suggestions for its improvement. We would also like to thank Bob Zmud, Professor and Michael F. Price Chair in Management Information Systems, University of Oklahoma, for comments made at an ethics seminar held during spring 1999. We are also grateful to the editors who gave guidance and help in revising the draft of this chapter.

References

American Society for Information Science (1999) *ASIS Handbook and Directory*, Washington, DC: American Society for Information Science.

Barlow, J. P. (1994) 'A Taxonomy of Information', *Bulletin of the American Society for Information Science*, 20: 5 (June/July), 13–17.

Borghoff, U. M. and Pareschi, R. (eds.) (1998) *Information Technology for Knowledge Management*, Berlin: Springer-Verlag.

Briet, S. (1954) 'Bibliothécaires et Documentalistes', *Revue of Documentation*, XXI, 41–5.

Briet, S. (1951) *Qu'est-ce Que La Documentation?*, Paris: Édit.

Broadbent, M. (1998) 'The Phenomenon of Knowledge Management: What Does it Mean to the Information Profession?, *Information Outlook*, 2: 5 (May), 23–35.

Brown, W. S. (1996) 'Technology, Workplace Privacy, and Personhood', *Journal of Business Ethics*, 15: 11 (November), 1237–48.

Buckland, M. (1998) 'Documentation, Information Science, and Library Science in the U.S.A.', in Hahn, T. B. and Buckland, M. (eds.), *Historical Studies in Information Science*, Medford, NJ: Information Today.

Buckland, M. (1992) *Redesigning Library Services: Moving to the Electronic Library*, Chicago: American Library Association.

Computergram International (1998) 'Knowledge Management Vendors Poised for Battle', *Computergram International*, 2 October.

Davenport, T. H. (1997) 'Known Evils: Common Pitfalls of Knowledge Management', *CIO*, 15 June, http://www.cio.com/archive/061597_think_content.html.

Davenport, T. H. and Prusak, L. (1998) *Working Knowledge: How Organisations Manage What They Know*, Boston: Harvard Business School Press.

DiMattia, S. and Oder, N. (1997) 'Knowledge Management: Hope, Hype, or Harbinger?', *Library Journal*, 122: 3 (15 September), 33–5.

Frolick, M. N., Wilkes, R. B. and Urwiler, R. (1993) 'Telecommuting as a Workplace Alternative; an Identification of Significant Factors in American Firms' Determination of Work-at-Home Policies', *Journal of Strategic Information Systems*, 2: 3 (September), 206–22.

Gordon, G. (1997) Administration and General Information About Telecommuting, http://www.gilgordon.com/telecommuting/faq/administration.html, 12 September.

Haeckel, S. H. and Nolan, R. L. (1993) 'The Role of Technology in an Information Age: Transforming symbols into action', in The Institute for Information Studies, *The Knowledge Economy: The Nature of Information in the 21st Century*, Queenstown, MD: The Aspen Institute.

Hansen, M. T., Nohria, N., and Tierney, T. (1999) 'What's Your Strategy for Managing Knowledge?', *Harvard Business Review*, 77: 2 (March–April), 106–16.

Harari, O. (1994) 'The Brain Based Organisation', *Management Review*, 83: 6 (June), 57–60.

Nation's Business (1999) 'Hiring Stellar Employees in a Tight Job Market', *Nation's Business*, 87: 3 (March), 14.

Hesse, B. W. and Grantham, C. E. (1991) 'Electronically Distributed Work Communities: Implications for Research on Telework', *Electronic Networking*, 1: 1 (Fall), 4–17.

Financial Times (1999) 'How to Map Knowledge Management,' *Financial Times*, 8 March. Accessed through Lexis-Nexis Academic Universe (11 March 1999).

Johnson, E. (1915) 'The Special Library and Some of its Problems', *Special Libraries*, 6: 10 (December), 157–61.

Computergram International (1998) 'Knowledge Management Vendors Poised for Battle', *Computergram International*, 2 October 1998. Accessed through First Search Business and Industry Database, 23 July 1999.

Koenig, M. E. D. (1996) 'Intellectual Capital and Knowledge Management', *IFLA Journal*, 22: 4, 299–301.

Lienert, A. (1998) 'Employees Benefit in Tight Job Market', *The Detroit News*, 24 August 1998, http://detnews.com/1998/biz/labor/monlead/monlead.htm.

McInerney, C. R. (1999) *Providing Date, Information, and Knowledge to the Virtual Office: Organisational Support for Remote Workers*, Washington, DC: Special Libraries Association.

Otlet, P. (1895–96, 1990) 'Sur la structure des nombres classificateurs', IIB Bulletin 1, Bruxelles: IIB, pp. 230–43, translated and edited by Rayward, W. B. (1990) 'On the Structure of Classification Numbers', *International Organisation and Dissemination of Knowledge: Selected Essays of Paul Otlet*, Amsterdam: Elsevier, pp. 51–60.

Otlet, P. (1907, 1990) 'L'Organisation systématique de la documentation et le développment de l'Institut International de Bibliographie', IIB Publication No. 82, Bruxelles: IIB, pp. 7–15, translated and edited by Rayward, W. B. (1990) 'The Systematic Organisation of Documentation and the Development of the International Institute of Bibliiography',

International Organisation and Dissemination of Knowledge: Selected Essays of Paul Otlet, Amsterdam: Elsevier, pp. 105–111.

Powell, J. H. (1999) 'Tight Job Market Tests Employers' Creativity', *Boston Herald*, 328, 30626 (22 April).

Ranganathan, S. R. (1949, 1989) *Philosophy of Library Classification*, Bangalore, India: Sarada Ranganathan Endowment for Library Science.

Rayward, W. B. (1983) 'Library and Information Sciences: Disciplinary Differentiation, Competition, and Convergence', in Machlup, F. and Mansfield, U. (eds.), *The Study of Information*, New York: John Wiley & Sons, pp. 343–63.

Rayward, W. B. (1998a) 'The History and Historiography of Information Science: Some Reflections', in Hahn, T. B. and Buckland, M. (eds.), *Historical Studies in Information Science*, Medford, NJ: Information Today, pp. 7–21.

Rayward, W. B. (1998b) 'The Origins of Information Science and the International Institute of Bibliography/International Federation for Information and Documentation (FID)', in Hahn, T. B. and Buckland, M. (eds. *Historical Studies in Information Science*, Medford, NJ: Information Today, pp. 22–33.

Rayward, W. B. (1998c) 'Visions of Xanadu: Paul Otlet (1868–1944) and Hypertext', in Hahn, T. B. and Buckland, M. (eds.), *Historical Studies in Information Science*, Medford, NJ: Information Today, pp. 65–80.

Rifkin, J. (1995) *The End of Work: The Decline of the Global Labor Force and the Dawn of the Post-Market Era*, New York: G. P. Putnam's Sons.

Rowley, J. E. (1988) *Abstracting and Indexing*, London: Clive Bingley.

Ruggles, R. L. (ed.) (1997) *Knowledge Management Tools*, Boston: Butterworth-Heinemann.

Ruggles, R. L. (1998) 'The State of the Notion: Knowledge Management in Practice', *California Management Review*, 40: 3 (Spring), 80–90.

Schor, J. B. (1991) *The Overworked American: The Unexpected Decline of Leisure*, New York: Basic Books.

Schrage, M. (1999) 'The Nightmare Of Networks: When Best Practices Meet The Intranet, Innovation Takes a Holiday', *Fortune*, 139 (29 March), 198.

Scott, P. J. and Kirby, A. E. (1999) 'The SLA Competencies: Raising the Bar on Performance', *Library Journal*, 124: 12 (July), 46–8.

Senge, P. M. (1990) *The Fifth Discipline: The Art & Practice of The Learning Organisation*, New York: Currency Doubleday.

Shera, J. (1966) *Documentation and the Organisation of Knowledge*, Hamden, CT: Archon Books.

Shera, J. (1983) 'Librarianship and Information Science', in Machlup, F. and Mansfield, U. (eds.), *The Study of Information: Interdisciplinary Messages*, New York: John Wiley & Sons, pp. 379–88.

Williams, R. V. (1998) 'The Documentation and Special Libraries Movements in the United States, 1910–1960', in Hahn, T. B. and Buckland, M. (eds.), *Historical Studies in Information Science*, Medford, NJ: Information Today, pp. 173–80.

Wilson, P. (1983) 'Bibliography R & D', in Machlup, F. and Mansfield, U. (eds.), *The Study of Information: Interdisciplinary Messages*, New York: John Wiley & Sons, pp. 389–97.

Zuboff, S. (1988) *In the Age of the Smart Machine: The Future of Work and Power*, New York: Basic Books.

Notes

1   'Special librarians' is a term for those who are librarians in corporations, government agencies, museums, associations, newspapers, hospitals, law firms and other

organisations where the clientèle is defined and the information functions are critical to the mission of the organisation.

2 The Gartner Group is a high-technology consulting firm: `http://gartner5.gartnerweb.com/public/static/home/home.html`.

3 Although the company is hypothetical, the example is based on real-life experience of the information professionals in an American *Fortune* 100 company, two *Fortune* 500 companies and a global management consulting firm (McInerney, 1999).

4 In a 1998 research project interviews revealed that in one large corporation employees assumed that the MIS Department was responsible for all the corporate Web sites and intranets, but in fact the librarians in the corporate information centre were the key Web developers (McInerney, 1999).

5 The biological sciences have traditionally been arranged in taxonomies of genus and species index terms for plants and animals. One can argue that the assignment of the taxonomies or cascading subject categories is inexact at best, using characteristics that may or may not be the best attributes in which to group plants or animals. The advantages of taxonomies are that they are recorded, standardised and understandable to users.

6 Rayward (1998b) reports that such a 'hypercard stack' was developed for the International Offices of Documentation for the Polar Regions, for Hunting and Fishing, and for Aeronautics.

7 The study was conducted by the Ernst & Young Center for Business Innovation (Ruggles, 1998).

8 All names of software products used here are fictional, but they are based on real software marketed for KM purposes.

9 EVE is a fictional name based on an actual product.

2 Intellectual Capital: Managing by Numbers

Ali Yakhlef and Miriam Salzer-Mörling

Introduction

Upon her arrival in Africa, a Swedish aid worker is greeted by a native black boy who eagerly and willingly starts to help her unpack. A long pen-like thing in one of her bags catches his attention:

'What's this?', he asks, carefully examining the object.

'It's a thermometer', replies the aid worker.

'What's it for?'

'Oh, it's a device that tells you how cold the weather is...'

The boy muses for a second and gazes at her.

'But why do you need that? Doesn't white skin *feel*?'

Throughout the history of management, the relationship between employees and their organisation has been the target of many programmes of rationalisation and reformation: 'scientific management', 'human relations', 'human resource management', 'Business Process Re-engineering' etc. Among the newcomers to this litany are what have come to be labelled 'knowledge management' and 'intellectual capital'. Whereas 'scientific management' sought to remedy the weaknesses associated with the employee's body and motion in time and space, 'knowledge management' is more specifically posed to target the mind of the employee. Against a background chorus chanting the advent of the information/knowledge society, it has become widely accepted that knowledge is a useful thing for companies to have, thereby taking centre stage in most strategic discussions.

Within the rapidly expanding field of knowledge management, accounting for intellectual capital has emerged as a distinct area aiming at turning knowledge into a calculable asset. In Foucault's (1972) terms, intellectual capital has become a *discursive formation* in that it has created professors, journals, conferences and many other enunciative authorities, such as consulting firms and industry analysts, whose sole business it is to devise and elaborate different measuring techniques, theories and concepts which are disseminated in the popular press as well as in more informed circles.

Consequently, the top concern of corporate managers today revolves around such questions as: What is knowledge? Where does it reside? How to secure it, spread it, develop it, manage it, measure it etc.? The ultimate aim – which can be traced to Taylor – is to displace knowledge from the body it inhabits to the balance sheet, where it is meant to feature as a new type of capital, commonly referred to as 'intellectual capital', rivalling and eclipsing the traditional concept of financial capital. The concept of 'intellectual capital' is today very much *en vogue*, getting all the headlines in the popular press as well as in more informed research publications. Hence, within the terms of the discourse on intellectual capital, knowledge has fallen prey to the vocabulary and practices of accounting. Knowledge has become the target of management, of control, of rational, calculative thinking and of the practices of accounting.

Aim of the Chapter

This chapter attempts to develop an epistemological questioning of the evolving discourse on intellectual capital. Beginning by analysing some of the assumptions underlying the discourse, we proceed to lay bare some of the intentions animating the attempts to turn knowledge into numbers. What are the implications of attempting to manage knowledge by numbers? The epistemological critique draws on ideas from post-structuralism, philosophy and the sociology of knowledge.

Within the hotly debated discourse on intellectual capital, organisational members' knowledge has come to be represented as assets and items of property as though they were discrete bundles of legally defined and enforceable property rights, and as if they could be transferred from one owner to another. Even though most philosophers and social scientists are hard put to agree what knowledge is, it is hoped that breaking it down into different categories and attaching these to various types of metrication will tell us something about the nature of knowledge. This point is epitomised in the following note: '...when you can measure what you are speaking about, you know something about it; when you cannot measure it... your knowledge is of a meagre and unsatisfactory kind' (Thomson, 1889).

We proceed to discuss some of the incoherent assumptions underlying the discourse on intellectual capital. For instance, we discern and question the practice of separation and exclusion (between various forms of knowledge) as a method to construct accountable worlds (Yakhlef, 1998), a lionisation of cognition to the detriment of other modes of knowing and experiencing the world (Calori, 1998), an un/natural bent to favour numbers as a mode of control (Porter, 1996) and a mode of being in an organisation. It is remarkable that mythopoetic and emotional aspects, as well as intuitive thinking, are conspicuous by their absence in this debate.

Finally, we turn to an analysis of the intentions and ambitions animating the discourse, where the main concern revolves around the purposes and functions that the discourse serves. For one thing, it could be said that the attempt at inventing the category of 'intellectual capital' as an object of thought arises out of an uncertainty. Such uncertainty has come to be widely shared across corporate landscapes. Intellectual capital, if it remains unknown to management, can be seen as an organisational (social?) danger: the spectre of employees holding most of the strategic resources underlying the corporation is too harsh a reality for managers to swallow. Knowledge is not to be insubordinate and hidden from the scrutinising gaze of any governing instance, otherwise managers cannot be held responsible for things lying beyond their immediate gaze and control. However, the nagging question is how one can put a price and an exchange value on human brains.

For another, the reduction of knowledge into numbers has a governing potential (Miller and Rose, 1994), leading to what Latour (1987) calls a centre of calculation. As noted in Power (1996), we need to recognise the deep relation between quantitative practices, such as statistics and accounting on the one hand, and administrative and managerial concerns on the other. To put it differently, the 'ambit of accounting... is first of all administrative and not cognitive' (Porter, 1992, quoted in Power, 1996). Hence the main concern of the discourse on intellectual capital is not to create or develop knowledge, but to control through an authoritarian fabrication of meaning (Salzer-Mörling, 1998).

The Discourse on Intellectual Capital

The formation of the discourse on intellectual capital is predicated upon the assumption that the traditional double-entry bookkeeping system is not able to reflect emerging realities. It is an inadequate tool for measuring the value of corporations whose value, it is claimed, lies mainly in their intangible components. The aim of the critique of the old system is to create a sense of urgency and necessity, thereby paving the way for, or legitimising the need for, alternative systems. The rhetoric is couched predominantly in apocalyptic terms: the implication is that there is no future for companies if they do not seriously address and manage their intellectual capital diligently:

> Step lively now and you will be in the vanguard of this movement, better prepared and more experienced than your competitors. Or wait, until it washes over you and tosses you forward, struggling to keep from being dashed and drowned. But make no mistake, whatever path you choose, Intellectual Capital is our future (Edvinsson and Malone, 1997, p. 22).

Furthermore, this call for a new system is not the making of researchers or of a small group, but rather, it is claimed, it comes from the environment which puts pressure on organisations to make their assets more visible so that the shareholders can exert more control over their ventures. Hence

...this lack of common practices for disclosing and visualising Intellectual Capital hurts all stakeholders and investors. They, too, can miss a subtle change in tenor or the loss of a key knowledge-carrying employee that signals the coming eclipse of a corporate star (Edvinson and Malone, 1997, p. 7).

In this connection, a number of enunciative authorities have contributed to the creation of this discourse, amplifying the significance of intangible assets to the detriment of financial assets. More recently, in a cover story in *Fortune*, Stewart (1994) heralds intellectual capital as the company's most valuable asset, the main challenge being how to operate and evaluate a business when knowledge is its chief ingredient. The claims posit that the value of intellectual assets exceeds by many times the value of assets that appear on the balance sheet, and that intellectual capital is the fount from which financial results are generated etc. Financial capital is hence made subsidiary to intellectual capital.

The notion that there is a value hiatus between the corporation's real value and the value shown on balance sheets has come to be referred to as *Tobin's q*. Tobin's q was introduced in 1969 by James Tobin to be used as a predictor of a company's future investments. It compares a company's market value to the replacement value of all its physical assets. The measure has been used to explain a variety of things, such as how to gauge a company's intangible value or the difference between a company's physical and monetary assets and its market value: Market Value $= q \times$ Asset Value, where q stands for the relation between the market value and the asset value. For example, if $q = 10$, then the market value is meant to be 10 times higher than the asset value. As examples of companies that are assumed to have a high *Tobin's q*, Sveiby (in Bontis, 1997) mentions that 'Shares in Microsoft, the world's largest computer software firm, changed hands at an average price of $70 during the fiscal 1995 at a time when their so-called blood value was just $7. In other words, for every $1 of recorded value the market saw $9 in additional value for which there was no corresponding record in Microsoft's balance sheet'.

These statements, multiplied though they may be, are often reinforced by, and reinforce, a set of larger social discourses such as the transition to a post-Fordist, post-industrial economy which puts a premium on knowledge and information rather than on raw material. Within this context, knowledge is redefined as an asset that can be identified, and that management has been called on to enhance it and measure it in order to contribute to the value of the corporation. Skandia AFS was one of the first enthusiastic companies to embrace the idea and practice of intellectual capital, having gone a long way towards making the *human assets* visible in the financial reports. In fact, Skandia was the

first company to submit a supplement to the traditional annual report on intellectual capital and to institutionalise the new category of 'Director of Intellectual
Capital', to refer to the manager who is made responsible for controlling the so-
called knowledge assets.

Having depicted the background against which the discourse on intellectual
capital has arisen – a background problematising and marginalising prevailing
valuation techniques – let us now proceed to describe the various efforts
deployed in translating the complex and sticky domain concerning knowledge
into numbers. In this process, we focus on how the molten realm of knowledge
(Porter, 1996) is, against its natural bent, successively categorised and
subcategorised and subsequently converted into numbers. The category 'intellectual capital' should not be taken as a self-contained cognitive object resulting
from a natural unfolding of the history of accounting, but we need to ask how it
has found its way from its immediate, homely habitat (the body and mind) to
the annual report. As noted before, intellectual capital has arisen as a critique of
the assumably obsolete model of 'financial capital'. Hence the intellectual capital
discourse's motto is to capitalise on other subtler resources having to do with
knowledge and the intellect. This process will also lead to the invention of
criteria which will support and sustain the overall logic and purposes of the
discourse.

Divisions and Subdivisions

One of the organising principles underlying the discourse on intellectual capital
is that of division and separation. On the basis of Edvinsson and Malone's (1997)
definition of organisational economic realities, intellectual capital yields two
classes: *human capital* and *structural capital*. The division is based on the principle
of the location of that capital. Edvinsson and Malone (1997) define human
capital as the value of everything that 'leaves the company at five p.m.', that is,
the values of the employees. Notice that human capital stands for that part of
knowledge that could be made explicit, codified in words and figures, barring
from the debate other forms of implicit knowledge that resist mapping and
quantification. Human capital has been subjected to further division and subdi-
visions, such as *individual* and *shared capital* (Hudson, quoted in Bontis, 1997).

By contrast, structural capital is everything that remains within the company
after 5 p.m., when every employee has gone home. This is meant to be structured, encoded into documents and secured within the confines and culture of
the company. At this juncture, a distinction is made between *customer capital* and
organisational capital. By 'customer capital' reference is made to the company's
relationships with its customers. Organisational capital is claimed to include two
further aspects of capital: *innovation capital* and *process capital*. Whereas the
former is described as the company's renewal strength 'expressed as protected
commercial rights, intellectual property, and other intangible assets and values'

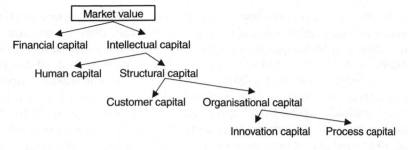

Figure 2.1   Skandia's intellectual capital model (Skandia CD-ROM, June 1996)

(Supplement to Skandia's 1996 Annual Report), the latter stands for the 'combined value of value-creating processes' (Supplement to Skandia's 1996 Annual Report), as represented in Figure 2.1. This figure displays the different components of intellectual capital as conceived of by Skandia. Further, in order to increase the prospects of calculability of this newly created cognitive category, the Balanced Scorecard, as a conceptual tool, is adapted for capturing the various aspects of a firm: *financial focus, customer, human, process* and *renewal and development* (Kaplan and Norton, 1996). Whereas the financial focus is assumed to represent the past and the customer and process foci represent the present, the renewal and development focus is posited to stand for the future. Within this arrangement, the human focus takes centre stage, around which all other components revolve (see Figure 2.2).

To illustrate the logic underlying the intellectual model and how it is supposed to work, let us consider an investment in new IT media, for example. Such an investment will be shown in the financial annual report as a cost, thereby reducing the financial value of the company. On the opposite side, the investment will affect the other components positively. It is hoped, for instance, that it will improve customer service, rationalise internal processes, amplify

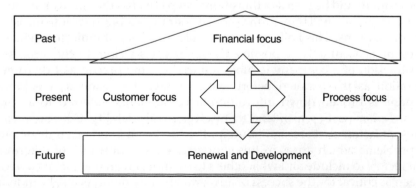

Figure 2.2   The Skandia Navigator (a version of the Balanced Scorecard)

research and development, and make people more productive and more creative. The 'Balanced Scorecard' (Kaplan and Norton, 1996) is a measurement and management technique which seeks to capture the total value – financial and intellectual. The Balanced Scorecard is only one facet, or mode of manifestation, of the intellectual capital. Notice that there is no consensus concerning these descriptions, which we are unable to explore or much less to arbitrate within the limited scope of this chapter. Rather, we intend to provide an understanding of the logic underlying the construction of the category of intellectual capital and some of the accessory devices deployed to operationalise it as an intellectual tool for managing and controlling organised action.

So far we have been concerned with the practices of division and classification deployed in order to bring forth the different components of intellectual capital. As we shall see later, underlying such cognitive operations (or discursive practices) is the logic of division and separation. Before that, our immediate concern in what follows is to explore how the various categories, made visible through the practices of division and separation, are converted into numbers – an inscription form that is readily amenable to quantification and calculability. Numbers constitute the thread of accounting techniques.

Developing Indicators

The ambition of visualising the category of intellectual capital and of translating it into numbers has led to the invention of a new category – 'indicators'. Indicators are different from the traditional key ratios in that they do not display any value in themselves. What they actually measure is change. Edvinsson and Malone (1997) provide the following example of an indicator: the number of customer visits to the company. In itself this indicator says little about the strategic thrust of the firm. However, when compared with the other indicators within the same focus and the flows among the other foci and between the top-down flows, one can attach, it is claimed, a strategic value to its impact.

Indicators could be seen as a transitional step towards the realm of numbers. It is hoped that they will transform vision and strategic objectives into measurable inscription forms. This boils down to developing a set of indicators which will represent as accurately as possible the company's vision. In this process, the overall vision of a company is subjected to the same practices of division and separation as those noted before. Accordingly, the vision or mission of a company is broken down into different components, referred to as *Critical Success Factors* (CSF) which lend themselves to calculability. CSFs are meant to represent factors that are significant for the success of a certain strategy. One of the problems which arises in this connection is the difficulty of determining what factors to include and what others to exclude, given that factors that could be seen as critical for the success of any strategy may theoretically be indefinite. The only way of circumventing this difficulty is to develop the criterion of relevance. Hence if these indicators are to be of any use, it is argued, one should restrict oneself to those criteria that are most relevant. Table 2.1 displays a set of samples of indicators used by Skandia.

The selection of relevant criteria is an arbitrary process, which is attendant upon the perception and attitudes, and favouring, of those who are entitled to make the selection. As noted by Roos *et al.* (1997) 'it is extremely rare for managers to sit down and try to understand where the company's value comes from'. Hence both the identification and selection of CSFs involve a process resting upon the whims and priorities of those doing the selection. The meaning of indicators is derived from their relation to the flows of the CSFs. For instance, the flows linking a certain indicator to the overall strategy are assumed to exhibit the extent to which the indicator is in concordance with the company's strategy.

Table 2.1   Examples of indicators used by Skandia

Financial focus

Value added/employee ($)

IT expenses/administrative expenses (%)

Return on net asset value (%)

Customer focus

Customer visits to the company (#)

Market share (%)

Customer lost (%)

Process focus

Change in IT inventory ($)

Processing time, out payments (#)

Application filed without error (#)

Renewal and development focus

R&D expenses /administrative expense (%)

Training expenses/employee ($)

Premium from new launches (%)

Human focus

Employee turnover (%)

Number of women managers (#)

Average age of employees (#)

The flows among the different foci (from the Processes to the Human, Renewal and Development, the Customer and finally the Financial) are meant to show the extent to which indicators can be used in the measurement process. For instance, the flow is assumed to show how well an increase in an indicator belonging to the Renewal and Development focus correlates with the Financial focus. It is important to note that the latter flow shows the input–output relationship between investment in intellectual capital and the financial outcome ensuing from it. However, the logic of this correlation can be questioned. To what extent can the relation among the various foci (especially that between the Financial focus on the one hand and the other foci on the other) be established? Indicators are generated from changes in the Financial focus. An improvement in the Financial focus may not be connected to an improvement in intellectual capital, thereby casting some doubt over this correlation.

Indices

Indices are devised to address some of the limitations just mentioned above. The expression *intellectual capital index* (IC index) is the contribution of the London-based consultant company Intellectual Capital Services (ICS). The underlying assumption is that indices can be developed to capture in numbers indicators, perspectives and other areas of interest, or into a consolidated index for the whole company (Roos *et al.*, 1997). The IC index is meant to capture the total capital of a company, ranging from its knowledge to its strategy and business. The idea behind the index approach is simple: a number of indicators are expressed in numbers and weighted together into an index for a whole perspective or focus. The indices representing each focus are then aggregated into a compiling IC. When consolidating the different indicators, these have to be of the same dimension, expressed in an index value. The consolidated index will then measure the aggregated relative change of the indicators. The same weights are ascribed to all indicators within a perspective or a focus. For instance, if five indicators are used, each indicator should be weighted by 0.2, given that the sum of the weights should always be 1. As summarised in the following equation, the return on intellectual capital equals the transformation efficiency between the intellectual and the financial capital divided by the positive effects of an investment on the intellectual capital:

ROIC = Flows from IC to FC/Flows from FC to IC

This sketchy outline of the logic underlying the discourse on intellectual capital displays a number of cognitive practices. Prominent among these is the assumption that reality is can be divided into ever smaller components and that these components can unproblematically be turned into figures. To recap: the process of developing these figures is arbitrary, and in no way seeks to grasp any reality or value that is independent of the relations and interrelations constructed by the discourse itself. Furthermore, the principle of division and separation is predicated upon the assumption that reality is dichotomously structured, ordered in a binary logic (Foucault, 1970, 1972). The indicators and the indices deriving from the vision and the strategy of the company translate critical success factors into intellectual capital changes and show how these changes interplay with financial resources. The choice of such success factors is geared towards favouring too cognitivist a view of the intellect and towards forms that can be reduced to figures and amenable to calculability and measurements, as discussed in the next section.

The Ordering of Intellectual Capital

So far we have briefly depicted the main features of the discourse on intellectual capital. What if we were to begin by posing the question of how this discourse is constructed and what purpose it serves? What is proposed here is then to search out the dynamics of the process that constitutes the category of 'intellectual capital'. Any critique should start with an examination of the definition of the object and the classification of its subcategories. It is to be noted from the outset that there are other ways of telling the story of intellectual capital, depending on the various schools of thought and theorists. Therefore, in this presentation, we try as much as possible to draw on one version of this discourse, focusing mainly, but not solely, on the work of Edvinsson and Malone (1997).

Within this evolving discourse, the expression 'intellectual capital' is defined, by Edvinsson and Malone (1997, p. 44), in the following way:

> Intellectual Capital is the possession of the knowledge, applied experience, organisational technology, customer relationships and professional skills that provide Skandia with a competitive edge in the market.

From this it would emerge that it is unproblematic to establish a correlation between the possession of these resources and a competitive edge. While it is possible that Skandia enjoyed a high growth rate from the beginning of the 1990s onward, can we attribute this to the implementation of the practice of intellectual capital? During that period, the economic situation in general is claimed to have improved significantly, not necessarily as a result of the implementation of intellectual capital. It is therefore difficult to establish such a causal link between the practice of intellectual capital and competitive edge, as implied in the definition.

Intellectual capital, according to the authors, consists of two categories: 'human capital' and 'structural capital', and as noted before, the distinction between them lies in that the former constitutes the value of everything that leaves the company at 5 p.m., and the latter is everything that stays in the company when the human capital has left. Hence by structural capital is meant the company's documenta-tion, customer databases, software, structures, trademarks, manuals etc. – all of which are aspects that the company can purport to possess. Now, these defini-tions are not detached descriptions of the nature of these two phenomena. Rather, they are prescriptive, functioning as the basis for action: since human capital implies uncertainty for the company – being unalienable and hard to measure – the challenge is to extract it and transform it into structural capital, which can be amenable to control, measurement and deliberation.

On this view, the human capital is a corporate risk, since it can go out through the door and never come back. Therefore part of the task of the practice of intel-lectual capital is to enforce routines of documentation, of transferring knowl-edge from humans to machines where it can be articulated into more endurable and stable forms. From this perspective, the discourse is not only concerned with visualising the total value of a company, but primarily with creating the very value that it purports to visualise. Hence it is the structural capital that is more interesting, not because it opens up new vistas of knowledge and insights for the employees, but because it offers more prospects for control and measurement.

On the other hand, the overall distinction between human and structural capital is not a hard and fast one. Recall that intellectual capital is manifested in five foci, or perspectives: financial, customer, process, renewal and development, and human. The human focus picks up such dimensions as staff turnover, number of women managers and average age of employees. In this connection, human components emerge under the guise of structural capital, casting a cloud over the overall distinc-tion between human and structural capital (Olve *et al.*, 1997).

Critical Discussion of Intellectual Capital

The way in which the discourse on intellectual capital is organised in dichoto-mies – human *or* structural, organisational *or* customer, process *or* renewal (see Figure 2.1) – is remarkable. It is as though there was no ambiguity, no vagueness, no overlapping between the dichotomous concepts. Can we talk of a human-less structural capital, a renewal activity without processes, and organisational capital which excludes its customer capital? Where do the boundaries of human capital stop and where do those of structural capital begin? Is it defined in terms of transportability? How about software or databases existing in computers? These too can be transported home after work. The law of excluded middle (A or not A) presupposes that the symbols used are precise, which they are not (Russell, 1923, in Calori, 1998). The mode of reasoning in terms of *either or* displays antinomies without synthesis.

Another way of questioning this dichotomous thinking, this reduction of social and organisational activities into a conceptual model, is by invoking some post-structuralist ideas, drawing on what has come to be referred to as 'radical relationalism' and 'non-closure'. From a relationalist perspective, 'nothing can be specified independently or outside of a set of differential articulation' (Daly, 1991). Any definition is the articulation of difference; hence it is only by developing this relational logic in this relational formation (established between categories and spaces) introduced by the authors that the intellectual capital is created. Hence the identification of the class of intellectual capital is attendant upon how it is articulated in a set of practices and categories within this relational formation.

Non-closure implies that, assuming that any object identified is the outcome of a discursive relational formation, the identity of any object can never be fixed or closed, 'but is under constant threat of subversion/recovery from alternative differential articulations' (Daly, 1991). For example, the class of 'woman' will be constructed as a particular difference within the relational pattern 'family', 'mother', 'passive' etc., and as a countervailing difference in respect to the relational sequence 'oppressed', 'angry', 'equal rights' etc. These two relational orderings exist in the infinite play of differences. From this relationalist perspective, any separation between spheres will be contingent and precarious, depending solely on the historical construction and not on any *a priori* division of necessity. Put differently, the language in which intellectual capital is couched, as well as its truth claims, are not already 'out there' waiting for the authors to discover them. Rather, they are the outcome of the discourse itself.

Predominance of Cognitivism at the Expense of Emotions

One of the assumptions underlying the discourse on intellectual capital is that knowledge could be transmitted from individuals to structures. On this count, one can question whether the form of knowledge that could be verbalised and encoded into organisational structures is actually the source of competitive advantage. Is there more to knowledge than just the objective, codifiable, explicit side of it?

Indeed, most theorists are at one that individuals – and by extension, organisations – know more than they can tell. For Polanyi (1966) all knowledge has a tacit dimension. At one extreme of a continuum, knowledge is almost completely tacit, semiconscious and unconscious in people's heads and bodies, and at the other extreme it is almost completely explicit, or codified, structured and accessible to people other than the individuals originating it (Leonard and Sensiper, 1998). To the extent that the tacit dimension is not publicly available and hence difficult to imitate, should not this be the source of competitive advantage, rather than the components that are accessible to consultants and partners as well as competitors? Spender (1996), Grant (1996), Bennett (1998) and others, argue for the importance of tacit knowledge in constituting competitive advantage. On this view, the rationale for the existence of the firm comes from a fundamental *asymmetry* in the economics of knowledge (Grant, 1996). To the extent that codifiable knowledge can easily migrate and diffuse over borders, this asymmetry comes from tacit knowledge, which is immobile and intrinsically bound up with the individuals working side by side in an organisation. Markets are at a disadvantage because they cannot create conditions under which multiple individuals can integrate their tacit knowledge.

In this sense, intellectual capital seems to be concerned merely with the kind of knowledge that is explicit, codifiable and ready to be put into any of the cognitive boxes constructed by the discourse itself. Whatever can be encoded into what is constructed as intellectual capital would then by any measure be regarded as a part of that capital. Apparently this assumes an objectivist mode of knowing, suppressing other alternative ways of knowing and experiencing the world. Intellectual capital would not represent the share nor the say of individuals who are 'feelers', that is, who deploy heuristics and intuition in enacting and solving problems. Feeling and emotion have been conspicuous by their absence in this debate; this is so even though many efforts today are being deployed by many theorists to bring emotions into the domain of intelligence (usually referred to as 'emotional intelligence' (such as treated in Salovey and Mayor (1990) and Fineman (1993)).

Privileging Numbers as a Mode of Knowing and Controlling the World

> The perspective taken in this book is that these two concerns [measurement and management] are two sides of the same coin: what you can measure, you can manage, and what you want to manage, you have to measure. (Roos *et al.*, 1997)

Not only does the discourse on intellectual capital invent the category of intellectual capital, but also the tool for measuring it. Therefore the next part of our critical discussion will focus on how the discourse turns knowledge into the calculable form of numbers, subjecting them to the language of accounting.

Within the terms of this discourse on intellectual capital, there is a concerted effort to make intellectual assets visible and to show their value in financial and annual reports. The problem begins when you try to capture in numbers the secrets of tacit knowledge that employees hold. Increasingly, managers of organisations have become aware of the fact that translating human capital into structural capital is itself an investment. If knowledge is safely stored in the organisational databases and structures, an organisation stands to lose less money if one of its experts leaves it with all the knowledge and information that he or she may have.

In an attempt to make these newly invented categories and subcategories amenable to control, they have become the target of quantification, whereby these are inscribed in quantifiable inscription forms, namely numbers. Once divided up into subsets and purified from fuzziness and ambivalence, it is only a small step to reduce them to numbers. Recall that the passage from categories to numbers is via the concept of indicators. Indicators involve a number of Critical Success Factors which are meant to derive from the overall strategic vision and extend to the various foci or perspectives. We have also noticed that indicators are aggregated into indices. Remember further that the process of converting the strategic vision into indicators and indices is arbitrary in that the identification and the selection of Critical Success Factors are attendant upon the interests of those doing the selection. Subjective though this process may be, it brings intellectual work to rationality. By translating knowledge into the economic – supposedly rational – language, managers are hoping to improve the prospects of rational behaviour and control. As it were, accounting has the particularity of turning inherently subjective components into institutional objectivities by virtue of being widely presupposed to be true (Porter, 1996). Numbers are 'objective because they are stable, not the other way around' (Porter, 1996).

As noted by Porter (1996), '[n]atural knowledge is rarely conceived in terms of objects that can be equated with money, the universal substance of accounting'. Measuring knowledge is not simply a matter of applying a metre stick. First there is the problem of defining the status of intellectual capital and the form of knowledge that is part of that capital and what is not. Then one has to decide about the choice of the parameters to be included in the calculation. Most of the time, quantifying a quality necessarily means to 'ignore a rich array of meanings and connotations. This recalls Nietzsche's observations on history: the form of life epitomized by quantification depends on the art of forgetting' (Porter, 1996). Quantifying a quality abstracts away from it contextual and conventional cues. In the case of intellectual capital, the effort pursued to mathematise knowledge has mainly focused on what can be verbalised, codified and communicated. In some way, what can be articulated and communicated to other specialists has given rise to a standardised, common language concerning intellectual capital concepts among people in different places. Standardisation is one way of formalising and making impersonal and stable the meaning of the concepts used. The creation of stable successful concepts implies the creation of 'cognitive objects', or new entities. Converting the molten and diffuse realm of organisational knowledge into neatly delineated arrays of entities creates new things, or at least changes old ones (Porter, 1996).

However, the reduction of intellectual capital has a constitutive effect. It would be naïve to assume that indicators and indices related to intellectual capital merely act as a mirror reflecting or representing the value of a company. Citing to Gigerenzer *et al.* (1989), Porter (1996) observes that '[n]umbers react back on the process they are designed to measure, and are themselves important actors in the economic process'. If, for instance, Microsoft releases positive figures, these will serve to emphasise to shareholders and investors the success of their ventures, strengthening their commitment and confidence in the company's thrust. Bad figures will send a shiver down the spine of the local stock exchange, if not the world economy as a whole. Figures, positive or negative, will be interpreted and used as an input in many a decision concerning investments, personnel policies, strategies etc. In that way, they are resurrected in more impactful and tangible ways. In the long run, the form and strategy that a company takes are dependent upon the nature of such numbers. Hence, rather than the numbers representing the company, we will find that the company, as an entity, will be shaped by numbers. This does not, however, imply an all too deterministic view of numbers. As Porter (1996) observes, the world does not always yield to the 'forms impressed on it by some quantitative *force majeure*'. That is, just because numbers can take on such a powerful status, their power can easily be challenged and undermined by actors seeking to circumvent them. In accounting practices, this technique is usually referred to as 'creative accounting'.

Concluding Remarks

The function of accounting techniques is to expose knowledge, to make it visible to internal as well as external agencies, and to subject it to the practice of exchange. The creation of the category of intellectual capital draws knowledge closer to the market (Porter, 1996), making its value subject to the laws of the market, of competition etc. By inventing the techniques for calculating it, managers and corporations have become responsibilised for its creation and deployment. Furthermore, the invention of this category implies not only the invention of new metrication instruments, but also a disciplining and disci-plined category of managers and employees, be it 'manager of intellectual capi-tal', 'knowledge executive' or 'knowledge worker'. Managers of intellectual capital are responsibilised for the efficient deployment of knowledge.

Furthermore, a closer look at the logic underlying the intellectual capital discourse will reveal more incoherence and inconsistencies. Although the authors define intellectual capital as a 'debt', they do not provide for some cate-gory which may stand for 'intellectual credit', for instance – if we are to preserve the system with double-entry bookkeeping. What are the implications of conceiving of intellectual capital as a debt? Above all, we need to establish a more comprehensive balance sheet of the wounded and injured, as a result of reducing the three-dimensional, hustle and bustle of the complex, social and organisational activities into abstract numbers. Not only do numbers describe the phenomena that they are meant to grasp, but they also change these phenomena, creating many more.

Acknowledgements

We appreciate the suggestions and comments on a previous version of this chapter by the editors of this book. We would also like to thank the Swedish Council for Work Life Research for funding this research project.

References

Bennett, R. H. (1998) 'The importance of tacit knowledge in strategic deliberations and decisions', *Management Decision*, 36: 9.

Bharadwaj, A. and Konsynski, B. R. (1997) 'IT Value: Capturing the Intangibles', *Informationweek 500*, 22 September.

Bontis, N. (1997) 'Intellectual Capital: An Exploratory Study That Develops Measures and Models', *Management Decision*, 36: 2.

Calori, R. (1998) 'Philosophising on Strategic Management Models', *Organisation Studies*, 19: 2, 281–306.

Daly, G. (1991) 'The discursive construction of economic space: logics of organisational and disorganisation', *Economy and Society*, 22.

Edvinsson, L. and Malone, M. (1997) *Intellectual Capital: Realising Your Company's True Value by Finding its Hidden Brainpower*. New York: HarperCollins.

Fineman, S. (1993) *Emotions in Organisations*, London: Sage.

Foucault, M. (1970) *The Order Things: An Archaeology of the Human Sciences*. London: Tavistock.

Foucault, M. (1972) *The Archaeology of the Human Sciences*, London: Tavistock.

Foucault, M. (1993) *Madness and Civilisation*. London: Routledge.

Grant, R. M. (1996) 'Toward a knowledge-based theory of the firm', *Strategic Management Journal*, 17, 109–22.

Jackson, M. W. (1996) 'Natural and Artificial Budgets: Accounting for Goethe's Economy of Nature', in Power, M (ed.) *Accounting and Science: Natural Inquiry and Commercial Reason*, Cambridge: Cambridge University Press.

Kaplan, R. S. and Norton, D. P. (1996) *The Balanced Scorecard*. Boston, MA: Harvard Business School Press.

Latour, B. (1987) *Science in Action*. Cambridge, MA: Harvard University Press.

Leonard, D. and Sensiper, S. (1998) 'The Role of Tacit Knowledge in Group Innovation'. *California Management Review*, 40: 3 (Spring).

Miller, P. and Rose, N. (1994) 'Accounting Economic "Citizenship" and the Spatial Reordering of the Manufacture', *Accounting, Organization and Society*, 19: 1.

Olve, N.-G., Roy, J. and Wetter, M. (1997) *Balanced Scorecard i svensk Praktik*, Malmö: Liber Ekonomi.

Polanyi, M. (1966) *The Tacit Dimension*, New York: Doubleday.

Porter, T. M. (1996) 'Making things quantitative', in M. Power (ed.) *Accounting and Science: Natural Inquiry and Commercial Reason*. Cambridge: Cambridge University Press.

Power, M. (1996) 'Introduction: from the science of accounts to the financial accountability of science', in M. Power (ed.) *Accounting and Science: Natural Inquiry and Commercial Reason*. Cambridge: Cambridge University Press.

Roos, J., Roos, G., Edvinson, L. and Dragonetti, N. C. (1997) *Intellectual Capital: Navigating in the New Business Landscape*. London: Macmillan.

Salovey, P. and Mayer, J. D. (1990) 'Emotional Intelligence', *Imagination, Cognition and Personality*, 9, 185–211.

Salzer-Mörling, M. (1998) 'As God Created the Earth... A Saga that Makes Sense?', in D. Grant, T. Keenoy and C. Oswick (eds.), *Discourse and Organisation*. London: Sage.

Spender, J. C. (1996) 'Competitive Advantage from Tacit Knowledge? Unpacking the Concept and its Strategic Implications', in B. Moingeon and A. Edmondson (eds.), *Organisational Learning and Competitive Advantage*, London: Sage, pp. 56–73.

Stewart, T. (1994) 'Your Company's Most Valuable Asset: Intellectual Capital', *Fortune*, 3 October.

Thomson, W. (1889) 'Electrical units of measurement', in *Popular Lectures and Addresses*, London.
Yakhlef, A. (1998) 'IT Outsourcing and the Construction of Accountable Worlds', *Organisation*, 5: 3, 426–46.

3 Bugged: the Software Development Process

Lynne F. Baxter

Introduction

Critical theorists have for over two decades been concerned with the tensions surrounding the encoding of embodied and embedded knowledge in manufacturing technology (e.g. Noble, 1979), but little work has been undertaken on the encoding process itself as represented by software writing, and how it may fail (Lyytenin *et al.*, 1991).

Software development as an activity and computer programs as an outcome have increasingly central parts to play in organisations; indeed, they could be viewed as a hinge between the product and service dimensions of the market offering. Friedman and Cornford's (1989) time-based phasing would suggest that by now software writing would be unproblematic and that constraints from meeting users' needs would predominate, but Collins and Bicknell's (1998) accounts of a wide range of projects would imply that it is basic programming which is still generating many difficulties.

Software developers can be construed as a particular variant of the term 'knowledge workers' (Zuboff, 1988). The kind of 'knowledge'-generation process involved marshals several of the images identified by Blackler (1995). There is an interplay between embrained and encoded knowledge which is realised in the activity of writing programs. A software developer's ingenuity is mediated through programming languages to create new routines. The scarcity of programmers, degree of skill and general lack of visibility of the task creates space in the organisation for them and their way of doing things that may well assume the status of a normalising discourse that legitimates the division of labour (Knights *et al.*, 1993).

This chapter addresses how developers have routinised this division in one setting, and how they manage to sustain this in the face of a faulty outcome to the knowledge production process. I trace an active process 'which is: (a) manifest in systems of language, technology, collaboration and control (i.e. it is mediated); (b) located in time and space and specific to particular contexts (i.e. it is situated); (c) constructed and constantly developing (i.e. it is provisional); and (d) purposive and object-oriented (i.e. it is pragmatic)' (Blackler, 1995, p. 21). In order to do this I make no apology for allocating a major part of the chapter to describing the business context, organisation structure and daily routines of the individuals working in software development.

Before this, elements of Callon and Latour's actor network theory are discussed. The theory is not without its critics, and alternative frameworks could have been used to analyse the data (e.g. Clegg, 1989). Although contested and quite simplistic, the Callon and Latour framework allows the analysis of network formation in a way which captures the dynamic nature and does not lose the specific organisation context. It is used in this instance to help theorise why bugs in software are 'acceptable', and how the software development process itself constitutes one of a series of cases of mobilisation (Callon, 1986). Bugs, which are after all defects, are considered a normal part of software in contrast to the intolerant attitude to defects in manufacturing operations.

Previous work (Baxter, 1996) examined the social construction of what constitutes a bug in software, using Callon and Latour's concept of symmetry (criticised by Collins and Yearley writing in Pickering (1992)). Briefly, software developers are often remote from the ultimate users. The software can 'crash' a system when the users press a sequence of keystrokes, and later when the developers try to replicate the sequence the same result cannot be achieved. The software is bugged from one perspective, not from the other and could be seen to be an actant in its own right. This work probes in more depth the organisation and socially constructed context to this and concludes that although there may well be intrinsic reasons as to why software may never be perfect, software developers are able to create power and space for themselves through claiming special knowledge bases to handle software, despite the continued delivery of software with bugs. The software artefact is inextricably linked to its development process in such a way that makes software developers highly resistant to management control strategies (Friedman and Cornford, 1989).

The Sociology of Translation

Callon and Latour's (1986) 'Sociology of Translation' can be used to explain the way new technologies are developed, and this process affords space for a dynamic conception of power. They would assert that other ideas of power contain the following foci: (a) the initial force from those who have power; (b) the completeness of the transmission, and (c) the ability of the medium to reduce this by creating resistance and friction (Latour, 1986, p. 267). An example Latour quotes is where a manager gives an order that is carried out by 200 people. The order may change slightly, and the people may carry it out differently, but that is just part of the process. This model applied to the study of power results in people focusing on the individual or group who starts the process and any resistance to it, which would certainly characterise much of the early Labour Process Debates.

The contrasting model is what Callon and Latour would call translation. This is where every step in the spread of a technology is a separate act of a person, and it is only in very peculiar circumstances that a smooth, obstacle-free process occurs. There is no initial impetus to create inertia; each person has to add some energy to the process. Latour uses the analogy of a rugby game. The energy that propels the technology cannot be hoarded, and for it to progress individuals have to take an active role, which frequently changes the nature of the technology; instead of the first model, where the technology is transmitted, the technology here is transformed.

If one subscribes to the translation model, the carrying out of an order by a large number of people would seem to be a rarity. Latour concludes that sociologists have taken the wrong starting point in their studies, and should abandon studying power, and purely social phenomena, and instead consider a range of 'associations' between the social and science and technology.

Callon (1986) and Latour (1986) note that a key decider on whether a technology becomes popularised is if the people involved in creating it are skilled at forming coalitions of like-minded people to guard and guide the development forward. The 'sociology of translation' comprises this idea of power with four phases or 'moments'. The first moment is problematisation. One group of people try to show another that they have the correct solution to their problem. They have to lead the target group through a series of practices that the original group can define and control. These are known as 'obligatory passage points'. The next phase is where momentum is developed through the enrolling group positioning itself between the target group and other groups, and fostering relationships that the enrolling group has control over; this is known as 'interessement'. The phase after that is known as 'enrolment' and occurs when the alliances and coalitions agree on what they want the outcome of the process to be. The last phase is called mobilisation, where the enrolling agencies control the enrolled to preserve the pattern of interests that is satisfactory to the enrolling agency. Callon and Latour do not expect the process to be successful every time. The usual illustration quoted is Callon's (1986) one of scallop fishing off Brittany, where scientists were able to create a reputation and thus marshal interested parties such as government bodies, fishermen and, apparently, scallops into agreeing to participate in the scientist's preferred solution. The scallops were treated as actants in the process with similar status to the others, and indeed it was their action or lack of it which contributed in this instance to the failure of the translation process. The labelling of phases in network development, its accomplishment and ability to fall apart are very appealing, and there are obvious parallels between this and the software development process.

The promotion of the scallops to a full actor in the process gave a different perspective on the analysis which other writers on technology have not done. Latour (1993) develops this position more fully to argue that the boundary between humans and things is a false one. However attractive this may be, some criticisms can be made. The success or otherwise of the theory depends on the perspective adopted. In this instance, one could have made the fisherman's representatives the enrollers; it was Callon's (1986) decision to target the scientists. A related point comes with an author's role in the process. The actors being studied have all been given equal status, but I have a part in the process as I label the actors, define the passage points, judge when the moments are changed and so on. My thoughts and influences are only partially articulated. There is a logical extension to this theory to include a more reflexive approach within the methodology, which Callon and Latour do not.

The implications for any study undertaken with these theorists in mind are that almost irrespective of the merits of the technology itself, a technology will be developed if the appropriate coalition forms around it to drive it forward, and that the development is a difficult accomplishment which could at any time be broken. The next section introduces the organisation setting.

Background

The company is a division of a global organisation, and it makes autotellers. The business is extremely profitable, with gross margins exceeding a third of turnover, although over the 50 years that the company has been located in the area this has not always been the case. Several quite diverse products have been made in the area, with a fluctuating number of staff and sites. At its peak, there were 6,000 people working on several sites; now there are just over 1,500 working on two sites. A recent chief executive is attributed with changing the site from a 'screwdriver' plant to one responsible for a product on a global basis, with research and development (R&D) closely allied to manufacturing and distribution. As evidence of this, just under a third of the workforce are graduate engineers.

The core of the main plant is a large manufacturing area, which is surrounded by office accommodation housing the management, research and development (including software development) and specialised test activities. Space in this plant is at a premium. R&D takes place adjacent to the manufacturing operation, and it is impossible to work on software development without seeing the end product and how it is made. There are approximately 150 people involved in software development, with additional capacity being bought in from time to time. Up until the mid-1990s, the manufacturing and software elements of the product development organisation were organised as separate groups within the business, but more recently they have been formed into a single organisation.

This has highlighted the differing perspectives on manufacturing and software development as activities. Manufacturing the hardware is viewed by the company as less problematic. The operations have received awards and the process is more open and subject to scrutiny. The hardware has evolved through minor improvements, the software has become far more complex, varied and written to carry out additional functions. The volume of products is not that great, so there is no 'assembly line'. Sub-components are assembled in cells and transported to a large test area where the electromechanical and software components are put through a lengthy battery of tests. To the observer, it appears as if there is a high amount of finished inventory, as from time to time devices are stored at the side waiting for software to be installed or rewritten to complete the assembly process. For example, two devices were 'parked' in the software developers' office space for three months, waiting for a software bug to be mended. Mechanical failure has largely been designed and tested out, with both product and process failures open to scrutiny and the subject of improvement processes, as they are viewed as intolerable and preventable: 'zero defects' may be a slogan but it reflects the mentality and measurement systems. This can be contrasted with the software process. The organisation as a whole subscribed to a particular variant of the popular phase-gate development process (see for example Wheelwright and Clark (1992) and Cooper (1993)), which had been recently implemented in the site. However, even given this, software projects were taking two to three times the duration estimated when the projects were given the go-ahead. It actually took the length of the three-year project that this chapter is based on to obtain specific information about this; the management of the organisation were clearly embarrassed about it.

Software Development and its Management

Software is needed to operate the device itself and to connect to and be managed by the network. Everything revolves around single projects. In autumn 1996 there were 70 projects in progress. Projects are labelled in three ways: new product developments (NPDs) for the open market, advanced product developments (APDs) and specific customer requests (SCRs), where a customer has asked for something new. In autumn 1996, 51 (73%) of the 70 projects were NPDs, 16 (23%) APDs and 3 (4%) SCRs. Clearly, very few projects are at the behest of customers: the impetus for new projects comes from within. The size of the project can vary from three to five developers taking eight months to produce one program, to 10–16 developers taking almost four years to produce seven to nine 'information products'. There are six developer groupings in software, four depending on the type of software a developer works on and two quality and product management ones. Projects comprise a spread of developers from each group.

Tasks

Although the variety and complexity of programs have grown over the years, most of the programming is done with standard languages and environments. For example, Windows NT will be used as the environment for coding in C++ using an iterative development process for Systems Management software to indicate when the hardware unit has run out of consumables for example.

Alternatively, OS/2 will be used as the environment for coding in C using a waterfall (Sommerville, 1992) development process for platform group software. The basic product is a series of lines of code, and the outcome of a project can amount to several thousands of lines. These can be printed out and subjected to tests, but the whole atmosphere and attitude surrounding this process are different from those of its electromechanical counterparts. At the core of how the software is produced is that it is talked about as though it can 'behave' and that 'behaviour' is not wholly controllable. In Callon and Latour's (1986) terms the software is viewed as an actant in the process. People who have moved into managerial jobs view this as the 'real' task and talk fondly of 'keeping their hand in'. The lines of code may or may not contain bugs, but combining sets of lines of code is usually where the bugs come in. As practically all projects involve this linking together it is easy to see how any one individual might have difficulty in tracing the ultimate source of a bug. Computer-assisted software engineering tools are used, but as the projects are all labelled 'new' in some form or another the possibility of starting from scratch is available and used, as it ties into the individual's sense of competence and creates space.

The customer is integrated into the development process through having a representative from the marketing department on the project team from the early stages. The idea will normally come from within, but the marketing department fanfares new developments to customers. 'Customer delight' may be associated with perfect devices in one part of the building, but the whole relationship is far more open when it comes to software.

It seems reasonable to assume that the customer wants defect-free software running in the hardware, but they seem socialised into accepting something less. When asked why they will put up with lengthy delays in the completed projects, a process manager in software development said that they were given beta versions with the promise of an upgrade, or given a previous more robust version of the software in the interim. This can be contrasted with the substantial investment in new hardware R&D test facilities that the company made after one customer showed that the product sometimes could not operate below − 20 °C. The company is not unusual in providing 'beta versions'. 'Versions', 'upgrades' and 'patches' are part of the lexicon of software usage, and a review of the cases contained in Collins and Bicknell (1998) would suggest that customers are remarkably patient and tolerant where this is concerned. But can the reader imagine having a 'beta' set of wheels on their car? A patch of metal being installed on the car door? A newer version of electric windows being offered after three months of using the car?

The phase-gate management of the process consists of development 'phases' which culminate in 'gates', where a senior team set criteria that should be met before the project continues to the next phase. This is intended to filter projects which are not meeting a need or going to plan in order to reduce project 'inventory' and speed development cycle time for the remainder. There are strong parallels between this and manufacturing 'best practice', embodied in the

Toyota system. Cognitive mapping of developers revealed that the first gate was the only one which was perceived to close, so most of the effort was spent in launching a project, which if it passed the gate was almost never cut. All projects were deemed essential, so the management process did not work as intended. Instead of a development funnel, there was a development tub.

Passing the gate was not dependent on the 'quality' of the idea as such, but whether the individual developer had a sufficient reputation or could attract a more powerful sponsor to align with. Once this was achieved, a team was formed at least on paper and a detailed project plan was submitted to the management committee, including an estimate of when the software would be ready. Many of the figures in the plan were known to be very loose guesses. The committee frequently asked for modifications to the proposal. What was striking was that the least informative part of the project proposal was the information about what the software would do. The management team were prepared to wait for this. The phase-gate process was followed and time was spent writing reports and 'meeting' criteria, but projects were never cancelled: too much was at stake. The management committee was under the impression that it had set priorities among projects, but the developers felt they were too abstract and did not relate to individual ones. The only time a project left the 'inventory' was when it was finished, though it could return for 'maintenance' later.

It was clear that the most important aspect was the formation of an acceptable team at the start, which had to include people with 'reputations' in the different specialisms. The company collated 'effort recorder' data and I analysed it. The data consisted of arrays of time booked by individuals by specialism on projects in week units over the period of 18 months. The developers were initially asked, and then ordered, to fill in forms. However inaccurate the data is likely to be, it did show that individuals on teams were frequently transferred out to other projects. The profile of a team working on a project changed considerably over its lifetime, and this did not mean that particular specialism was no longer required. For example, on a large project which had 34 developers recording time worked on it, only three people worked for the entire span of the effort-recording period. The rest ramped up time, left after a period, joined for two months and then left for a spell etc. People frequently returned to projects. Any project had a shifting population of developers, with people new to the team joining all the way through. One might expect a funnelling of effort, with a tailing off when it was nearing completion, but this was not the case.

Whereas workers and machinery on the assembly floor were 'flexible', software developers were not. Launching new projects involved poaching, trading and sustaining the link with developers with reputations. The team formation and profile of the portfolio of projects one had were more important than writing bug-free software on time, it appeared. Coupled with the view of software being an actant, the lengths of the overruns are in retrospect unsurprising.

There seem obvious parallels between this and Callon (1986), with the software embodied in the project being the centrepiece of a network which was interested and mobilised, but which, like the scallops, eventually did not collude. This is explored in more detail in the next section.

Discussion

It is possible to identify three intersecting network translations involving the company. The first translation process occurs at a meta level between the company and the customer, the second is where consultants are trying to mobilise the organisation along their cycle time reduction 'technology' and the third is the day-to-day software development activity. The next section examines the phases of the networks in turn before exploring where they may overlap or intersect.

The company, as outlined above, has an extended relationship with its customers, and arguably holds the more powerful position. This is exemplified by the 'technology push' nature of new product development, the bounded nature of customisation and the extent to which customers will accept software with bugs, however camouflaged, and lastly the high profitability in the business. The company has successfully mobilised its customer base. How is this position arrived at?

The highly competitive nature of the customer market facilitates the problematisation phase of translation. Cost reduction is a major emphasis for customers and the company can argue that its technology can reduce the cost base for the customer while improving end-customer service. This benefit is realised if the system is well managed, and increasingly the company is trying to carry out that service for the customer. The customer is more likely to conduct business with the case company (interessement), as it is global, is the market leader and has an attractive product offering in the shape of robust hardware coupled with customised software and network management skills. The agreed outcome for the 'enrolment' phase is a contract for multiple hardware units complete with software to be delivered several months hence. Small orders for additions and replacements form the minority of the business. Despite missing deadlines and delivering incomplete or imperfect software the company is successful in mobilising the customers.

Senior management in the company are aware of the failings in the development process, and the company as a whole is noted for its close relationships with universities, consultants and other ways to foster the conditions for 'business improvement'. The second 'translation' process represents just one of these activities. At a corporate level 'time to market' was perceived to be an area for improvement and the company as a whole embraced a different way of managing new product development, sold to them by consultants. The specifics of the early phases of the consultant's engagement of the company are not known, but it is possible to construct an account for the problematisation phase. A management idea with widespread and sustained interest was time-based competition (Blackburn, 1991; Stalk and Hout, 1990; Rich and Hines, 1997). This, together with disquiet about the meeting of performance targets inside the corporation, and its willingness to avail itself of new technologies, would be sufficient for the area to be perceived as a problem. Why the specific network relationship was set up (interessment) with these consultants could be attributed to their track record in the area and the nature of their offering. The phase-gate framework has academic backing (Cooper, 1993, 1994), as does the organisation structure they propose (Finger *et al.*, 1992). The high degree of formalisation in the roles and activities must have been appealing as a way to manage the maverick R&D process.

The enrolment phase consisted of the delivery, training and cascading of the frameworks and structures across the corporation with the prescribed outcome of shortening the development cycle times. The mobilisation appears to have limited success. Initially, the impression gathered at meetings and interviews was that the new *modus operandi* was well embedded; however, over the extended research period it became clear that the lexicon, organisation and start of the framework were being used, but the project termination and prioritisation rules were not. Something else had precedence. The consultant had not mobilised the company effectively.

I would argue that the translation process which had primacy over the two described above was the most mundane, namely the software development process. To recap briefly, the process consists of an idea coming to a developer and the developer forming a coalition to meet the initial framework criteria; then, when the proposal passes this 'gate' in the process, lines of code are written by coalitions of developers who leave and rejoin the project. The development process eventually extends to include the customer, and although in a formal sense the program might be finished, it returns for maintenance and upgrade. The problematisation phase is triggered normally by an individual developer, who identifies a new idea to improve existing software or supplement the current range, and has to convince other developers and the management committee of its merit. The interessement phase is very clear-cut, with the scarcity value of good programmers, the formal framework and the lack of success outsourcing this activity reinforcing the legitimacy of the in-house developers to tackle the new problem. The product development process reinforces this phase strongly. The enrolment phase is highly formal as well, and can be said to have occurred when the new project has passed the first 'gate' in the development framework. Mobilisation takes place from the developer perspective in a way in which the company would not expect. Instead of the framework and corporate objectives guiding the process, the developer's preferred activities of idea generation and forming and dissipating coalitions do, and this is assisted by the widely held view that software is uncontrollable and ultimately an actor in its own right.

The partial adoption of the phase-gate framework has reinforced the *status quo*, rather than undermining it. Gate criteria intended to render development activities more visible and open to scrutiny have instead been used to prolong and intensify them. The third network has operated to undermine the second, but is substantially constitutive of the first network. Bugs and modifications to software serve to create more transactions with customers, who, in the light the business performance figures, are bound to the company rather than considering stopping the relationship.

The case can be located in traditional debates concerning power and powerlessness in the labour process, but it highlights contradictions and provides far greater detail on how some outcomes are achieved. For example, the case shows that under circumstances which Friedman and Cornford (1989) would argue would engender a 'responsible autonomy' strategy, senior management implemented a project control process which attempted to bring a group of professional people into more 'direct control'. The company was highly profitable and not undergoing serious market pressure. Senior management employed a blanket strategy for all projects, although different people and groups within the organisation could employ differing resources and contexts to amend or resist the strategy. Friedman (1990) would maintain that it is difficult to change an overarching strategy from direct control to responsible autonomy in an organisation, and this case could be seen to be supporting that view, but a closer reading of the material would reveal that elements of both strategies coexist within the organisation, and have done so for some time.

The integrity of software developers as a group also raises interesting points. Friedman identified that responsible autonomy was the most reasonable way of managing software developers and that several attempts had been made to encroach on this autonomy through the use of 'structured programming' (Kraft, 1977) and computer-assisted software engineering (Friedman and Cornford, 1989) to affect the task that programmers undertake, which they have resisted or co-opted into their knowledge domain, thus enhancing their reputation. Indeed software developers share many contextual elements and characteristics of Whitley's (1984) organised groups in science. According to Whitley (1984) 'Reputations are won by persuading the relevant audience of the importance of one's work and so affecting their own priorities and procedures' (p. 26). Clearly it is not difficult to persuade people of the *importance* of a software developer's work, with the cost of this element of a product or service being exceedingly high (Collins and Bicknell, 1998). What the case adds is that reputations can be sustained although the software produced need not necessarily contain a high degree of novelty or be reliable. Indeed, the reputations are not even challenged.

Friedman and Cornford (1989) and Whitley (1984) were able to make their points without referring to any specific technologies, in this case the actual programs written. It has been argued that there is something intrinsic to software which makes perfect results impossible. For example, Mackenzie (1996) noted that ten to twenty lines of software could yield a possible 10^{14} execution paths, with a concomitant number of bugs. Testing for bugs is also a largely fruitless exercise. Early work carried out by Dijkstra (1972) stated that testing only shows the bugs which are in the code: the lines of code may not meet the intended objective.

However difficult it is to detect bugs after they are written, this does not obviate the point that there are techniques to prevent at least some of these bugs being realised in the first place, techniques which have been used in other areas of manufacturing. The reasons why they have not been applied lie in the power and position that software developers have mobilised for themselves, both consciously and subconsciously.

Conclusions

It is impossible to say whether software could be entirely open to the same kinds of scrutiny and rendered docile in the way that more traditional manufacturing process are, but it is possible to conclude that this is unlikely to happen when problems are actually constitutive of relations with customers (Woolgar, 1991). Software may appear to behave as an actant in its own right, which creates organisation space and kudos for developers. The way developers are organised and operate has similarities with information systems departments in Beer's work long ago (1981). This chapter is intended to show the daily accomplishment of the developers in maintaining the mobilisation of interests along their chosen path. Attempts by the more senior management to reduce 'embrained' knowledge (Blackler, 1995) by altering the 'encultured' routines has been incorporated by the developers rather than resisted. The purposeful activity of creating software is mediated by the programming languages and organisation routines in such a way as to construct a more intense relationship with the customer in a specific set of business circumstances to the profit of the developers and currently the company as a whole.

References

Baxter, L. F. (1996) Power Relations in Organisations, *PhD Thesis*, University of Manchester.

Beer, S. (1981) *Brain of the Firm: the Managerial Cybernetics of Organisation*, Chichester: John Wiley.

Blackburn, J. D. (1991) *Time-Based Competition: The Next Battle Ground in American Manufacturing, The Business One*, APICS Series in Production Management, Irwin.

Blackler, F. (1995) 'Knowledge, Knowledge Work and Organisations: an Overview and Interpretation', *Organisation Studies*, 16: 6, 1021–47.

Callon, M. (1986) 'Some Elements of a Sociology of Translation', in J. Law (ed.) *Power Action and Belief: A New Sociology of Knowledge*, London: Routledge & Kegan Paul, London, pp. 196–233.

Clegg, S. (1989) *Frameworks of Power*, London: Sage.

Collins, T. and Bicknell, D. (1998) *Crash*, London: Simon & Schuster.

Cooper, R. G. (1993) *Winning at New Products: Accelerating the Process from Idea to Launch*, Reading, MA: Addison-Wesley.

Cooper, R. G. (1994) 'New Products: the Factors That Drive Success', *International Marketing Review*, 11: 1, 60–76.

Dijkstra, E. (1972) The Turing Award Lecture, *Communications of the ACM*, 5.

Finger, S., Fox, M. S., Prinz, F. B., Rinderle, J. R. (1992) 'Concurrent design', *Applied Artificial Intelligence*, 6: 3, 257–83.

Friedman, A. L. (1990) 'Managerial Strategies, Activities, Techniques and Technology: Towards A Complex Theory of the Labor Process', in D. Knights and H. Willmott (eds.), *Labor Process Theory*, London: Macmillan, pp. 177–208.

Friedman, A. L. and Cornford, D. S. (1989) *Computer Systems Development: History, Organisation and Implementation*, London: John Wiley.

Knights, D., Murray, F. and Willmott, H. (1993) 'Networking As Knowledge Work: A Study of Interorganisational Development in the Financial Services Sector'. *Journal of Management Studies*, 30, 975–96.

Kraft, P. (1977) *Programmers and Managers: The Routinisation of Computer Programming in the United States*, New York: Springer-Verlag.

Latour, B. (1986) 'The Powers of Association', in J. Law (ed.), *Power Action and Belief, a New Sociology of Knowledge?*, London: Routledge & Kegan Paul, pp. 264–80.

Latour, B. (1993) *We Have Never Been Modern*, Cambridge MA: Harvard University Press.

Law, J. (1986) *Power Action and Belief, a New Sociology of Knowledge?*, London: Routledge & Kegan Paul.

Lyytinen, K. and Hirschheim, R. and Klein, H. (1991) 'The Effectiveness of Office Information Systems – a Social Action Perspective', *Journal of Information Systems*, 1: 1, 23–42.

Mackenzie, D. (1996) 'Computers, 'Bugs' and the Sociology of Mathematical Proof', in W. H. Dutton (ed.), *Information and Communication Technologies: Visions and Realities*, Oxford: Oxford University Press, pp. 69–85.

Noble, D. (1979) 'Social Choice and Machine Design' in D. Mackenzie and J. Wajcman (eds.), *The Social Shaping of Technology: How the Refrigerator got its Hum*, Milton Keynes: Open University Press, pp. 109–24.

Pickering, A. (ed) (1992) *Science as Practice and Culture*, Chicago: Chicago Press.

Rich, N. and Hines, P. (1997) 'Supply-chain Management and Time-based Competition: the Role of the Supplier Association', *International Journal of Physical Distribution & Logistics Management*, 27: 3–4, 210–26.

Sommerville, I. (1992) *Software Engineering*, Wokingham: Addison-Wesley.

Stalk Jr, G. and Hout, T. M. (1990) *Competing Against Time*, New York: The Free Press.

Wheelwright, S. C. and Clark, K. B. (1992) *Revolutionising Product Development*, New York: The Free Press.

Whitley, R. D. (1984) *The Intellectual and Social Organisation of the Sciences*, Oxford: Clarendon.

Woolgar, S. (1991) 'Configuring the User: the Case of Usability Trials', in J. Law (ed.), *A Sociology of Monsters, Essays on Power, Technology and Domination*, London: Routledge, pp. 58–99.

Zuboff, S. (1988) *In the Age of the Smart Machine: the Future of Work and Power*, New York: Basic Books.

4 Knowledge Management and the Conduct of Expert Labour

Richard Hull

Introduction

Knowledge management has quickly come to mean many things to different people, which is one of the reasons why it has often been dubbed as merely a 'new management fad', encouraged by consultants seeking a new label under which to sell much the same services and systems. Indeed, it could easily be argued that the focus on knowledge management arose from the perceived failures of business process re-engineering, where both the initial enthusiasm, including new IT systems, and the following problems were heavily touted by the main management/IT consultancies. The 'problems' were, crudely, that BPR projects often resulted in the loss of layers of middle management (Coombs and Hull, 1995), which were in hindsight alleged to be the organisation's most 'valuable asset', or rather, what was lost was the knowledge and experience of middle management. The focus on knowledge management was then an ideal opportunity for consultancy firms to restore their tarnished image, as they turned to enhancing the 'leverage' of such knowledge and experience to the benefit of the organisation. Although there is undoubtedly an element of truth to this, and to the concomitant criticism that knowledge management is merely another form of the intensification of white-collar work, there is also no doubt that many firms are adopting significant new practices, altering existing operations, appointing specific knowledge management personnel, and installing new systems. In combination with these developments there has been a proliferation of academic and practitioner journals and newsletters centred on knowledge management, the establishment of many academic research centres, the development of postgraduate courses, the appointment of academics with the title of 'Professor of Knowledge Management', and the establishment of government units focused on disseminating best practice to firms. Clearly then, the phenomenon is not merely some passing fad, but is in the process of establishing itself as a new aspect of management and organisations and a new form of expertise.

This chapter discusses knowledge management from a perspective on 'expert labour'. While other chapters in this book focus on broader aspects of knowledge work, learning and so-called 'intellectual capital', this chapter treats knowledge management as an emergent form of expert labour, which as such has an identifiable professional or disciplinary background and a set of observable everyday practices. Putting this another way, the analysis presented here discusses knowledge management as *merely* a new form of expertise, rather than from any particular understanding of the nature and characteristics of knowledge or information. Accordingly, the first half of the chapter develops a perspective on expert labour by means of a critique of one of the key recent contributions, the 'critical realist' perspective outlined by Reed (1996, 1997), which is shown to entail a non-productive contradiction between its ethics of evaluation and its sociology of knowledge. Following this critique a perspective is outlined on the conduct of expert labour which does not suffer this contradiction. The second half of the chapter then applies this perspective to knowledge management, and demonstrates how the emergent discipline suffers from philosophical and political problems that are rooted in the history of 'knowledge as a unit of analysis'. However, practitioners are often coping with these problems through the generation of a wide variety of new and redefined practices, some of which have the potential to alter power relations for knowledge workers in new and interesting ways.[1]

Evaluating Expertise

Experts get it wrong sometimes – this much is especially evident at present. A common-sense response would be to attempt to ensure that experts make fewer mistakes – to ensure that, for instance, phenomena like BSE are recognised earlier and acted on. A common-sense perspective would acknowledge, without necessarily accepting, the increasing dependence on experts and hence the increasing importance of ensuring that they don't make fatal mistakes. There are currently a number of such perspectives, or rather practical interventions: attempts to 'democratise' expert decision-making, to 'involve more stakeholders', to constitute 'citizen juries', or to 'strengthen the networks of relevant actors'; the consequent attempts to 'increase public understanding' of expert knowledge; and finally attempts to introduce or reform professional Codes (of Ethics, Conduct, Practice, etc.), often using 'insights' from prominent so-called 'moral and political philosophers'.[2]

However pragmatic or effective these may be – and I don't wish to be too unduly critical of most of these developments – they cannot escape from making an impossible choice between the two currently available forms of reasoning that we might apply to understand and evaluate expertise, *prior to intervening*. Social and political theory is fond of telling us that we can choose either the rationalism and realism of 'enlightened modernity' (including critical versions such as 'critical realism') or the relativism of postmodernity, which assigns the negotiation of fact and justice to local context; this is 'reason as pluralism', and consequently calls for a 'postmodern ethics' (Baumann, 1993) or a 'new ethics'. The problem with the latter is that it gives us no grounds for evaluating and hence improving expertise: it cannot tell us how to legislate.[3] The former, on the other hand, is very good at telling us how to legislate, but as Baumann is fond of saying, it legislates constantly within its method, and that is its downfall: its failure to recognise the hidden, discarded and newly emergent aspects of social life.

Expert Labour

The impossible choice between rationalism and 'new ethics' is neatly, if unintentionally, illustrated in a recent and comprehensive review of empirical and theoretical approaches to contemporary expert power and control (Reed, 1996). One of the main achievements of this work is to locate work on the sociology of professions and professionalisation 'within the political economy of expertise' (Reed, 1996, pp. 578–9). The argument is that the established forms of professionalism, professional organisation and professional power have recently been radically altered by the combined impact of economic, technological and ideological changes. Among other factors, the growth of 'organisational professions', such as managers and administrators, together with the financial crisis of the welfare state, are forcing challenges to the traditional professions associated with welfare, and to other professions; they are heralding and enhancing the emergence of new forms of expertise and new 'expert divisions of labour'; and they are breaking the links between the State and professional expertise which once legitimated and guaranteed the neutrality of those professions.

Reed further suggests that neo-liberal policies impose 'market-based disciplines' on labour markets and work practices, resulting in the commodification of expert labour. He also highlights the degree to which different groups within the expert division of labour rely on complex interactions between 'social-political control strategies' on the one hand, and economic and technological changes on the other hand. Chief among those technological changes are the new information and communication technologies (ICTs), which both disable traditional forms of control and enable the emergence of new forms of expertise and new means for challenging established expertise. This technological, economic and political restructuring is primarily manifest through the new phenomenon of 'institutional reflexivity' – a term from Giddens which describes the way that modern institutions and organisations 'systematically monitor and control their own performance in such a way that their strategic effectiveness and operational efficiency are greatly enhanced' (Reed, 1996, p. 573). Indeed, for Reed, 'organisations become *the* strategic social units for generating, storing and manipulating knowledge so as to secure the planned reproduction of social systems' (Reed, 1996, pp. 573–4). These developments in combination, it is argued, lay open some of the foundations of expert power, and render them more subject to challenge and division, more subject to 'micro-political power struggles'. It is those power struggles, and more generally the 'interpenetration of global change and local re-ordering', that should consequently, he argues, be the focus of future research.

While one must welcome Reed's achievement in taking discussions of expertise out of the narrow confines of the sociology of professions, the argument leads us to ask a number of questions. Firstly, if there was one prime advantage to working within the sociology of professions it was that the object of study was clearly defined and delimited. Professions have the trappings of formal procedures, entry requirements, occupational structures, written codes or guidelines, membership lists, official histories, clear and not-so-clear linkages with academic disciplines, the existence or otherwise of engagements with labour market issues, etc. These all provide rich empirical material which, in combination with other objects of study, provides the basis for broader inferences (see for example Whitley (1984)). But for Reed, what exactly is 'expertise' if it can no longer be defined with reference to existing or emergent professions? It soon becomes clear that expertise is essentially defined with reference to power.

He first quotes Simon Schaffer: 'experts can gain authority if they can convince their society that they have access to esoteric matters only to be reached through their specialised skills and yet of general potential utility' (Schaffer, 1994, p. 17). Reed then reinterprets this as:

> Schaffer is identifying the interrelated dimensions of political, cognitive, technical and organisational power that define and legitimate the position of experts within traditional and modern societies... modern expertise has a specific form and content that reflects the particular socio-technical conditions and organisational configurations that define 'late modernity'. That is, it becomes a, if not *the*, defining feature of [late modernity] to the extent that it generates, applies and protects the codified specialised knowledge necessary for the reflexive monitoring of social activity on a global scale (Reed, 1996, pp. 575–6).

We can simplify this complex formulation somewhat if we refer to Reed (1997), where he sets out his support for the 'critical realism' of Bhaskar (1974, 1993), Archer (1995) and others. This philosophical position rests on positing the real but not directly observable existence of 'structures' or 'tendencies' (in both 'nature' and 'society') which are generative mechanisms which have an 'interplay' with other causal objects such as human agents, such that there are explicable, if not entirely predictable, outcomes which can be empirically observed. Given that position we can see that Reed (1996) is essentially suggesting that expertise and expert power are in part the outcomes of the interplay between local power struggles and broader structural mechanisms or tendencies, and also one increasingly important element of those broader changes – expertise is one of the 'mediating systems' that Bhaskar (1979) postulates as the 'point of contact' between agency and structure. To put it more bluntly and in old-fashioned terminology, Reed (1996) is suggesting that the *content* of expertise is socially constructed[4] – what counts as expertise is *only* that which experts have successfully been able to mobilise through the exercise of expert power.

The problem with this formulation is that it would now seem that the only distinguishing feature of expert labour – as against any other form of labour – is defined with respect to its power effects, its ability to 'carve out' areas of action. Because, by accepting the argument that knowledge and skill – the content of expertise – are socially constructed, we lose what were once (and still are, for most people) the defining characteristics of expertise. Knowledge and skill are instead now understood to be social products and hence defined in terms of the interplay between local socio-political control strategies and broader generative mechanisms, and thus they lose their ability to act as defining features of expert labour. To see this, imagine the following scenario: within an organisation being studied, one person claims to be an expert in X-ology, and claims that her perspective on line management procedures is the only correct one. However, no one can be found within the organisation to support her claim, and against that claim there are ten people mobilising Y-ology. In time, it is apparent that the latter win the argument, by whatever means, and that this is a generalised phenomenon – those very rare people who attempt to mobilise X-ology invariably lose the argument. Who then is to judge whether X-ology really counts as 'knowledge and skill' or not, and hence how can we judge whether the attempts to mobilise and practice X-ology constitute expert labour? In other words, constituting expert labour only with respect to features of its socio-political context is severely limiting – expert labour on this account is that which other people have successfully defined and mobilised as expert labour, and *nothing else*. This is a far cry indeed from the sociology of professions.

It is also a deeply problematic juxtaposition of the two perspectives on reason. 'Reason as rationalism' is utilised in order to identify the characteristics of expertise, expert power, expert labour. But the reason *of* expertise, its coherence or otherwise and its relationship to the world, that reason is socially produced, so that on the surface the argument would appear to deny the possibility of rational judgement of the content of expertise, would appear to imply some form of 'reason as pluralism', or more precisely an 'explanatory pluralism' (Reed, 1997, p. 33).

The impossible choice has apparently been fudged, but in fact it has been made but obscured. We can see this in a number of ways. Firstly, 'the explanatory pluralism entailed within a realist position has definite limits: it *cannot admit* substantive theoretical approaches to the study of organisation that dissolve structure into agency and consequently remain blind to the structural contextualisation and conditioning of social interaction' (Reed, 1997, p. 33, emphasis added). In other words this is only the pretence of pluralism. Secondly, and perhaps more importantly, what guidelines do we have for making judgements about those processes of the social production of the content of expertise, that 'interplay between local political struggle and broader generative mechanisms'? Here we have to look for small clues in Reed (1997), where we find the imperative that 'if we fail to recognise these realities [of the complex interplay between agency and structure] and to incorporate them within our analyses, then we will severely limit our capacity to acknowledge, much less explain, the nature of the phenomena that constitutes the subject matter of our field or *to provide well-informed critiques of their restrictive influence and emancipatory potential'* (Reed, 1997, p. 34, emphasis added); and later we have the imperative that 'any theory of organisation [must remain] sensitive to the stratified nature of social reality *and its implications for social action'* (Reed, 1997, p. 37, emphasis added). In other words, the reason *of* expertise, or rather its proxy, the social processes of its production, are to be judged firstly within the 'limits' of perspectives that do not 'dissolve structure into agency', and secondly by reference to 'emancipatory potential' and 'implications for social action'.

So, regardless of the extent of the micro-politics and the social struggles over expert labour, the real picture is only revealed through 'reason as rationalism'. In addition, however, what is hidden but constantly implied are firstly the *judgements* that there is something terribly wrong with the 'contemporary world' and with the expert labour which has been 'directed' to produce it, and something wonderfully right about the 'emancipatory potential' that can only be revealed through correct analyses. But more importantly, what is hidden but constantly implied is that the role of the intellectual is to straightforwardly reveal those mechanisms, as if the intellectual is not an 'expert' and is able in some way to rise above the micro-politics and social struggles that construct the knowledge of 'other' experts.

In attempting to establish how, precisely, Reed (1996) would come to judgements about expert labour, by following his own chains of 'reason', we have demonstrated that the 'rationalism' cannot be sustained: it collapses into a set of essentially *ethical* appeals and *sovereign* assertions: about the wrongness of the 'contemporary world', the need for 'emancipation', the role of the intellectual and correct analysis, and an absolute, sovereign assertion that reality is structured. Both the ethical appeals and that sovereign assertion are placed outside our jurisdiction, beyond the possibilities of judgement. In other words this work is essentially a combination of two contradictory positions: on the one hand, a sociology and political economy of expertise and knowledge that sees all expertise and knowledge as being structured by particular socio-economic situations and 'generative structures'; but on the other hand an ethics that is posited as being absolutely true and somehow outside of any such structuring. As we shall see below, in the discussion on the emergence of 'knowledge as a unit of analysis', this same contradiction has been present with many attempts to counter logical positivism.

This critique has firstly demonstrated that any attempt to understand and evaluate expertise must pay serious attention to its own forms of reasoning, precisely because one is attempting to develop one's own particular expertise. This much has been clear within debates on the sociology of scientific knowledge for many decades (see Pickering, 1992).

However, as those debates have also demonstrated, there are severe problems when analysis of expertise attempts to incorporate political and ethical considerations (see for instance the special issue of *Social Studies of Science*, on 'The Politics of SSK', May 1996).

We have consequently demonstrated that there is a requirement to *suspend* ethical and political judgements about, for instance, the absolute need for 'emancipation', while being able to work towards 'good enough justice', towards small, tentative advances in judgement and evaluation.

> If metaphysics is the aporia, the perception of the difficulty of the law, the difficult way, then ethics is the development of it, the *diaporia*, being at a loss yet exploring various routes, different ways towards the good enough justice, which recognises the intrinsic and the contingent limitations in its exercise (Rose, 1995).

This means not adopting any absolute position about the 'complex interplay between agency and structure'. We might wish to pragmatically say that some structures do have partial effects and that people will exercise their agency – their choices, their freedoms, their powers and their resistance to powers – in often unpredictable ways. However, we have seen that posing the dichotomy of agency and structure requires absolute sovereign assertions that cannot be justified. This means abandoning this dichotomy.

In terms of evaluating expert labour, then, we require forms of analysis that do not reduce the content of expertise to the outcome of socio-economic forces, institutional structures or political struggles, but which are instead sensitive to the quite particular and specific ways in which different forms of expertise emerge, and, based on such analyses, are able to make initial evaluations of the validity of that content, for instance about its coherence and its 'objects of study'. Secondly, however, we require analysis of the ways in which the expertise is applied in practice, because allowing for the possibility of 'unpredictable activity' requires allowing for significant changes in that expertise as it is applied and adapted. While many contemporary and extremely valuable perspectives on scientific and technological expertise have emerged from such 'local' and 'micro' studies (e.g. Actor Network and ethnomethodological approaches), they have however tended to ignore the specific characteristics of the long-term emergence of particular forms of expertise.

The Conduct of Expert Labour

> Perhaps the equivocal nature of the term *conduct* is one of the best aids for coming to terms with the specificity of power relations. For to 'conduct' is at the same time to 'lead' others... and a way of behaving within a more or less open field of possibilities (Foucault, 1982, pp. 220–1, original emphasis).

At first sight this might appear to reintroduce the agency–structure dichotomy, but the difference lies in Foucault's focus on 'the specificity of power relations': unlike those who demand the primacy of 'resolving' the agency–structure dichotomy, Foucault consistently refused to define or assert what the powers of structures or of agents were, and instead repeatedly demonstrated that power relations could only be understood for specific cases, and could only be general-ised in terms of different modes of *attempts* to govern conduct, or governmentality. Again, at first sight this might appear to invalidate any general approach to expert labour. However, when we also incorporate Gillian Rose's focus on judgement we can arrive at such a general approach.

Very briefly, Gillian Rose (1981, 1984, 1992) argues that understanding the processes and outcomes of judgement does, *contra* Foucault, require assertions about one particular form of power relations, namely the power of law, broadly conceived as both formal regulation and as any sets of concepts and supporting institutions which declare 'the way things are and should be'. Crucially, this thus includes metaphysical and ethical concepts, and the various ways these are supported and reinforced. It is, if you like, a very drastic reformulation of the old concept of 'ideology' but without the baggage of contrasting 'ideology' to 'truth', or to the 'base' of material relations. Of course this power is mediated by specific historical circumstances, but again this is not to posit a distinction between 'ideas' and 'material reality' because of course the law constitutes, through its concepts, our understanding of 'material reality' but its concrete judgements are much more than merely 'ideas'. This focus on law – or rather, her focus on the 'broken middle' between law and ethics – also entails a speculative, equivocal approach to social theory that is yet able to work towards 'good enough justice' (see Hull (1998) for the full argument in relation to expert labour).

When we combine this with Foucault's focus on conduct we can now argue that conduct understood as 'to lead others' is tightly bound to, but quite distinct from, conduct understood as 'a way of behaving'. These two are not a dichotomy, opposites, or ends of a spectrum, because they are both essentially about what people do, about people's attempts to govern the conduct of others, especially by defining the law, and people's responses within a field of possibili-ties. But they do, however, require different forms of analysis, especially in the case of understanding and evaluating expert labour, and consequently I suggest we distinguish between 'discipline' and 'practices' as being two related but distinct aspects of the conduct of expert labour. This will thus enable us to make initial judgements about the disciplinary background and the everyday prac-tices, both separately and in conjunction – the coherence of the disciplinary theoretical basis, the fit of that theoretical basis with other available perspectives on similar objects of study, the organisation and institutions of the discipline, and its degree of resistance or openness to novelty especially as revealed through everyday practices.

Discipline

Contrary to the 'populist' interpretations of Foucault's works, which posit 'disci-pline' as a generalised but diffused tendency of modernity, the emphasis here is on discipline as an observable set of quite specific ways and means for attempting to conduct (lead) the expert activities of experts. In general, we can think of the discipline of expert labour as the formal and informal social, institutional and artefactual arrangements for maintaining and developing that form of expert labour; for ensuring compliance with what are seen as the established formats of that expert labour, but also for allowing the development and change of those formats. Academic disciplines are one paradigmatic example; and another would be the various trappings of a profession – formal procedures, entry requirements, training arrangements, occupational levels and structures, written codes, guidelines or manuals, membership lists, official histories, clear and not-so-clear linkages with academic disciplines, and the existence or otherwise of methods of engagement with labour market and employment issues.

However, we must also be able to include those forms of expert labour which are either nascent and emergent, or have been 'hidden' or 'unrecognised' or classed as 'craft traditions'. Thus, for instance, for nascent expertise we would also look for (a) populist commentary, rhetoric and prescription addressing an identifiable 'problem', or (b) the promotion and utilisation of an identifiable technique or 'skill'. In earlier work (Hull, 1997) I described how the 'conduct of computing' has been (and continues to be) governed through the inseparable involvement of a variety of social science concepts, forms of language and techniques. I was thus able to discuss the emergence of new concepts and practices within computing – such as the notion of 'interaction with a computer' – concepts and practices which were often seen initially as forms of critique or resistance to 'established' computing. That work suggests, then, that one appropriate way of identifying and analysing particular disciplines of expert labour is 'historical sociology' (Dean, 1994) and the delineation of 'problematisations' (Castel, 1994) in the manner of the governmentality studies (e.g. Barry *et al.*, 1996; Burchell *et al.*, 1991).

Practices

Practices can, of course, take a variety of forms, and this creates a need for a flexible approach to describing and classifying them, able to cope with practices which are both formal and informal; weakly or strongly specified; reliant on artefacts, or not; regularised by time, or regularised by event; and so on. It is perhaps worth offering a formal definition of practices at this point. Practices encompass the variety of ways in which labour is regularised and routinised, whether formally in recognised techniques, tasks and processes – which are sequences of tasks – or informally in acknowledged ways of 'getting by' and 'getting the work done'. This definition thus includes both 'traditional' organisational analysis, and more recent ethnomethodological approaches (e.g. Turner, 1994; Lynch, 1993), but without making any appeal to the importance of 'tacit knowledge', for reasons that become clear in the discussion below on 'knowledge as a unit of analysis'.

There are of course extensive methods for 'task analysis' within a variety of academic and operational fields, and there will often exist Guidelines, Codes of Practice, or Codes of Conduct, which specify in fine detail the normative descriptions of a wide range of specific practices. There are also the methods and models within Organisation Studies which focus on categories of activities, most notably the venerable 'Aston Studies' (Pugh, 1988); and of course Weber's original characterisation of 'bureaucracy' rested on a large number of organisational variables, many of which concerned the nature of activities within organisations (Clegg, 1994). The pragmatic approach we have adopted – aimed primarily at developing simple taxonomies from ethnographic studies – involves delineating three attributes or dimensions of practices which are amenable to empirical analysis: (a) specific immediate objective or intention; (b) the overall long-term or strategic aim; and (c) the degree of formality. The first two attributes are self-explanatory, and relate specific practices to features of the discipline (and, of course, to features of the organisational context). The third attribute will cover habitual, traditional or informal practices as well as formal rules, task divisions and explicit standards.

The Conduct of Knowledge Management

The disciplinary contours

How has it become possible for anyone to even *consider* the idea of 'managing knowledge'? As mentioned in the introduction, it is possible to construct a narrative which traces the rise of knowledge management through the activities of the management/IT/accounting consultancies over the last decade or so – the enthusiasms, the new technologies and techniques, the failures, and the ways these failures were then problematised and packaged up into new offerings and services, new technologies and techniques. However, although there is undoubtedly an interesting story to tell here, it would not be able to tell us how and why these consultants and their supporting academics decided to focus on 'knowledge', rather than say 'expertise', 'truth' or 'reason', and why they decided that it was possible to conceive of 'knowledge' as an entity that could be managed, an entity that could be stored, made to flow from one place to another, and put to use in the same way one uses a tool. How was it, in other words, that 'knowledge' became a discrete entity?

'Knowledge as a unit of analysis' – a post-positivist problematisation of knowledge?

One of the astonishingly unremarked features of the 20th century is the growth, especially since the 1960s, of attempts by social scientists and others to utilise knowledge as a unit of analysis. These range from the simplest attempts to cate-gorise knowledge, for instance into tacit and explicit, to the complex formula-tions we see today. They are all, I would argue, attempts to deal with what are *perceived* to be the problems with positivism and especially with the 'traditional' picture of scientific method, so they include such formulations as 'tacit knowl-edge', 'falsifiable and non-falsifiable knowledge', 'subjective knowledge', 'bounded rationality', 'embodied knowledge', 'organisational or social knowl-edge' or 'situated knowledge'. At this point it is important to remember that Polanyi developed his notion of the distinction between explicit and tacit knowledge in deliberate and explicit opposition to the arguments from J. D. Bernal and other Marxists that science should be centrally planned by the State (see Prosch (1986, p. 16)). This led him to discuss the 'social nature of science' and the ways in which scientific communities reach consensus, which he saw as being in stark contrast to the supposed 'ideal' of logical positivism which he rejected, in company with Mannheim, Popper, Hayek and numerous other academics who feared the links during the 1930s between logical positivism and 'scientific Marxism'. Hayek later introduced into economics the 'problems' of the 'division of knowledge' and the 'use of knowledge in society', which were taken up by his colleague Machlup in the 1960s. Daniel Bell also famously adapted the problematisations from Hayek, Polanyi and Mannheim in formu-lating his thesis on the new importance of scientific and technical knowledge (see Hull (2000b) for a more detailed description).

We see here the emergence of a particular 'post-positivist' problematisation: the notion that knowledge is an important entity, a unit of analysis, which presents particular types of problem which can no longer be left purely to philosophers, but which require the attention of various other experts. This provides for a variety of concepts, linkages, investigations, commentaries, labels, new language and re-definitions of old language, and changes in prac-tices and techniques. However, once we see how this problematisation has emerged we can also see both political and philosophical problems with it. The philosophical problem is that positivism has been 'misrecognised' (Rose, 1981): it has wrongly been cast as an epistemological and methodological error, rather than being seen to be based on notions of the 'sovereignty' of truth, perception and method that are tightly bound to similar notions of the 'sover-eignty' of monarchs and the State, as Foucault also demonstrated. Conse-quently, much of this 'post-positivist' problematisation of knowledge retains sovereign, absolute notions of 'freedom', 'the subject' and 'natural laws' that can only be justified by appeal to ethical imperatives that are themselves not open to challenge. In this sense, we can see that there are many similarities with the 'critical realism' of Reed. Both critical realism and the much broader problematisation of knowledge can now be seen to embrace a non-productive contradiction: they each advocate a post-positivist epistemology, combined with a positivist ethics, a combination which is bound to yield bizarre and unpredictable outcomes.

This leads us to the political problem: alongside this unpredictable combination of positivist ethics and post-positivist perspectives on knowledge, we have, with Hayek, Machlup, Polanyi and Popper, an essentially neo-liberal politics which seeks to reduce the role of established political government and increase the role of markets and a variety of forms of expertise, whether scientific, technological, economic, psychological or more recently accounting, auditing and 'bio-economic' (cf. Rose, 1993). The 'knowledge society' thesis, with the post-positivist problematisation of knowledge and accompanying arguments about the increased economic importance of knowledge, can thus be seen as a 'knowledge-based' justification for liberal market-based democracies. It thus places immense barriers in the path of developing any radically alternative political arrangements, any alternative forms of understanding and putting into practice the complex and constantly shifting relationships between knowledge and power.

These then are some of the disciplinary contours of the conduct of knowledge management. Whatever activities and practices are associated with knowledge management, they take place within a broad body of discourse, the 'post-positivist' problematisation of knowledge, with its accompanying political and philosophical problems. Knowledge management is rapidly becoming an identifiable discipline, with journals, newsletters, research centres, professorships and government 'best practice' units. This discipline can be interpreted in a number of ways. I have suggested that one feature is the utilisation of knowledge as a rhetorical justification for particular forms of political and economic coordination. How then does this discipline compare with what actually happens in practice, with what people do when they say they are doing knowledge management? As we shall see below, there are some significant mismatches.

Knowledge management practices

The formal results of the case-study research on specific Knowledge Management Practices (KMPs) has been extensively reported elsewhere for a variety of different audiences (Coombs and Hull, 1998; Coombs *et al.*, 1998; Hull, 1999a,b; Hull, 2000a). One of the key observations is the sheer variety of KMPs across a number of dimensions. From just five R&D settings we identified over 130 KMPs which could be aggregated into over 80 different practices, with consequently very little duplication. There was a considerable variety of formats for 'processing knowledge', in stark contrast with the traditional classification of knowledge processing as merely the three forms of 'creation, dissemination and utilisation'. Some examples were:

- Identification of knowledge that 'may be useful'.
- Capture or retrieval of knowledge.

- Altering the format – e.g. codifying knowledge by transferring it onto paper or IT systems, which also had various formats ranging from limited fields to hypertext.

- Validation of knowledge – for instance, through discussions with peers within or outside the organisation.

- Contextualising and re-contextualising – for instance, looking for common aspects and differences between the original context of the knowledge and the intended context.

- Achieving 'closure' – e.g. agreeing common definitions, for instance between R&D practitioners and Patent Attorneys, or between different project disciplines.

Around half the KMPs were to some degree 'informal' – *ad hoc*, reliant on initiative rather than being directed, or having a low degree of specification, standardisation or specialisation. In two cases the importance of these 'informal' practices was, as it were, 'formally recognised'. In one unit the phrase 'we're very informal here' was repeated so often and in the same way that it appeared more of a mantra than a shared perception. In another unit 'formalised informality' was encouraged, whereby bottom-up initiatives from R&D practitioners became sanctioned by senior management, but without attempts by them to formalise or direct those activities. With many of these 'informal' practices there was a complex mix of *post hoc* rationalisations in terms of improving 'performance', together with clear attempts to advance the relative profile or position of particular groups or individuals. In one case the library and information support specialists were taking initiatives to counter the tendency of R&D practitioners to gather information from the Internet. This was bypassing the expertise of the library/information unit and hence placing its position in danger. The initiatives were rationalised in terms of countering the possibility of R&D staff 'reinventing the wheels' of information gathering and sifting. In another case, a market research unit was repositioning itself by mapping competitors' R&D trajectories, with the expressed intention to just 'survive' – the existence of the unit was in danger unless they could demonstrate their indispensability.

Knowledge Management and ICTs

Many new KMPs had clearly been enabled through new Information and Communication Technologies (ICTs): electronic archiving of technical documents; electronic 'Patent Watch' bulletins; email, especially for specific discussion lists; and of course intranets for facilitating and advertising clusters of R&D expertise, for Web publishing of interim and final project results, and their extension towards collaborators through 'extranets'. Of course this observation must be tempered by awareness of the 'situated' and 'negotiated' usage and implementation of ICTs (Suchman, 1987), but these ICTs could be classified according to the different 'frameworks of computing', which have different approaches to the nature, role and context of knowledge and communication (Hull, 1997).

However, in one of the organisations the role of ICTs was minimal, primarily because of the importance for practitioners in this organisation of contextualising and re-contextualising what had been learned on specific projects – it was strongly felt that much of the knowledge gained within one project was highly specific or contextual to that project, and for aspects of that knowledge to be applicable to other projects it had to be carefully re-contextualised. In addition, in this organisation there was a strong emphasis on relations between experts being based on confidence, reputation and reliability, which echoes earlier studies of the 'reputational basis' of different scientific and engineering disciplines (Whitley, 1984).

There were also problems and disasters, for instance with electronic document management systems, and with implementing intranets, and in general a high degree of scepticism for 'technical fixes' to knowledge management issues. Indeed, in some cases there was concern that such technical fixes would merely *harden* already existing practices and routines, rather than opening up new directions. This scepticism was reflected in the finding that the role of ICTs was significant for only about 30% of the distinct KMPs. This is despite the tendency, as noted above, for knowledge management to be most often promoted by management/IT consultants or internal units. Many R&D centres are currently under pressure to re-think their strategic use of IT, although in one case the person responsible for knowledge management, recently recruited from a large consultancy, shifted his focus fairly dramatically over the year away from such 'technical fixes'.

Knowledge in context

A key observation is the extent to which practitioners emphasised the importance of the context of knowledge, and the relationships between knowledge and a variety of other factors within and outside the organisation. We have already mentioned the contextualising and re-contextualising of knowledge gained during projects, and this practice was noted in other organisations to a lesser extent. In addition a large group of KMPs were focused explicitly on what we labelled as 'mapping knowledge relationships' – deliberate attempts to understand the relationships between separate sets of knowledge. These sets of knowledge were separated for various reasons – different project teams which had no reasons to interact, different scientific and technical disciplines, different functional units, and within and outside the organisation. An example of mapping within the organisation is the 'formalised informality' mentioned above, which was focused on allowing the emergence of informal discussion groups on specific topics, comprising people from different projects, disciplines and units. 'Competitor intelligence' is a good example of mapping across organisations, with another being the encouragement to staff to 'offer' their expertise to external standards and regulatory bodies and judicial hearings, with the dual intention of keeping track of regulatory and legal developments and offering the organisation's own perspective on specific issues. Another example was the practice of deliberately recruiting people with extensive networks of friends and ex-colleagues in other organisations.

These KMPs are based on an understanding that there are highly complex interactions and interdependencies between different aspects of knowledge: between *types* of knowledge, for instance explicit and tacit, *domains* of knowledge (knowledge of technologies, of customers, of competitors etc.), and the *sources* of the knowledge – inside or outside the organisation, in this or that discipline, from a journal, magazine or friend in another organisation. Such an understanding or perspective flies against the simplistic descriptions and prescriptions from the consultants and academics constituting the discipline of knowledge management. The R&D practitioners and managers were, in a sense, putting into operation various self-taught versions of the sociology of knowledge. At the most basic level, this was expressed to me as, to paraphrase, 'of course we recognise that knowledge and power are connected, that's why simple ideas about knowledge management and about intranets and extranets and all the various "guidebooks" are insufficient'. These practitioners are clearly attempting to accomplish a very difficult balancing act between 'recognising the partiality of knowledge', and 'knowing the truth of a situation'. Secondly though, the discussions and debates about 'the social construction of skill and knowledge' are clearly not reserved for academics, and are instead diffused through organisations in complex ways. This would seem to pose some problems for those academics who would presume to have specialised or privileged access to understanding 'the social construction of skill and knowledge'.

Knowledge management and career development

Leading on from the last point, one of the key issues to emerge from the case studies, especially where intranets were being actively developed, was the relationship between KMPs and career development. Put simply: on the one hand many R&D practitioners saw their promotion prospects depending, in large part, on the specialised knowledge they 'held' or 'owned'; on the other hand, there were various initiatives, ICT developments such as intranets, and indeed pronouncements from senior management, to the effect that 'sharing knowledge' was a 'good thing' and sometimes a 'necessity' for the health and development of the unit as a whole. In one case this dilemma had reached such 'serious' proportions – in the sense that 'knowledge hoarding' was seen to be a resistance and an impedance to the health of the unit – that there were currently moves to radically restructure the 'Reward and Recognition' systems. Interestingly, though, these moves were in combination with moves to build in to the R&R systems a greater degree of equal opportunities (or rather a 'diversity policy'), with the connection being that the tendency to 'hoard' knowledge reinforced the privilege of those already privileged, for example through gender or race, while the initiatives in 'sharing knowledge' generally came from those attempting to 'level the playing field'. In this case, then, the emergence, development and debates about knowledge management within the unit had to some extent altered the parameters of internal power struggles, to the benefit of those who saw themselves as marginalised in some way, who had been able to rhetorically combine their interests with those of the unit as a whole.

Conclusion

One could construct a complex set of financial, institutional, industrial, technological and global explanandums which, interacting in various ways, would explain away the phenomenon of knowledge management and its manifestation in specific KMPs. One could alternatively, perhaps, construct arguments about tendencies and tensions in the relationships between knowledge management and the 'responsibilisation' of R&D practitioners, their internalisation of particular corporate problematisations and orientations. Certainly the first argument may be partly appropriate in discussing, for example, the two units (library and market research) apparently struggling for survival. The second argument, on the other hand, may hold some water when discussing the 'mantra' of informality and the managerial sanctioning of 'formalised informality'. Neither, it seems to me, could 'explain away' the picture painted in the last observation, of KMPs and career development.

More importantly, neither of those potential sets of explanation/discussion are of any use if we wish to suggest how KMPs may assist the operations of research, development and day-to-day running in, for instance, the NHS, Social Services Departments or Education Authorities. Certainly, some people may wish to merely condemn out of hand the emergence and continued operation of KMPs. That, to me, is real nihilism. What then can we say about the conduct of knowledge management, arising from this work?

Firstly, it is clear that people, R&D practitioners and others in R&D settings, are having to cope with the consequences of a discipline which, in many ways, got it wrong when it posed 'knowledge' as an entity that could be managed. While the terms of that discipline remain as they are, there will inevitably be many instances where KMPs are straightforwardly ineffective – for anyone. If ICT systems are built strictly along those lines they will fail. If procedures, processes and 'cultural systems' of knowledge management are constructed along those lines they will encounter immense difficulties, not least of which will be the well-known problems associated with attempting to mobilise subjectivity – 'the knowledge one has' – in furtherance of aims remote from the subjects. This was graphically illustrated in the discussion about 'knowledge hoarding versus knowledge sharing'.

Secondly, however, often precisely because of those errors within the original discipline, people are developing a range of new practices, many of which are far more interesting and potentially more effective than the original knowledge management literature. This is shown in the variety of 'knowledge processing characteristics' that emerged, the variety of formats deployed, and the variety of strategic aims associated with KMPs. This variety, together with the issues raised about knowledge management and career development, suggest moreover that knowledge management – understood as a group of KMPs rather than as a top-down system – has the potential to enable people in R&D settings to challenge some existing organisational features, to do more effective R&D, and hence possibly to do R&D that is more socially responsible (perhaps that's wishful thinking). However, the prime, overriding lesson here is that detailed analysis of very specific KMPs, and the context in which they are or might be located or might be allowed to emerge, is a prerequisite for effective judgement of the possible value of any particular form of knowledge management. One cannot and should not, in other words, attempt to come to any overall evaluation without that level of empirical detail. Of course these are extremely preliminary observations – the result of only five studies – so there is a clear need for further more extensive study of KMPs, particularly studies of organisations which have attempted to introduce formalised knowledge management systems.

References

Archer, M. (1995) *Realist Social Theory: the Morphogenetic Approach*, Cambridge: Cambridge University Press.

Barry, A., Osborne, T. and Rose, N. (eds.) (1996) *Foucault and Political Reason: Liberalism, Neo-liberalism and Rationalities of Government*, London: UCL Press.

Baumann, Z. (1993) *Postmodern Ethics*, Oxford: Blackwell.

Bhaskar, R. (1974 [1977, 2nd edn]) *A Realist Theory of Science*, Brighton: Harvester Press.

Bhaskar, R. (1979), *The Possibility of Naturalism*, Hemel Hempstead: Harvester Wheatsheaf.

Bhaskar, R. (1993) *Dialectic: the Pulse of Freedom*. London: Verso.

Burchell, G., Gordon, C. and Miller, P. (eds) (1991) *The Foucault Effect: Studies in Governmentality*. Hemel Hempstead: Harvester Wheatsheaf.

Callon, M. and Latour, B. (1992) 'Don't Throw the Baby Out with the Bath School! A Reply to Collins and Yearley', in A. Pickering (ed.) *Science as Practice and Culture*, Chicago: Chicago University Press, pp. 343–68.

Castel, R. (1994) '"Problematisation" as a Mode of Reading History', in J. Goldstein (ed.), *Foucault and the Writing of History*, Oxford: Blackwell, pp. 237–52.

Clegg, S. R. (1994) 'Max Weber and the Sociology of Organisations', in L. J. Ray and M. Reed (eds.), *Organising Modernity: New Weberian Perspectives on Work, Organisation and Society*, London: Routledge, pp. 46–80.

Coombs, R. and Hull, R. (1995) 'BPR as "IT-enabled Organisational Change": An Assessment', *New Technology, Work and Employment*, 10: 2, 121–31.

Coombs, R. and Hull, R. (1998) '"Knowledge Management Practices" and Path Dependency in Innovation', *Research Policy*, 27: 3, 237–53.

Coombs, R., Hull, R. and Peltu, M. (1998) 'Knowledge Management Practices for Innovation: An Audit Tool for Improvement', CRIC Working Paper No. 6, Manchester: ESRC Centre for Research on Innovation & Competition. Also Forthcoming in *International Journal of Technology Management*, 2000.

Dean, M. (1994) *Critical and Effective Histories: Foucault's Methods and Historical Sociology*, London: Routledge.

Foucault, M. (1982) 'The Subject and Power', in H. Dreyfus and P. Rabinow (eds.) *Michel Foucault: Beyond Structuralism and Hermeneutics*, Brighton: Harvester. Quoted in Owen, D. (1994). *Maturity and Modernity*, London: Routledge, p. 153.

Hindess, B. (1996) *Discourses of Power: From Hobbes to Foucault*, Oxford: Blackwell.

Hull, R. (1997) 'Governing the Conduct of Computing: Computer Science, the Social Sciences, and Frameworks of Computing', *Accounting, Management and Information Technologies*, 7: 4, 213–40.

Hull, R. (1998) 'The Conduct of Expert Labour: Knowledge Management Practices in R&D', CRIC Discussion Paper 22. Manchester: ESRC Centre for Research on Innovation & Competition.

Hull, R. (1999a) 'Actor Network and Conduct: The Discipline and Practices of Knowledge Management', *Organisation*, 6: 3, 405–28.

Hull, R. (1999b) 'Knowledge Management and Innovation: A Focus on Practices', *Measuring Business Excellence*, September.

Hull, R. (2000a) 'Knowledge Management Practices and Innovation', in Andersen, Howells, Hull, Miles and Roberts (eds.), *Knowledge and Innovation in the New Service Economy*, London: Edward Elgar.

Hull, R. (2000b) 'Knowledge and the Economy: Some Critical Comments', *Economy & Society*, in press.

Irwin, A. (1995) *Citizen Science: A Study of People, Expertise, and Sustainable Development*, London: Routledge.

Irwin, A. and Wynne, B. (eds.) (1996) *Misunderstanding Science? The Public Reconstruction of Science and Technology*, Cambridge: Cambridge University Press.

Laredo, P. and Mustar, P. (1998) 'The Techno-Economic Network, a Socio-Economic Approach to State Intervention in Innovation', in Coombs, Green, Richards and Walsh (eds.), *Technology and Organisations*, London: Edward Elgar.

Lash, S., Szerszynski, B. and Wynne, B. (1996) *Risk, Environment and Modernity: Towards a New Ecology*, London: Sage.

Latour, B. (1996) 'On Actor–Network Theory – A Few Clarifications', *Soziale Welt-Zeitschrift Fur Sozialwissenschaftliche Forschung Und Praxis*, 47: 4, 369.

Lynch, M. E. (1993) *Scientific Practice and Ordinary Action: Ethnomethodology and Social Studies of Science*, Cambridge: Cambridge University Press.

Pickering, A. (ed.) (1992) *Science as Practice and Culture*, Chicago: Chicago University Press.

Prosch, H. (1986) *Michael Polanyi: A Critical Exposition*, Albany, NY: SUNY Press.

Pugh, D. S. (1988) 'The Aston Research Programme', in A. Bryman (ed.) *Doing Research in Organisations*, London: Routledge, pp. 123–35.

Reed, M. L. (1994) 'Expert Power and Organisation in High Modernity: An Empirical Review and Theoretical Synthesis', paper presented to the ESRC Research Seminar Series 'Transformation of the Professions'.

Reed, M. L. (1996) 'Expert Power and Control in Late Modernity: An Empirical Review and Theoretical Synthesis', *Organisation Studies*, 17: 4, 573–97.

Reed, M. L. (1997) 'In Praise of Duality and Dualism: Rethinking Agency and Structure in Organisational Analysis', *Organisation Studies*, 18: 1, 21–42.

Rose, G. (1981 [1995, 2nd edn with new Preface]) *Hegel: Contra Sociology*, London: Athlone Press.
Rose, G. (1984) *Dialectic of Nihilism: Post-Structuralism and Law*, Oxford: Blackwell.
Rose, G. (1992) *The Broken Middle: Out of our Ancient Society*, Oxford: Blackwell.
Rose, G. (1995 [1997, Vintage edition]) *Love's Work*, London: Chatto & Windus.
Rose, N. (1993) 'Government, authority and expertise in advanced liberalism', *Economy & Society*, 22: 3, 283–99.
Schaffer, S. (1994) 'In the know', *London Review of Books*, 10 November, pp. 17–18.
Schot, J. (1992) 'Constructive Technology Assessment and Technology Dynamics: The Case of Clean Technologies', *Science, Technology and Human Values*, 17: 1, 36–56.
Schot, J. and Rip, A. (1997) 'The Past And Future Of Constructive Technology Assessment', *Technological Forecasting And Social Change*, 54: 2/3, 251–68.
Sclove, R. E. (1995) *Democracy and Technology*, London: Guildford Press.
Sclove, R. E. (1998) 'Editorial – Better Approaches to Science Policy', *Science*, 279: 5355 (27 February), 1283.
Stenson, K. (1998) 'Beyond histories of the present', *Economy & Society*, 27: 4, 333–52.
Suchman, L. (1987) *Plans and Situated Actions: The Problems of Human–Computer Communication*, Cambridge: Cambridge University Press.
Turner, S. (1994) *The Social Theory of Practices: Tradition, Tacit Knowledge, and Presuppositions*, Chicago: University of Chicago Press.
Whitley, R. D. (1984) *The Intellectual and Social Organisation of the Sciences*, Oxford: Clarendon Press.
Wilkinson, J. (1997) 'A New Paradigm for Economic Analysis? – Recent Convergences in French Social Science and An Exploration of the Convention Theory Approach with A Consideration of its Application to the Analysis of the Agrofood System', *Economy & Society*, 26: 3, 305–39.

Notes

1 The case-study research was funded by the UK Economic and Social Science Research Council, Grant Number L125251008. Aspects of this chapter have been presented to the 19th Annual Labour Process Conference, Manchester 1998 and the conference 'Actor Network and After', Keele University, 1997. I would also like to acknowledge the many various comments, especially from Mike Chumer, Hugh Willmott, Craig Prichard, Vivien Walsh, Rod Coombs (my collaborator on the case-studies) and my ex-colleagues at the Centre for Research on Innovation and Competition, Manchester.

2 On attempts to involve citizens in scientific and other areas of expertise, see Irwin (1995); for a description and critique of 'public understanding of science' see Irwin and Wynne (1996) and Lash *et al.* (1996); on 'democratising policy' see Sclove (1995, 1998). 'Strengthening the networks of actors' is a reference to the Actor Network approach of Callon, Latour and others, which has been applied in specific attempts to intervene in both the deployment and the development of expertise (Laredo and Mustar, 1998), and especially within the technique of Constructive Technology Assessment (Schot, 1992; Schot and Rip, 1997). On the rise of attempts to develop and reform professional Codes, see such journals as *Business Ethics, Science and Engineering Ethics, Applied Philosophy, Science* and *Nature*, in addition of course to the many discussions of 'infoethics', medical ethics and 'bioethics'.

3 Governmentality studies (Burchell *et al.*, 1991; Barry *et al.*, 1996) have always focused strongly on the role of expertise in new modes of governing populations, but stopped short of normative evaluations of specific forms of expertise. Such studies are

generally characterised by critics as 'postmodernist' or 'post-structuralist', but in practice vary widely from the historical and genealogical to the development of new and 'exemplary' forms of intervention in contemporary disputes. Recently there have been some calls precisely for more normative judgements (Stenson, 1998; Hindess, 1996). This chapter can thus be viewed as a contribution to those calls.

4 Reed (1996) does not use the phrase 'socially constructed', although he did in an earlier version (Reed, 1994). And of course Bhaskar himself talks of 'knowledge as a social product'.

5 Safe Enclaves, Political Enclaves and Knowledge Working

Niall Hayes and Geoff Walsham

Introduction

Commentators on contemporary themes of organising have suggested that organisations have increasingly become dependent on the exercise of specialist resources and on workers that ply their trade through their cognitive abilities and their specialist knowledge (Blackler, 1993, 1995). Reich (1991) terms these 'symbolic analytical workers', whose intellective abilities are varied, difficult to duplicate and who frequently command high rewards. Contemporary organisations which comprise a high proportion of qualified staff who trade in knowledge itself through peer to peer collaboration are referred to as knowledge-intensive firms (KIFs) (Blackler *et al.*, 1993, 1997; Boland and Tenkasi, 1995). Dominant accounts in the knowledge work literature portray knowledge as being an entity that can be possessed and traded, viewing learning as a process by which a learner internalises knowledge, whether 'discovered', 'transmitted' from others or 'experienced in interaction' with others (Bell, 1973, 1978; Nonaka and Takeuchi, 1994). In contrast to this, the less dominant relational view adopted in this chapter portrays knowledge as being provisional and context bound (Lave, 1988; Orr, 1990). Relational writers view knowledge as residing in an evolving, continuously renewed set of relations of persons, their actions and the world, and thus in contrast to dominant accounts, they contend that knowledge cannot be divorced from its context (Tsoukas, 1996; Lave and Wenger, 1991).

Several relational writers argue that many 'expert dependent' organisations are increasingly going through a shift to becoming communication intensive (Barley, 1996; Blackler *et al.*, 1998). This shift, in part, is attributed to the emergence of ubiquitous low-cost distributed technology (Ruhleder, 1995; Blackler *et al.*, 1997). Zuboff (1996) concurs with this view, by noting that as technologies, such as groupware systems, become more ubiquitous, they are 'fully imbuing tasks of every sort and providing ever more powerful opportunities for the kind of learning that translates into value creation'. Indeed, some scholars view knowledge work as being inseparable from the development of contemporary technologies (Knights *et al.*, 1993; Star and Ruhleder, 1994; Ruhleder, 1995).

Several writers within the relational tradition view *power/knowledge* as being inseparable. Critical writers, such as Alvesson (1993), indicate that organisations lay claim to knowledge rather than possess knowledge (Willmott, 1995). Alvesson (1993) further argues that the notion of knowledge-intensive firms is no more than an institutionalised myth, which seeks to ensure employee conformity with the institutionalised expectations of their environments. Most influential in this domain has been Foucault's (1977) writings on the panopticon, and how knowledge is always bound up with technologies of power. The panopticon created the effect of 'universal transparency' within a prison, which aimed to induce 'in the inmate a state of consciousness and permanent visibility that assures the automatic functioning of power [Foucault, 1977, p. 201). Zuboff (1988, p. 319) draws on this concept, and suggests that information systems, due to their technical arrangements, provide similar possibilities for the threat of continuous observation, which reduces the need for discipline so that finally: 'discipline, regulation and surveillance are taken for granted'. At present, accounts of the political and normative issues in the mainstream knowledge working literature, particularly with reference to the role of information systems, are not as plentiful as these issues warrant.

This chapter explores how the political and normative context was implicated in knowledge working in a UK selling division of a multinational pharmaceuticals company. Compound UK (the selling division) introduced Lotus Notes, a leading groupware product, to assist employees to work more qualitatively within and between functions. Employees used Lotus Notes to share views and perspectives with members of their own and other functions. Specifically, this chapter will consider why it was that some shared databases had more of a political air than others, and how the political and normative context was implicated in influencing the character of interaction of employees working within and between functions. Furthermore, the chapter will draw on, and extend, Boland and Tenkasi's (1995) communities of practice approach, which conceptualises how communication technologies are implicated in knowledge working with reference to political and normative issues.

This chapter will first outline the particular communities of practice approach drawn upon in the study, as well as the conceptualisation of power that underpins the analysis. Following this, the principles which underlie the ethnographic research method used will be explained. We will then introduce Compound UK. The next section will discuss how the visibility that Lotus Notes provided was implicated in influencing the character of interaction within and between boundaries, and we will then explore how the political use of Notes was implicated in knowledge working. The final section will discuss the implications and conclusions arising from this study.

Conceptualising the Role of Groupware Technologies in the Knowledge Work Process

The communities of practice school is largely attributed to the work of Lave and Wenger (1991), Brown and Duguid (1991) and subsequently Chaiklin and Lave (1993). Boland and Tenkasi (1995) have subsequently drawn on these foundations specifically to conceptualise the role of communication technologies in the knowledge work process. They see organisations as being characterised by a process of distributed cognition in which multiple communities of specialised knowledge workers, each dealing with a part of an overall organisational problem, interact to create the patterns of sense making and behaviour displayed by the organisation as a whole (Boland *et al.*, 1994). Each community of knowing consists of specialised knowledge workers, and includes divisions, functional areas, product lines, professional specialities, project teams and issue-based committees. These communities interweave with each other across various levels of the organisation, as 'individuals will find themselves as members of several communities of knowing operating within a firm and its environment'.

Boland and Tenkasi (1995) developed the concepts of perspective making and perspective taking to refer to the ability to reconfigure the knowing of experts. *Perspective making* refers to the process whereby a community develops and strengthens its own knowledge domain and practices. As a perspective strengthens, it complexifies, which involves a shift from a global and undifferentiated construct to a more precise explanation, and a more coherent structure of meaning. The process of *perspective taking* refers to the process of collaboration between experts working across boundaries, when they are able to appreciate and synergistically utilise their distinctive knowledge (Blackler *et al.*, 1999). Boland and Tenkasi (1995) suggest that making their own understandings visible for self-reflection is vital to the perspective-taking process, and advocate communication technologies to support this process. They further note that perspectives need protection from other demands while they are forming. They suggest that a new expanded sense of activity and community needs to emerge, born of an awareness of the changing context and a willingness to construct new meanings and methods.

No accounts from a communities of practice perspective have explicitly explored how the political and normative context is implicated in knowledge working, though both Boland and Tenkasi (1995) and Lave and Wenger (1991) do indicate that this indeed is an important consideration. To develop the analysis of the political character of interactions within and between boundaries, this chapter has drawn on Goffman's (1959) work on front and back regions to develop a conceptual distinction between safe and political enclaves and to explore the implications of the political use of cooperative technology. Political enclaves are akin to what Goffman terms 'front regions'. He likens these settings to being front of stage, where actors portray a public facade. Political enclaves in this study are portrayed as being used as a resource by all politically orientated actors who seek to further their own agendas.

Safe enclaves are akin to what Goffman terms 'back regions', which he likens to being the back of stage, where employees feel safe to express their own underlying views of an activity. These settings are conducive to discussion and reflection surrounding the ongoing activities and events. However, a cautionary note surrounding this distinction between safe and political enclaves needs to be mentioned at the outset. The distinction refers to the character of the use of the shared databases and other encounters between employees, and consequently safe enclaves are political in so far as they are shared social spaces. For example, opting out of political enclaves in preference to safer ones is itself a political act.

Methodology

This section presents the ethnographic methodological approach that has been drawn upon to undertake this research. An ethnographic account seeks to produce detailed descriptions of the everyday activities of social actors within specific contexts. It is a naturalistic method relying on material drawn from the first-hand experience of a field worker in some setting (Skeggs, 1994). Its main concern is to present a portrait of life as seen and understood by those who live and work in the domain concerned (Steier, 1991). Ethnographers believe in the power of their questions and the use of representations to construct the lives of the people they are studying (Steier, 1991). By doing this, an ethnographic account provides access to the everyday ways in which participants understand and conduct their working lives.

The primary research in Compound UK was carried out in two phases over a two and a half year period. However, one of the authors had previously conducted an action research project over a six month period in the year previous to the primary research period, which, although not directly related to the focus of the subsequent study, did provide valuable background and awareness of the context of this study. The first phase of fieldwork was undertaken between October 1995 and February 1996. During this phase, 33 in-depth interviews were carried out, lasting from 1 to 3 hours each, as well as considerable informal interaction. Between February 1997 and May 1997, 21 follow-up interviews were conducted in order to try to understand the use of cooperative systems over time, and to provide the longitudinal element that is seen as highly desirable for ethnographic research.

In the first phase, interviews were relatively structured. They sought to glean the changing perceptions and work practices that had emerged as a result of the introduction of Lotus Notes. As an increased awareness about both Compound UK's operations and a provisional understanding of the emerging issues was gathered, the interview questions were not followed as rigidly as they were at the outset of the research. In the second phase of interviews, any emerging themes and issues that remained unresolved from phase one were pursued in a more unstructured way. This flexibility allowed for the modification of the research design in the light of emergent or unanticipated analytical problems thrown up by the context or the data (Layder, 1993). In addition, interviews were confidential and conducted in private. The initial part of the interview would be spent explaining the identity and purpose of the researcher(s), and reassuring interviewees that no attribution would be given to their views in any subsequent discussion or reports. Relatedly, detailed field notes were preferred to the use of a tape recorder, as it was thought that tape recording would have led to less candid responses.

Interviews were supplemented by social interactions in the cafeteria and during drinks in the evening with employees. The aim of this social interaction was to gain a feel for what it is like for the people in the situation being studied. In particular, by undertaking these social interactions at every possible moment, it allowed a way to compensate for any limitations arising from undertaking interviews. These extensive interactions were intended to further reveal a 'rich under life' that is usually seen as being masked to quantitative researchers (Geertz, 1973), and to those qualitative researchers that place their emphasis solely on undertaking interviews.

Compound UK

Compound UK is concerned primarily with selling products to hospitals and general medical practices, while also undertaking clinical trials of new drugs with participating doctors in Great Britain and Northern Ireland. The selling division had undergone considerable change over the decade prior to the restructuring as a response to reforms in the UK health care sector, as outlined below.

During the late 1980s there was an acceleration in the reform of the UK National Health Service (NHS) (Connah and Pearson, 1991). Government controls on public expenditure meant that for a number of years the health care budget had not kept pace with inflation, and thus had reduced in real terms. To try to achieve cost savings, the NHS attempted to mirror market principles by introducing an internal market-place (Robinson and Le Grand, 1994; Flynn and Williams, 1997). This led the NHS to rethink the purchase of pharmaceuticals products; the criteria for purchasing such products no longer concentrated solely on their efficacy, but also on their cost and efficiency.

The introduction of these market reforms has split the health care sector between primary care and specialist care. The primary care sector covers general medical practices, while the specialist care sector covers hospital markets. Since the reforms, many primary care doctors have become fund-holders. They have budgetary responsibilities for drugs, hospital referrals, and staff, as well as for their fixed costs. Hospitals are also more autonomous from the Department of Health, and are responsible for their own budgets. As a consequence, specialist care doctors are part of a large group of decision makers, including managers and accountants. From the point of view of Compound UK, at the time of the research study not only had the criteria for purchasing pharmaceuticals products added cost savings to each drug's efficacy, but sales situations had also become far more complex, since client groups such as hospitals now included a wider range of actors in their purchasing decisions.

Much of this chapter focuses on the commercial function of Compound UK. In 1993, this was reorganised into eight regions. It was thought that this would provide each region with considerable autonomy to plan and respond to its own locality, and thus to make the organisation more responsive to the new marketplace. In 1996, the commercial function consisted of its director, Tom Saunders, eight regional managers, twelve area managers, and around 150 sales representatives (reps). All members of the commercial function, apart from the director, worked from their own homes, while employees working in other departments were located at the head office, Compound Square.

As part of the response to the environmental changes in Compound UK, senior management felt that the selling division could become more competitive by encouraging employees to draw on all areas of the organisation to work and share information and knowledge across functional and geographic boundaries. Lotus Notes was seen as a software package that could assist with sharing information and improving group working.

In addition to an electronic mail (email) facility, there were three main uses of Notes after its introduction in Compound UK. First, databases to support the cooperative activities involved in strategic selling were created. These databases allowed employees to input their views and information in a structured way with the aim of bringing together the employees' shared knowledge so that they might contribute to a successful sale. Issues were recorded on electronic strategic selling sheets. A second use of Notes was the provision of a wide variety of discussion databases which focused on issues, products or a particular role. The final and most prevalent use of Notes was the contact-recording database. This database provided a shared resource for employees to record details of customers. This is a widely used practice in selling companies, and had been present in various paper and electronic forms in Compound UK since the early 1970s. We will focus on contact recording and strategic selling as the empirical basis for much of the rest of the chapter. It was the use of these aspects of the technology that displayed the themes of this chapter most clearly.

Visibility and Invisibility

This section discusses the differing ways that employees responded to the visibility that the introduction of Lotus Notes brought to their activities. The visibility arose from employees working discursively on Lotus Notes' shared databases and provided a means for much more of the employees' day-to-day work lives to be made transparent to managers. This transparency provided a resource for senior managers to coordinate and control employees, as had happened with the previous contact recording system.

Although contact recording on Lotus Notes had considerably more scope for sharing perspectives and details than the previous contact-recording system, it still provided the facility to monitor the number of contacts that reps made with doctors. Not long after Notes was introduced, the commercial director instructed the Lotus Notes developer to devise a league facility which could indicate centrally how many contact records and strategic selling sheets had been completed by each sales representative. Once the contact records had been collated centrally in the form of league tables, Robert Cross, the strategic selling manager, would send out electronic messages to field force managers to inform them about the number of contact records and strategic selling sheets that each rep had completed. Area managers felt obliged to inform members of their sales team that their low contact recording rates had been noticed centrally. This confirmed many of the reps' suspicions about the intention behind the reintro-duction of an electronic contact recording system.

Extended capacity to monitor and control

However, contact recording on Lotus Notes not only allowed reps to represent the number of calls they made; unlike its predecessor, it also had the scope to record employees' observations and comments. Some senior managers would regularly review not only the league tables, but also the detailed comments and observations that reps had recorded, so that they could gain a deeper insight before meeting particular doctors or other stakeholders. It also provided an insight into how their products were faring. This meant that with reps recording not only the number of visits, but also the content of their visits, the storage capacity of Lotus Notes expanded the degree of authoritative resources that senior managers could draw on to sanction reps compared with that which existed with Jaguar, the previous contact-recording system.

Many of the more cynical reps were negative about the use senior managers made of the details stored on Lotus Notes. They suggested that it had intention-ally brought senior management, located in Compound Square, into their own homes. This point is best explained by one primary care rep, who reacted angrily when the author asked if he felt closer to what was going on in Compound Square as a result of the introduction of Lotus Notes, saying:

> It is the people based in headquarters who feel isolated; this is why they use tech-nology, so they can monitor what people in the field are up to. The computer allows them a handle on what we do. How would they have known that I was sat in a hotel

meeting you before they introduced Notes? Now I will put it into my contact recording database.

The introduction of the strategic selling database similarly extended the ability for senior managers to exercise tight control over sales reps. All employees, but most notably the sales reps, were required to input details discursively on the shared database, to structure their visits, and to draw on the expertise of other employees. Strategic selling sheets represented a simplification of the selling process; they provided a way to visibly structure their more complex work. By developing strategic selling sheets, reps could prove to senior management that they were following guidelines by planning their more difficult sales in a way that senior management, and the strategic selling manager in particular, could monitor and control. As one area manager mentioned:

> Robert Cross looks randomly at everyone's strategic selling sheets to check up on the quality of them. Robert will send me a note saying that the reps' use of the strategic selling sheets was either appropriate or not appropriate! Sometimes he will write more detailed comments.

Prior to the introduction of Notes, there was more reliance on area managers to supervise and control much of the reps' work due to the limited awareness that those in Compound Square had of a rep's day-to-day activities. The only direct information that senior managers could draw on to monitor the reps' activities, were the contact rates recorded on Jaguar. However, as discussed above, Notes not only indicated the number of contacts made, but also allowed senior managers a more detailed indication of the activities that reps were undertaking through the detailed fields that reps completed on the contact recording and strategic selling databases. This allowed senior management in Compound Square to coordinate more of the reps' day-to-day activities, which had previously been exercised locally by area managers. Consequently, the authority of senior management was increased and the autonomy of the field force management was reduced.

The career reward structure

Some reps welcomed the reintroduction of contact recording and the extended surveillance capacity, and harnessed this increased visibility for their own individual purposes. These reps would record a considerable number of contact records regardless of whether they were relevant, so that they could register a high position on the league tables. They would record all the doctors, managers, accountants and even nurses that they met in general practices and hospitals. This went contrary to the ethos that arose in tandem with the restructuring and the introduction of Lotus Notes that emphasised only recording 'relevant' calls. Many non-career-orientated reps were quite resentful of some other sales reps and of those working in Compound Square, who they saw as using Notes to try to further their careers. Non-careerist reps were generally those that had been doing the job for some time, and had mostly given up any hopes they had for career advancement, while careerist reps were ambitious, and tended to be younger.

Non-career-orientated reps were generally favourable to the move away from only recording the quantity of calls, and saw this approach to working as being appropriate to the new health care environment. However, they feared that as a result of the activities of the ambitious reps, senior management might revert to explicitly directing reps to record high contact rates. As one experienced rep noted:

> Younger people just see repping as temporary, as a way to pass through to the head office. They think they can put up with it for a few years, and are quite happy to input loads of contacts, and work flat out; this has an impact on the long-term reps, who have to keep up with them.

Many career-orientated reps would seek to gain favour with Robert Cross, Tom Saunders and Martin Garratt (the general manager), by working on a considerable number of strategic selling sheets at any moment in time. As with the contact-recording database, many non-career-orientated reps felt frustrated with their peers, as they saw them legitimating the extensive use of strategic selling, regardless of whether they had any complex sales accounts in their territory at that time or not.

This was particularly the case for primary care reps, who did not see the benefit of having too many strategic selling sheets open at any particular time. Primary care was not seen to consist of as many stakeholders as specialist care, and in effect, primary care reps only had one or two general practices that could be classified as complex sales situations within their territory. Thus, with many primary care reps keeping active a considerable number of strategic selling sheets, non-career-orientated reps resented this. They felt they were merely doing this to gain favour with the strategic selling manager who reviewed how well or how poorly the rep had used the strategic selling database. As one rep mentioned:

> There are not that many complex sales situations in my area, and I only need to keep active a few strategic selling accounts at a time, unlike some of the shining stars!

In specialist care, the extensive use of the strategic selling database was seen as more justified and less politically orientated, because of the increased complexity of the sales situations since the health care reforms. Also, most specialist care reps had already 'served their time' as primary care reps, and generally were the more experienced and less ambitious reps.

A further component of Notes that was used by some employees as a resource to politicise was the electronic mail facility. Many of the electronic messages that senior managers received informed them of something mundane that had been completed by lower level employees, and were described by senior managers, and their personal assistants, as being pointless. They saw these ambitious reps as just trying to gain 'brownie points' with the senior managers for the amount and nature of work they had undertaken, or planned to undertake. By using email in this way, they thought that they could be noticed by senior managers, and would be viewed favourably in any future promotion opportunities. One medical liaison manager (MLM) highlighted the political character of the use of Notes, saying:

> There are a lot of highly career-orientated and cut-throat people in Compound UK, and they have taken every chance to portray themselves to the senior managers in a good light. There are a lot of yes men, and this is encouraged in Compound UK by one manager in particular. If you look at the use of the technology, it mirrors their ambitions.

The discussion databases, which had a national and cross-functional audience, were also used with similar intentions. Politically orientated employees were aware that the national discussion databases were reviewed and contributed to by many senior managers, including the commercial director and the general manager. Those employees who wanted their comments to be noticed by senior managers felt that contributing to these databases would be beneficial to their career development. The national discussion databases were occupied, in the main, not only by ambitious reps, but also by employees based at Compound Square. Indeed, several reps referred sarcastically to these discussion databases by terming them 'Compound Square News'! As one rep mentioned:

> There is a political element, definitely. People hijack databases to make political state-ments. They want to be seen and heard. The national discussion databases are where the political animals are to be found. These include some reps, but mostly those in Compound Square contribute to them. Tom Saunders, Martin Garratt and other senior managers look at the national databases, and these tend to be used the most. The regional databases are not the same. They are about local and regional issues, and are more concerned with sharing than anything else.

As the previous quotation indicates, a consequence of this political use of the shared databases was that this often led to employees' comments reaffirming the views of senior management, rather than providing a way to explore under-standings and meanings that different groups of employees held across the organisation.

Though the functional or role-specific discussion databases did not generally share the same political character, a few had high levels of visibility. For example, on the MLM's discussion database, all ten MLMs would contribute and review the changing issues on a regular basis. However, the medical director discovered the success of this database and asked if he could take part in the discussions. Consequently, soon after he had access to this database, its use petered out. As one medical liaison manager mentioned:

The MLM database was really well used but has petered out now. This happened soon after our boss, the medical director, asked if he could be included in it because he had heard how successful it was. No one felt that they could comfortably share views in the knowledge that he was reviewing the database.

Many employees felt less uneasy sharing their views on the functional or regional specific shared databases. For example, several of the regional and role-specific databases were used extensively to express and share views and comments between colleagues in the same function. This was in contrast to the use of national shared databases, where many employees felt uneasy working discursively with employees that they were unfamiliar with, or suspicious of their motives, and as a consequence limited the opportunities for crossing boundaries in Compound UK.

Political and Safe Enclaves and Perspective Making and Taking

This section will draw on the conceptual distinction between political and safe enclaves to consider how the nature of use of Lotus Notes was implicated in knowledge working, and specifically the perspective-making and taking process. This conceptual distinction will be further clarified throughout this section through an additional construct of optionality and non-optionality. Non-optionality refers to those shared databases that employees felt that they had to use in order to legitimate their activities, whereas optionality refers to those shared databases that they did not feel normatively bound to use. More specifically, the first subsection will explore how an employee's optional and non-optional inclusion in, and optional exclusion from, political enclaves was implicated in knowledge working. The second subsection will explore similar issues for the safe enclaves.

Political enclaves and knowledge working

The previous section explored in detail the varying ways that employees at all levels of the organisation harnessed the visibility that Notes provided as a resource to further their own positions. Table 5.1 summarises how the individualistic motivations that surrounded many employees' use of Notes were implicated in limiting the perspective-taking process.

Several senior managers viewed the contact recording and strategic selling databases as a way to ensure that reps worked in the ways they promoted, while ambitious reps harnessed these aspects of Notes, as well as the national discussion databases, to prove to senior managers they were working hard, and complying with their directives. This meant that the nature of the use of Notes merely reinforced the dominance of these senior managers' perspectives. Consequently, much of the use of Notes was driven by individualistic concerns, rather than engaging in collaboration with employees in other communities in order to appreciate and synergistically utilise their distinctive knowledge.

These difficulties were further reinforced due to the optional exclusion of non-careerist reps from the national discussion databases, and due to the limited nature of their non-optional inclusion in the contact-recording or strategic selling databases. Not only did they view the use of these political enclaves as being futile, they also saw contributing their views and recording their activities on the non-optional contact recording and strategic selling political enclaves as being time-consuming. In addition, many employees were fearful that any non-consensus-forming contributions that they made to the national discussion databases might be misunderstood or seen as irrelevant. By not contributing, or only contributing in a limited way, they reinforced the political nature of these enclaves. As Table 5.1 indicates with reference to the perspective-taking process, many employees' non-optional inclusion in, and their optional exclusion from, the shared databases led to a homogenising of expressed perspectives that merely reflected the dominant positions in the organisation. Consequently, the dominance of these consensus-forming views did not assist others with different expertise to recognise and accept the different ways of knowing of others (Boland and Tenkasi, 1995).

As Table 5.2 summarises, the homogenising of expressed perspectives that arose from the careerist *optional inclusion* in, and non-careerist *optional exclusion* from, community-wide databases, not only restricted the perspective-taking process, but was also implicated in limiting the perspective-making process. The consensus-forming nature of the comments recorded and viewed on the community-wide databases restricted the extent to which each community could make unique representations of their understandings available on the shared databases. This resulted in employees based in the differing functions being unable to distinguish how their own community's views differed from those recorded by members of other functions. Consequently, communities

Table 5.1   **Political enclaves and perspective taking**

Concept	Issues stemming from the cases
Optional inclusion	• By senior managers in the contact recording and strategic selling databases in order to ensure that reps worked in the ways they advocated.
	• By career-oriented reps to prove that they were working hard and complying with their wishes.
Non-optional inclusion	• By non-ambitious reps, who only made the minimum use they felt they had to of the contact recording and strategic selling databases.
Optional exclusion	• By employees from the national discussion databases, which they saw as being optional.

Table 5.2   **Political enclaves and perspective making**

Concept	Issues stemming from the cases
Optional inclusion	• Career-oriented employees replicate the views of senior management
Optional exclusion	• Non-careerist employees either excluded themselves entirely, or only contributed minimally to national discussion databases. This reconfirmed the political nature of many of the databases.

were unable to establish their own identity by locating their views within the diversity of perspectives.

Safe enclaves and knowledge work

This subsection will discuss the implications for knowledge work stemming from the use of safe enclaves. Table 5.3 summarises how the use of safe enclaves presented opportunities for the perspective-taking process, albeit in a limited way.

As Table 5.3 indicates, although there were no community-wide databases that were deemed safe, some employees did *optionally include* themselves in those shared databases that were viewed by, and contributed to, exclusively by members of their own community. In these safe enclaves, those employees who had experience of working with members of other functions would discuss and provide advice to less experienced members of their own community on how they could best interact with members of other functions.

However, although the opportunities for perspective taking were few, some enclaves did present opportunities for the perspective-making process. Table 5.4 summarises the issues surrounding safe enclaves and perspective making. Though non-careerist reps did not normally include themselves in political enclaves, they did *optionally include* themselves in the regional databases that they perceived to be safe to express their underlying views. On community-specific safe enclaves, many non-ambitious reps would discuss the ways in which they had approached sales situations and other areas of interest that they shared. The safe enclaves allowed for some discussion and reflection to occur

Table 5.3   **Safe enclaves and perspective taking**

Concept	Issues stemming from the cases
Optional inclusion	• Debate in community-specific databases about how they go about their work with others.

Table 5.4   **Safe enclaves and perspective making**

Concept	Issues stemming from the cases
Optional inclusion	• Some discussion and reflection leading to the strengthening of perspectives within a community (e.g. regional databases).
Optional exclusion	• Ambitious reps excluded themselves from the perspective-making process, as they did not see them as beneficial to their career development.
	• Experts' feelings of safety on some enclaves was only temporary.

about how they went about their work, and for the strengthening of perspectives within communities.

However, as noted above, some ambitious reps *optionally excluded* themselves from the use of these community-specific safe enclaves, as they did not see their time spent using them as being beneficial to their career development. In addition, due to the resentment of non-ambitious reps for having to use the non-optional political enclaves, and the additional workload this presented, many did not use these safe enclaves extensively. With these employees not taking part, or their participation being marginal, the amount of debate that centred on how a community went about their work was limited, and this restricted the strengthening of perspectives within communities.

The divide between optional inclusion in and optional exclusion from safe enclaves also led to competing views about how members of the commercial function should go about their work. Ambitious reps still felt that they should reinforce senior management perspectives by making considerable use of the contact-recording, strategic selling and national discussion databases, while non-career-orientated reps felt that they should work qualitatively rather than quantitatively, and not necessarily follow senior management perspectives. This led to a competing perspective that members of the commercial function had of themselves. Developing more coherent meaning structures than the preceding ones is vital to the perspective-making process, yet due to the optional exclusion of a significant number of reps from the community-specific databases, it left the field force with a weakly developed perspective of themselves.

One further comment on safe enclaves and perspective making is that most feelings of safety on some enclaves were only temporary. For example, on the medical liaison managers' database, as discussed previously, open and frank discussion was prevalent until the director of the clinical and medical function asked if he could be included in the debate. Following this, the use of this database petered out, as MLMs were fearful of what they recorded. This again signified the importance of having safe enclaves in which employees are able to express their underlying views.

Implications and Conclusions

This final section will consider the implications and conclusions arising from this study. We will first consider the implications and conclusions relating to the theoretical conceptualisation of knowledge adopted in this study, before reflecting on the specific implications arising from the micro-level study of Compound UK.

First, due to the inadequacy of the existing theoretical conceptualisations of how the political use of information systems is implicated in knowledge working (Blackler *et al.*, 1997, 1998, 1999), this study drew on Goffman's (1959) work on front regions and back regions to develop the conceptual distinction between safe and political enclaves. These theoretical concepts acknowledge the importance of looking at the nature of the social performances that are carried out in different shared databases and other encounters. Central to Goffman's conceptual distinction is the operation of normative sanctions. This study provided further clarification through the distinction between optionality and non-optionality. This development demonstrates how pragmatic acceptance is sustained through the control of the front region setting. Though Boland and Tenkasi's (1995) and Blackler *et al.*'s (1997, 1998, 1999) accounts of perspective making and taking do indicate that cultural and political issues are worthy of consideration in this process, they have not indicated how the consequences arise or what they are for the perspective-making and taking processes. The theoretical constructs and distinctions developed in this chapter may be drawn upon to sensitise future empirical studies informed by the original innovative accounts. More generally, these distinctions may inform future studies that consider how the character of interaction within and between boundaries emerges.

In relation to the specific issues emerging from the micro-level empirical study of Compound UK, the character of interaction varied from enclave to enclave, some having a more political air than others. As is summarised in Table 5.5, safe enclaves were characterised as being shared social spaces which allow one's underlying views to be expressed, allowing for discussion and reflection on the different ways of working. In Compound UK, all safe enclaves were optional and community specific. However, many careerist reps optionally excluded themselves from the use of community-specific enclaves, as they saw their time as being better spent using the community-wide political enclaves for their own individualist agendas. This limited the extent and nature of participation, and resulted in the irony that safe enclaves which presented opportunities for the perspective-making and taking processes were used in a limited way,

Table 5.5   Safe enclaves/political enclaves

Safe enclaves	Political enclaves
• Express one's underlying views	• Portray a public facade
• Discussion and reflection on ways of working	• Politicising by senior and ambitious employees
• All-optional	• Exclude some employees
• All community-specific	• Optional and non-optional
	• Community-wide

while the political enclaves which restricted the knowledge work process were used extensively.

Political enclaves were distinguished as being shared social spaces which were characterised by participation resembling a 'public facade'. This study indicated how the career reward structure, the surveillance activities that senior managers undertook, and the minimal or non-use that non-ambitious employees made was deeply implicated in influencing the consensus-forming character of interaction within and between boundaries. However, knowledge work, from the conceptualisation adopted in this study, seeks to value and integrate the diversity of expertise across boundaries in organisations (Boland and Tenkasi, 1995), and the homogenisation of perspectives runs contrary to this. Furthermore, as a result of the normative discipline and regulation that arose from the threat of continuous observation which Lotus Notes provided, we suggest that groupware technologies may well be deeply implicated in the homogenisation of perspectives (Hayes and Walsham, 2000; Foucault, 1977; Knights and Murray, 1994). Being aware of how the dominance of senior management discourses may limit knowledge working is vital (Bloomfield and Coombs, 1992; Suchman, 1994; Willmott, 1993). The conceptual distinction between political and safe enclaves is presented as a way to sensitise future researchers and practitioners as to how the use of technology in organisations may be implicated in the character of interaction, and in turn in knowledge working.

A further implication to emerge from the micro-level study of Compound UK relates to the increasing workloads that may be associated with the use of groupware technologies. Much of the optional exclusion on community-specific databases by careerist reps arose because of the extensive use they made of community-wide databases. Conversely, the optional exclusion of non-careerist employees in some community-wide shared databases was not solely due to their frustration with the politicising, but also due to the degree of work that many undertook in completing the detailed fields that they saw as crucial to present and future sales opportunities, often for the benefit of others. This finding concurs with some early groupware research, which found that often groupware applications may 'fail' due to the additional work that is required to be undertaken by one group of employees for the benefit of others in order to 'keep the network working' (Bowers, 1991; Grudin, 1988, 1990). Being aware of how the extra workload may limit knowledge working when there is an emphasis on the use of groupware technologies is thus an important consideration to bear in mind.

To summarise, this study has indicated that rather than groupware technologies being viewed as democratic, their use should be viewed as being historically contingent and inherently political. Further critical empirical studies are advocated that consider the implications arising from how the use of groupware technologies are shaped by the interests of those that seek to contrive their own desired outcomes at the expense of others.

Acknowledgements

The authors gratefully acknowledge the critical insights provided by Frank Blackler, Brian Bloomfield, Peter Checkland and Norman Crump at Lancaster University, and Matthew Jones at the University of Cambridge, during the development of the ideas reported in this chapter. We also wish to thank those members of Compound UK who participated in this longitudinal study.

References

Alvesson, M. (1993) 'Organisation as Rhetoric: Knowledge-Intensive Firms and the Struggle with Ambiguity', *Journal of Management Studies*, 30: 6 (November), 997–1015.
Barley, S. (1996) 'Technicians in the Workplace: Ethnographic Evidence for Bringing Work into Organisation Studies', *Administrative Science Quarterly*, 41: 1 (March), 146–62.
Bell, D. (1973) *The Coming of Post-Industrial Society*, New York: Basic Books.
Bell, D. (1978) *The Cultural Contradictions of Capitalism*, London: Heinemann.
Blackler, F. (1993) 'Knowledge and the Theory of Organisations: Organisations as Activity Systems and the Reframing of Management', *Journal of Management Studies*, 30: 6, 863–84.
Blackler, F. (1995) 'Knowledge, Knowledge Work and Organisations, An Overview and Interpretation', *Organisation Studies*, 16: 6, 1021–46.
Blackler, F., Reed, M. and Whitaker, A. (1993) 'Editorial, Knowledge and the Theory of Organisations', *Journal of Management Studies*, 30: 6 (November), 851–61.
Blackler, F., Crump, N. and McDonald, S. (1997) 'Crossing Boundaries: Some Problems of Achieving Expansive Learning in a High Technology Organisation', *Working Paper For the EIASM Conference On 'Organising in a Multi-Voiced World'*, Leuven, Belgium, 4–6 June.
Blackler, F., Crump, N. and McDonald, S. (1998) 'Knowledge, Organisations and Competition', in G. Kroght, J. Roos and D. Kleine (eds.), *Knowing in Firms: Understanding, Managing and Measuring Knowledge*, London: Sage.

Blackler, F., Crump, N. and McDonald, S. (1999) 'Organisational Learning and Organisational Forgetting', in M. Easterby-Smith, J. Burgoyne and L. Araujo (eds.), *Organisational Learning and the Learning Organisation: Developments in Theory and Practice*, London: Sage.

Bloomfield, B.P. and Coombs, R. (1992) 'Information Technology, Control and Power: The Centralisation and Decentralisation Debate Revisited', *Journal of Management Studies*, 29: 4, 459–84.

Boland, R. and Tenkasi, R. V. (1995) 'Perspective Making and Perspective Taking in Communities of Knowing', *Organisation Science*, 6: 4, 350–72.

Boland, R., Tenkasi, R. V. and Te'eni, D. (1994) 'Designing Information Technology to Support Distributed Cognition', *Organisation Science*, 5: 3, 456–75.

Bowers, J. (1991) 'The Janus Faces of Design: Some Critical Questions for CSCW', in J. Bowers and S. Benford (eds.), *Computer Supported Co-operative Work: Theory, Practice and Design*, Amsterdam: North-Holland.

Brown, J. S. and Duguid, P. (1991) 'Organisational Learning and Communities of Practice: Towards a Unified View of Working, Learning and Innovation', *Organisation Science*, 2: 1, 40–57.

Chaiklin, S. and Lave, J. (1993) *Understanding Practice: Perspectives on Activity and Context*, Cambridge: Cambridge University Press.

Connah, B. and Pearson, R. (1991) *NHS Handbook*, 7th edn, London: Macmillan.

Flynn, R. and Williams, G. (1997) *Contracting for Health: Quasi-Markets and the National Health Services*, Oxford: Oxford University Press.

Foucault, M. (1977) *Discipline and Punish: The Birth of the Prison*, Harmondsworth: Peregrine.

Geertz, C. (1973) *The Interpretation of Cultures*, New York: Basic Books.

Goffman, E. (1959) *The Presentation of Self in Everyday Life*, Garden City: Doubleday Anchor.

Grudin, J. (1988) 'Why CSCW Applications Fail: Problems in the Design and Evaluation of Organisational Interfaces', *Proceedings of the Conference On Computer-Supported Co-operative Work*, Portland, Oregon, 26–28 September. New York: ACM Press.

Grudin, J. (1990) 'Groupware and Co-operative Work: Problems and Prospects', in B. Laurel (ed.), *the Art of Human–Computer Interface Design*, Cambridge, MA: Addison-Wesley.

Hayes, N. and Walsham, G. (2000) 'Competing Interpretations of Computer Supported Cooperative Work in Organisational Contexts' *Organization*, 7: 1, 49–67.

Knights, D. and Murray, F. (1994) *Managers Divided: Organisation Politics and Information Technology Management*, Chichester: John Wiley & Sons.

Knights, D., Murray, F. and Willmott, H. (1993) 'Networking as Knowledge Work: A Study of Strategic Inter-Organisational Development in the Financial Services Industry', *Journal of Management Studies*, 30: 6 (November), 975–95.

Lave, J. (1988) *Cognition in Practice: Mind, Mathematics and Culture in Everyday Life*, Cambridge: Cambridge University Press.

Lave, J. and Wenger, E. (1991) *Situated Learning: Legitimate Peripheral Participation*, Cambridge: Cambridge University Press.

Layder, D. (1993) *New Strategies in Social Research*, Cambridge: Polity Press.

Nonaka, I. and Takeuchi, H. (1994) *The Knowledge Creating Company: How Japanese Companies Create the Dynamics of Innovation*, Oxford: Oxford University Press.

Orr, J. E. (1990) 'Sharing Knowledge, Celebrating Identity: Community Memory in a Service Culture', in D. Middleton and D. Edwards (eds.), *Collective Remembering*, Newbury Park, CA: Sage, pp. 169–89.

Reich, R. (1991) *The Work of Nations: Preparing Ourselves For 21st-Century Capitalism*, London: Simon & Schuster.

Robinson, R. and Le Grand, B. (1994) *Evaluating the NHS Reforms*, London: King's Fund Institute, Policy Journals.

Ruhleder, K. (1995) 'Computerisation and Changes to Infrastructures for Knowledge Work', *The Information Society*, 11: 2, 131–44.

Skeggs, B. (1994) 'Situating the Production of Feminist Ethnography', in M. Maynard and J. Purvis (eds.), *Researching Women's Lives from a Feminist Perspective*, London: Taylor & Francis.

Star, S. L. and Ruhleder, K. (1994) 'Steps Towards an Ecology of Infrastructure', *Proceedings from CSCW'94*, Chapel Hill, NC. New York: ACM Press.

Steier, F. (1991) 'Introduction', in F. Steier (ed.), *Research and Reflexivity*, London: Sage.

Suchman, L. (1994) 'Working Relations of Technology Production and Use', *Computer Supported Co-operative Work (CSCW)*, 2: 1–2, 21–41.

Tsoukas, H. (1996) 'The Firm as a Distributed Knowledge System: A Constructionist Approach', *Strategic Management Journal*, 17 (Winter Special Issue), 11–25.

Willmott, H. (1993) 'Strength is Ignorance; Slavery is Freedom: Managing Culture in Modern Organisations', *Journal of Management Studies*, 30: 14, 515–52.

Willmott, H. (1995) 'The Odd Couple?: Re-Engineering Business Processes; Managing Human Relations', *New Technology, Work and Employment*, 10: 2, 89–98.

Zuboff, S. (1988) *In the Age of the Smart Machine*, New York: Basic Books.

Zuboff, S. (1996) 'The Emperor's New Information Economy', in W. Orlikowski, G. Walsham, M. R. Jones and J. I. Degross (eds.), *Information Technology and Changes in Organisational Work*, London: Chapman & Hall.

6 Intranets and Knowledge Management: De-centred Technologies and the Limits of Technological Discourse

Sue Newell, Harry Scarbrough, Jacky Swan and Donald Hislop

Introduction

An important current trend in the business environment is the tendency for applications of technology to be 'bundled' together with legitimating discourses aimed at senior management. For example, many applications of Information Technology (IT) in the early and mid-1990s were either stimulated or justified by a discourse of Business Process Re-engineering (BPR), which held that old functional structures needed to be swept away in favour of streamlined 'business processes'. Although BPR was subsequently subject to scathing criticism from academic and practitioner commentators alike, the trend continues in the wake of BPR with an exponential increase in managerial interest in 'knowledge management'. The discourse of 'knowledge management' is one in which the ability to manage 'knowledge assets' is seen as increasingly important for organisations (Offsey, 1997). In particular, knowledge sharing across departments, functions or geographical locations is discussed as a core organisational competence for many (if not all) organisations, not just knowledge-intensive firms (Newman, 1997).

The coupling of IT with these more or less nebulous concepts centring on organisational performance can be provisionally explained in a number of ways. The increasing pervasiveness and malleability of IT vastly extends the different ways in which technology can be applied to organisations – becoming increasingly implicated in organisational redesign and shifts in business strategy. These features mean that IT applications not only cut across existing managerial specialisms – creating ambiguity – but also increase levels of uncertainty about the relationship between the use of technology and the pursuit of organisational goals. The discourses first of BPR and then of knowledge management can thus be seen as attempts to assuage the uncertainty and ambiguity surrounding IT use (though at the same time increasing it to the benefit of consultants and others).

By bundling IT applications within an overarching discourse, this current trend raises new questions about technological innovation. The influence of management discourse on the adoption and design of technology is relatively neglected in the literature on IT and organisations. The latter is still centred on a dichotomy of technological determinism versus social choice, which is increasingly difficult to apply to the fluid interactivity of IT innovation processes (although it should be noted that recently several writers have moved beyond this simple dichotomy; for example, Dutton (1996) and Bloomfield *et al.* (1997)). This chapter seeks to explore this relationship between discourse and technological implementation through an empirical focus on the discourse of knowledge management and its technological realisation within one large multinational organisation.

Given our initial comments, it is not surprising to find that the growth in interest in the topic of knowledge management has been dominated by an IT perspective (Scarbrough *et al.*, 1999). From this perspective, the focus is on developing and implementing KM databases, tools (e.g. decision support tools) and techniques for the creation of 'knowledge bases', 'knowledge webs' and 'knowledge exchanges' (Bank, 1996). In particular, corporate intranets are depicted as a key part of the solution to the 'knowledge management problem'. The rapid diffusion of intranets, however, is beginning to pose important questions about the development and effects of this technology, including concerns about the process and effectiveness of intranet implementation (Gartner Group, 1997). Examining the innovation process surrounding the diffusion, design and implementation of intranet technology is therefore particularly timely.

Intranets can be defined in a number of ways, but most agree that there are three essential features of this technology (Bansler *et al.*, 1999). Firstly, an intranet is a network based on the Internet protocol suite TCP/IP and runs common Internet applications, such as the World Wide Web. This means that, unlike traditional client–server configurations and network technologies, which run proprietary software and use different protocols, intranets allow communication across different operating systems and equipment. Users can thus access corporate data through a Web browser. Intranets offer 'a seamless way to integrate text, graphics, sound and video' (Bansler *et al.*, 1999, p. 751). Secondly, unlike the Internet, an intranet is a private network, giving access on a selective basis. This restriction is achieved by creating firewalls (Oppliger, 1997) or by physically separating the intranet from external networks (a firebreak strategy). Intranets can be created centrally in an organisation (as a corporate intranet) with access to all or by organisational units who can create 'child intranets' (Bhattacherjee, 1998). Thirdly, unlike traditional intra-organisational information systems, intranets do not address any specific well-defined need (Damsgaard and Scheepers, 1999), but the main use of an intranet is for more general communication and collaboration among organisational members. Intranets can thus be used to publish (e.g. home pages, newsletters, documents, employee directories), to search (for a variety of information), to transact (with functionality on intranet pages and other organisational computer-based information systems), to interact (e.g. via discussion groups and other collaborative applications) and to record (e.g. best practices or frequently asked questions) (Damsgaard and Scheepers, 1998). Thus, an intranet uses Internet technology to build internal computer networks, offering the potential for information sharing and collaboration across departments, functions and different information systems within the organisation (Bernard, 1996). As will be shown in this chapter, these features of intranet technology are essential in understanding its diffusion, implementation and usage.

In this chapter we consider in particular the extent to which the adoption of intranet technology facilitates organisation-wide knowledge management defined as 'the broad processes of locating, transferring and more efficiently using information and expertise within an enterprise' (Offsey, 1997, p. 113). We address these questions by focusing upon the way in which intranets are diffused, designed and implemented within a specific organisational context. This analysis thus highlights the way that intranets interact with and change relations among organisational actors and contexts, and examines the emergent organisational effects of such interactions. As will be shown in the case study, these emergent effects were exactly the opposite of what was intended, creating electronic fences rather than the global electronic network that was envisioned. Thus, despite initial aims of knowledge sharing, our study found that intranet developments encouraged fission, not integration, and tended to reinforce powerful centrifugal forces operating on the strategic development of the firm. Such effects are explained in terms of the de-centred logic of intranet development and, in particular, its implementation within highly differentiated 'knowledge communities'. This suggests that there are limitations on the application of intranets to practices of knowledge management. The study thus suggests a cautious approach to intranet developments that aspire to knowledge integration. In certain highly decentralised contexts, they may have the ironic effect of further reinforcing geographical and functional barriers to knowledge exchange.

Theorising Intranets

User services facilitated by intranet technology are very wide-ranging, including communication, collaboration, navigation and access to information (Boettcher, 1998). It could be argued that the scope and character of these user services facilitated by intranet technology is distinctive. Where other IS innovations are relatively discrete in their impact, the distributed character of intranet technology has extensive implications for a wide range of user groups. Moreover, intranet design not only has effects on workflow and communication patterns but also on the wider array of knowledge management practices within organisations. The scope and character of intranet developments thus poses important questions for our understanding of the interplay between technology and organisation. In theorising these complex interactions, the recent emergence of the 'structurationist' approach provides a useful framework. This highlights the recursive and interactive relationship between user groups, technologies and the pre-existing organisational context (Orlikowski, 1992).

These interactions include both structural and processual elements. In processual terms, the development of intranet technology can be understood in terms of flows and combinations of different types of knowledge. To design and develop the hardware and the software for an intranet, technical IT knowledge and expertise will be required. Such technical knowledge can be described as a relatively codified form of knowledge, as demonstrated by the many do-it-yourself books which describe how to create Internet or intranet sites. On the other hand, to design and develop the content for an intranet, so that it fulfils its espoused communicative and collaborative objectives, depends on an understanding of the important knowledge flows within the organisation. This will be much more dependent on tacit knowledge, which is embedded in the shared understandings of particular user groups (Nonaka, 1994). Thus, the effective implementation of a Corporate intranet will require the blending of generic technical knowledge with the contextualised local knowledge of the user (Leonard-Barton, 1988). This knowledge is unlikely to be located in a single individual. Rather, the design and development of an intranet will rely on networks to provide the forum for integrating the knowledge and information needed for making the necessary technological and organisational changes. Some of this required knowledge may not exist internally, so that both internal and external networking is important to elicit the different types of knowledge (Kreiner and Schults, 1993). In understanding the design, development and implementation of intranets, it is therefore necessary to consider the ways in which the critical forms of knowledge have been combined through networking processes.

The process of technology design and use cannot be abstracted, however, from the structure of the organisation or the roles played by designer and user groups within that structure. In this perspective, the adoption of information technology is seen as closely intertwined with organisational issues (Fulk and DeSanctis, 1995). This acknowledges that the institutional properties of the organisation, such as pre-existing relationships and the distribution of resources may exert an important influence on the design and use of technology. As Orlikowski (1992, p. 405) notes: 'Technology embodies and hence is an instantiation of some of the rules and resources constituting the structure of an organisation'. Walsham (1993), using Giddens' (1984) original work, categorises such rules and resources under three headings: structures of signification, legitimation and domination. Structures of legitimation are to do with the espoused values prevailing within an organisation. They thus relate to what is seen as legitimate discourse and may be reflected in an organisational vision or mission statement. Structures of domination reflect the distribution of power within an organisation and so and will influence the concentration of resources needed for collective action. Finally, structures of signification are to do with the meanings circulating within the organisation and reflect the underlying norms within which behaviour is enacted. Thus, although the espoused value may be to encourage knowledge sharing within an organisation, this may be prohibited by an inability to mobilise the resources needed for this or because this espoused value conflicts with prevailing reward structures, which encourage knowledge hoarding rather than sharing. The existing structural context may therefore shape the use of technology and lead to rather different outcomes from those intended.

Ciborra and Patriotta (1996, p. 9) refer to such emergent outcomes as 'drifting', since they occur because of '...the matching between plasticity of the artefact and the multiform practices of the actors involved'. Users of intranet technology in particular seem to be able to exert a high degree of influence over its development and use. As such, intranet technology can be seen as relatively 'open-ended' and 'equivocal' (Weick, 1990), offering high levels of 'interpretative flexibility' (Bijker *et al.*, 1987). At the same time, precisely because of this flexibility, such open-ended systems also need to be more carefully adapted to their context. Thus, Orlikowski *et al.* (1995, p. 424) note: 'This open-endedness offers benefits of flexibility but also creates the possibility that – without adaptation of the technology to the context and vice versa – the technology will not reflect local conditions or communication norms and hence be under-utilised or inappropriately utilised'.

In understanding intranet innovation processes, a structurationist perspective thus directs us to focusing on the interactions between the technology, the users and the organisation. Given the high level of interpretative flexibility inherent in intranet technology, the prediction would be that these interactions could be very different in different situations. This suggests that it would be useful to consider a variety of intranet design and development projects so that these differences can be examined. In structural terms, it is necessary to assess the structures of legitimation, domination and signification and the associated key resources and in processual terms to assess the knowledge flows and networking relationships that are activated during the adoption process within a specific intranet project. It is the interaction between these different elements, in combination with the distinctive features of the technology itself, which will affect the ways in which the intranet is implemented and used in each particular situation.

The case example discussed below allows us to consider different intranet projects within the same organisation. By using multiple projects within a single organisation, we can control for sectoral and national institutional factors influencing the adoption process and focus on organisation and technology interactions. As will be seen, the process of innovation was very different across these projects, with clear variations in terms of the observed interactions. These different intranet projects achieved varying levels of success in terms of facilitating the knowledge sharing which was sought, although in no case was the technology fully appropriated (Clark and Staunton, 1989). The aim of this chapter then is to explore different intranet design and development projects in order to explore the different ways in which the technology, the users and the organisation interact and to consider the implications of these different interactions. It is argued that, in understanding the outcomes of these different intranet projects, it is useful to focus on the distinctive features of intranet technology, which created tensions between the interactions relevant for different aspects or layers of its development. A propositional model is developed which summarises the contradictions between these different layers of intranet development.

Ebank: a Meta-Case Study

Exploratory project probes were used within a single case company, which we call Ebank. These probes were conducted at three different times over a two and a half year period. Thus, while the research focuses on a single company, we were able to collect longitudinal data from a variety of relatively independent intranet implementation projects, which were occurring at about the same time within Ebank in different departments.

Background to Ebank

Ebank is one of the largest European banks and was created six years ago with the merging of two independent banks of the same nationality. It is located across 70 different countries worldwide. It has not grown organically but via acquisitions of existing banks across these countries. It consists of a number of different product divisions, including domestic, international and investment banking.

Two years ago a major global client left the bank because it did not feel that it was getting an integrated service across countries. Thus, despite Ebank calling itself 'the global bank', the reality was very different. It was rather loosely coupled, with each country and division operating relatively independently and having its own systems supporting unique structures and processes. This meant that clients were offered very different services across countries. The vision from the top (articulated as 'Vision 2000') was to create a truly global, networked bank. A paper was written by members of the corporate business strategy committee in 1996 recommending that Ebank develop a worldwide communications network (infrastructure) connecting all of its businesses and promoting knowledge sharing across the bank. 'Knowledge Management' was central to the vision discourse.

The discourse surrounding Vision 2000 was communicated widely within Ebank, as demonstrated by the fact that virtually all those interviewed discussed this as central to their own intranet project. In all the interviews the central theme of knowledge sharing was apparent, with individuals accepting Vision 2000 as a legitimate strategic intent. The immediate response to Vision 2000 was to set up an intranet pilot project. This project was centrally resourced and brought together individuals from different divisions across the bank. This pilot was a very technically focused project to test out the infrastructure.

The formal evaluation of the project occurred after about 18 months. One of the main conclusions from the pilot was that there was a need for greater overall coordination in the development of IT systems across the bank. Ironically, the actual impact of the pilot was the commencement of a multitude of independent intranet projects (a conservative estimate was that there were 150 independent intranet sites). Thus, during the pilot project many of those involved had recognised the benefits of intranet technology for their own department and so had started to develop their own independent systems, not even waiting for the formal evaluation of the pilot. Funding was not available centrally for these developments, so they were supported at the departmental level. This meant that a whole range of intranet projects sprang up almost spontaneously and with very little linkage across these projects. While the interviews made it clear that the different intranet projects were basically operating independently of each other, paradoxically they all nevertheless saw these independent projects as part of the common organisational initiative to encourage global knowledge sharing – Vision 2000. Nevertheless, the actual impact of developing these independent intranets was to reinforce existing functional and geographical boundaries with what could be described as 'electronic fences'.

The next section provides details of three of the independent intranet projects that we had information about. These have been selected specifically because they expose very different patterns of interactions between the technology, the users and the organisation. We are not trying to argue that they are in any sense typical, but simply that they illustrate different examples of intranet innovation design, development and use.

Examples of different patterns of intranet design, development and use

The intranet for the domestic division: Officeweb
Officeweb was being designed for the Domestic Division (DD) of Ebank – the national branch network. At the time, the level of IT in the branches was very low, with the vast majority of internal communication via fax and internal mail. The idea was that an intranet would support the more decentralised approach which was being sought within this division – making the branches more entrepreneurial and innovative so that they could respond to their own regional conditions and rely less on the corporate centre. However, despite considerable resources put in to the development of Officeweb, and its strategic importance for the domestic division, the project was eventually abandoned (after considerable development costs had already been spent) because test trials of Officeweb showed that it could not work on the existing branch infrastructure.

Relevant structural factors: Intranet technology appeared to offer scope for supporting the more decentralised, entrepreneurial, organisational structure which the DD was trying to move towards. The ability of an intranet to support this new structure thus provided the Officeweb project with considerable strategic significance.

Resources: Resources for the project were very limited. Experts from the IT department were involved at the outset, but then moved away, leaving just one full-time person working on the project. This person did not have any IT expertise and was not particularly powerful within the DD. Nevertheless, given that the project was seen as significant by the branch managers who would be the eventual users of Officeweb, they were more than willing to discuss how they saw the potential of an intranet. Through such discussion, the project leader was able to gain the managers' support and enthusiasm for the intranet as well as develop a clear understanding of their business needs.

Networks: During the early phase of this project there was wider networking which introduced some technical expertise. For the subsequent development of Officeweb, however, given the limited resources, there was no real opportunity to network widely. The only real networking that occurred was therefore between the project team leader and the community of DD managers who were going to be the end users of the system.

Knowledge: Networking with the end users was extremely important in gaining access to the localised user knowledge about what content should be on Officeweb to make it useful. Thus, when the managers saw the content that was proposed for Officeweb they were extremely keen and felt that it would be a very useful tool for knowledge sharing across the domestic division.

Use of the IS: So Officeweb was developed into what was considered to be a useful intranet package, with content that was needed at the branch level. However, the project leader then moved forward to an online trial in two branch offices. This was the first time the system had been used on the TCP/IP infrastructure which the IT function had been installing. The outcome was a disaster because the bandwidth of the infrastructure was too narrow for the traffic they were attempting to send via Officeweb – it took 20 seconds to change pages! The root of the problem lay in the fact that those involved in developing Officeweb had not anticipated the amount of bandwidth the system would require given the amount of information they wanted to send. At the time of the first visit to Ebank, these problems had only just been uncovered and the team leader was searching for solutions. However, by the time of the second research visit, the project had actually been abandoned. It had been decided that the problems uncovered by the Officeweb trial were insurmountable. So even though Officeweb had strategic significance and had encouraged a great deal of enthusiasm among the potential community of users, it was effectively abandoned.

The intranet for Global Transaction Services: GTSnet
GTSnet was the intranet that was developed for Global Transaction Services (GTS). GTS was a new division of Ebank set up to provide an integrated service for global customers. GTSnet had been developed and implemented in 17 countries. It contained information on countries, on trade and cash management, and on people in the network, and general Ebank and GTS-specific information. None of the information was new. People could simply now obtain their information from one integrated source and have the possibility to feedback and set up discussion groups. However, there had been complaints that the content was not always up-to-date and there were clearly problems of both the supply and demand of information on GTSnet.

Relevant structural factors: The GTSnet project was certainly seen as legitimate in terms of the globalizing strategy of the bank. Setting up the GTS division and providing an IT tool for the communication of data across the globe so that information on a particular global customer was accessible in the same format in any country was an accepted part of the Vision 2000 discourse. GTSnet would provide that communication tool.

Resources: The business case for setting up GTS as a separate division was done by external consultants and as soon as the business case was approved they moved forward to developing the intranet to support this dispersed division. Financial resources for the GTSnet project were abundant, and these resources were used to bring in external consultants. Thus the GTSnet project was staffed almost exclusively by external IT consultants. There were 140 consultants from the selected external company working on the GTSnet project, together with only a handful of Ebank employees. As an indication of the size of the project, it is worth noting that the GTSnet project was bigger than the yearly turnover of this consultancy.

Networks: Unsurprisingly given the composition of the GTSnet project team, there were communication problems – 'whatever obvious problems you can think of with such an arrangement – we had them' (Ebank GTSnet project member). The intranet project itself was divided into a number of sub-projects, and the coordination between these different sub-projects was very poor. Moreover, given that there were so few internal people involved in the project, there was very little networking with those who would be the end users of GTSnet.

Knowledge: While the external consultants had the technical expertise to develop the IT needed for the GTSnet intranet, they did not have the relevant business knowledge. This was recognised by the project leader of GTSnet, but his problem was that there were few 'spare' Ebank employees as so many of them were involved in other big projects like the introduction of the euro for 1999 and Year 2000 projects.

Use of the IS: In the original business case for the creation of GTS, there was recognition of the importance of knowledge management to make the new division a success. The consultants involved had pushed the idea that knowledge management was not about building an IT system but about changing the culture so that people were willing to work together and share knowledge. It was acknowledged that this conflicted with current practices which rewarded individuals for their personal knowledge, not their sharing. However, the initial thrust had been to develop the intranet system itself – GTSnet. As with most of the other intranets considered, the information being put on to GTSnet was not new, just collected together electronically for the intranet. People could thus obtain their information from one integrated source and have the possibility to feedback and set up discussions etc. GTSnet was operational and had been rolled out to 17 countries. However, there were problems. For example, there had been complaints from users that the information on the intranet was not up-to-date. This was because there had been no control over what was put on the system. There were also more general problems of both the supply and demand of the information on GTSnet. Specifically, very few, if any, individuals were actually making use of GTSnet to share their knowledge or access the knowledge of others.

The intranet for IT: Iweb
Iweb was an intranet specifically designed for the IT function. It was one of the first intranets to be developed within Ebank and the initial justification for developing it was related to gaining expertise in intranet technology. Iweb was being used to store information centrally that was previously available in other forms, often as written documents. When asked to give an example of the kind of knowledge which users were finding useful on Iweb, the best example that could be found was of the corporate bus timetable. This gives information on when the company bus will be at the three different city sites of the bank! The bus travels between the different sites, and so is at any one site about once every 20 minutes. There was no evidence that the intranet had promoted any sharing of personal knowledge or expertise even within the IT division, never mind more broadly across Ebank. It was limited to a digital repository of existing information, which was used by some, but not all, of the staff within the IT division.

Relevant structural factors: Much of the rationale for designing and implementing Iweb had to do with the importance of developing intranet expertise within the IT function. Given the general acceptance of Vision 2000 discourse, the development of intranet expertise was clearly seen to be legitimate.

Resources: Members of the IT function had a heavy presence on the initial pilot project and, recognising the potential of intranet technology, quickly started their own departmental project to develop Iweb. Even though resources for

Iweb came from within the department, the project was well-resourced. The technical skills were abundant and, since the intranet was being developed within the IT department, they were able to purchase state-of-the-art servers to provide the system platform. The project was sponsored by a very senior manager within the IT function, which meant that the project team had significant power to enrol support from across the department.

Networks: As originally the project team did not have its own internal intranet expertise, two external consultants were brought in to work full-time with the internal project team members. The project team did not undertake an extensive search of potential sources of expertise both because they believed their existing networks already enabled them to identify the most appropriate external source and because it was initially only an experimental project. In the event this proved problematic, as within three months the external experts had been dismissed because they were unable to supply the organisational (as opposed to the technical) expertise which was needed (see below).

Knowledge: These external experts worked with a small ($n = 6$) group of internal individuals from the IT department. Given the background of the internal project team members, however, the intranet technical expertise was soon appropriated internally. Moreover, beyond the immediate Iweb project team, many individuals within the IT function began to 'play' with HTML during their spare time. These 'hobbyists' were frequently referred to during interviews and were an important spur to Iweb development.

Use of IT: At the time of the interviews, the Iweb infrastructure was fully operational and they had also developed fairly well-established rules governing what was put on the intranet and how to keep it updated. However, there were problems in the actual use of the intranet across the group of potential users within IT. Many individuals continued to use alternative sources when they wanted particular information. This was recognised as a problem, and indeed had been part of the reason for working with the external consultants at the outset. The selected consultancy was believed to be one of the few national firms that had successfully developed its own intranet. However, it had been able to force people to use its intranet by first requiring all employees to purchase their own PC and modem (at a reduced cost) and then simply using only the intranet to communicate and exchange information. This had worked for the consultancy company, but it was not considered to be an appropriate solution for the bank, which included a much broader range of individuals, even within the IT group. Iweb was not therefore being used to share knowledge and experience across individuals and groups even within the narrow functional IT group. There was certainly no sharing beyond this boundary.

Meta-case conclusions

The three examples of intranet development were very different and demonstrate the importance of the interactions between technology and organisation. GTSnet was able to call upon a huge pool of resources, while Officeweb struggled for even limited internal resources in the form of person-hours to be made available. Iweb fell in-between these two extremes. In terms of networks and knowledge, GTSnet made extensive use of a variety of external contacts, but failed to involve internal actors in these networks so that the knowledge was never transferred or appropriated. Officeweb had good internal business links but failed to develop strong networks to link in with the technical expertise that it lacked. Finally, Iweb did involve external networks and managed to acquire technical knowledge so that it could support the intranet technical development internally, but the project team did not manage to similarly appropriate the organisational knowledge required to support a culture of knowledge sharing.

In none of the three examples had the intranet been fully appropriated by its users. Officeweb had been thwarted by basic technical problems, which stemmed from a lack of technical expertise on the project team. GTSnet had been successful in developing the system itself. However, the development of GTSnet had relied almost exclusively on external expertise for both content and structure and there had been no real attempt to acquire this expertise internally. This created problems, as there was no recognition internally about the importance of keeping the system up-to-date and therefore informationally useful. Iweb had also used external expertise but had at least managed to acquire the technical expertise internally and had managed to impose a set of rules and procedures for creating and utilising the content on the system. However, Iweb had not done anything to produce the attitude change needed for encouraging the creation and sharing of knowledge using the intranet, despite the fact that the importance of this was acknowledged. They had attempted to 'buy in' this expertise, but had failed, as the Ebank culture was so different from that of the company whose expertise they were trying to appropriate.

While there were severe limitations to the effective utilisation of all three intranets considered, what is even more apparent is the lack of any synergy and knowledge sharing across the various intranet projects. Far from creating a global network integrating functions and groups across Ebank, the development of these independent intranets could be said to be increasing the barriers, with electronic fences reinforcing the already existing functional and national barriers. The introduction of intranets had effectively created knowledge silos. There had been little transfer of learning across the group as a whole – the design process had been negotiated at the local level, bridging, at least in some cases, the external and local internal expertise, often quite successfully. However, the main problem was the wider communication of this expertise across the different business groups, primarily because the different business groups operated so autonomously. This severely limited the broader enactment of the Ebank vision to create a global knowledge-sharing network.

Discussion

The conclusions from the meta-case suggest that the development of intranets needs to be viewed not as a tool of integration or even of management control, but as the expression of the fissile and Balkanising tendencies within the fragmented knowledge base and power structures of the organisation. This effect can be understood in terms of the distinctive 'de-centred' nature of the technology. This relates to the way in which its design, development and use represents a context in which multiple layers of interaction between technological and organisational factors will be relevant. This poses important questions for our understanding of the interplay between knowledge, technology and organisation. Where mainframe computers encouraged centralised forms of control and standardised meanings in user interactions, and distributed computing promoted more decentralised control but retained some standardisation of meaning, intranet technology, and other forms of groupware, involve multiple constituents and meanings. One way of understanding the distinctiveness of intranets is to consider three different layers of functionality and practice incorporated within such technology (Bressand and Distler, 1995):

- Infrastructure: the hardware/software which enables the physical/communicational contact between network members.

- Infostructure: the formal rules which govern the exchange between the actors on the network, providing a set of cognitive resources (metaphors, common language) whereby people make sense of events on the network.

- Infoculture: the stock of background knowledge which actors take for granted and which is embedded in the social relations surrounding workgroup processes. This cultural knowledge defines constraints on knowledge and information sharing.

Although other studies identify various levels in the design, development and use of information technology, they are usually specified in terms of the different functional or managerial requirements associated with each level (e.g. Earl, 1996). The value of considering these three distinctive layers of intranet development is that it exposes the divergent and potentially contradictory relationships between these different spheres of activity. This is not to say that these layers are not conflated in practice; rather, different technology, user, organisation interactions are implied by each level. For example, at the infrastructure layer, the relevant actors, resources, relationships and forms of knowledge associated with intranet development are likely to vary significantly from the most important contextual factors and active groups implicated in the formation of 'infoculture'. One would anticipate a greater emphasis on financial resources, on legitimising structures, and on technical as opposed to user knowledge. Although these issues do not cease to operate for the development of intranet 'infoculture', it seems likely that the crucial enablers and constraints will differ markedly. Discursive resources, structures of signification and localised user knowledge seem likely candidates for the critical success factors in this setting. That is, each layer of activity requires a different configuration of network relationships, resources and knowledge deployment. In other words, to say that information technology and organisation are homologous is also to say that these different layers may be as loosely coupled as the different sub-systems of the organisation (Weick, 1979). Table 6.1 develops a propositional model of these configurations of strategic factors at each layer of intranet development.

Although this is a highly schematic analysis, it does offer a template to apply to the analysis of the various projects presented above. Firstly, in terms of Officeweb, the focus was on interactions at the infoculture layer. The desire was to increase the autonomy of the local branches so that they could respond to their own regional conditions and rely less on the corporate centre. The development of an intranet was seen as structurally significant to support such devolution. The project team concentrated on bringing together the relevant branch managers to create a community of users where local knowledge could be shared in order to start to produce the cultural changes necessary for this new more entrepreneurial structure. However, despite considerable effort put in to the development of Officeweb, and its strategic importance for the domestic division, the project was effectively abandoned because test trials of Officeweb showed that it could not work on the existing branch infrastructure. That is, Officeweb had failed to enrol the strategic organisational factors necessary for the development of the infrastructure layer of an intranet.

At the other extreme, GTSnet had operated extremely successfully at the infrastructure layer, integrating the necessary structures and processes to develop the basic intranet system for the Global Transactions Services division. However, it had failed either to enrol the necessary political support internally to bring together the technical and business expertise (infostructure) or to get users to see the intranet system as strategically significant to the success of the division (infoculture).

The development of Iweb was perhaps the most successful of the three projects in that it had managed to achieve two of the three layers of intranet development. The Iweb project was seen as legitimate, and the relevant IS expertise had been acquired, originally by bringing this expertise in from outside through using consultants, but then appropriating this knowledge internally. The Iweb team had also managed to demand that all users of Iweb used the same editorial standards so that Iweb intranet sites were compiled using some basic, shared configurational rules. This had not been achieved on any of the other intranet projects considered during the research. This was possible because the Iweb project was supported by a senior manager of the IT function who was able to insist that users followed the rules developed by the Iweb steering committee. However, the Iweb project team had not managed to change people's basic attitudes to knowledge sharing and encourage users to

Table 6.1 Intranet development – key factors

Layers of development	Relevant structural factors	Key resources	Dominant networks	Critical forms of knowledge	Use of information system
Infrastructure	Legitimation	Financial, technological	Technology suppliers and consultants	IS expertise	Communication of data
Infostructure	Domination	Political	Consultants, cross-functional networks	Technical and business knowledge	Exchange of information
Infoculture	Signification	Cultural and discursive	Communities of practice	Localised user knowledge	Sharing of knowledge

see the intranet as strategically significant to their business. Applying the propositional model to the three independent intranet developments, the differences
are clear, as illustrated in Table 6.2.

The propositional model serves to illustrate the distinctive features of intranet
technology. So various are the actors and meaning systems associated with
these different layers, it could almost be argued that intranets are not so much a
technology but rather an ensemble of sometimes divergent or contradictory
practices. It is in this sense that we say that intranets are a de-centred technology
(Derrida, 1981); that is, loosely coupled systems with no core or essential characteristics or significance but rather multiple and distributed meanings and actors
(Grint and Woolgar, 1996).

Of course, these distinctive characteristics of intranet technology interacted
with the particular organisational context within Ebank. Thus, the organisational context influenced intranet developments in a number of ways. At one
level, decentralisation as both a structural attribute and a discourse prompted
different groups to use intranet technology to promote their own autonomy.
This meant that these differing intranet initiatives tended to promote centrifugal tendencies within Ebank as each group privileged their own radically
differing needs and world-views. While understanding the tensions between
the technology and the existing organisational context, is certainly one way of
considering the contradictions that were evident in Ebank, the observed centrifugal effect was not attributable to the institutional context alone. There appear
to be inherent contradictions across the three technology layers, which limit an
IT-driven approach to knowledge management, since these contradictions
problematise the conventional distinction between infrastructure and application. Thus, the de-centred nature of intranet technology itself seems to have
militated against whatever integrative functions it might serve. Given the
requirements of the infrastructural, infostructural and infocultural elements of
the intranet, our project groups found it difficult to achieve the requisite
blending of knowledge and resources capable of linking and assimilating
different layers of design and use. Infrastructural development, for example,
implied standardisation and some reliance on the centralised expertise of the IT
function, but a truly meaningful infoculture seemed more likely to grow out of
the localised sensibilities of different user groups. Further, structuring and
formalising the use of intranets (developing the infostructure) creates rigidities,
which contradict the ability of the tools to improve collaborative work and
knowledge sharing (the infoculture).

It may be that the de-coupling of these multiple intranet fuctionalities therefore reflects a more fundamental problem to do with the distributed and highly
tacit nature of useful organisational knowledge (Tsoukas, 1996). The qualities of
useful knowledge may themselves subvert attempts to achieve a standardised
approach (as demanded by the infrastructure and infostructure layers of
intranet development) to the sharing of knowledge (infoculture development).
Arguably, information systems aimed at knowledge management need to

Table 6.2　Implementation and usage of the three intranets developed within Ebank

Case study	Relevant structural factors	Key resources	Dominant networks	Critical forms of knowledge	Use of information systems
Officeweb	Signification	Limited – time with users	Some internal networking, but very limited external networking	Some business and organisational knowledge acquired but lacking technical expertise	Infrastructure problems limited any use
GTSnet	Legitimation	Huge – external technical involvement	Much external networking, but limited interaction with internal networks	Knowledge not internally appropriated	Infrastructure developed but infostructure problems limited use
Iweb	Legitimation and domination	Moderate – internal functional involvement	Some external networking interacting with internal networks	Technical knowledge acquired but lacking organisational knowledge	Infrastructure and infostructure developed but infoculture limited use

maintain the integrity of the social communities in which such knowledge is embedded. As Boland and Tenkasi (1995, p. 359) put it: 'Communication systems must... support diversity of knowledge through the differentiation provided by perspective taking within communities of knowing'.

Following this argument, the notion of a centralised IT-driven approach to knowledge management as an integrating mechanism needs to be critically scrutinised. If it is not to be homogenising or de-skilling, knowledge management must incorporate the diversity of perspectives developed by different groups: 'The problem of integration of knowledge... is not a problem of simply combining, sharing or making data commonly available. It is a problem of perspective taking in which the unique thought worlds of different communities of knowing are made visible and accessible to others' (Boland and Tenkasi, 1995, p. 39). Whether it is possible to make visible these different communities of knowing within a large globally decentralised organisation remains an empirical question, but it is certainly not unproblematic, as demonstrated by the Ebank case. Against a backdrop of a de-centralised organisation, grown through acquisition, with a highly distributed knowledge-base, the discourse of intranets as technological solutions to knowledge management only strengthened the centrifugal tendencies within the bank. This demonstrates that intranets as knowledge management tools may have profoundly equivocal effects, constituting neither an electronic panopticon nor the liberating cyberspace commonly depicted. Intranets may actually advance the sedimentation of existing localised and distributed knowledge communities.

References

Bank, D. (1996) 'Technology (A Special Report): The New Worker – Know-it-Alls – Chief Knowledge Officers Have a Crucial Job: Putting the Collective Knowledge of a Company at Every Worker's Fingertips', *Wall Street Journal*, Eastern Edition, 18 November, p. R28.

Bansler, J., Havn, E., Thommesen, J., Damsgaard, J. and Scheepers, R. (1999). 'Corporate Intranet Implementation: Managing Emergent Technologies and Organisational Practices', paper presented at the *7th European Conference on Information Systems*, Copenhagen.

Bhattacherjee, A. (1998). 'Management of Emerging Technologies: Experiences and Lessons Learned at US West', *Information and Management*, 33, 263–72.

Bernard, R. (1996). *The Corporate Intranet*, Chichester: John Wiley.

Bijker, W. E., Hughes, T. and Pinch, T. J. (eds) (1987) *The Social Construction of Technological Systems*, London: MIT Press.

Bloomfield, B. and Coombs, R. (1992) 'Information Technology, Control and Power: The Centralisation and Decentralisation Debate Revisited', *Journal of Management Studies*, 29: 4, 459–84.

Bloomfield, B., Coombs, R., Knights, D. and Littler, D. (1997) *Information Technology and Organisations: Strategies, Networks and Integration*, Oxford: Oxford University Press.

Boettcher, S. (1998) *The Netscape Intranet Solution: Deploying the Full-Service Intranet*, New York: John Wiley.

Boland, R. J. and Tenkasi, R. V. (1995) 'Perspective Making and Perspective Taking in Communities of Knowing', *Organisation Science*, 6: 4, 350–63.

Bressand, A. and Distler, C. (1995) *La Planete Relationelle*, Paris: Flammarion.

Ciborra, C. and Patriotta, G. (1996) 'Groupware and Teamwork in New Product Development: the Case of a Consumer Goods Multinational', in C. Ciborra (ed.), *Groupware and Teamwork*, New York: John Wiley.

Clark, P. and Staunton, N. (1989) *Innovation in Technology and Organisation*, London: Routledge.

Damsgaard, J. and Scheepers, R. (1998) 'Intranet Implementation in Large Organisations', in N. J. Buch *et al.* (eds.), *Proceedings of the 21st Information Systems Research Seminar in Scandinavia*, Aalborg, Denmark.

Damsgaard, J. and Scheepers, R. (1999) A 'Stage Model of Intranet Technology: Implementation and Management', paper presented at the *7th European Conference on Information Systems*, Copenhagen.

Derrida, J. (1981) *Positions*, Chicago: University of Chicago Press.

Dutton, W. H. (ed.) (1996) *Information and Communication Technologies: Visions and Realities*, Oxford: Oxford University Press.

Earl, M. J. (ed.) (1996) *Information Management: The Organizational Dimension*, Oxford: Oxford University Press.

Fulk, J. and DeSanctis, G. (1995) 'Electronic communication and changing organisational forms', *Organisation Science*, 6: 4, 337–49.

Gartner Group (1997). 'Meeting the Intranet Challenge: Technologies, Organizations, Processes', *Inside Gartner Group This Week*, XIII: 49, 1–4.

Giddens, A. (1984) *The Constitution of Society*, Cambridge: Polity Press.

Grint, K. and Woolgar, S. (1997) *The Machine at Work: Technology, Work and Organization*, Oxford: Polity Press.

Knights, D. and Murray, F. (1994) *Managers Divided: Organisational Politics and Information Technology Management*, Chichester: John Wiley.

Kreiner, K. and Schults, M. (1993) 'Informal Collaboration in R&D. The Formation of Networks Across Organisations', *Organisation Studies*, 14: 2, 189–209.

Leonard-Barton, D. (1988) 'Implementation As Mutual Adaption of Technology and Organisation', *Research Policy*, 17, 251–67.

Newman, V. (1997). 'Redefining knowledge management to deliver competitive advantage', *Journal of Knowledge Management*, 1: 2, 123–8.

Nonaka, I. (1994) 'A Dynamic Theory of Organisational Knowledge Creation', *Organisation Sciences*, 5, 14–37.

Offsey, S. (1997) 'Knowledge Management: Linking People to Knowledge for Bottom Line Results', *Journal of Knowledge Management*, 1: 2, 113–22.

Oppliger, R. (1997) 'Internet Security: Firewalls and Beyond', *Communications of the ACM*, 40: 5, 92–102.

Orlikowski, W. J. (1992) 'The Duality of Technology: Rethinking the Concept of Technology in Organisations', *Organisation Science*, 3: 3, 398–427.

Orlikowski, W. J., Yates, J., Okamura, K. and Fujimoto, M. (1995) 'Shaping Electronic Communication: the Metastructuring of Technology in the Context of Use', *Organisation Science*, 6: 4, 423–44.

Scarbrough, H., Swan, J. and Preston, J. (1999) *Knowledge Management: a Review of the Literature*, London: Institute of Personnel and Development.

Tsoukas, H. (1996) 'The Firm as a Distributed Knowledge System: a Constructionist Approach', *Strategic Management Journal*, 17 (Special Issue), 11–25.

Walsham, G. (1993) *Interpreting Information Systems in Organisations*, Chichester: John Wiley.

Weick, K. E. (1979) *The Social Psychology of Organizing*, Reading, MA: Addison-Wesley.

Weick, K. E. (1990) 'Technology as Equivoque: Sensemaking in New Technologies', in P. S. Goodman, L. S. Sproull and Associates, *Technology and Organisations*, Oxford: Jossey-Bass.

7   The Bearable Lightness Of Control: Organisational Reflexivity and the Politics of Knowledge Management

Alan McKinlay

Introduction

Foucault's conception of power/knowledge insists that neither category can be considered independently. More than this, his historical studies of the clinic, the asylum and, most famously, the penitentiary imply not just that 'power' and 'knowledge' are mutually constitutive but that they necessarily develop with a devilish synchronicity. In this chapter we suggest that Foucault's gloomy prognosis that 'knowledge' always empowers the already powerful is neither necessary nor inevitable. Indeed, an acceptance of the gap between 'power' and 'knowledge' – a gap occupied by tacit knowledge and unregulated social processes – may be a precondition for managements attempting to enhance the reflexivity of the labour process. Reflexivity, the ability of individuals and workgroups to critically assess and alter work organisation, has emerged as a crucial objective of contemporary management. The 57 varieties of employee involvement, empowerment and teamworking are all geared to enhancing the scope and depth of reflexivity in work organisation. Empowerment programmes were about engaging employees' tacit knowledge exclusively in the service of corporate agendas of quality, efficiency and competitiveness. Critical assessments have stressed both the hegemonic victory of empowerment and the resilience of worker resistance. The labour process tradition has spoken eloquently of the victory – more or less complete – of managerial power, but has remained silent about managerial knowledge.

Pharma is an American-owned, increasingly global drug company. Accelerating the drug development programme both by compressing distinct functional phases of the process and by globalising key aspects of clinical testing is a key corporate goal. Achieving faster 'molecule to market' both reaps huge financial gains through longer patent protection and enlarges Pharma's portfolio of commercially attractive drugs. Pharma's drug development cycle is approximately fourteen years. A central corporate objective is to reduce cycle time to eight years inside the next two years. While automated screening has radically

107

altered the nature and pace of the drug discovery process, the development phase remains heavily reliant on the management of long-term clinical trials and the documentation required by the regulators (Chiesa and Manzini, 1997; Pisano, 1998). Refining management control systems through the development phase is critical to overall corporate success. Corporate management has concluded that there are no structural or technological mechanisms left to be utilised. The language is significant – it betrays its Taylorist roots. Tacit knowledge has not just to be employed, mobilised, or harnessed but *captured*.

There are two main alternatives vying for supremacy inside Pharma's knowledge management initiatives. There is, on the one hand, real support among corporate executives for the development of a technological vehicle for knowledge management, a comprehensive database of the experiences of key decision-makers. By using hypertext, the relevant piece of 'knowledge' would be accessed by other Pharma technicians at a similar decision point in a parallel project. Conversely, senior operational managers are sceptical about the cost and value of such a venture. Whatever the practical difficulties in constructing such a comprehensive experiential database, however, the key objection to such a technological approach is not that it would fail but that it would succeed. The codification required by a comprehensive database would necessarily limit the range of permitted responses. Codification would compromise the tacit knowledge it was designed to capture (Button *et al.*, 1995, pp. 185–6).

The alternative approach to knowledge management that has significant support among operational management is much more modest. Effective knowledge management, they contend, is based on identifying the fora, organisational positions, and chronological moments at which individual and organisational learning is greatest in scope, depth and intensity. Project managers, for example, occupy an ambiguous position between functions and the managers of specific development phases. Project managers are conduits for the transmission of tacit knowledge between functions and programmes and over time. Mentoring, extensive debriefing and reaching back into earlier phases of the drug development programme are key knowledge management initiatives. Equally important is an acceptance that unregulated social spaces – such as 'knowledge fairs' – have to be increased with minimal intervention or attempt to standardise their format. While operational managers endorse this modest approach on practical grounds, among the management group responsible for evaluating these alternatives there is an appreciation that knowledge management must map, monitor and enable the transfer of tacit knowledge. Any attempt to standardise or control the process would inevitably fail or fatally compromise the very possibility of organisational reflexivity.

This brings us back to the question of power/knowledge. The dominant strand of Foucauldian studies of new work regimes stresses their hegemony: resistance is futile, serves to extend managerial control, or allows individuals only ironic distance from corporate discourses as a routine refuge. Pharma is debating how to increase both the reflexivity of the labour process and knowledge transfer. There is a contradiction between corporate pressure for uniformity and control and local management's determination not to damage the existing informal patterns of knowledge transfer. In other words, this is a debate within management about the scale and importance of the gap between 'power' and 'knowledge'. This gap is, for local management, the critical space in which reflexivity becomes possible and, for corporate management, a challenge for organisational control. This debate pivots on questions of power, knowledge and identity. Drawing on workforce surveys, interviews, and non-participant observation, this chapter allows us to eavesdrop on the voices of the powerful and of the objects of their knowledge. But, extending the reach of Foucault's own research, which neglected the furtive whispering of the prisoner and the penitent, we also listen to the voices of the technicians aware that their capacity for reflexivity is both essential to their identity and threatened by the knowledge management programme.

Working With Foucault?

> Our society is not one of spectacle, but of surveillance;... it is not that the beautiful totality of the individual is amputated, repressed, altered by our social order, it is rather that the individual is carefully fabricated in it, according to a whole technique of forces and bodies. We are... in the panoptic machine, invested by its effects of power, which we bring to ourselves since we are part of its mechanism (Foucault, 1977, p. 217).

That the convergence of computer and telecommunications technologies offers new possibilities for surveillance is beyond question. But so too does this technology open up the prospect of enhanced coordination and participation in civil society. The emerging debate over the impact of these technologies is polarised between panglossian optimists and the gloomy fatalists who masquerade as 'radical' theorists of the information age. Cities, Boyer (1996, p. 163) concludes, are so densely wired that control 'acts like a sieve... a (computerised matrix) whose mesh transmutes from point to point, undulating and constantly at work. The code, not the norm, becomes the important device. Discourses and architectures seem to be dislocated from space, deeply hidden within the electronic matrices of a global computer network that connects all points in space and directs our lives from some ethereal "other" location'. It is not simply the growth in panoptic possibilities inherent in the convergence of information and communications technology but the *centralisation* of personal data (Robins and Webster, 1988; Gandy, 1993). More than this, extensive and intimate surveillance is compiled, codified and compared to permit ever more subtle classifications of human behaviour. Listen to Robins and Webster's (1988, p. 47) influential argument that 'on the basis of the "information revolution", not just the prison or factory, but the social totality, comes to function as the hierarchical and disciplinary Panoptic machine'. Just so: digital mystification occupies the same space in social theory that was once colonised by one-dimensional man. Foucault's use of the panopticon as the defining image of modernity is completely transcended as surveillance becomes truly systemic, freed from the troublesome confinement of time and space: control is everywhere and nowhere.

No doubt Foucault's disclaimers about the over-definition of panopticism pale beside the centrality of surveillance in his histories of the prison, asylum and clinic. After restating the importance of Bentham's innovative panopticon design he adds, 'but the procedures of power that are at work in modern societies are much more numerous, diverse and rich. It would be wrong to say that the principle of visibility governs all technologies of power used since the nineteenth century' (Foucault, 1980, p. 148). Inescapably, however, Foucault was systematically dazzled by the dangers of panopticism and blind to its limits and opponents (Jay, 1994, pp. 415–16). But, whatever his failings, Foucault directed our attention to material practices and never to mysterious 'others', 'ethereal' or otherwise. The final irony here is that Bentham – unlike Foucault – offers the panopticon as a physical and social architecture that is not solely punitive. Just as the benign cruelty of the prison regime is as redemptive as it is vindictive, so Bentham envisaged panopticon designs increasing industrial efficiency, underwriting the scruples of public officials and as a force for extending democratisation. Equally, in a particularly chilling passage, Bentham observes that the impersonal discipline of the panopticon would occasionally have to be supplemented by the personal intervention of the gaoler – or, to use Foucault's term, that 'monarchic' power be exercised to underscore the illusion of constant surveillance. 'I will single out the most untoward of the prisoners', wrote Bentham, 'and keep an uninterrupted watch on him'.

> I will watch until I observed a transgression. I will note it down. I will watch for another: I will note that down too. I will lie by for a whole day: he shall do as he pleases that day.... The next day I will produce the list to him. You thought yourself undiscovered: you abused my indulgence: see how you were mistaken. Another time, you may have rope for two days, ten days: the longer it is the heavier it will fall upon you. Learn from this, all of you, that in this house transgression can never be safe (Bowring, 1838–43, iv, 81–2).

The danger of such writing is that it is all too easy to construct a convincing pastiche but impossible to refute on its own paranoid terrain. Indeed, so elusive is theorising in the area of the new simulation/surveillance technologies that some influential writers eschew the conventions of academic debate altogether. Only by escaping from the confines of logic and evidence – apparently – can one capture the range and depth of surveillance technologies. Except, of course, for an impressive array of references to French post-modernism. Take Bogard's (1996) *The Simulation of Surveillance*, for example. Bogard offers a 'provocation' rather than an analysis, a 'social science fiction' that takes dystopia to an entirely novel pitch. If Weber's 'iron cage' offers a conservative regret at the disenchantment of modernity, then Foucault provides an austere vision in which resistance is pushed to the edge of panoptic institutions. Or rather, in Foucault's case, resistance must necessarily *seek* the margin if it is to retain that elusive character that avoids strengthening centres of power/knowledge: only inconsequentiality and obscurity can ensure the survival of specific acts of resistance. As Sawicki (1998) notes, however, while this led the later Foucault to concentrate on the politics of identity, this did not blind him to the persistence of structural inequalities. But even this sympathetic reading of Foucault leaves him standing to one side of collective projects, concerned with an ethic of self-development or the aestheticisation of the personal. Bogard's (1996, p. 66) fantasy is a deliberate device to convey both the 'lightness' of panopticism in which surveillance is signalled, the shadow of a central observatory that produces real disciplinary effects. If the immateriality of monitoring is implicit in Bentham then information technology liberates surveillance from the limitations of time and space. So profound and ubiquitous is the blurring between the real and the virtual that surveillance no longer follows a dialectic of control and resistance but traces 'a logic of virtualisation and hyperrealisation'. 'This is an imaginary', Bogard insists (1996, p. 17), 'that is already very much a real part of our everyday lives'. The mere anticipation of surveillance is sufficient to guarantee the reality of self-discipline and mutual control. More specifically, with respect to databases, Poster (1990) frets that the coding, manipulation and linking of data have become the cornerstone of more enveloping forms of surveillance than the panopticon of the industrial age. 'The discourse of databases, the Superpanopticon, is a means of controlling masses in the postmodern, postindustrial mode of information.' This leads Poster (1990, p. 97) to the 'uncomfortable discovery' that 'the population participates in its own self-constitution as subjects of the normalising gaze of the Superpanopticon'. And you thought that you were simply buying a shirt, not consolidating the corporate surveillance of consumption.

There is something in this, but not much. The contrast between Poster and Bogard is instructive. Poster's analysis is technologically premature: how much deeper would his pessimism be now that hypertext allows the monitoring of qualitative data and database content is easily separated from its initial software. Bogard, on the other hand, finds the realities of 'telematic' societies so overwhelming that they can only be approached obliquely. Bogard's fiction does not even aspire to be a parable. Indeed, the logic of the 'fiction' is that it can offer only impotent fatalism: no alternative reading is imaginable. We shall confine ourselves to the preliminary observation that power/knowledge is a much more complex concept than this reading allows. Even in Bentham, far less Foucault, monitoring does not of itself deliver knowledge or automatically enhance the powerful. Rather, Foucault is insistent that gaolers, doctors and psychiatrists must guard against complacency lest their charges become knowledgeable about the chinks in their armoury of surveillance. Equally, the powerful must constantly remake the normalising gaze if it is to retain its intensity and so capability to shape behaviours and morals. While corporate managements can now amass huge quantities of data about consumers there remains a yawning gulf between the aspiration of, say, relational marketing and the reality of data mining techniques that – so far – leaves knowledge overwhelmed by information. The same holds true for employees. Attitude surveys are widely used but more commonly broken down into component parts to highlight the performance of management teams than to understand the subtle dynamics of teamworking. By the mid-1980s the proliferation of PCs and haphazard growth of applications had undercut the possibilities of durable, centralised control of databases. While database software has made it possible to 'lash together' previously discrete applications, there is little sense of the permanence or intimacy that gave the panopticon its claustrophobic power to grind down recalcitrant souls (Cortada, 1996, pp. 210–13; Rule, 1996). In truth, much of the writing about social control in 'telematic' or 'information' societies is little more than technological determinism dressed in Parisien *haute couture*. This technological determinism obliterates all traces of human agency: managers become ciphers or themselves targets of surveillance; workers are not just powerless but their agency is permitted only in so far as it renders control ever more perfect.

Increasingly, electronic surveillance is being elevated far beyond the possibilities of bureaucracy, signifying nothing less than the birth of a new era of the workplace as a totalising regime (see Simpson (1999) for example). Sewell (1998) offers a final refinement on the theme of all-seeing electronic surveillance. Electronic surveillance of industrial work can never be complete, concedes Sewell, and can also be subverted and ignored, at least for a time. But if the gaze of peers, one's immediate workgroup or team, is added then hidden spaces inside the workplace become far fewer. This inter-penetration of comparative electronic and intimate social surveillance is what Sewell terms 'chimerical control'. So profound is electronic and social surveillance that management can devolve much routine decision-making to shopfloor teams without compromising their power or authority. 'Chimera' is a curious label for such searching disciplinary processes. On the one hand, chimera conveys the enveloping, perhaps grotesque nature of control, but on the other hand, it also suggests the imaginary, or the delusional. But there is nothing illusory or hallucinatory about the dynamics of control and resistance inside the electronics factories that Sewell describes. On the contrary, the parallel processes of electronic and social control are all too real, and cannot be imagined away. One irony of Sewell's approach is his misuse of the PhoneCo studies of peer review in a microelectronics factory, an example *not* of the perfection of team control but rather of the way that workgroups inverted the disciplinary gaze to subvert management control and maintain their solidarity (McKinlay and Taylor, 1996, 1998). The only gain from Sewell's intervention is that he reminds us of the need to understand not just the *interface* of the social and digital realms but their interrelationship; that is, the *digitisation* of the social realm of work and the *social* nature of the digital world.

In truth, much of what passes for Foucauldian analysis owes far more to Bentham than to Foucault (see, for instance, Sewell and Wilkinson (1992) and Lacombe (1996)). By itself, the capacity to accumulate vast stores of information about efficiency, quality or employee attitudes is not the construction of knowledge. Management knowledge relies upon the ordering, normalisation and reflection upon information, much more than simply storage. There is, in other words, no *automatic* coupling of power/knowledge. Rather, one has to look for the mechanisms by which management gathers, stores, interrogates and reflects upon information about the shopfloor. Nor – obviously – can one simply assume that management has effective means of transforming information into power/ knowledge. But although this seems such a commonsensical observation, it is one that ignored by so-called Foucauldian analyses of industrial work, call centres and the like.

There was a real debate inside Pharma over the meaning of knowledge management. The group within Pharma responsible for developing knowledge management techniques was Central Knowledge Support (CKS). CKS played two roles inside Pharma. On one level it provided a range of essential information-handling services to corporate clients, from clearing printer jams to 'handshaking' different software platforms. The fraught period immediately before filing a new drug with the regulatory authorities was crucial to CKS's reputation. CKS was also represented at every project meeting across functional boundaries. Beyond this, CKS had successfully developed a package for the electronic submission of drug protocols to the regulators, an enormous time and cost saving. Routine competence, high visibility within the corporation at all levels, and a major innovation in regulatory relations all combined to give CKS enormous influence far beyond its formal service function.

For CKS, the driving concern was not how to build a corporate database of tacit knowledge but how to understand, construct and extend 'communities of practice'. The term 'communities of practice' reflected CKS's determination to make knowledge management *practical* and their dismissal of the idea of a 'virtual warehouse' of tacit knowledge as fundamentally flawed. Specifically, CKS pondered how to ensure that tacit knowledge which was dialogic and ephemeral by its very nature could be captured, codified and, just as important, jettisoned once it had lost its value (Boje, 1991). 'Communities of practice' is a term popularised by Brown and Duguid (1991) who offer a quite different image of the development and transfer of knowledge from that of Foucault. Again, echoing classic Taylorism, they portray a profound imbalance in knowledge in – as opposed to of – work. That is, workers, not managers, effectively monopolise knowledge about how work is actually done, a knowledge that has proved doggedly invisible to the scrutiny of the techniques of job design. They begin with the startling discovery that actual work practices often differ markedly from that prescribed by company manuals. More than this, they observe that workers deploy, share and develop tacit knowledge through sharing their experiences and telling stories. So far, so predictable. The twist, however, is that management should understand – and appropriate – these informal exchanges; that formal organisational structures and manuals should engage with 'communities of practice' to maximise the innovative potential of the organisation. While there is due acknowledgement of the need to maintain the 'healthy autonomy' of communities since they 'cannot reasonably be expected to surrender their knowledge freely', Brown and Duguids' (1991, pp. 54–5) overriding aim is to 'harness innovative energy' (similarly, Hedlund, 1994). But accessing the tacit knowledge that was once the exclusive domain of craft workers, which was the target of Taylorism, is fraught with difficulty. Finding ways to link disparate 'communities' through, for example, the dissemination of rich narratives, becomes an important aspect of corporate planning. And here the notion of 'communities of practice' intersects with the concerns of Poster and Bogard. For the inescapable irony is that participatory control that seeks to elicit not just compliance but endorsement requires the active engagement of participants. There is a very real sense in which this entails, as the management texts would have it, volunteers not conscripts (Brown and Duguid, 1991, p. 54):

> In some form of another the stories that support learning-in-work and innovation should be allowed to circulate. The technological potential to support this distribution – email, bulletin boards, and other devices capable of supporting narrative exchanges – is available. But narratives... are embedded in the social system in which they arise and are used. They simply cannot be uprooted and repackaged for circulation without becoming prey to exactly those problems that beset the old abstracted canonical accounts. Moreover, information cannot simply be assumed to circulate freely just because technology to support circulation is available.

Roots of Knowledge Management

> Teams are last year's thing – been there, done that, got the tee-shirt. It's all about going beyond teams – way beyond teams – it's all about creating communities. Communities are larger, looser, more inclusive, more transient (CKS Interview, 2 November 1998).

In Pharma the successor to empowerment is the first faltering steps in 'knowledge management'. Knowledge management refers not so much to the scientific techniques of drug development as to the administrative processes that generate the extensive documentation required by the regulators. Tapping into the tacit knowledge of gatekeepers between the different functions, project teams and phases of the development programme has become the focus of major corporate investment. Knowledge management, one American corporate planner reflected, will have succeeded to the extent that it 'really drills *down* into the team experience'.

> Executives in Pharma do not control Pharma. They recognise that. They go out of their way to demonstrate that fact. They take contradictory decisions in order to demonstrate their relative powerlessness and to force ground level people to think, to

improvise, to acknowledge their empowerment. That's a deliberate Pharma policy that accepts – even celebrates – the gap between 'knowledge management' and 'real knowledge' – the stuff that people actually do'

The CKS team leader, an advocate of a highly decentralised system to allow 'conversations between experiences', was highly critical of corporate management's determination to retain 'a control mentality', a mentality he concluded was unlikely to deliver the necessary step-change in development times.

> I'm an innovator, but I'm surrounded by colleagues who are accelerators. I think it's time to really push back the boundaries; my colleagues want to do what we do already [pause] just faster (CKS Project team interview, 3 November 1998).

Of course, the issue was polarised between CKS 'radicals' and corporate 'conservatives', guardians of a system in which management's exclusive access to certain forms of knowledge maintained or enhanced an individual's power and authority.

> One of our problems is we have gatekeepers who restrict access to information. This is a constant frustration. But if we get rid of them then everyone has access to everything and we have opened up a Pandora's Box because we've surrendered control over knowledge – there would be no management of knowledge (PA interview, 10 November 1998).

CKS was given the task of finding a compromise position that would balance control and radical decentralisation. Even basic electronic mail systems render parts of formal organisational structures and control processes irrelevant to actual patterns of communication and work organisation (Ciborra, 1993, p. 77). The textualisation of communication that formerly was largely, if not exclusively, interpersonal both makes the process more collective and necessarily provides a novel platform for reflexivity (Zuboff, 1988). A technical evaluation of the different groupware products and their relationship to the Internet and intranets concluded that any extension of functionalities to cover workflow management and knowledge management required participating in the development of 'groupweb' products. Lotus Notes remains the lynchpin of the groupware movement towards building collaborative digital environments that combine collaboration and developmental capabilities with coordination and control. For Pharma, the central decision was how to categorise user populations so that routine administration is maintained in sites at the individual level. Corporate sites, on the other hand, will be based on groupware systems and reserved for internal documents that either settle a state of expertise, on products say; or internal documents which establish a platform of administrative expertise, Standard Operating Procedures or *ad hoc* amendments to working practices. Routine processing of information is conducted in Documentum, a system based on maximising the transparency and control of linear and well-established workflows. Only corporate sites are responsible for creating or disseminating knowledge, and groupware would be the shared global platform. Even in a firm that regards leveraging innovation as critical to competitive advantage, there was a cleavage between employees processing information in highly controlled software systems and others creating knowledge using more collaborative systems.

These decision processes were paralleled by the US parent company hiring consultants to install a knowledge management system – 'Lessons Learned'. 'Lessons Learned' is a database of tacit knowledge, of tips generated by individuals and, more usually, workgroup debriefings at the end of a project. This was the $12 million electronic suggestions box. The 'Lessons Learned' process is segmented by function, site, project and status. There is no linkage between the separate processes nor a robust common platform for data gathering. The 'Duke' report on the CompoundX development programme, for example, offered a series of detailed additions to the administrative canon and methods of resolving previous difficulties, but without considering ways of improving future capability to improvise or innovate. What emerged from an extensive process was a balance sheet that registered the pros and cons of specific administrative practices. Study diaries were now physically improved but overly complex in layout and used different paper sizes in different national locations – standardising stationery would make compilation easier. More seriously, the 'Duke' report highlighted a serious of interface tensions between functions, projects and external contractors. The contributors concluded that all tensions could be resolved by enforcing tighter standard operating procedures across functions and projects. The search was for closed administrative solutions that eliminated the very possibility of future interface tensions. Rather than accept that not all difficulties could be eliminated in such a complex, communication-intensive process, the 'Duke' report effectively externalised 'solutions' as the prerogative of the corporate planning function. There was little sense in which this was a reflexive process, in which workgroups not only identified improvements to administrative procedures but developed a fuller understanding of how to cope with inherent uncertainty. Overlaying the huge 'Lessons Learned' database would be textual links that would allow users to search chronologically, functionally and thematically.

Against this technological, systems-driven approach stood an alternative vision of a more conscious elaboration of current methods of knowledge management, a system whose great strength lay in deep interpersonal relationships but that was increasingly strained by fast growth. In comparison to 'Lessons Learned', one is struck by the modesty of this alternative. In essence, this involved first opening up additional social spaces for informal exchanges. Management's role is mapping and monitoring and, above all, avoiding unnecessary disruption to current informal modes of tacit knowledge transfer (see Davenport and Prusak, 1998, pp. 70–1). 'We have to use a hands-off approach', said the Knowledge Initiative manager, a corporate ally of CKS – struggling for a phrase – 'a very light touch, any initiative has to be light, almost imperceptible'.

> We have to accept that we cannot manage knowledge in the sense of hard wiring a system. We have to allow people to make their own links, to give them the techniques to allow them to construct, interact with knowledge. We can't put in a technological fix. It's not about finding specific answers but allowing people to problem solve, gain knowledge in unexpected ways (CKS, 3 November 1998, Interview 4).

The extensive use of digital technologies to exchange information between functions, development phases and international locations had generated considerable management understanding of the importance of 'soft' interpersonal skills in digital media. Indeed, Pharma project managers went to considerable lengths to socialise virtual exchanges. One coordinator of a transatlantic project team routinely had the American participants open birthday cards or boxes of European biscuits during videoconferences. This was deliberately intended to symbolise the small exchanges that are the daily experience of workgroups sharing the same physical space. This practice was extended to virtual coffee breaks in which low-level employees performing similar tasks in parallel in Europe and America would meet for 'online coffee' in a designated chat room. The explicit management aim was twofold: to socialise the digital world and to extend the reach of digital communication into the social world of the workplace. The real importance of this small-scale exercise is, however, not so much in its rich symbolic content. Rather, the point is that a chance gesture by an individual manager quickly became part of his managerial style. From this, through the weekly meetings of project managers such practices were rolled out across *all* international projects. The speed and thoroughness with which the socialisation of digital exchanges became an explicit target are indicative of the sophistication of project management and their willingness to experiment with social technologies of knowledge management. For CKS such experiences reinforced their conviction that large-scale databases were antithetical to knowledge management. The key to effective knowledge management was not perfecting surveillance techniques but opening up, as the CKS team leader put it, 'a storyworld, a place where people hold conversations, where one person's throwaway remark has the chance to become invaluable for someone else. We've got to give people the opportunity to scavenge. Looking is just as important as finding'.

Internal surveys of drug development teams revealed a widespread appreciation of the importance of tacit knowledge – practical experience – over explicit knowledge – of standard procedures. The surveys, conducted by the consultants Oracle, concluded that 'tacit knowledge is perceived (38%) to be twice as valuable day-to-day as explicit (19%)'. But, the consultants warned, Pharma 'must issue a challenge to ensure that knowledge is indeed tacit by nature, and not by practice':

> it is usually discovered that the knowledge is not tacit in nature. Rather, there is a reluctance on the part of staff members to codify their knowledge, thus rendering that knowledge tacit. In reality, this knowledge could be made explicit, with employee cooperation.

There is a hint here that Pharma's consultants define the hoarding of practical knowledge by workgroups as a form of passive resistance and a mute acceptance that this 'resource' cannot be extracted but must be freely given (see Blackler, 1995, p. 1041).

> All we're doing is producing a reservoir of information. The swimmer is not the knowledge – the act of swimming is the knowledge (CKS team meeting, January 1999).

Such organic, fluid imagery recurred time and again in CKS: it was intended to convey the immersive nature of deep participation in a communnity, however transient. But this imagery was not always used with approval, far less positive engagement. In reply to a question about the positive, self-development possibilities offered by knowledge management, a project manager first agreed that this was the case, but quickly added that 'this is about corporate reach, about reaching in to that pool of tacit knowledge, drawing from that well of experience. What that means, of course, is that Pharma owns the well itself'.

The Realities of Knowledge Management

> It's like drawing a picture in the air with your finger. As soon as you've finished, it's gone (CKS team meeting, December 1998).

The central image of technological knowledge management was that the face of all participants is used as the electronic page upon which information is written. Words are superimposed on the image of a face, the face of the 'donor' of this knowledge. Or are the words the backdrop to the image? This was the palimpsest, the electronic parchment upon which 'knowledge' was to be written and rewritten, accessed and shared. For the Web designers, this was a device to humanise the exchange between an individual and the database. But another reading is possible. As the ghostly face and words swim before the interrogator's eyes, first the image and then the text is on the surface.

But we should be extremely sceptical of the immediate practicality of such panoptic tools. During an informal exchange between two members of the Central Knowledge Support team about how best to ensure maximum use of the informational 'Magic Kingdom', there was a pause while they contemplated the scale of their task to build a truly effective, truly participatory database of tacit knowledge.

> Just now KM is about capturing 'Lessons Learned' and locking them away somewhere safe. And there's nothing safer than a 'Lessons' database because nobody, but nobody tries to break into it. We give them the tools, tell them how valuable these 'Lessons' are, but still they're left untouched.

With a mixture of gloomy resignation and bemused regret, the two laughed that these surveillance databases were so seldom used that the majority of hits on the sites were by the original Web designer and those curious about the menu in the plant canteen. The conclusion was that they would remove the hit counter from the sites to disguise its limited use. The reality falls far short of panoptic dystopia and management's vision of employee participation in emancipatory digital communities.

Internal surveys revealed a clear reluctance to commit personal experiences to recordable media, both because this was contrary to sharing tacit knowledge only with one's immediate workgroup and opened up the individual to scrutiny beyond existing structures. Fewer than one-third of respondents felt that current electronic knowledge capture and transfer procedures were effective. In response to the question 'what is the primary repository for divisional best practices and experiences', 18% cited the 'electronic knowledge base' compared with the 56% who replied 'the brains of Pharma employees'.

And this is the dilemma that confronts knowledge management as a corporate project. Tacit knowledge is gained and exchanged through interpersonal contacts and is typically context- and time-specific. More than this, tacit knowledge is the currency of the informal economy of the workplace, a currency devalued by management appropriation of even small change. The highly formalised 'Lessons Learned' process does not engage with the social processes of work in any real sense: 'lessons' are torn from their social and temporal context. At best, management can hope to refine some standard operating procedures, but cannot strip out tacit knowledge and lay it bare to inspection by all. Nor do the more sophisticated attempts to allow dialogue through shared work narratives necessarily overcome these barriers to panopticism. For only senior project managers and their nominees will be permitted to take place in these virtual conversations. Metaphorically, these are conversations between 'gaolers' and do not include 'prisoners' – save for a handful of temporary 'trustees' – and cannot hope to produce a totalising gaze of the 'penitentiary'. No surveillance system – real, virtual, or chimerical – can deliver tacit knowledge without the *willing* participation of the knowledgeable. Tacit knowledge, by its very nature, remains elusive from the corporate gaze.

Conclusion

We began by reviewing some of the wilder shores of Foucauldian scholarship interpreting technology and organisation. The overblown fears that the combination of teamworking, peer scrutiny and database technologies would leave little or no space for individual or collective resistance. Further, for companies such as Pharma seeking to develop more reflexive labour processes, maintaining private social spaces was essential for the development of tacit knowledge. Nor can technology-driven systems of knowledge management resolve this paradox. The most sophisticated databases can capture 'knowledge bytes' but cannot appropriate the subtle and ephemeral social processes that constitute tacit knowledge. One side of the debate surrounding knowledge management in Pharma *is* about extending surveillance and control into the informal world of work. But this is countered by more sophisticated arguments from the CKS team that to intrude on the private spaces in which tacit knowledge emerges is to fatally compromise knowledge management as a project. Indeed, the validity of the term 'knowledge management' is coming into question. The alternative is to open up more of the social and virtual spaces that make tacit knowledge possible. Knowledge fairs – events that draw people from similar functions in parallel projects – and temporary intranet chat rooms – including anonymised exchanges – are but two examples. Management's role is to develop methods to monitor and measure the content of the social processes in such spaces. Analysis would not be about outputs but the quality of the exchanges in terms of the demographics of participants, linguistic analysis, and the scope of the conversation. At most this much softer approach would deliver more refined facilitation skills, and a sense of the limits of management's knowledge and power over informal social processes. To compromise the dialogic basis of tacit knowledge was to jeopardise the routine innovations that skirt official procedures and, indeed, allow formal procedures to function. As the CKS team leader put it, 'we have to make control *bearable*'.

References

Blackler, F. (1995) 'Knowledge, Knowledge Work and Organisations: An Overview and Interpretation', *Organisation Studies*, 16: 6, 1021–46.

Bogard, W. (1996) *The Simulation of Surveillance: Hypercontrol in telematic societies*, Cambridge: Cambridge University Press.

Boje, D. (1991) 'The Storytelling Organisation: A Study of Story Performance in an Office-Supply Firm', *Administrative Science Quarterly*, 36, 106–26.

Bowring, J. (ed.) (1838–43) *The Works of Jeremy Bentham*, Edinburgh: Simpkin Marshall.

Boyer, C. (1996) *Cybercities: Visual Perception in the Age of Electronic Communication*, New York: Princeton Architectural Press.

Brown, J. S. and Duguid, P. (1991) 'Organisational Learning and Communities-of-Practice: Towards a Unified View of Working, Learning, and Innovation', *Organisation Science*, 2: 1, 40–57.

Button, G., Coulter, J., Lee, J. and Sharrock, W. (1995) *Computers, Minds and Conduct*, Cambridge: Polity Press.

Chiesa, V. and Manzini, R. (1997) 'Managing Virtual R&D Organisations: Lessons from the Pharmaceutical Industry', *International Journal of Technology Management*, 13: (5,6), 471–85.

Ciborra, C. (1993) *Teams, Markets and Systems: Business Innovation and Information Technology*, Cambridge: Cambridge University Press.

Cortada, J. (1996) *Information Technology as Business History: Issues in the History and Management of Computers*, Westport, CT: Greenwood Press.

Davenport, T. H. and Prusak, L. (1998) *Working Knowledge: How Organisations Manage What They Know*, Cambridge, MA: Harvard Business School Press.

Foucault, M. (1977) *Discipline and Punish: The Birth of the Prison*, Harmondsworth: Allen Lane.

Foucault, M. (1980) *Power/Knowledge*, London: Harvester.
Gandy, O. (1993) *The Panoptic Sort: A Political Economy of Personal Information*, Boulder, CA: Westview Press.
Graham, S. (1998) 'Spaces of Surveillant Simulation: New Technologies, Digital Representations, and Material Geographies', *Environment and Planning D: Society and Space*, 16, 483–504.
Grey, C. (1994) 'Career as a project of the self and labour process discipline', *Sociology*, 28: 2, 479–98.
Hedlund, G. (1994) 'A Model of Knowledge Management and the N-form Corporation', *Strategic Management Journal*, 15, 73–90.
Jay, M. (1994) *Downcast Eyes: The Denigration of Vision in Twentieth-Century Thought*, Berkeley, CA: University of California Press.
Lacombe, D. (1996) 'Reforming Foucault: A Critique of the Social Control Thesis', *British Journal of Sociology*, 47: 2, 332–52.
McKinlay, A. and Taylor, P. (1996) 'Power, Surveillance and Resistance: Inside the "Factory of the Future"', in P. Ackers, C. Smith and P. Smith (eds.), *The New Workplace and Trade Unionism*, London: Routledge.
McKinlay, A. and Taylor, P. (1998) 'Through the Looking Glass: Foucault and the Politics of Production', in A. McKinlay and K. Starkey (eds.) *Foucault, Management and Organisation Theory: From Panopticon to Technologies of the Self*, London: Sage.
Pisano, G. (1998) *The Development Factory*, Cambridge, MA: Harvard Business School Press.
Poster, M. (1990) *The Mode of Information: Poststructuralism and Social Context*, Cambridge: Polity Press.
Robins, K. and Webster, F. (1988) 'Cybernetic Capitalism: Information, Technology, Everyday Life', in V. Mosco and J. Wasko (eds.), *The Political Economy of Information*, Madison, WI: University of Wisconsin Press, pp. 44–75.
Rule, J. (1996) 'High-Tech Workplace Surveillance: What's Really New?', in D. Lyon and E. Zureik (eds.), *Computers, Surveillance, and Privacy*, Minneapolis, MN: University of Minnesota Press.
Sawicki, J. (1998) 'Feminism, Foucault and "Subjects" of Power and Freedom', in J. Moss (ed.) *The Later Foucault: Politics and Philosophy*, London: Sage.
Sewell, G. (1998) 'The Discipline of Teams: The Control of Team-Based Industrial Work through Electronic and Peer Surveillance', *Administrative Science Quarterly*, 43, 397–428.
Sewell, G. and Wilkinson, B. (1992) 'Someone to Watch over me: Surveillance, Discipline and the JIT Labour Process', *Sociology*, 26, 271–89.
Simpson, I. H. (1999) 'Historical Patterns of Workplace Organisation: From Mechanical to Electronic Control and Beyond', *Current Sociology*, 47: 2, 47–75.
Zuboff, S. (1988) *In the Age of the Smart Machine*. New York: Basic Books.

8 Human Capital or Capitalising on Humanity? Knowledge, Skills and Competencies in Interactive Service Work

Paul Thompson, Chris Warhurst and George Callaghan

A knowledge economy is one 'where economic value is found more in the intangibles, such as new ideas, software, services and relationships, and less in the tangibles like physical products, tonnes of steel or acres of land' (Scottish Enterprise, 1998, p. 3). Policy-makers and academics alike (Reich, 1993; DTI, 1998; von Krogh *et al.*, 1998; Byers, 1999; Vickery, 1999), endlessly repeat the mantra that knowledge work offers a rationale for the development of human capital in the workplace, a blueprint for the creation of competitive 'world class' firms, and a way of preventing advanced economies that are restructuring away their sunset industries from becoming peripheral low-wage, low skill national economies.

Practically and theoretically, knowledge work and services are seen to go hand in hand (see, for example, Barley (1996)). This chapter challenges the way in which that link is presented and understood. Building on existing critiques of the idea of a knowledge economy (Warhurst and Thompson, 1998a), it argues that key growth areas of service work are drawing on knowledge and creating skills that, though innovative, bear little resemblance to the dominant model. In particular, such work draws on broader social competencies and aesthetic qualities possessed by potential employees. Two case studies of interactive service work in central Scotland constitute the empirical focus. Scotland generally has a larger proportion of service work than the UK as a whole, and is making concerted efforts to promote this sector. Eighty-three per cent of jobs in the Glasgow economy are in the service sector and the largest firms in Glasgow are service-orientated. The three industries that are particularly prominent – tourism, retail and financial services – feature in the first case study. Call centres are now a characteristic growth area across the central belt of the country, with a total of 17,000 employees as a whole, and it is this work that features in our second case study.

Knowledge and Services: Disentangling the Wires

The importance of the service sector cannot be denied. World employment seems to be becoming dominated by the service sector, with forecasts that 90 per cent of all jobs created in the future will be in the service sector (Armistead, 1994). Within this trend, the creation of new tertiary occupations and the expansion of older ones, for example in financial services, medicine, education, leisure and technical services, is particularly notable. So is the growth of the retail sector. In Britain, employment in the retail distribution and service sector is close to 4.5m, only just behind the total for manufacturing (*Labour Market Trends*, 1996). Of the three sectors of the economy in Britain, agriculture now accounts for 2.3 per cent of employment, industry 24.3 per cent and services 73.4 per cent. To varying degrees, much the same pattern can be found in countries throughout Europe, North America, Japan and Australia as Table 8.1 illustrates.

The use of terminology such as a move from the *machine age* to an *information age* (Hamel and Prahalad, 1996), illustrates the inseparability of the service/knowledge pairing. Work in the new economy is no longer about the production of tangible goods, but concerned with the centrality of knowledge and manipulation of symbols, processes far more characteristic of services (Drucker, 1986). Little wonder then that Scottish Enterprise (1998) argues that the new skills to be developed are the 'thinking' skills associated with work in research, sales, marketing, management and information technology.

However, we need to disentangle these assumed links before rushing headlong into embracing the service/knowledge economy. Many writers have raised concerns about the fragility of employment in the service sector (Goodhart and Wood, 1994; Buckingham, 1995; Wallace, 1995; Donovan, 1996; Sinden, 1996), or

Table 8.1   Sectoral employment in developed economies

Country	Agriculture	Industry	Services
Australia	5.3	23.7	70.5
Belgium	2.6	27.7	69.7
Canada	4.4	22.2	73.2
France	5.1	27.7	67.2
Germany	3.0	37.1	59.9
Ireland	13.8	28.9	57.3
Japan	5.9	34.3	59.8
Sweden	3.4	25.4	71.1
Switzerland	5.6	33.2	61.2
USA	2.7	24.1	73.2

Source: *Labour Market Trends*, November 1996.

about the classification of service jobs, suggesting far closer links to manufacturing than are normally acknowledged (OECD, 1994; Warhurst and Thompson, 1998a). Of far more importance for our purposes is caution about the *nature* of this employment. Over the past thirty years, most service sector growth has occurred in low-skill, low-wage jobs such as serving, guarding, cleaning, waiting and helping in the private health and care services, as well as hospitality industries (Crouch *et al.*, 1999). Only 7 per cent of the fastest growing occupations in the USA could be classified as Reich's symbolic analysts, and for the most part these occupations are 'mundane', suggests Henwood (1996): engineers, computer professionals and associated technicians. Current trend predications suggest that all of those occupations that could be classified as symbolic analysts will account for only 13 per cent of employment growth in the USA. Keep and Mayhew (1999b) suggest that core organisational competencies in much of the service sector, for instance in retail stores, are found within a small subsection of senior managers. Store managers, let alone shopfloor workers, are given little opportunity to exercise discretion within the centralised planning framework. Moreover, the pattern of most growth in the low skill services jobs seems set not to change, as Figure 8.1 indicates for the USA – reputedly at the vanguard of transformation to a high-skill, high-wage knowledge work economy.

The percentages in the figure indicate the relative forecast growth areas in US employment. Inclusion of the absolute numbers of forecast increases (from the same article) indicates that although the numbers of computer analysts and programmers will grow significantly during the forecast period – up 737,000, the largest growth areas are in 'mundane' public sector teachers – up 773,000 – followed by nursing – up 765,000. Personal and protective services are also large growth areas, for example home-health and child-care workers and guards. Janitors' and cleaners' jobs will also expand greatly – an increase of over half a million.

Much the same pattern is true for the UK. During 1998 McDonald's opened 100 new outlets in the country, creating 5,000 new low-end service jobs; Bass Taverns, the managed pub operator created 4,000 similar jobs and Burger King 2,000 (Bannister, 1997). Within the UK, Scotland is no different. Although policy-makers such as First Minister Donald Dewar (Scottish Office, 1999) eulogise the importance of the knowledge economy and the growth of knowledge workers, data on employment growth in Scotland (actual and forecast) indicates a very different development (Scottish Enterprise, 1997). Rising from 68% in 1986, the service sector now provides 74.5% of jobs in the Scottish economy. Nevertheless, about one third are mainly in the public sector and over one fifth in distribution, hotels and catering. There will be job growth in associate professional and technical occupations, although caution is again required here, for this growth will occur mainly in the public rather than the private sector. The largest single area of job growth between 1996 and 2006 is expected to be in sales jobs within distribution, hotels and catering. The next biggest increase will be in personal and protective service jobs, again mostly within the public sector. As a

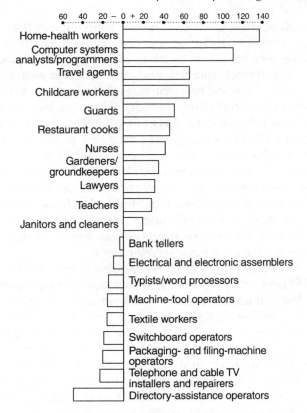

Figure 8.1   Forecast occupational trends in the USA 1992–2005 (%) (US Bureau of Labour Statistics, cited in *The Economist* (1995))

consequence, it is not technical or even thinking skills which are of increasing importance to most employers in the country but 'person-to-person' skills. Significantly, most of these jobs are expected to be filled by female part-time workers.

Crucially, for many employed in the expanding service sector, the content of their work remains highly routinised and stringently monitored (see, for example, Leidner (1993), Ritzer (1998) and Taylor (1998)) and often low paid. Part of the problem, noted by Braverman (1974) over 25 years ago, lies in official classifications of the occupational structure which focus upon the form of jobs rather then the content of labour. Relatedly, there is insufficient sensitivity to the heterogeneity of work and employment within the service sector – not just between knowledge work-type 'iMacJobs' on the one hand and 'McJobs' on the other, but also the heterogeneity that exists within similarly classified employment within the service sector

Knowledge and service work must be disaggregated conceptually as well as empirically. To achieve this it is necessary to do something that many commentators conspicuously avoid – specify something of the conditions and character of knowledge in work. The implicit model of the traditional knowledge *worker* is someone who has access to, learns and is qualified to practice a body of knowledge that is formal, complex and abstract. Knowledge *work* requires employment relationships and task structures that allow for creative application, manipulation or extension of that knowledge. However, the 'body' here is not a collection of abstract theories and facts but resides in part in the person (it is 'embrained' to use Blackler's term), and partly in a profession or occupational community that polices its content and boundaries. Professional intellect has, then, been assumed to be coterminous with knowledge work (Quinn *et al.*, 1996). Taking the argument a step further, many commentators assert that such professional and scientific–technical labour is becoming the characteristic feature of the service-based, information-driven economy (Handy, 1995; Barley, 1996). Knowledge work, with its distinctive labour process and employment relations, is thus inherent to contemporary economic development.

In terms of conceptualisation of knowledge itself, the most basic distinctions date back to Polanyi (1958, 1967). Tacit knowledge is based upon the 'indwelling' of awareness and understanding by individuals – 'we know more than we can tell' (Polanyi, 1967, p. 4). By analysis of action, other individuals can make this tacit knowledge explicit or stated in the form of rules and procedures. Theorists who have recently attempted to update and extend taxonomies of knowledge in work (Fincham *et al.*, 1994; Blackler, 1995; Frenkel *et al.*, 1998) largely reproduce traditional polarities, though often in new languages. There is knowledge that is abstract and pertaining to concepts, theories and formula. In contrast there is organisationally specific knowledge relating to that which is non-generalisable tacit, technical or formal, but which can be systematised in procedures, policies, routines and roles. Then there is societal or social knowledge derived from broader shared understandings, values and beliefs; or tacit knowledge that comes from practice and experience and that can be shared among work colleagues.

Such distinctions are useful and necessary and we have adapted them in Table 8.2, indicating in italics the terms used in these new taxonomies. The categories are not meant to be taken as fixed pairings. For example, theoretical and tacit are also a meaningful 'pair'. What we are trying to signal is the nature of the traditional hierarchy. Knowledge work has been based on that which is theoretical, technical (connected to tangible or intangible products and techniques) and explicit. In contrast knowledge which is contextual, social and tacit has been taken to be of lesser value, significance or centrality to work.

Problems arise when trying to apply traditional characterisations and hierarchies to contemporary knowledge economy arguments. Competitive advantage for firms is said to lie in developing abstract rather than practical knowledge, and in encouraging knowledge derived from shared understandings and values rather than that related to procedures and policies. Underlying this argument is the explicit or implicit notion that the conditions of traditional knowledge work

Table 8.2　**Categories of knowledge in work**

contextual	social	tacit
embedded	*encultured*	*embodied*
contingent	*cultural*	*informal*
theoretical	technical	explicit
abstract		*encoded*
formal		
embrained		

are spreading to ever-increasing categories of workers. Routine work is being abolished, upgraded or marginalised through such developments.

It is eminently possible to object to the assumptions about the nature of professional and technical labour itself (Warhurst and Thompson, 1998b), but that is not our purpose here. The problem is that knowledge economy perspectives are not representative of trends in service work. It is certainly true that examples can be found of innovative theoretical knowledges being produced in semi-autonomous employment relationships – for example by specialist IT professionals. Equally, as we have demonstrated, there can be found far greater numbers of routine fast food and other McJobs. While it would be easy to settle for the standard skills polarisation argument, the interesting developments are taking place in *interactive service work*, where different and often new knowledge and skill trajectories are taking place. Here firms are seeking to 'add value' through the identification and utilisation of tacit and social competencies, in a largely contextual knowledge framework. Though there are considerable practical and theoretical uncertainties attached to the term, it signifies a capacity to perform required tasks or activities (Cooper and Robertson, 1995) rather than specifically identifiable or demonstrated skills.[1]

Interactive Service Sector Work

Leidner (1993) defines interactive service sector work as involving face-to-face or voice-to-voice interaction with customers, while Allen and du Gay (1994) characterise it as work which is intangible and heterogeneous and which involves simultaneous production and consumption. Although some of this work requires the use of technical knowledge (most often acquired through investment in human capital) the majority of interactive service sector jobs are highly routinised and repetitive.

Unlike manufacturing work, where employees produce products for sale in the market-place, in interactive service sector work the employees, and the way they look, sound and act, *are themselves* part of the product. Two examples of this type of work, which form the case studies analysed later in this paper, are retail and call centre work. In call centres the emphasis is almost exclusively on the quality of vocal communication, with customer satisfaction being strongly influenced by the energy and enthusiasm of the call centre operative. Product knowledge has a role, but in all except the most specialised call centres, the managerial focus is on the use of empathy to create rapport with the customer. Likewise in retail work the 'aesthetic' capacities and attributes of employees – language, dress codes, manner, style, shape and size of the body – are deliberately used to appeal to the senses of customers, most obviously in a visual or aural way. Again, detailed product knowledge may play a part, but in most cases management want the comfort and trust which are supposed to accompany a pleasant manner and appearance.

This has implications for recruitment to interactive service work, for although the majority of this work requires little technical knowledge, there is a need for particular social skills and competencies – abilities which are difficult to identify and extract. This has led to recruitment, selection and training being particularly important. In order to identify workers with the personal characteristics likely to make them interact spontaneously and perform effectively (that is, to choose people with intangible qualities – such as sociability, drive, honesty, adaptability and a sense of humour – which make them 'the right kind of person for the job'), many call centre managers have devised intensive recruitment and selection processes. Such applicants are screened *in* rather than unsuitable ones screened out. The training that follows takes these embodied capacities and attributes and shapes them into conscious tools for use in the service interaction.

The existence of such work complicates the discussion surrounding human capital. Traditionally this is associated with technical knowledge, where people study to gain a theoretical or practical understanding of a specific field of learning which is, importantly, publicly and privately recognised, most usually through a qualification. The labour process of interactive service sector work, however, draws on capacities and attributes located (often unconsciously) *within* each worker. These workers draw on limited technical knowledge during their work, but they do have to develop a consciousness of their social skills and an awareness of when and how to deploy these. *In extremis* this personal awareness could be described as tacit knowledge, where workers develop an understanding of themselves which allows them to consciously use their emotions to influence the quality of the interactive service sector product.

Case 1: All Style and No Substance?

Within the shift to services in the Glasgow economy, the creation of 'style labour market' jobs is at the forefront. The material presented here is drawn from Warhurst *et al.* (2000)'s research on interactive service work within this style labour market (although in the course of the research it became obvious that the practices associated with aesthetic labour were also to be found, to a lesser degree, in other service sector companies in the retail industries). In conjunction with documentary analysis, a qualitative research methodology was adopted involving a series of interviews and four focus groups of male and female managers and employees, predominantly in the 20–30 age bracket, and who were involved in face-to-face or voice-to-voice customer interaction. The primary research examined the retail, hospitality and banking industries. Three areas of interest were analysed within these industries, namely recruitment and selection; training, working and management practices; and the service encounter.

Aesthetic labour is defined as a supply of 'embodied capacities and attributes' possessed by workers at the point of entry into employment. Employers then mobilise, develop and commodify these capacities and attributes through processes of recruitment, selection and training, transforming them into 'competencies' and 'skills' which are then aesthetically geared towards producing a 'style' of service encounter deliberately intended to appeal to the senses of customers, most obviously in a visual or aural way.[2] Aesthetic labour encompasses individual attributes and task requirements to produce a favourable interaction with the customer and to complement social and technical skills. Employer demand for aesthetic skills and competencies is becoming more prevalent because of its perceived commercial utility: 'Unlike the labour force of many large industrial corporations, retail sales assistants [for example] are constantly "on display" to purchasers of their products... the employment of particular types of individuals to "front" the retail store is essential... the retail assistants... increasingly comprise the actual product on sale' (Lowe and Wrigley, 1996, p. 24).

The research affirmed that management was looking for a matrix of skills from their employees: aesthetic, social and technical. However, technical skills could be developed with training once employees were in the organisation. At the point of entry it was the former two skills that were desired. And it was in the area of recruitment and selection that aesthetic labour had the most obvious resonance, as this process allows for the filtering out of 'inappropriate' people.

> On paper her application was fine [and] she'd been interviewed by our personnel people... [but]... this woman walked in.... How she looked and how she spoke... it was even the way she wore her uniform, the way her hair and her make-up was... my manager took an instant dislike to her and the woman lasted seven weeks.... I mean she was brilliant at [bank telling] but because of the way she looked and the way she spoke he took an instant dislike to her and it all went against her. (focus group respondent)

Each firm had a 'model' employee that management sought to recruit. Sometimes this ideal was informal and implicit; in other cases it was formal and explicit. In the recruitment literature of the hotel within the study, it was a person description, not a job description that featured, asking prospective employees to assess themselves by the 14 words that were claimed to characterise that company's 'personality': 'stylish' and 'tasty' for example. A number of the participants in the focus group also suggested that there had been a distinct shift in what organisations were now seeking in the potential employee. In particular, they noted the need for applicants to have the ability to present a certain type of persona that encompassed many of the 'dispositions' suggested by Bourdieu (1984) – language and dress codes; manner; and style, shape and size of the body.

Consequently, organisations were looking for the 'right' sort of appearance and disposition, the latter being more important than any technical skills. For example, the personnel manager of the hotel, in discussing the recruitment of staff for a new café within the hotel, commented that: 'we didn't actually look for people with experience... because we felt that wasn't particularly important. We wanted people that had a personality more than the skills because we felt we could train people to do the job'. The hotel was ideally looking for male and female graduates between 19 and 25 years old. 'There is probably a Hotel Elba look', said the manager, 'not an overly done up person but very, quite plain but neat and stylish... young, very friendly... people that look the part... fit in with the whole concept of the hotel'.[3] For other companies in the hospitality industries, employees had to be 'well groomed, smart, clean and tidy... well spoken... trendier people...' (bar manager).

Corporealness was not the only desired aesthetic in recruitment. In relation to customers' aural aesthetic, the voice and accent of employees was important. In the hotel, the personnel manager was adamant; 'We didn't want someone who spoke in a very guttural manner'. In the banks, again, one respondent claimed that having a 'clear accent' was an absolute essential.

Once past the recruitment and selection stages, a common theme that emerged was the extent to which organisations, through training, continued to seek to mould people into the desired personas. This moulding was most obvious in the 'style' hotel. After the telephone interview, application with CV and then face-to-face interview to be selected as waitering staff, there was a ten day induction in which extensive grooming and deportment training was given to the staff by external consultants. Such sessions encompassed haircuts/styling, 'acceptable' make-up, individual makeovers, how men should shave and the standards expected in relation to appearance. The person-to-person skills – the usual communication, verbal, personal and teamworking skills identified by Hesketh (1998) – were also important in the companies studied here. Once employed, it was then that technical skills and product knowledge were imparted on-the-job to employees: how to present food, take orders, use equipment etc. In most cases this training was provided at a very basic level and often through new employees shadowing existing employees.

Regulation of appearance and adherence to company standards was, in one company, overseen by the 'grooming standards committee', or in the words of one of the employees, the 'uniform police'. Their function was to monitor things such as the employees' skirts, shoes, stockings and jewellery to ensure that they all conformed to the company ideal. Role-playing was a recurring feature of employee training. Such methods sought to impress upon employees the importance of their own aesthetic capacities and attributes from the customers' perspective and also then develop and mobilise these capacities and attributes as knowledge, skills and competencies so as to be able to differentiate and so better serve customers. The companies instructed their employees in how to approach customers by 'reading' those customers' signifiers, such as body language, for example. An employee of another up-market fashion retail company, Donnatella, related how 'the supervisors do a wee act kind of thing and pretend they are a customer and say "This is a bad example" and "This is a good example", and the good example is when you smile at them as soon as they walk in'. Working for Leviathan, another respondent claimed, 'is a bit like acting. I mean it's like being in drama school, being taught how to stand and how even to look at customers'.

Echoing Van Maanen's (1990) comment about employees as 'talking statues' at Disney, dressed in company clothing, employees in one retail outlet, when not serving or replenishing stock were required to stand at 40 degrees near to the entrance of the store, smiling invitingly at prospective customers. Posture here was also prescribed. In another store, employees were required to stand in front of a mirror and go though a prescribed appearance checklist before entering the shopfloor. Many of the retail employees talked of the 'performance' involved in their work, not only managing their emotions, as Hochschild (1983) has noted, but also their appearance. 'I think that we've all got the qualification how to present ourselves. I mean that how we're getting training, part of your training is actually how to perform', said one such employee, continuing: '...we've all got to present the company now. We're not workers as such – we're ambassadors now'.[4] Perhaps even more, some companies, such as Hotel Elba, want their staff to be the embodiment of the company, and the human software is transformed into corporate hardware.

Practices are frequently justified with reference to the customer. Within a well-known restaurant chain a respondent recalled how a colleague was dismissed for being 'too common', although the ostensible reason was poor performance. In questioning the decision the respondent (an assistant manager at that time) was told that, 'She wasn't what they considered right for the company, what the customers were expecting'. An interesting variant on whether employees may reflect the required image was found, again, in an up-market fashion retailer. In this organisation employees were constantly entreated to use words such as 'exquisite' and 'luxurious' instead of more prosaic terms such as 'nice' and 'lovely'. In part this was a reflection of the fact that 'There's a type of customer who would really like that language'. Failure to use this and other similar elaborate language in the customers' presence was again a source of sanction and disciplinary action from management.

Interestingly, the employee who described the operation of the 'uniform police' in her company found it largely unproblematic: 'But I think it's necessary for someone who is in uniform, you know the fact that they have to have their hair tied back or whatever. What's the point in giving somebody a corporate image and then having big bits of hair everywhere'. It was 'a good thing', she insisted. Moreover several participants, representing a range of service industries, suggested that peer pressure would also ensure conformity to company standards on appearance and deportment, as individuals who did not comply were felt to be letting their colleagues down. This socialisation was reflected in the view of a participant working when she explained how she had confronted management on this issue: 'I said that I feel as though I'm being watched and they said "Well it's making sure the Leviathan standards are being kept up. If someone fails, the whole shop is affected by it". And it's true', she reflected.

Case 2: Call Centre Work

Call centres represent important new forms of work, both in terms of the number of employees and through the nature of the labour process. Drawing on the work of Callaghan and Thompson (1999) we examine Telebank, a company that has four integrated call centres throughout the UK. These call centres receive all incoming calls to the bank. In total they employ 2,000 people, 500 of whom work in the case study location. Data collection took the form of taped semi-structured interviews with 24 customer service representatives (CSRs) and 14 managers. In addition there was non-participant observation of recruitment, training and the labour process. Repeat visits were made to the research site over a period of nine months.

The content of call centre work has already proven controversial, with descriptions of perfect control in electronic sweatshops (Fernie and Metcalf, 1997) contested by more traditional labour process accounts (Taylor and Bain, in press). Questions of recruitment, selection and training have been relatively neglected, therefore leaving issues of changing knowledge and skills under-explored. At the outset it is important to recognise that there are many different types of call centre, with the differentiating factors being whether calls are inbound or outbound, the degree of product complexity and variability, and the depth of technical knowledge required to deal with the service interaction. Taylor and Bain (1998) found that 47.3 per cent of Scottish call centres deal only with inbound calls, and Telebank, the case study research site, is one of these, receiving 20,000 incoming calls a day.

In common with many call centres, Telebank uses an automated call distribution system (ACD). These systems receive inbound calls, automatically allocate them to CSRs, place calls in a queue and (in conjunction with other software) offer sophisticated management information packages. The more developed systems, such as the one used at Telebank, operate over a number of sites, creating a virtual 'super group' of CSRs within which calls are spread. Within such a system each CSR takes an average of 120 calls per day. Each call lasts around 180 seconds and is split into two main parts: talk time (160 seconds) and post call wrap-up time (20 seconds). The time between calls is also measured and, reflecting its non-productive nature, is known by management as 'white space'.

CSRs aim to deal with 80% of all incoming calls, with the remaining 20% being passed on to branches or other areas of the bank. Of the calls dealt with by CSRs, two thirds relate to requests for specific account information (such as balances), requests for simple actions (moving money between accounts) and charge queries. Most of the calls are therefore similar and simple: CSRs have limited discretion with customer accounts, with scripts and screens largely determining what they can see and do.

Yet despite such routine work Telebank uses a sophisticated recruitment and selection process: a job and person specification were designed; appropriate recruitment channels selected; application forms collected and analysed; telephone interviews given; role plays assessed; two-person structured interviews undertaken; references and credit checks collected and finally job offers made. The ratio of people who complete an application form to those being offered a training place can be as high as 20:1. We argue that this process reflects the centrality of social skills and competencies to the nature of the tasks in routine interactive service work. This leads to the potential 'performance gap' associated with the indeterminacy of labour being addressed outside the labour process itself through rigorous selection and training, as well as inside through rules and controls.

Telebank's recruitment process is designed to assess applicants in three areas: personality traits; communication (especially verbal) skills; and, with less emphasis, technical skills. On technical skills, Telebank managers look for keyboard skills, basic numeracy and the ability to move around a system. More time and thought, however, are put into assessing social characteristics and competencies:

> I think the communication skills are the most important, very important. The difference between what they do and what the people on the phones in other banks do is down to their personality, their communication skills. That is the only substantive differentiator between the banks – the personality of the individuals on the telephone. That's the highest skills. Their guys know all about banking products, my guys know all about banking products. Their guys will have to know about systems, my guys will have to know about systems. That's all roughly the same. The differentiator is how they communicate with that customer. It is the overriding skill that they've got to have. (Manager 6)

Personality and attitudinal predispositions are deemed more important. Management wants people who can continually communicate with energy and enthusiasm and who can recognise nuances in conversations with customers and vary their voice accordingly. Such abilities draw on broader social knowledge: the skills of active listening, about knowing when and how to speak, that are part of a more common understanding of communication norms and values. As Telebank states in its recruitment literature, it is looking for people with 'life experience... for example running a house and raising children requires many of the skills we are looking for', skills which include vocal, verbal, visual communication, excellent listening ability and being able to work under pressure. Such skills are more difficult to identify and quantify than technical knowledge, but are crucial to interactive service work.

Telebank not only recruits attitude, it tries to shape and dictate it. Social competencies identified through the selection process are built upon during Telebank's six-week, full-time training programme. With reference to products and systems, trainees are given a folder which specifies what they can and cannot do: an alphabetical index containing details of procedures (known as 'cookery cards') and a file for more complex procedures (known as 'added ingredients'). This limited and highly contextual knowledge is complemented with classroom-based training, where trainees are shown how to navigate through these systems.

However, the main emphasis is on communication skills to 'build rapport' with the customer. This is split into two parts – managing a conversation (techniques of conversational control) and managing yourself (control over energy and enthusiasm). Taken together, the techniques are geared to giving trainees an awareness and influence over the regulation and management of feelings. As one manager stated:

> Tone gives away just about everything that's going on in your mind... if a customer is stupid you need to become quite clever in your acting abilities... enthusiasm and tone give away your mood; if you are five minutes from the end of a shift, or having a bad day... you'll have to fight these reactions, shut them out, push them out. The good thing is if you can do this, eventually you will be able to change yourself. Or on the 'bad days', unless it is very serious, put up with it.

CSRs are told that sufficient concentration will improve sincerity – once rapport is built 'you're there'. Such attitudes reveal that management are encouraging CSRs to change their underlying feelings and values, to provide emotional labour (Hochschild, 1983). Telebank employees, like those described by Richardson and Marshall (1996), are required by management to continually 'smile down the phone'. This appears to be consistent with evidence for the existence of 'deep acting' elsewhere in interactive services. For example, Taylor (1998, p. 98), in his research into a telephone sales operation of a British airline, comments: 'service sector employers are increasingly demanding that employees deep act – actively work on and change their feeling to match the display required by the labour process'.

The extent to which acting extends beyond the surface level in our case appears to be limited. Interviews revealed considerable scepticism about the significance or nature of 'building rapport': 'I can see it's [building rapport] important, but most customers just want to come on and get their query dealt with, they don't really care whether you're they're best friend with them at the end of the call (CSR 2).

Rapport is undermined both by the routine nature of the tasks and the relentless pace of work. It requires time and discretion, qualities that are heavily constrained by the nature and extent of call monitoring. Statistics on how many calls, how they are handled and where they are directed are collected and graded as a basis for feedback and discipline. Not surprisingly, adverse reaction to 'the stats' was the most consistent feature of CSR interviews. Contrasts with expectations at interview and in training were noted:

> What they don't tell you when you come to the interview is the emphasis they put on stats. They are very statistics oriented – how long your average call is, your average wrap time... the emphasis in the call centre and other call centres is on the number of calls, the quality of the calls, yes, but not this rapport thing where you chat with someone (CSR 1).

CSRs' perceptions of the skill requirements of the job also differed in part from management. While there was consensus about social rather than technical skills, employees also placed more emphasis on the ability to survive stressful and repetitive work: identifying patience, tolerance, level-headednesss, sense of humour, listening, flexibility and emotional self-management. One CSR noting that, 'You've got be very tolerant, I think. You have to be able to take a deep breath, the customer is always right, kind of thing. But it's very repetitive. I've been here for six months now and it's very mundane – just waiting for the next beep!' (CSR 8).

Management's attempted utilisation of social competencies and mobilisation of emotions is therefore the beginning, not the end, of the story. The contradictions are too near the surface for it to be effective or experienced positively. Telebank employees are certainly aware of the need for pretence, but there is little evidence of deep acting, of CSRs actually changing themselves. Rather, they make conscious decisions about engaging in customer service – with varying degrees of enthusiasm: 'I sit on the phone and put a face across to the public. Some people can't distinguish between stopping their emotions. Some people come in here feeling really down, and go on the phone feeling down. Other people can switch' (CSR 3). Some close down parts of themselves to deal with the repetition; many leave the industry dissatisfied with its particular effort bargain; and others engage in strategies of call avoidance (Bain and Taylor 1999). Interactive service work requires the presence of social and tacit knowledge, but the profitable practice of such knowledge is still a matter of negotiation between workers and managers.

Conclusion and Policy Implications

Both case studies allow an analysis of labour that moves beyond traditional conceptions of knowledge and skill by exploring how service employers are defining, eliciting and developing social and aesthetic competencies in their workforce. There were considerable continuities of managerial intent and employee experience across the two cases, particularly in the kinds of social competencies required and the recruitment and training mechanisms initiated. However, in call centre work employee attributes are less embodied, despite the emphasis on voice and accent, and more focused on performance. Not surprisingly, therefore, management relies more on traditional targets and controls. Perhaps the key difference is in the response of employees. Although call centre workers identify with the goals of service quality, there is little evidence from this or other cases that they are 'seduced' by the product or process. In style labour market jobs people recruited for their appearance appear to embrace the image and the means of policing it more readily. It is important to note that both aesthetic labour and call centre work are not homogeneous. High-end call centre work, for example, selling complex financial products, is likely to require quite different working knowledge, and therefore different employment conditions. Our purpose has been to raise critical questions about the spread and significance of knowledge work, not to ignore its importance in some sectors.

We also need to recognise the broader growth of knowledgeability in work. Though it takes particular forms in interactive services, employers more generally have been trying to address some of the limits of Taylorism and bureaucracy through accessing what had traditionally been tacit, informal knowledge. As Lew Platt, chairman of Hewlett-Packard put it (quoted in Caulkin (1997, p. 10), 'successful companies in the twenty first century will be those that do the best job of capturing, storing and leveraging what their employees know'. While some of this process may involve abstract knowledge, much of it seeks to draw on uncultured knowledge or that which arises from shared understandings among people (Blackler *et al.*, 1998). This is less a case of investing in human capital than capitalising on the 'humanity', or the social capacities of employees.

The fact remains that most companies 'lever' knowledge in ways that bear little resemblance to the literature or official corporate and governmental pronouncements. Figure 8.2 attempts to map how companies typically lever knowledge in routine work situations, including typical assembly and low-end service work. Managers seek to identify employee competencies, systematically utilise what has traditionally remained tacit, and then abstract from knowledgeable practice regulatory systems that seek to formalise and assess that knowledge. Studies show that workers' capacity to contribute to innovation and 'value-adding' tends to be stifled by management in the UK and the USA. While a few 'high road' companies in the UK and the USA elicit and utilise their employees' knowledge to improve company products or processes, most

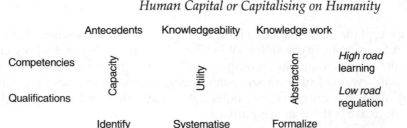

Figure 8.2 The production of routine workplace knowledge

companies opt for the 'low road' of regulation rather than learning (Appelbaum and Batt, 1994; Milkman, 1998; Warhurst and Thompson, 1998b).

The findings of the case studies have significant implications, not just for conceptualisations of work and employment, but for policy debates. There has been a welcome shift by left-of-centre governments to either renew or refashion active labour market policies in new political and economic conditions. While improving employability and enhancing human capital through training and other measures are reasonable objectives, current policy formation is over-influenced by over-hyped knowledge economy theories.

There are a number of problems. First, the 'real' knowledge economy, such as high-tech clusters in biotechnology or advanced electronics, is vital to the contemporary economy, but relatively small in scope and potential for employment growth. We therefore cannot generalise too far in terms of knowledge and skill requirements (Keep and Mayhew 1999b; Crouch *et al.*, 1999). Second, while high-skill employment is growing in social, community, personal and business services, it is being outstripped by the growth of new low-skilled jobs such as those in interactive services (Crouch, 1999).

In policy terms, such trends have significant implications for the existing supply-side training policies. On the one hand if we want to change direction, it is necessary that 'attention is paid to the demand side of the labour market, to issues like the quality of jobs, their availability, pay rates and so forth' (Peck, 1999, p. 7). State-led incentives to invest in progressive and innovative uses of human capital must be combined with policies to protect the employment conditions of the many low-skill jobs that will inevitably remain. On the other hand, supply processes themselves have to be re-thought. Existing provision by agencies intending to make the young and unemployed attractive for firms has tended to be IT, IT and more IT. And yet there is some evidence that employers rank such IT skills very low as a criterion of employability generally (Hesketh, 1998). It is often the 'person-to-person' skills that determine employee selection at the point of entry to, and are crucial in, interactive service work (Keep and Mayhew, 1999a). Vocational education needs to address more seriously the social competencies that contemporary work requires, but which many school leavers appear to lack. Here, two problems emerge. The first is the appropriateness of allocating public funds to perfect the pretence of emotional labour or compound the obvious discrimination issues arising from aesthetic labour. The second, arising from this potential funding, is the feasibility of devising credible vocational education and training accreditation that would enable the recognition and reward of such labour.[5] Admittedly, such measures raise difficult questions about the purposes and potential of education and work, but difficult questions are better than easy answers.

Acknowledgements

The authors gratefully acknowledge the contributions of Anne Witz, Dennis Nickson and Anne Marie Cullen in the research of the first case study reported here.

References

Allen, J. and du Gay, P. (1994) 'Industry and the Rest: the Economic Identity of Services', *Work, Employment and Society*, 8, 2.

Appelbaum, E. and Batt, R. (1994) *The New American Workplace: Transforming Work Systems in the United States*, Ithaca, NY: ILR Press.

Armistead, C. (1994) *The Future of Services Management*, London: Kogan Page.

Bain, P. and Taylor, P. (1999) 'Employee Relations, Worker Attitudes and Trade Union Representation in Call Centres', *Paper to 17th International Labour Process Conference*, Royal Holloway College, London.

Bannister, N. (1997) 'Thousands of McJobs planned', *Guardian*, 30 December.

Barley, S. (1996) *The New World of Work*, London: British-North American Committee.

Blackler, F. (1995) 'Knowledge, Knowledge Work and Organisations: An Overview and Interpretation', *Organisation Studies*, 16, 6.

Blackler, F., Crump, N. and McDonald, S. (1998) 'Knowledge, Organisations and Competition', in G. von Krogh, J. Roos and D. Kleine (eds.), *Knowing in Firms*, London: Sage.

Bourdieu, P. (1984) *Distinction: A Social Critique of the Judgement of Taste*. London: Routledge.

Braverman, H. (1974) *Labor and Monopoly Capital*, New York: Monthly Review Press.

Buckingham, L. (1995) '1,000 Jobs Go at WH Smith', *Guardian*, 24 August.

Byers, S. (1999) 'People and Knowledge: Towards an Industrial Policy for the 21st Century' in G. Kelly (ed.) *Is new Labour working?*, London: Fabian Society.

Callaghan, G. and Thompson, P. (1999) 'Proceeding to the Paddling Pool: the Selection and Shaping of Call Centre Labour', paper to the *17th Annual International Labour Process Conference*, School of Management, Royal Holloway, University of London.

Caulkin, S. (1997) 'So, a little knowledge is not quite so dangerous', *Observer*, business supplement, 28 September.

Cooper, D. and Robertson, I. I. (1995) *The Psychology of Personnel Selection*, London: Routledge.

Crouch, C. (1999) 'The Skills Creation Triangle Out of Balance', *Renewal*, 7: 4.

Crouch, C., Finegold, D. and Sako, M. (1999) *Are Skills the Answer? The Political Economy of Skill Creation in Advanced Industrial*, Oxford, Oxford University Press.

Department of Trade and Industry (1998) *Our Competitive Future: Building the Knowledge Driven Economy*, Cm4176, London, The Stationery Office.

Donovan, P. (1996) 'Thousands Go in NatWest Branch Cuts', *Guardian*, 31 July.

Drucker, P. (1986) 'The Changed World Economy', *Foreign Affairs*, 64, 4.

Economist (1995) 'A World Without Jobs', *The Economist*, 11 February.

Fernie, S. and Metcalf, D. (1998) '(Not) Hanging on the Telephone: Payment Systems in the New Sweatshops', *Discussion Paper 390*, Centre for Economic Performance, London School of Economics.

Fincham, R., Fleck, J., Proctor, R., Scarbrough, H., Tierney, M. and Williams, R. (1994) *Expertise and Innovation*, Oxford: Clarendon Press.

Frenkel, S., Korczynski, M., Shire, K. and Tam, M. (1998) 'Customer Service Representatives and Work Organisation in Call Centers', paper prepared for *Wharton Financial Institutions Center Conference on Call Center Management Science*.

Goodhart, D. and Wood, L. (1994) 'Sock Shop Puts All Full-time Staff on Part-time Contracts', *Financial Times*, 26 January.

Handy, C. (1995) *The Future of Work*, WH Smith Contemporary Papers 8.

Hamel, G. and Prahalad, C. K. (1996) 'Competing in the New Economy: Managing Out of Bounds', *Strategic Management Journal*, 17.

Henwood, D. (1996) 'Work and its Future', *Left Business Observer*, 72, Internet edition.

Hesketh, A. (1998) 'Reward in this Life', *Guardian*, Higher education supplement, 24 February.

Hochschild, A. R. (1983) *The Managed Heart: Commercialisation of Human Feeling*, Berkeley, CA: University of California Press.

Keep, E. and Mayhew, K. (1999a) 'The Assessment: Knowledge, Skills, and Competitiveness', *Oxford Review of Economic Policy*, 15, 1.

Keep, E. and Mayhew, K. (1999b) 'Towards the Knowledge Driven Economy – Some Policy Issues', *Renewal*, 7: 4.

Labour Market Trends (1996) November, London: Office for National Statistics.

Leidner, R. (1993) *Fast Food, Fast Talk: Service Work and the Routinisation of Everyday Life*, Berkeley, CA: University of California Press.

Lowe, M. and Wrigley, N. (1996) 'Towards the New Retail Geography', in N. Wrigley and M. Lowe (eds.), *Retailing, Consumption and Capital: Towards the New Retail Geography*, Harlow: Longman.

Marshall, K. (1994) 'NVQs: Training for Competence, or a Process for Deskilling?', *International Journal of Lifelong Education*, 13: 1.

Milkman, R. (1998) 'The New American Workplace: High Road or Low Road?', in P. Thompson and C. Warhurst (eds.) *Workplaces of the Future*, London: Macmillan.

Norris, N. (1991) 'The Trouble with Competence', *Cambridge Journal of Education*, 21: 3.

OECD (1994) *Jobs Study: Evidence and Explanations* Pts 1 & 2, Paris: OECD.

Peck, J. (1999) 'Getting Real With Welfare-to-Work: (Hard) Lessons from America', *Renewal*, 7: 4.

Polanyi, M. (1958) *Personal Knowledge*, London: Routledge & Kegan Paul.

Polanyi, M. (1967) *The Tacit Dimension*, London: Routledge & Kegan Paul.

Quinn, J. B., Anderson, P. and Finkelstein, S. (1996) 'Managing Professional Intellect: Making the Most of the Best', *Harvard Business Review*, March–April.

Reich, R. (1993) *The Work of Nations*, London: Simon & Schuster.

Richardson, R. and Marshall, J. N. (1996) 'The Growth Of Telephone Call Centres in Peripheral Areas of Britain: Evidence from Tyne and Wear', *Area*, 28: 3.

Ritzer, G. (1998) *The McDonaldisation Thesis*, London: Sage.

Scottish Enterprise (1997) *Scottish Labour Market and Skill Trends*, Glasgow: Scottish Enterprise.

Scottish Enterprise (1998) *1998 Strategic Review Consultation Document*, Glasgow: Scottish Enterprise.

Scottish Office (1999) *Skills for Scotland*, Edinburgh: The Stationery Office.

Sinden, A. (1996) 'The Decline, Flexibility and Geographical Restructuring of Employment in British Retail Banks', *The Geographical Journal*, 162: 1.

Taylor, S. (1998) 'Emotional Labour and the New Workplace' in P. Thompson and C. Warhurst (eds.), *Workplaces of the Future*, London: Macmillan.

Taylor, P. and Bain, P. (1998) 'An Assembly Line in the Head: Work and Employee Relations in the Call Centre', *Industrial Relations Journal*, 30: 2, 101–17.

Taylor, P. and Bain, P. (in press) 'Entrapped by an "Electronic Panopticon"? Worker Resistance in the Call Centre', *New Technology, Work and Employment*, 15: 1.

Thompson, P. and Warhurst, C. (eds.) (1998) *Workplaces of the Future*, London: Macmillan.

Van Maanen, J. (1990) 'The Smile Factory: Work at Disneyland' in P. J. Frost *et al.* (eds.), *Reframing Organisational Culture*, Newbury Park: Sage.

Vickery, G. (1999) 'Business and industry policies for knowledge-based economies', *OECD Observer*, no. 215.

von Krogh, G., Roos, J. and Kleine, D. (eds.) (1998) *Knowing in Firms*, London: Sage.

Wallace, P. (1995) 'Safe at the Bank? Don't Count on It', *Independent on Sunday*, Business Section, 4 June.

Warhurst, C. and Thompson, P. (1998a) 'Hands, Hearts and Minds: Changing Work and Workers at the End of the Century' in P. Thompson and C. Warhurst (eds.), *Workplaces of the Future*, London: Macmillan.

Warhurst, C. and Thompson, P. (1998b) 'Shadowland: The Real Story of Knowledge Work and Workers', paper to the *16th Annual International Labour Process Conference*, UMIST.

Warhurst, C., Nickson, D., Witz, A. and Cullen, A. M. (2000) 'Aesthetic labour in interactive service work: some case study evidence from the "New" Glasgow', *Services Industries Journal* (forthcoming).

Wieczorek, J. (1995) 'Sectoral Trends in World Employment and the Shift Toward Services', *International Labour Review*, 134: 2.

Witz, A., Warhurst, C., Nickson, D. and A. M. Cullen (1998) 'Human Hardware: Aesthetic Labour in the New Workplace', paper to the *Work, Employment and Society Conference*, University of Cambridge.

Notes

1 Firms and HR practitioners are increasingly attempting to identity core or transferable competencies (such as 'adapting to change') as a basis for standardised recruitment and selection. Such practices have been extensively criticised as facilitating deskilling rather than developing learning and creativity (Norris, 1991; Marshall, 1994), but this debate is beyond the scope of this chapter.

2 An attempt to more comprehensively explore the conceptualisation of aesthetic labour, and its composites, can be found in Witz *et al.* (1998), as can a typology of aesthetics and organisation.

3 Pseudonyms for the case study companies are used throughout the chapter.

4 The performance required of employees in interactive service work is well noted. Usually, this performance is viewed through the lens of emotional labour. What is missing is an appreciation and examination of management's utilisation of employees' embodied competencies and skills - 'aesthetic labour'. The performance of employees requires then not just emotion management but also the management of their appearance, and this research demonstrates that management seeks to control both.

5 In conjunction with one of us writing here, plus Dennis Nickson, the Wise Group, a social enterprise, is engaged in such an attempt in order to enable the unemployed to re-enter paid work in the New Glasgow economy.

9 Re-Pairing Knowledge Worker and Service Worker: a Critical Autobiography of Stepping into the Shoes of My Other

Dorothy Lander

The pairing and paradoxes of service and knowledge are the stuff of my working woman autobiography. For 18 years until the mid-1990s, I was the manager of university student residences in Nova Scotia. I was responsible for personal services for students in residence, supervision of a unionized custodial staff, and a multi-million dollar contract with the caterer, Marriott Corporation. I am still struggling to articulate the many forces that had me walking away from this permanent, full-time, full-benefits job, but this I do know – my overwhelming 'stuckness' centred on a sense that service work would not count as knowledge any time soon. Was I stuck in women's work?

The following year I took steps to translate my frustrations and perplexities into doctoral research in the UK. My research questions were framed in feminist epistemologies: assumptions about how gender relations and gendered performances are implicated in how and why knowledge is (or is not) obtained, created, shared and valued. What can service workers (predominantly women) know? What if knowledge worker and service worker were not the Other?

My working story took an unexpected twist in 1998. My knowledge credentials in hand (PhD), I returned to this same university, turned left at the site of my former basement office, walked some forty yards to the west, and took up my post as assistant professor in adult education. My new ground-level working space with its arched window and Trinity motif is an architectural reminder that I now occupy the original academic and religious centre of the university. Here I work at a distance with graduate students who are practitioners in diverse, service-oriented workplaces – nurse educators, managers and administrators, police and military trainers, literacy educators, counsellors, HRD trainers and performance consultants, among others. The Internet is the usual medium for our one-on-one teaching–learning relationship. Am I suddenly a knowledge worker? The discourses on work in the global market-place characterise knowledge workers as people who own the knowledge in their heads as the key means of production, who convert their intellectual capital into goods and services, and who make decisions that will profit the organisation. These same

141

discourses implicate service workers as bodies that are ancillary to knowledge, bodies that clean up messes so that the knowledge worker can make the heady, profitable decisions. My former worklife in university management constituted these paradoxical identities and my present worklife as an academic is made up of something else again. Am I perhaps walking around in unpaired shoes?

As faculty-knowledge worker, I now engage with student *learners*. I approach my teaching practice as relational *service encounters*. I am both caught up in and resist the market language of contractual *transactions* related to satisfying student *customers* in the provision and payment for knowledge and learning *services* as commodities. Is the shoe on the other foot? Or is the shoe on the foot of my Other?

Critical Autobiography as Feminine Dialogic

The most admirable thinkers within the scholarly community... do not split their work from their lives. They seem to take both too seriously to allow such dissociation, and they want to use each for the enrichment of the other.... What this means is that you must learn to use your life experience in your intellectual work (C. Wright Mills, *The Sociological Imagination*, 1959, pp. 195, 196).

Narrative approaches to organisation and management studies have taken hold (Boje, 1994; Czarniawska, 1997, 1998; Hatch, 1996, 1997; Orr, 1987; Weick, 1995, 1996). Organisational researchers are giving increased attention to organisational stories as ways of knowing, analysing, diagnosing, critiquing, assessing, managing and changing organisation. Why then does the researcher's autobiography typically remain the untold story of organisational research? Ann Game's (1994) deconstructive approach to the university organisation is a remarkable exception. I readily identify with Ann Game and our shared culturally specific text of white women in Western universities. 'I *do* clean up academics' disorders, mess; and if my work is polluting to them, it is *their* mess displaced onto me that threatens' (p. 48).

The researcher's autobiography and subjective reflexivity, the sociological imagination that Mills (1959) values, are rarely featured in accounts of organisational research, even feminist approaches (e.g. Acker, 1990; Calás and Smircich, 1993, 1996; Holmer-Nadesan, 1996; Kanter, 1977; Probert, 1999). 'Not afraid to draw on personal, private experience when dealing in the public realm' (Calás and Smircich, 1993, p. 71) is a desired qualification in their wry 'Help Wanted' ad based on the 'feminine-in-management' rhetoric, but the authors do not then make their own personal, private feminine experience explicit. This stands in contrast to feminist qualitative research in which autobiography performs authentic theorizing on reflexivity, the gendering of knowledge and the plurality of women's ways of knowing (e.g. Church, 1995; Fletcher, 1994; Griffiths, 1994; Neilsen, 1998; Olesen, 1998; Richardson, 1994).

Czarniawska (1997) offers first-person accounts of her autobiographical acts in the conduct of organisational research, but carefully separate from the rest of her work and life. 'A self-reflective reading can be attempted' she writes, 'but I feel that after Ashmore's (1989) [*The Reflexive Thesis*], *not much new* can be achieved by following this direction. The critique is best done by others' (1998, p. 17, my italics).

I try to achieve 'something new' by explicating the dialogical, responsive knowledges of the autobiographical 'I' in my re-presentation of my own working autobiography. The 'something new' is tracing organisational knowledge production through the mediated, multiple selves of autobiography, the 'I' who is always responding to an-Other (Bakhtin, 1986, p. 69). The 'something new' is feminist dialogism, Irigaray's (1981) woman who is 'not One... "she" goes off in all directions and... "he" is unable to discern the coherence of any meaning. Contradictory words seem a little crazy to the logic of reason' (cited in Bauer and McKinstry, 1991, p. 11). The 'something new' is my striving for iconic resemblance (Lash, 1990, p. 194) and 'style as theory' (Van Maanen, 1995) by re-pairing my paradoxical and paired representational abstractions of service–knowledge/services–service with my tacit knowing and lived autobiography of service work and knowledge work (see Chia and Morgan, 1996).

Critical autobiography embodies the flexing of multiple positions that include my researcher self, my worker self, my teacher self, my learner self and my (step)mother–spouse–daughter self(s), to name just a few. Hatch (1996) cautions against overidentification between author and narrator, the effect of which she claims 'can be paralyzing, or at least embarrassing, self-consciousness' (p. 365). Yet Hatch validates 'narratives of the self' when she cites sociologist Laurel Richardson (1994), who in turn, validates my working paradox of standing in the Other's shoes, when I am the Other.

My critical autobiography is a performance of walking other-wise. My critical autobiography performs in the dialogical space of action and space of resistance, building on Holmer-Nadesan's (1996, p. 59) research into the striving of the cleaning service worker of the university 'to be the subject that decides, as opposed to an object that is decided upon'. The resistant discourses of these women who clean university residences destabilize the dominant relationship of knowledge over service. 'Resistance is the dialectic other of organisational control' (p. 57).

The departure point for translating my personal working autobiography into public issues and opening up alternative meanings in the organisational space of resistance is the management and service discourse on shoes and walking the talk.

What of Shoes? What of Walking? What of Footing?

That place-between-2-places, that walk-in-2-worlds: this is the space 'beyond' difference that I want to explore for feminist theory and praxis. The 'new patterns of relating across difference' that Audre Lorde called for in 1980 are still urgently needed as we cross the millennial border (Susan Stanford Friedman, '"Beyond" Difference: Migratory Feminism in the Borderlands', 1998, p. 67)

Derrida's (1987) question 'What of shoes? What, shoes? Whose are the shoes?' and his supplementary of whether the shoes in Van Gogh's painting are a 'pair' are questions that just might initiate millennial dialogue on the management of walking in 'that place-between-2-places'. I bring the shoes–feet–walking metaphor to bear on my position that the market discourse of customer services has appropriated and naturalized the moral rhetoric of service: standing in another's shoes and walking a mile in someone else's shoes translates 'serving others' into 'satisfying customers'. Knowing the other as other in 'generously loving relations' (Silverman, 1996, p. 43) is the rival discourse that I favour for resisting the dominant market discourse and destabilizing this dominant system.

Knowing the Other as Other

Service work and knowledge work constituted my tacit organiser for organisational research before this distinction emerged as an explicit organiser and generated my grid of binary oppositions and multiple gendered identities. There is a straightforward autobiographical influence in my allegorical breaching of the division of labour in my article (Lander, in press) entitled, 'Can Martha Know? Can Mary Serve?' The motherhouse of the religious order of the Sisters of St Martha is in Antigonish, Nova Scotia, where I worked as a university service operations manager for so long. At the beginnings of this residential campus, the Marthas were responsible for the service of cleaning, laundry and food for students and resident priests, continuing until staff were unionized in the 1950s and management became a lay responsibility. St Martha is the patron saint of cooks and servants and this religious order celebrates one hundred years of 'service' in 1999. The market orientation of services was anathema to this working environment.

My exposure to the Marthas colours my reading of exchange-value appropriating response–ability–value in the organisational literature on service leadership (e.g. Zeithmal *et al.*, 1990) servant-leadership (e.g. Greenleaf, 1977; Schuster, 1998) and stewardship (Block, 1993). From day one as manager, I worked alongside Sister Ann Aloyse, who as supervisor of the housekeepers and janitors in students' and priests' residences reported to me in terms of the organisation chart. My immediate image of her soft white curls and comfortable plumpness calls up her contradictory moniker of 'Sarge', a masculinist identifier that recognised her service in the women's division of the army during the Second World War. Probert (1999) contrasts apprenticeship, men's preserve in hierarchical workplace learning, to the lateral, informal learning of 'Sitting next to Nellie' (Butler and Connole, 1992). 'Walking next to Sister A.A.' across campus, I rehearsed, performed and came to know service as 'knowing second persons' (Code, 1991). I speculated privately that her approach might be in part a resistance to the hierarchical workplace learning of the military. I learned to value her judgement calls, which balanced private and public spheres, partiality and impartiality, in relationships with staff. We challenged the masculinist discourse of trade unions, specifically the impartiality principle of the collective agreement, when we re-scheduled the start time on the evening shift one hour later for one employee. Her husband, also in cleaning services, could then drive their one car back home to the county after his day shift, turn over the car keys in the yard, and take over child care responsibilities where she left off. Informal learning and partiality in making management decisions both rely on knowing the other as other, constituting 'generously loving relations with the other' (Silverman, 1996, p. 43). On another basis of 'knowing second persons', we would defer to the collective agreement and deny requests to change the schedule to accommodate a janitor's wish to take on a supplementary job during the lobster fishing season. Sister A.A. could strategically and contradictorily become the 'Sarge' of the hierarchical workplace.

The organisational logic of impartiality that Acker (1990) brings to job evaluation in gendered organisations also applies to the masculinist seniority principle of collective agreements with service workers:

> Both jobs and hierarchies are abstract categories that have no occupants, no human bodies, no gender.... The concept 'a job' [that] organisational logic presents as gender neutral... already contains the gender-based division of labor and the separation between the public and the private sphere (p. 149).

When Sister Ann Aloyse retired, I also came to know that her subject position as a Martha distanced her from disembodied abstract principles and bestowed on her privilege and agency in making decisions and value judgements *in context* and *in relationship* with persons. As a Martha, she was *supposed to* relate to the whole, embodied person, not the abstract, universal worker. Balancing the public and private in decision-making involved much more negotiation between context and contract in the matrices of power in my years as manager following her retirement. The Marthas' vocation of service combined with their vows of poverty had the lingering effect of naturalizing low pay for non-religious workers in these occupations. Yet the lingering effect of cherishing 'service' as vocation in its original sense is manifest on the annual Staff Appreciation Day for service workers: the occasion is marked by humorous stories of everyday practice that celebrate embodied workers. These stories confer 'ideality on the face and lineaments' (Silverman, 1996, p. 96) of the other.

Knowing the Other as Knower

Schuster's (1998) pronouncement on service work as having 'little to do with using your head and everything to do with pushing a broom, or cleaning a toilet, or... shining shoes' signals the body–mind dualism and the singular use-value of servant-leadership for dismantling hierarchies or perceptions of hierarchy. The dualism of the service-worker body and the knowledge-worker head is echoed in what Webb (1998, p. 2) suggests 'could be the simplest definition of all: that knowledge is 'organised information in people's heads (Stonier, 1990)'. The juxtaposition of 'competitive advantage' and 'female advantage' embeds the head–body dualism and naturalizes the feminine-in-management; the rhetoric works to create 'the appearance of a radical rethinking' while maintaining the same gendered power imbalances (Calás and Smircich, 1993, p. 72). It is borne out of not knowing women and service workers as knowers. When I lived the everyday life of a manager, professors of business administration did not call upon me once in 18 years, either formally or informally, to share my knowledge of management with their undergraduate students. It is a tribute to the power of the gendering of knowledge and the exclusivity of service and knowledge spheres that I could have daily conversations about my management practices with business students over a meal in the student dining room and at committee meetings without ever being known as a knower of management. By contrast, the Food Services Director of Marriott Corporation, who had no higher education 'knowledge credits' to his name and whose management experience in contract food services was relatively recent, was invited regularly to make presentations in business courses and nutrition and consumer studies seminars, and to judge management students' case study presentations. I am not diminishing Eugene Vidito's outstanding management knowledge; indeed he received Marriott's top corporate award for management in North America. But could it be that 'real men(agers)' work for corporations, not universities and non-profit organisations? Business professors did ask me to volunteer myself and my department for student practicums by becoming the 'client' for their students-as-management consultants. The teacher in me (my Master's degree was in adult education) was delighted to advise students on their learning projects. They developed very useful proposals related to designing a Call for Tenders for the university food service contract, making recommendations for enhancing the computer database for residence and board students' financial transactions, and for launching a campus-wide recycling program. My established service worker identity had the effect of rendering me primarily the needy client who did not know, very secondarily the manager of a complex, computerised service operation, and invisibly as a teacher-advisor.

My identity and involvement with these university students *qua* customers learning management skills just happens to be a close-to-the-bone example of the use-value of the feminine-in-service leadership as the means to an end. The end and object of knowledge is exchange-value that can 'create product, guarantee quality, or serve customers' (Block, 1993, p. 8). Zeithmal *et al.* (1990) are blunt about the use-value of service to create exchange-value. I can readily substitute my own name and other service workers and the feminine-in-management for 'service' in the following passage:

[Service leaders] *use* service to be different; they *use* service to increase productivity; they *use* service to earn the customers' loyalty; they *use* service to fan positive word-of-mouth advertising; they *use* service to seek some shelter from price competition (p. 2, my italics).

Throughout these management theories of service, there is an implicit assumption that knowledge workers do not have to learn the service skills of responding to an-Other. As Holmer-Nadesan's (1996) research confirms, 'Cleaning and "looking after students" are both skills that management assumes service workers "naturally" know how to perform' (p. 75). Block (1993) finds it 'beguiling' that 'we [organisational leaders and knowledge workers] already know a lot *about* service, *about* partnership, and *about* empowerment' and yet there 'has been disturbingly little fundamental change in the way business, government, health care, and education manage themselves' (p. 11, my italics). 'About' signals knowing in the abstract. My 'allegorical breaching' (Van Maanen, 1995) of 'about' is a reminder that service workers live, breathe and walk service, in short, 'know' service, and in the process 'know a lot *about* service', should anyone care to ask. De Certeau (1984) unlaces the epistemological hierarchy of the knowledge worker and service worker: the knowledge of the service worker 'is known only by people other than its bearers' (p. 71).

I am building towards re-pairing knowledge and service as processes that involve knowing the Other as other, and knowing the Other as knower. In the process, I re-pair and re[as]semble my vocations of manager and teacher. The past and the present converge as I 'translate' my service manager's textual practices and trajectories into my current textual practices and trajectories as a teacher and knowledge worker with adult education practitioners. This is Bruner's (1990) sense of human reflexivity that orients toward the past to reconceptualize 'other ways of being, acting, and striving' (p. 109).

Human reflexivity, our capacity to turn around on the past and alter the present in its light, or to alter the past in the light of the present.... The 'immense repository' of our past encounters may be rendered salient in different ways as we review them reflexively, or may be changed by reconceptualisation (pp. 109–10).

My translation plants one foot firmly in the service university (e.g. St Martha's University; Lander, in press) of useful, meaningful, response-able knowledge and tiptoes with the other foot around the brave new enterprise university of performativity. The translation requires constant and contradictory changes in my footing. The impartiality of services and the partiality of service are broad translations of the contradictions that move in the between spaces of everyday practice. I re-present an appreciative email from a student and adult education practitioner as testimony to the management of co-response-ability that is the universal of both my past service work as a manager, and my present service work as a teacher. In other words, I reconceptualize service work as the universal of knowledge work and of management. Cathy Healy's email bears witness to my position that service and co-response-ability create value and generate knowledge. This is her response to my written responses to her first learning assignment, and as she tells about a student complaining to a teacher about marks, my teacher identification with her story co-exists with my manager self responding to a grieving employee or a dissatisfied residence student. Note how Cathy attaches 'complaint' to marks (and to value-for-money *services*) and 'reflection' to appreciation of responsive *service*. Cathy brings her experience in the history classroom and her current work with educators in volunteer agencies in Bosnia to bear on the contradictory knowing of service and services.

> As a teacher of history, I have marked many, many essays.... I always write comments,... make suggestions for improvement, and provide a very detailed evaluation scheme.... In ten years of teaching, though, I have only had a few (maybe half a dozen) students come in voluntarily to see me to go over their paper thoroughly.... I have only had one other professor who took such time reflecting over student work.... When he returned the papers, he warned students about coming to him to complain about marks.... He welcomed the opportunity to meet with students to help them learn how to improve writing and analytical skills, but he would not tolerate efforts to negotiate marks once he had spent so much time deciding upon them (Healy, personal correspondence, 1999)

Undoing Division and Prizing Difference

> The imaginary of my asymmetrical shoes-walking-footing metaphor inaugurates my performance of leverage on the binaries of the university organisation, the unlacing of my off-balance service and knowledge shoes. Leverage embodies multi-directional movement and combined with critical reflexivity enables walking-in-2-worlds (Friedman, 1998).

In unlacing the left and right pairings, I rely on Leigh Star's ideas of trajectory (Strauss, 1993) that converge with leveraging, walking-in-2-worlds, and finding meaning other-wise. Leverage upsets the symmetry of the pairings; leverage re-pairs.

> Trajectory is one way of capturing the between-ness without leaving the specious present, of noticing the pattern and shape. But beware! Between-ness is an elusive and fragile thing to describe. Even though it's the most robust and necessary thing in the world to experience (p. 47).

Readings' (1996) critique of the university and the emptiness of the pervasive quality rhetoric relies on the dualism of *calculation* and *meaning*. My response perhaps qualifies as describing and leveraging elusive and fragile between-ness: meaning *moves* with dialogical, responsive trajectories, whereas meaning *stands still* with calculation. In the capitalist context, a commodity is a calculated moment in 'the circulation process of value.... It is the material embodiment of dead, congealed, labor, and, by extension, information' (Curry, 1997, p. 6). Auto-biographical storytelling exerts leverage on the calculation of quality that like the monolithic pyramid of the organisational chart stands still until it is re-storyed. Yes, I am playing with the twin trajectories of re-*storey*ing hierarchies and re-*story*ing the organisational narrative.

Embodied binary logic is implicit in Shields' (1996) application of Bakhtin's dialogical imagination in which difference as otherness demonstrates the impossibility of fully standing in another's shoes, the impossibility of fully vacating one's own left–right, forward–backward binary steps, the impossibility of *speaking as* or *speaking for* the Other. Goffman's (1981) concept of dynamic changes in footing brings dialogue and footing together and resonates with non-essentialist theories of positioning as a way of 'focus[ing] attention on dynamic aspects of *encounters* in contrast to the way in which the use of 'role' serves to highlight static, formal and ritualistic aspects' (Davies & Harré, 1990, p. 243, my italics) of *transactions*.

My autobiographical un-pairing and re-pairing of my service and knowledge shoes helps me distinguish between texts that are ordered around oppositional categories that name the hegemonic other in devalued difference and texts that name and value the other as different by conferring 'ideality on the face and lineaments of another' (Silverman, 1996, p. 96). Service boots are made for walking and for going 'beyond the correct naming of our difference as the *sole* pattern of developing new relations' (Friedman, 1998, p. 68, my emphasis). Imagine my delight in taking up the double nuances of 'sole'! My autobiography traces my efforts at linking and unlinking, entangling and disentangling, lacing and unlacing, the 'blending as well as clashing that takes place in the contact zones between difference' (Friedman, p. 68); see Figure 9.1.

Walking and Working in 2-Worlds

Like Wittgenstein (1980), 'I find it important in philosophizing [and working] to keep changing my posture, not to stand for too long on *one* leg, so as not to get stiff' (p. 27). I did stay too long on one leg as a university services operations manager, and I did get stiff. I did get stuck. I spent 18 years in the work of delivering services to student customers, and I have spent the last five years trying to re-pair commodified services with the service of managing co-response-able relationships. I got so caught up in the *services* discourse of exchange-value transactions that at first I barely noticed that the relational-value and learning-value of the *service* encounter had been appropriated by and subordinated to the university 'enterprise'. I carried the management and market language of 'stakeholders' and 'transactions' and 'service delivery' and 'customers' and 'branded concepts' (e.g. Pizza Hut, Tim Hortons and Taco Bell are available throughout Marriott accounts in Nova Scotia universities) into my doctoral research related to the university as a service organisation. I was conversant in the acronyms, TQM, POS (point of sale) and f.c.p.m (food cost per meal) as they related to PIs (performance indicators) for quality in the student board program.

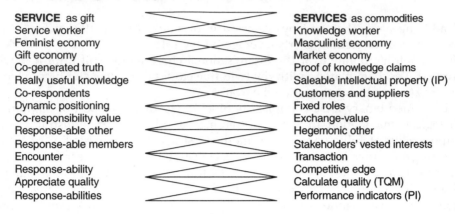

SERVICE as gift	SERVICES as commodities
Service worker	Knowledge worker
Feminist economy	Masculinist economy
Gift economy	Market economy
Co-generated truth	Proof of knowledge claims
Really useful knowledge	Saleable intellectual property (IP)
Co-respondents	Customers and suppliers
Dynamic positioning	Fixed roles
Co-responsibility value	Exchange-value
Response-able other	Hegemonic other
Response-able members	Stakeholders' vested interests
Encounter	Transaction
Response-ability	Competitive edge
Appreciate quality	Calculate quality (TQM)
Response-abilities	Performance indicators (PI)

Figure 9.1

The critical autobiography of my doctoral research started me on the way to re-pairing service and services, service and knowledge. I can revisit my momentous learning, which like James Joyce's 'epiphanies of the ordinary' or Kierkegaard's Moment break into the ordinary time of the past, present, and future and 'in the blink of an eye, it brings about a qualitative change within the temporal sequence' (Perkins, 1985, p. 19). My neatly laced-up chart of left and right shoes of service–services unfolded out of so many epiphanies of the ordinary. One early Moment was articulating the distinction between goods and services. Services are acts or processes that play out in experiences more often than in having a thing, the product of manufactured goods. The customer-learner participates in the production of the services they receive. There is usually no lag between the time a service is produced and the time it is delivered and consumed. As a food service manager, I lived these services and consumption principles every day in my co-response-able encounters with tray-toting, tool-using, meal-devouring students. Did my tacit knowing really need explicating? This reflexive question generated another startling Moment and came in *response* to the editors of this book asking me to rework this chapter by 'performing a reflexive analysis of [my] own reflexivity and *explicating* the value of that for managers in general' (Mike Chumer, my emphasis) so that '[my] own narrative become[s] more grounded or brought together more' (Craig Prichard, email, 9 August 1999). I re-present my subsequent reflexive dialogue with my Other as an implicit parallel dialogue of co-response-ability with these two editors and with imagined manager-readers:

I/i: Am I a better person by virtue of making my tacit knowing *explicit*?

Me/me: NOT!

I/i: Would I become a better manager once I was able to articulate [read *explicit* and *abstract*!] the distinctions between goods-services, service-services, service-knowledge and indeed my whole binary grid?

Me/me: It depends. I think tacit knowing and intuitive judgement performed the functional work that made up my dialogical encounters and transactions as a service operations manager. But ah, *dys*functional work, that's another story: my tacit agonized knowing of the gendering of knowledge and the commodification of knowledge in the university, ill equipped me for initiating my rival discourse of response-ability-Value and relationship-Value to the dominant discourses of use-value, exchange-value, patriarchy and capitalism. I was ill equipped to make judgements about the comparative Value of staying with my management job or fleeing.

I/i: Would I have got to take the 40-yard walk across the courtyard from my service worker job to my knowledge worker job if I hadn't got on to the knack of translating my tacit knowing into representational abstractions (a.k.a. PhD thesis)?

Me/me: Not a chance! Do you detect the irony that *after* I signified as a knowledge worker and professor, the now Director of Student Services but formerly Chair of Business Administration, asked to read my autobiographically based PhD thesis on the university as a service organisation?

I/i: Am I a better teacher and researcher because I have developed a knack for making my own tacit knowing explicit and for encouraging others to articulate what they know?

Me/me: A definite maybe! The 'better' is not because I recognise knowledge work as 'organised information in people's head' (Webb, 1998, p. 2) or know how to organise information in my own head. The site of organising is much more bodily distributed. The 'better' is coming to know and honour the tacit knower as knower. I appreciate that the tacit ways of knowing of managers, practitioners, service workers, and research participants entail embodied, sensory, response-able, relational, experiential knowing; and that tacit knowing gives rise to those imaginative stretches including linguistic stretches that serve to destabilize knowledge that is commodified, gendered, static, representational, abstract, and explicit (see Chia and Morgan, 1996).

I/i: Do you think the autobiographical *resemblance* between my teacher self, my researcher self, and my manager self, service workers all, might qualify for Chia and Morgan's (1996) understanding of pre-Enlightenment Renaissance knowledge and understanding of management 'in the wider sense as the *management of life*' (p. 59)? Do you think that autobiography and reflexivity might be reconceptualized as explicit representational knowing that signifies tacit knowing iconically? Chia and Morgan cite Lash (1990, p. 194): '"Images or other figures which signify iconically do so through their *resemblance* to the referent", emphasis added' (p. 53).

You/an-Other: Yes   ❏

No   ❏

Maybe   ❏

Other   ❏ _____ (respond to dlander@stfx.ca)

My positioning with the feminist dialogic of relationship-value and response-ability-value can engage with the feminist analytic of human capital theory and exchange-value (e.g. Donovan, 1991; Hart, 1992; Mies, 1998); this is walking in the place-between-2-worlds. Reconstituting the value of service work and knowledge work as co-response-ability and 'knowing second persons' (Code, 1991) rescues Value from the capitalist equation of 'Knowledge = Value' (K = V) (Curry, 1997, p. 8), where Value is exchange-Value.

Re-Pairing Knowledge and Service: a Performance of Contradictory Knowing

> She [Lily] knows that it is possible to love everyone the most. Even if she can't help loving Frances most of all (Ann-Marie MacDonald, *Fall On Your Knees*, 1997, p. 302).

To re-pair knowledge-as-service with knowledge-as-services is to leverage the 'contradictory knowing' (Davies, 1992; Davies and Harré, 1999) involved in the feminist dialogic of knowing an-Other as other, and knowing an-Other as knower. It involves re-pairing partiality and impartiality in the workplace, by coming to know 'that it is possible to love everyone the most' *and* to love the One Other 'most of all'. I read Ann-Marie MacDonald's novel in the midst of writing this chapter. As I was pruning the caragana tree in our front yard and remembering this story of three generations in a Cape Breton, Nova Scotia, family, I experienced yet another 'epiphany of the ordinary'. My Moment emerged from engaging in dialogue between this text and my working autobiography, as I pruned away. I had been waiting for the other shoe to drop, for epigrammatic closure. This contradictory way of knowing challenges the traditional paired shoes and collapses the steel-toed service boot and the tasseled knowledge loafer into multicoloured footwear whose wearer can make contradictory truth claims and other-wise choose all manner of contradictory paths and discourses.

Contradiction abounds in *instituted* cultural pairedness, and in language, as Derrida's (1987) insight bears witness, 'You don't say a pair of feet. You say a pair of shoes' (p. 264). The imaginary of my contradictory working autobiography includes the contradictory 'fact' that I get/got to wear knowledge loafers in both my management position and my teacher-researcher position. Yet I stand, walk and take my identity from service boots in the sense that as a service operations manager, I, like front-line service workers, walked in unclean, unsafe places.

I turn to feminist social theory and moral philosophy for scholarly commentary on partiality-impartiality contradictions involved in decision-making that involves the Other (Code, 1991; Blum, 1994). David Blum calls on Iris Murdoch's concept of 'loving attention' to assert that 'the moral task is not to generate action based on universal and impartial principles but to attend and respond to particular persons' (p. 13). I wonder if these philosophers could hold on firmly to the love and friendship model in managing a contract with the universal worker or the universal customer. Rose, who was the manager of catering and cleaning in the UK hall of residence that was the site of my doctoral study, offers eloquent testimony to the contradictory knowing that service work entails. Rose's response to a first year student's/customer's lament that there were 'no stodgy puddings' on his first day in hall, which he was 'used to' from home, articulates the contradictions of service and services, partiality and impartiality, public and private spheres:

> But equally there's somebody else who sits on the other side of the table and says, 'I can't eat stodgy puddings. I can't eat...'. ...Remember, I think we have to, it's always in a way, a compromise situation.... We would never please everybody because everybody's got their own, they, they all come from their own home environment where things are often different. But we've got to please as many people as possible.

In my reading of this passage, I identify with Rose. How intuitively (and tacitly) she draws Jerome, her student addressee, into the dialogue on the partiality–impartiality dilemma with her imperative, 'Remember, I think *we* have to...'. How often had I given virtually the same 'for the greater-good' response to board students in my Canadian situation! My own experience became explicit author-ity in asserting in my PhD thesis that 'we' service operations managers and service workers 'tend to the bureaucratic discourse of equality and impartiality when called upon to make public pronouncements, but in service practice,... [we] commonly extend unequal, partial treatment' (Lander, 1997, p. 259). What is this but the explicating of tacit contradictory knowing?

I am taking the position that contradictory knowing is moral knowing that demands that we walk and perform in unpaired, multicoloured footwear in order to re-pair the 'sole pattern', while still managing to keep our changes in footing on common ground. Relationship skills and communication skills of service work dominated numerically by women demand multi-skilling. Poynton (1993) reminds us 'Forget about acknowledgement of multi-skilling – the first step is to... gain acknowledgement for [women's skills] as *skills* rather than as personal attributes' (p. 86). Contradictory knowing involves changes in footing and authentic resistance when the contradictions do not neatly lace up and conflate on the left–right boundaries.

I hold critical autobiography and critical reflexivity response-able for my other shoe dropping. Moving my tacit knowing of contradictory knowing towards explicit, representational abstraction is a work-in-process. Let me both begin and close by performing reflexivity and contradictory knowing as a walking trajectory in between 2-worlds and 2-times, by responding on the eve of the millennium to 19th century capitalist analysis of the distribution of labour. The feminist dialogic extends co-response-ability to dead white European male theorists in the reflexive process of 'turn[ing] the past upon itself and alter[ing] the present in its light' (Bruner, 1990, p. 109).

Karl and Frederick (1845):

> As soon as the distribution of labour comes into being, each man [*sic*] has a particular, exclusive sphere of activity, which is forced upon him [*sic*] and from which he [*sic*] cannot escape. He [*sic*] is a hunter, a fisherman, a shepherd, or a critical critic and must remain so... [in contrast to an unalienated society after the revolution, where it would be] possible for me to do one thing today and another tomorrow, to hunt in the morning, fish in the afternoon, rear cattle in the evening, criticise after dinner... without ever becoming hunter, fisherman, shepherd or critic (Karl Marx and Frederick Engels, *The German Ideology*, 1970, p. 53).

I/i/Me/me (1999):

> *Au contraire*, it is possible for me, I, she [*sic*] right now to do service work and knowledge work today, tomorrow, and everyday; to clean and cook, hunt and fish, teach and write, research and criticise response-ably in generously loving relations in the morning, noon and night time too... without ever stepping into the shoes of my Other, which is impossible anyway. I step into my knowledge-able and service-able re-paired shoes; I walk in the re-paired and re[as]sembled shoes of my Other knowing I have become my Other. I don't want to seem ungrateful, for indeed you men have also tapped my tacit knowing: Yes, 'escaping' the gendering and commodifying of knowledge in the 'exclusivity' of public

and private spheres will take some enormously powerful, co-response-able flexing. Dankeschön, meine Herren for inadvertently explicating the intertwined signifying chains of capitalism and patriarchy. How about rethinking 'dialectic' as the co-response-able Value of the feminist dialogic brought to bear in overthrowing hierarchies, finding meaning elsewhere, and destabilizing these entrenched signifiers of knowledge work?

I/i–You/you–An-Other (2000+):   ...

References

Acker, J. (1990) 'Hierarchies, Jobs, Bodies: A Theory of Gendered Organisations', *Gender and Society*, 4: 2 (June), 139–58.

Ashmore, M. (1989) *The Reflexive Thesis: Wrighting Sociology of Scientific Knowledge*, Chicago: University of Chicago Press.

Bakhtin, M. M. (1981) *The Dialogical Imagination*, Austin: University of Texas Press.

Bakhtin, M. M. (1986) *Speech Genres & Other Late Essays*, Austin: University of Texas Press.

Bauer, D. M. and McKinstry, S. J. (eds.) (1991) *Feminism, Bakhtin, and the Dialogic*, New York: State University of New York Press.

Block, P. (1993) *Stewardship: Choosing Service over Self-Interest*, San Francisco: Berrett-Koehler.

Blum, L. (1994) *Moral Perception and Particularity*, Cambridge, MA; Cambridge University Press.

Boje, D. (1994) 'Organisational Storytelling: The Struggles of Pre-modern, Modern and Postmodern Organisational Learning Discourses', *Management Learning*, 25: 3, 433–61.

Bruner, J. (1990) *Acts of Meaning*, Cambridge, MA: Harvard University Press.

Butler, E. and Connole, H. (1992) 'Sitting Next to Nellie', In *What Future for Technical and Vocational Education?, International Conference Papers*, 2, Adelaide: NCVER.

Calás, M. and Smircich, L. (1993) 'Dangerous Liaisons: The "Feminine-in-Management" Meets "Globalisation"', *Business Horizons*, March, 71–81.

Calás, M. and Smircich, L. (1996) 'From "The Woman's" Point of View: Feminist Approaches to Organisation Studies', in S. R. Clegg, C. Hardy, and W. R. Nord (eds.), *Handbook of Organisation Studies*, London: Sage, pp. 218–58.

De Certeau, M. (1984) *The Practice of Everyday Life*, Berkeley, CA: University of California Press.

Chia, R. and Morgan, S. (1996) 'Educating the Philosopher-Manager: De-Signing the Times', *Management Learning*, 27: 1, 37–64.

Church, K. (1995) *Forbidden Narratives: Critical Autobiography as Social Science*, Toronto: Gordon & Breach.

Code, L. (1991) *What Can She Know? Feminist Theory and the Construction of Knowledge*, Ithaca, NY: Cornell University Press.

Curry, J. (1997) 'The Dialectic of Knowledge-in-Production: Value Creation in Late Capitalism and the Rise of Knowledge-Centered Production', *Electronic Journal of Sociology*, 2: 3. Available at: http://www.sociology.org/content/vol002.003/curry.html.

Czarniawska, B. (1997) *Narrating the Organization: Dramas of Institutional Identity*, Chicago, IL: University of Chicago Press.

Czarniawska, B. (1998) *A Narrative Approach to Organisation Studies*, Thousand Oaks, CA: Sage.

Davies, B. (1992) 'Women's Subjectivity and Feminist Stories', In C. Ellis and M. G. Flaherty (eds.), *Investigating Subjectivity: Research on Lived Experience*, Newbury Park, CA: Sage.

Davies, B. and Harré, R. (1990) 'Positioning: The Discursive Production of Selves', *Journal for The Theory of Social Behaviour*, 20, 43–63.

Davies, B. and Harré, R. (1999) 'Positioning and Personhood', In R. Harré and L. van Langenhove (eds.), *Positioning Theory*, Oxford: Blackwell, pp. 32–52.

Derrida, J. (1987) 'Restitutions', In *The Truth in Painting*, Chicago: University of Chicago Press, pp. 255–382.

Donovan, J. (1991) 'Style and Power', in D. M. Bauer and S. J. McKinstry (eds.), *Feminism, Bakhtin and the Dialogic*, New York: State University of New York Press, pp. 85–94.

Fletcher, J. (1994) 'Feminist Standpoint Research and Management Science', *Journal of Management Inquiry*, 3: 1 (March), 74–82.

Friedman, S. S. (1998) '"Beyond" Difference: Migratory Feminism in the Borderlands', in *Feminism and The Cultural Geographies of Encounter*, Princeton, NJ: Princeton University Press, pp. 67–104.

Game, A. (1994) '"Matter Out of Place": The Management of Academic Work', *Organisation*, 1: 1, 47–50.

Goffman, E. (1981) 'Footing', in *Forms of Talk*, Philadelphia: University of Pennsylvania Press, pp. 124–59.

Greenleaf, R. (1977) *Servant Leadership*, New York: Paulist Press.

Griffiths, M. (1994) 'Autobiography, Feminism and the Practice of Action Research', *Educational Action Research*, 2: 1, 71–82.

Hart, M. U. (1992) *Working and Educating for Life: Feminist and International Perspectives on Adult Education*, London: Routledge.

Hatch, M. J. (1996) 'The Role of the Researcher: an Analysis of Narrative Position in Organisation Theory', *Journal of Management Inquiry*, 5: 4, 359–74.

Hatch, M. J. (1997) *Organisation Theory: Modern, Symbolic, and Postmodern Perspectives*, Oxford: Oxford University Press.

Healy, C. (1999) Personal email correspondence, 4 March.

Holmer-Nadesan, M. (1996) 'Organisational Identity and Space of Action', *Organisation Studies*, 17: 1, 49–81.

Kanter, R. M. (1977) *Men and Women of the Corporation*, New York: Doubleday.

Lander, D. (1997) 'Telling Tales Out of School: Author-ising the University as a Service Organ-isation for First Year Students', *PhD Thesis*, University of Nottingham.

Lander, D. (in press). 'Can Martha Know? Can Mary Serve?', *Higher Education Perspectives*.

Lash, S. (1990) *The Sociology of Postmodernism*, London: Routledge.

MacDonald, A. M. (1997) *Fall on Your Knees*, Toronto: Vintage Canada.

Marx, K. and Engels, F. (1970) *The German Ideology*, New York: International Publishers.

Mies, M. (1986) *Patriarchy & Accumulation on a World Scale: Women in the International Division of Labour*, London: Zed Books.

Mills, C. W. (1959) *The Sociological Imagination*, London: Oxford University Press.

Morgan, G. (1994) 'How to Live with Contradiction', in *The Globe and Mail*, Toronto, 5 April. Available at: http://www.imaginiz.com/paradox.htm.

Neilsen, L. (1998) *Knowing her Place: Research Literacies and Feminist Occasions*, Great Tancook Island, NS: Backalong Books.

Olesen, V. (1998) 'Feminisms and Models of Qualitative Research', in N. K. Denzin and Y. S. Lincoln (eds.), *The Landscape of Qualitative Research: Theories and Issues*, Thousand Oaks, CA: Sage, pp. 300–32.

Orr, J. (1987) 'Narratives at Work: Story Telling as Cooperative Diagnostic Activity', *Field Service Manager*, 1: 1, 47–60.

Perkins, R. (1985) *International Kierkegaard Commentary: The Concept of Anxiety*, Macon, GA: Mercer University Press.

Poynton, C. (1993) 'Naming Women's Workplace Skills: Linguistics and Power', in B. Probert and B. W. Wilson (eds.), *Pink Collar Blues: Work, Gender & Technology*, Melbourne: Melbourne University Press, pp. 85–100.

Prichard, C. (1999) Personal email correspondence, 13 August.

Probert, B. (1999) 'Gender Workers and Gendered Work', in D. Boud and J. Garrick (eds.), *Understanding Learning at Work*, London: Routledge, pp. 98–116.

Readings, B. (1996) *The University in Ruins*, Cambridge, MA: Harvard University Press.

Richardson, L. (1994) 'Writing: a Method of Inquiry', in N. K. Denzin and Y. S. Lincoln (eds.), *Handbook of Qualitative Research*, Thousand Oaks, CA: Sage, pp. 516–29.

Shields, R. (1996) 'The Dialogical Challenge to Verstehen', *British Journal of Sociology*, 5. Available at: http://www.carleton.ca/~rshields.versdial.html.

Schuster, J. P. (1998) 'Servants, Egos, and Shoeshines: a World of Sacramental Possibility', in L. C. Spears (ed.), *Insights on Leadership: Service, Stewardship, Spirit, and Servant-Leadership*, New York: John Wiley & Sons, pp. 271–8.

Silverman, K. (1996) *The Threshold of the Visible World*, New York: Routledge.

Strauss, A. L. (1993) *Continual Permutations of Action*, New York: Aldine de Gruyter.

Van Maanen, J. (1995) 'Style as Theory', *Organisation Science*, 6, 133–43.

Webb, S. P. (1998) *Knowledge Management: Linchpin of Change: Some Practical Guidelines*, London: ASLIB.

Weick, K. E. (1995) *Sensemaking in Organizations*, Thousand Oaks, CA: Sage.

Weick, K. E. (1996) 'Speaking to Practice: The Scholarship of Integration', *Journal of Management Inquiry*, 5: 3, 251–8.

Wittgenstein, L. (1980) *Culture and Value*, Oxford, Blackwell.

Yeatman, A. (1994) *Postmodern Revisionings of the Political*, New York: Routledge.

Zeithmal, V. A., Parasuraman, A., and Berry, L. L. (1990) *Delivering Quality Service: Balancing Customer Perceptions and Expectations*, New York: Free Press.

10 Knowledge Workers 'R' Us: Academics, Practitioners, and 'Specific Intellectuals'

Deborah Jones

But what is new? There are no new objects so to speak; rather there are new relation-ships that one can draw from things, from the way people relate to one another, the ways things communicate among themselves and the way language reflects back on itself even when it is used to point to a reality outside itself (Trinh, 1994, p. 9).

Introduction

Work with knowledge is not new, and it is not new to think of this work as commodified in various ways, as a knowledge business. I take the new discourses of knowledge work as an opportunity to re-think who 'we' are, the critics of knowledge work. If language inevitably 'reflects back on itself even when it is used to point to a reality outside itself' (Trinh, 1994, p. 9), the language of knowledge work points back in a quite specific way to academics, to those who traditionally have knowledge as their business. This new discourse of knowledge work arises at a time when the traditional hold of academics on the knowledge business is being challenged, in western countries like my own, by broader discursive shifts showing up as, for instance, a new contestability in funding for research and teaching where the prior claims of universities are no longer quite as certain. The debates about who should have authority in the knowledge business tend to be organised by traditional binaries, by attempts to draw lines in the sand between academics and their others: managers, practitioners and technocrats.

In this chapter I aim to contribute to a 'critical analysis [of] the theoretical issues and empirical problems of learning, knowledge and work', in the words of the proposal for this book, by scrutinising the terms of these organising boundaries, and the distinctions they create between identity categories such as 'academics', 'knowledge workers', 'practitioners', 'managers' and 'intellectuals'. This is what feminist philosopher Judith Butler calls a 'denaturalizing critique' (Butler, 1990) – a strategy of interrupting assumptions about natural (-ized) identities, in order to open up possibilities for change. 'Only from a self-consciously denaturalized position can we see how that appearance of natural-ness has been constituted' (Butler, 1990, p. 110).

158

I take a reflexive approach to critical academic writing about knowledge work, considering the ways in which knowledge is our business, that 'knowledge workers "R" us', to consider the proposition that 'knowledge workers "R" us' has the effect of turning our critical scrutiny to our own practices of knowledge creation, knowledge commodification and knowledge diffusion. My starting point is Michel Foucault's notion of the 'specific intellectual' (Foucault, 1980).

Foucault's Notion of the 'Specific Intellectual'

Foucault emphasises that specific intellectuals operate 'at the precise points where their own conditions of life and work situate them' (Foucault, 1980, p. 126). My specific starting point was fieldwork research carried out with Equal Employment Opportunities (EEO) practitioners in the New Zealand Public service. I was dealing with two central issues. First, I was curious about what a feminist post-structuralist approach could offer these practitioners who wanted to change the organisations they worked in. How can we frame organisational intervention after post-structuralism – that is, the capacity 'to think and act within an uncertain framework... in a time marked by the dissolution of authoritative foundations of knowledge', as Patti Lather puts it (Lather, 1991, p. 13)?

Secondly, I shared with them a feminist agenda – that is, we shared a commitment to changing organisations *for women* and for minorities. I invite readers to put this question of relationships with the 'objects' of study at centre stage. For me, the shared commitment – no matter how problematic in various political terms – blurred the boundaries between our identities as academic and practitioners. It also exacerbated the distinction at times – especially early on, when several practitioners were afraid that I would repeat earlier feminist critiques which made them wrong (they felt) for their contamination by the forces of bureaucracy. Reflexive fieldwork strategies offer important opportunities to problematise knowledge production. They give us the chance – even force us – to re-think 'them/us'. Questions that this fieldwork raised for me were: in what ways are we (my subjects and I) involved in the same kinds of work? How can we theorise what it is that we are doing?

In *Truth and Power*, Foucault (1980) argued that a new kind of relationship between theory and practice is embodied in a new kind of 'specific' intellectual. Unlike the previous type of 'universal' intellectual, this subject does not work in the realm of the 'just-and-true-for-all', but 'within specific sectors, at the precise points where their own conditions of life and work situate them' (Foucault, 1980, p. 126). Foucault sees them as types of specialised experts, who have, 'willy-nilly', political responsibilities – that is, authoritative knowledge has political effects. This way of looking at specific intellectuals is inseparable from Foucault's concept of 'governmentality', and the kinds of expertise that regnerate and sustain it.

Specific intellectuals work in specific institutions, where 'truth is linked in a circular relations with systems of power which produce and sustain it, and to effects of power which it induces and which extend it'. Their job as critics, then, is 'ascertaining the possibility of constituting a new politics of truth' (Foucault, 1980, p. 133). In setting out the task of the specific intellectual, Foucault explicitly rejects the project of thinking in terms of 'what's in [people's] heads' (i.e. 'consciousness') and turns our attention instead to 'the political, economic institutional regime of the production of truth' (Foucault, 1980). Foucault's interest is in the discursive rules that make it possible for the position that 'can and must' be occupied by the subject of a given statement (Foucault, 1972, pp. 95–6), that is, in regimes of truth. This discursive positioning generates both complicity and agency – if you are the subject of a specific discourse, you are inseparable from it, and at the same time are enabled to take certain kinds of action.

Foucault rejects the split between the externally situated intellectual and the internally situated practitioner. There is no defensible boundary between intellectuals as free subjects and intellectuals as practitioners – defined as 'competent instances in the service of the state or capital' (Foucault, 1980, p. 127). The specific intellectual is not invalidated ethically or politically by complicity in institutional power/knowledge regimes, but rather becomes politically important *through* her complicity. Whether or not we claim that Foucault's specific intellectual is a premature attempt on his part to conceptualise emerging practices of knowledge work, the concept works as a way to think about possibilities for critical engagement with knowledge work practices. What Foucault's notion of the specific intellectual does is to pull the rug out from underneath the 'just-and-true-for-all' intellectual; to problematise the academic/practitioner relationship in new ways; to rewrite the identity of the intellectual as that of a certain kind of practitioner; and to rewrite the identity of the practitioner as that of a certain kind of intellectual. The notion of the specific intellectual draws together a range of challenging questions about academics and practitioners as knowledge workers.

To return to my fieldwork situation: the EEO practitioners and I could *all* be seen as politically engaged specific intellectuals, 'at the precise points where [our] own conditions of life and work situate [us]' (Foucault, 1980, p. 126). The distinction between intellectual and practitioner is erased within a broader frame where the key distinction becomes the explicitly politicised engagement – or refusal to engage – with 'constituting a new politics of truth' (Foucault, 1980, p. 133). To take an example that has broad resonances for knowledge work: EEO practitioners were actively engaged with contesting the terms by which merit was accorded to certain types of work rather than others, both in terms of individual promotion criteria and, more broadly, in terms of occupational segregation. They drew attention to the *political* effects of these terms. This, to me, is work at the level of 'the political, economic institutional regime of the production of truth' (Foucault, 1980).

Critical Management Academics As Specific Intellectuals

My title, 'Knowledge Workers "R" Us', refers in various ways to changing discourses of knowledge and of public service. Discourses of the market and of managerialism increasingly permeate the work not only of academics, but of a number of professional groups in publicly owned enterprises (Kelsey, 1993, 1997; Peters, 1997). In New Zealand, changes in funding structures have increasingly put academics in new relation to other researchers or knowledge workers outside the universities, who are also competing for government research funding. The tension of this relationship has been cranked up by government policies which attempt to address the perceived needs of a developing knowledge economy. In these new scenarios, knowledge starts to be more and more explicitly identified with work in science and technologies. 'End users' of research are predetermined and must be shown to be satisfied. Students are reconfigured as customers, and private providers compete with universities to meet their requirements. New forms of commodifying knowledge objects marginalise academics who are not identified with new discourse of knowledge work. Two possible – and currently occurring – responses from academics are to (a) seek to define their projects within the new discourses of knowledge work and/or (b) seek to identify and to defend what it is that makes academics different from other knowledge workers. In New Zealand the latter project currently centres around the notion of academic freedom, and of the role of universities, currently written in the legislation, 'as critic and conscience of society' (Education Amendment Act, 1990, 161: 4(a)v). This debate tends to centre around versions of the academic as autonomous intellectual – that is, a 'just-and-true-for-all' intellectual who resists the commodification of the market and the contamination of managerialism.

As critical scholars of management and of organisations, we are in a particularly acute situation in relation to market and managerial discourses – a situation that we share in many key respects with our non-critical colleagues. Although we may come from a range of disciplinary backgrounds, our employment is usually focussed, more or less directly, around business schools and management education. We are at the very least in relationship with managers as students, frequently as research subjects, and sometimes as clients for consultancy or research projects. We are also staff in institutions that are run by managers, and may be at times ourselves directly involved in management work in our workplaces.

Management studies more generally involves a range of practices by which relationships between academics and managers are organised, by which academic and management knowledges are distinguished. Within this range, practices of Critical Management Studies (CMS) involve distinctive anxieties about collaboration (Fournier and Grey, 1988; Lilley, 1997).

The Foucauldian concept of the specific intellectual draws attention to ways that *both* academics and practitioners are complicit in aspects of governmentality, whether or not they have dirtied their hands through too-close association with managers, or through themselves taking on management practices. For Foucault, governmentality is the template of all modern organisational power, not just the operations that we think of as 'government' (Foucault, 1991a). As academics, critical or not, we are positioned as subjects within this field of power. For instance, Australian cultural studies academics have hotly debated the involvement of cultural studies academics in policy analysis and advice (Bennett, 1998). In these debates, parallel in many ways to debates within Critical Management Studies, academics have been concerned with issues of political purity and integrity, of getting involved in government processes and accusations of selling out. Bennett objects strongly to the 'antinomies of critical theory' which:

> splits the world into two – critical reason and practical reason – in a way which fore-closes on the possibility of there being mutually productive relationships between them, except, of course, for ones in which the former lords it over the latter (Bennett, 1998, p. 5).

Against these tendencies in critical theory, Bennett emphasises the importance of Foucauldian perspectives which have 'undercut and disabled' ways of thinking which put the intellectual 'outside' the site of critique. Rather than seeing the involvement of academics in government as contaminating the academic project, Bennett calls cultural studies and policy formation 'two branches of government, each of which is deeply involved in the management of culture' (Bennett, 1998, p. 6). He argues that we cannot as academics 'connect productively' with 'other branches of government' if we see ourselves as located in some kind of (ideally) 'uncontaminated realm of critique' (Bennett, 1998). Bennett calls for a 'productive international dialogue' on ways of thinking about the 'specific nature of the political, intellectual and administrative ground that has to be negotiated to produce useful points of connection' between the two 'branches' of governmentality (Bennett, 1998, pp. 7–8).

The 'specific nature' of any 'ground' of knowledge must be its articulation through specific bodies in specific times and locations.

The split between the mind and body is a hallmark of modernism. The body is 'the unspoken of Western abstract theory', assumed to exist on a biological plane which is 'transcended to free the mind for the intellectual pursuits of fully rational subjectivity' (Shildrick and Price, 1999, p. 2). In recent versions of this binary, the 'white-collar body' (Zuboff, 1998) of twentieth-century clerical work is being reconfigured as the knowledge-worker's body in which knowledge is 'embrained, encultured and encoded' (Blackler, 1995). The mind/body split thus returns as the problematic connection between the knowledge (mind), and the worker (body) in the discourse of knowledge management – that frustrating difficulty whereby the knowledge is (inconveniently) embrained in the worker, and there is a terrific tension between wanting to extract and own the knowledge while disposing at will of the worker.

Attention to exploitation and commodification in knowledge work is part of the bread and butter of a critical management studies approach drawn from post-Marxist and labour process discourses. Issues of ownership of labour products in the context of the employment relationship are salient. I argue, however, that a version of this same politicised mind/body split returns repeatedly in critical scholarship which separates and distances itself from practitioners – as Bennett puts it above (1998), scholarship which allows a place for what he calls 'practical reason' only as subject to 'critical reason'. There is a tacit collapse here of critique with high theory, and, often, of practitioners with agents of capitalism. Against this, I am advocating a lot more specificity about power relations in the contexts of our work relationships; an explicit focus on the tacit distinctions that we bring to our practices (even or especially where these diverge from our academic writing); and new ways of theorising theory/practice from a critical perspective.

The knowledge work literature reminds us that knowledge work consists of a series of productive organising practices, as well as particular knowledge products (Blackler, 1995; Cortada, 1998; Fisher and Fisher, 1997). In other words, practices such as managing the academic career, organising collaborative work, and selecting and excluding colleagues, are crucial *specific* aspects of our engagement in institutional power/knowledge regimes. In a reflexive piece for the first issue of *Organization*, Ann Game has emphasised how important it is to look in a very specific way at 'precisely how 'academic', 'intellectual', 'work' and 'organisation' are articulated with each other' (Game, 1994, p. 47). In a piece based on her own experience as Head of School, Game argues that in academic life the intellectual self is constituted so that its 'other' is 'organisation', whether in the form of personal or institutional practices. It seems that academics – including management academics – do not want to be involved in 'the infrastructure, the material conditions of academic work: that which underpins the system but must remain invisible to maintain the status and authority of the academic' (Game, 1994, p. 48). Like the delegation of housework to women, or of paperwork to secretaries, this work must meet the rarely articulated standards of academics, while preserving the boundaries between academics and their others. The explicit discussions of management in universities threaten this comfortable distinction. I can hardly see how, as practising academics, we can avoid having to think about organisation and academic work, and in terms which acknowledge our locations and interests inside it.

For the critical management academic, a political recoil from managers, both inside and outside the university, may converge with rewriting a traditionally privileged academic ownership of knowledge and its production. It is crucial to think quite specifically here about our locations in management or business schools, and the sites where we come into contact – or avoid coming into contact – with management practitioners. For us – compared with our academic colleagues in other disciplines – the perceived risk of contamination is especially strong, and may be explicitly resisted. The questions that arise for me here are:

do we as critical academics want to create change? If not, what do we see as critical about our work? If so, how do we see our scholarly practices as leading to change? Do we see themselves as practitioners in any context?

I have invoked a 'we' here in order to open up questions of differences *within* Critical Management Studies, rather than to assume identity. Feminist philosopher Lorraine Code critiques her own field in saying that: 'There are no problems, no politics of 'we-saying' visible here; this is an epistemology oblivious to its experiential and political specificity' (Code, 1996, p. 198). The turn to language in CMS – deconstructions of the management canon, the discourse analysis of published texts in various media – presents a kind of temptation to engage with 'regimes of truth' from a location somewhere in critical outer space. This 'obliviousness' is harder to maintain through the in-your-face relationships of fieldwork. Meanwhile the practices of CMS perpetuate a kind of totalising critical perspective which prefers not to pay much attention to whose authority is privileged – to differences of gender, ethnicity or geographies *within* the critical, for instance (Calás and Smircich, 1989; Sotirin and Tyrell, 1998).

Towards the end of her piece, Game proposes that her 'story' could 'just as well' have been about 'a theoretical text, a literary text, a shopping centre, a domestic space, a field of study, or a journal called *Organization*' (Game, 1994, p. 49). However, a 'story about my office', told by an academic, does something different from other kinds of story, in directly applying our attention to the material aspects of our knowledge work practices. Game talks in some precise ways about her positions as female/academic/Head of School in (characteristically feminist) ways that do justice to the complexities of their differences and their implicated power relations. Her analysis puts the writer – and so the reader – in a particular and *specific* relationship to 'the way people relate to one another, the ways things communicate among themselves and the way language reflects back on itself even when it is used to point to a reality outside itself' (Trinh, 1994, p. 9). To me, this is some of the work of specific intellectuals.

Expert Knowledges

'We "find" ourselves in the mirror image of the other' (McKinlay and Starkey, 1998, p. 238), and Game's piece proposes one version of the process as it plays out in academic discourses. What does it mean to be an academic now? What is the unique expertise that distinguishes us from other knowledge workers, that justifies taxpayer support for our particular forms of knowledge production and our particular products? The concept of the specific intellectual helps unsettle the distinction between academics and practitioners. The unproblematised distinction between academics and practitioners claims rationality and the mind for academics, and relegates desires and the body to practitioners. It is indefensible politically, because critical management studies cannot ignore the violence that is done by reinstating intellectual elitism and suppressing differences within; as well as theoretically, because the theoretical boundaries cannot be definitively drawn between intellectuals and others in the absence of foundationalist knowledge. As critical management academics we need to be re-working the discourses of academia so that we do not simply or even primarily bounce off managerialism. Academic anxieties focus around modernist notions of academic freedom as individual autonomy and/or as advocacy for others. I do not necessarily advocate the abandonment of the rhetoric of academic freedom, but I do advocate a closer look at how it might, for instance, indefensibly main-tain privilege, or take a disingenuous or morally elitist stance about knowledge, power and subjectivity. While traditional organisation scientists can attempt a defence on the grounds of science, upping the ante on an unproblematised expertise based on research, critical management scholars need to be reflexive of what our current practices are and how we might re-work our discursive resources to create new knowledge orders where 'new versions of the self are experienced and practiced' (McKinlay and Starkey, 1998, p. 238).

I have discussed above Foucault's proposition that discourses of governmentality and the power relations that they implicate, are constitutive of academic expertise as they are of practitioner expertise. In both cases power/knowledge are inseparable, and there is no 'just-and-true-for-all' intellectual who stands outside the contamination of the will to truth. Governmentality is closely associated with certain kinds of professional subjects – experts in the technologies of governmentality.

I propose another approach to the question of what we have to offer practitio-ners. I am inspired by Foucault's description of his work as '"propositions", "game openings" where those who might be interested are "invited to join in", rather than "dogmatic assertions"' (Foucault, 1991b, p. 74). I like his idea of 'philosophical fragments put to work in a historical field of problems' (Foucault, 1991b). 'Philosophy' – or rather 'philosophical activity', is defined as 'work which is critical of thought itself... Instead of legitimising that which we already know, it... consist[s] in finding out how and how far it might be possible to think differently' (Foucault, 1992, pp. 8–9). Our collaboration with practitioners might then be this kind of invitation to put our philosophies to work. I suggest that we could offer expertise in terms of carrying out inquiries, of interrogating the rela-tionships between action and reflection, 'philosophy' and the 'historical field of problems'. We are not identical in expertise or location with the practitioners that we teach and do research about. I see no future in striving to be upholders of bodies of theory which perpetuate canons of positive knowledge and is applied to practice. I can't see what basis we have for claiming to unmask truths unseen by others. This specific expertise resides in reflexivity, and in abilities to create relationships with practitioners which will generate experimental action. As I have explained, the 'reflexivity' I have in mind involves a sophisticated knowledge of relevant discursive contexts – which in this case include the management 'canon'. We are in effect teaching students to be certain kinds of knowledge workers, and our best contribution to them is the capacity to develop this reflexivity 'at the precise points where their own conditions of life and work situate them' (Foucault, 1980, p. 126) – in effect, to be specific intellectuals.

Re-thinking Practice

Specific intellectual work requires ways of re-thinking practical knowledges which trouble the boundaries between theory and practice. While Foucault renders the 'just-and-true-for-all' intellectual obsolete, the idea of the 'specific intellectual' does not totally conflate intellectual and practitioner. Care is needed here to avoid equating the idea of expertise only with governmentality, and both with the (same old) bad guys. In a carefully nuanced discussion of the Foucauldian notion of expertise, Australian cultural analyst Jeffrey Minson argues that the 'will to truth' is not 'irreducible to a vehicle for powerful interests to create a monopoly of domineering expertise' (Minson, 1997, p. 413). Nor is all expertise premised on a truth claim: 'it is possible to see the role of expert knowledges as *truce-oriented as well as truth-oriented...* based in the procedural and ethico-rhetorical skills of the troubleshooter, negotiator or umpire, rather than purporting to cloak itself in the mantle of positive scientific objectivity' (Minson, 1997, p. 412, my italics). Minson here argues that many organisational practitioners *do* already operate like this, with an expertise 'akin... to the calculating know-how of diplomacy' (Foucault, cited in Gordon, 1991, p. 14). What is interesting here is the possibility of thinking of a kind of 'expertise-in-action' as not *necessarily* generated by 'regimes of truth'. Minson suggests that Foucault's work on the ethics of the self provides a basis for thinking about an 'ethical persona' for the practitioner, and Townley (1995) makes similar suggestions in discussing Foucault's work on 'self-formation'. I flag these suggestions as resources for the further development of theorising practice and its knowledges within a critical framework.

There are also potential resources in the management literature, in the domains of 'reflective practice' and 'action research'. Donald Schon's 'reflection-in-action' is an epistemology conceived as a response to Taylorist management science, and to what Schon saw as a split between 'rigor or relevance'. He describes this split as embodied in the field of management such that in some cases 'representative of the two tendencies – the professors of management and the practitioners of case-method – no longer speak to one another' (Schon, 1987, p. 305). Schon's device of taxonimising 'the field of management' based on who speaks to each seems a fruitful one for looking at embodied management knowledge practices. Schon presents managers as both 'partners' in the new 'body of techniques' that constitute 'technical rationality', and also as 'sensitive to' and 'aware of' 'nonrational, intuitive' elements in management – that is, he sees possibility in the critical approach that practitioners often take towards the truths of organisation science' (Schon, 1987, pp. 304–5). Schon wants to create a 'dialogue' between 'the art of managing' and 'management science' (Schon, 1987, p. 306). Schon's 'knowing-in-practice' (Schon, 1987) is in some ways reminiscent of Minson's formulation of a type of expertise that is 'truce-oriented as well as truth-oriented... based in the procedural and ethico-rhetorical skills of the troubleshooter, negotiator or umpire, rather than purporting to cloak itself in the mantle of positive scientific objectivity' (Minson, 1997, p. 412). While it suggests the possibilities of being re-theorised as 'Foucauldian self-formation' practices (Townley, 1995), 'reflective practice' currently sits in an uncritical relationship with 'management science', its will to truth and its 'mantle of positive scientific objectivity' (Minson, 1997, p. 412). Schon's 'alternative epistemology of practice' (Schon, 1994, p. 244) is a 'constructionist' one, in that communities of practitioners are seen as continually involved in '[making] and [maintaining] their worlds matched to their professional knowledge and know-how' (Schon, 1994, p. 245). His epistemology is not critical, in that identity, agency, professionalism and its knowledges are not located politically. Schon's notion of 'dialogue' has the effect of reinforcing the theory/practice binary, and so lends itself to anti-intellectual appropriations, and the possibility of collapse into a kind of unacknowledged functionalism.

The experimental tone of Foucault's 'philosophy in a field of action' has strong resonances with some aspects of action learning (action research, action science). In the management context, techniques of action learning are deployed across a range of interpretive contexts, critical and otherwise (Marsick and O'Neil, 1999). An emphasis on ownership by practitioners, and on knowledge generated in specific sites of practice, is shared in the explicitly critical streams of the action learning literature. The privileged subjects of action research are 'those whose action constitutes the practice' and 'those affected by the practice' (Kemmis and Wilkinson 1998, p. 35).

The quality of the critique afforded by action learning practices lies largely in the kinds of truth claims they are framed by, their ontological and political consequences. Critical questions would focus on the ways that lines are drawn or contested between theory and practice, and the power effects of a given piece of research. For instance, are they seen as giving access to some kind of essentialised practitioner knowledges, where practitioners are not differentiated or located? How are participating groups such as 'users' or 'clients' defined?

For me the critical potential of 'action learning' is that this literature is concerned with practice, rather than with developing a body of theory that is prior, and then applied to, practice. That is, it opposes 'just-and-true-for-all' theory. Feminist theorist Judith Butler argues that 'theoretical presuppositions are articulated only in and through [political] action and become available only through a reflective posture made possible through that reflection in action' (Butler, 1995, p. 129). This argues for a kind of action-learning approach to 'work done at the limits of ourselves' (Foucault, 1984b, p. 46). It opens up for me the possibilities of using post-structuralist theory for collaborative work with practitioners which addresses ongoing change projects in an 'ironic spirit' (Riley, 1988). This requires the double movement, the ironic stance of being committed to action without being committed to a positive or foundationalist account of the reasons for that action.

The Price of Critical Authority

Foucault's power/knowledge nexus means that governmentality works by producing some subjects as authorities. His idea of a specific intellectual is someone positioned in a specific power/knowledge nexus, and therefore uniquely qualified and empowered to reflexively critique the nexus itself. Foucault tends not to talk about why certain specific intellectuals would have an interest in taking on a critical task, but lurking in all discussions of crucial scholarship is the question of what the basis of this interest would be. This question gets harder when we destabilise the idea that the intellectual speaks for others or for some grand narrative of justice or truth.

Feminist writers have been consistently concerned with this question of position and interest, recognising the hegemonic impetus of claims to represent 'women' (e.g. Riley, 1988), and the risk of naturalising a 'female' identity (e.g. Butler, 1990). I have therefore turned to feminist writers for ways to theorise a specific critical speaking position, and its relationship to its others. Feminist formulations of reflexivity are grounded in the body – the designated site of gender difference, the trash left behind when the mind has been split away and appropriated for intellectual work. This form of reflexivity involves recognising specific bodies in specific contexts as the sites where knowledge is created. This specific reflexivity does not mean writing the same old unproblematised, individual 'I' back into the text as its author: as Elsbeth Probyn acknowledges,

> we cannot pretend that [being reflexive] is an easy thing to do, that there is an unmediated innocence to the self. The possibility of the self rests within a filigree of institutional, material, discursive lines that either erase or can be used to enable spaces in which 'we' can be differently spoken (Probyn, 1993, p. 4).

This 'politics of "we-saying"' (Code, 1996, p. 198) involves specifying both identity and difference *in context*. Reflexivity is relational – it is not just about the self, but about the other. These are 'the necessarily double and urgent questions of feminism: not merely who am I? But who is the other woman?' (Gallop, cited in Probyn, 1993, p. 10). It is about the possibilities of critical communities, and about fronting up to differences and power relationships within these communities, and between these communities and their others. This question of community must be historicised and critically located: for instance how is Critical Management Studies currently embodied? Does it consist of, as Fournier and Grey (1988) indicate, what Probyn describes as 'middle-aged tenured university professors, dressed in black leather jackets, cut loose from an idea of the 'public' or 'organic' intellectual, desperately going through their personal crises of lost authority' (Probyn, 1993, p. 10)? Or perhaps they are wearing ties (with feigned reluctance) and teaching post-modern strategy to CEOs? Or do they occupy both positions? I slip into 'they' here from 'we' – as a woman located in the post-colonial antipodes – is Critical Management Studies also located here? (Craig Prichard carries out a similar inquiry, in the next chapter, when he asks how knowledge workers are popularly embodied).

My interest, in this chapter, is to create possible positions from which to critique knowledge work. At the beginning of the chapter I quote Trinh Minh Ha's assertion that 'there are no new objects so to speak; rather there are new relationships that one can draw from things...' (Trinh, 1994, p. 9). Meaghan Morris argues that the point for feminist scholars must be 'to argue how and why a particular event of rewriting might matter' in feminist terms (Morris, 1988, p. 5). This rewriting process means using 'strategies of reference', to rewrite existing texts in producing a new speaking position in a 'particular polit-ical, critical and publishing context' (Morris, 1988, p. 6). This exercise is not 'a matter of inventing a 'personal voice' for 'me', but of 'developing enunciative strategies within the existing discourses' (Morris, 1988, p. 7). What has mattered to feminists is to create a theory of the embodied self which opens up new ways for women to speak as intellectuals, to reflect usefully on our own experiences and create versions of authority which are alert to the political implications of authority in a given context. At the same time, feminist writers are concerned with questions of exclusion and complicity, with whether or not, by positioning oneself in a specific discourse, an author takes up practices which marginalise others. Jana Sawicki asks:

> What is the price of the authority that we do attain?
> How is it constituted?
> To what extent does it require identifying ourselves with capitalist or patriarchal forces? Does it reproduce and legitimise patriarchal discourses and practices?
> Does it suppress other voices? (Sawicki, 1991, p. 107).

How do these questions look in the context of Critical Management Studies? *These interrogations are only intelligible in a community of subjects to the extent that there is a commitment to change power relations, and that this commitment recognises that de-centring authority of various kinds is crucial to this change.*

Looking Critically at Others as Knowledge Workers

Back to fieldwork as a 'useful point of connection' (Bennett, 1998, pp. 7–8).

The processes of mirroring – and the processes of othering that go with it – crys-tallised for me in my fieldwork with EEO practitioners, as I came to see that they and I were all complicit in discourses of equality that I had previously seen myself as exterior to (i.e. more radical). I saw a different other in the mirror when I worked soon after with an elite group of senior managers.

To take one example, the mirroring process showed up in my work to interpret accounts of the extremely long hours worked by senior managers in an information technology company. Rather infuriatingly, they articulated all the commitment and intrinsic motivation of empowered textbook knowledge workers. For instance:

> I enjoy the job I'm doing. I enjoy the environment. Ah job satisfaction is absolutely vital. I work because I enjoy it and... you know if I won Lotto I'd still come to work. Because fundamentally the job I do really suits my skills.

The same manager commented that she had worked every weekend so far that year. Another example:

> The commitment to the company and to the people in the company I think is very strong and if you come here on the weekend, like it's a normal work day... it is concerning because they're giving up their private life... I think it's a personal thing, because you manage your own job... it's like a drug. I mean I wake up some Saturday mornings and I'm thinking I'd better go to work, I've got so much to do. And you spend half of Saturday morning feeling guilty that you're actually at home.

How might a critical management academic interpret this kind of statement? From my critical colleagues, I got two kinds of interpretation:

1   They (the managers) are unknowingly brainwashed, disciplined (pick your theoretical stance) – in any event, in some way being exploited by the company, the discourses of empowerment, etc., or:

2   'It's alright for them' – they are privileged by being core workers in the globalised knowledge economy; they do not acknowledge how privileged they are by the dispossessed, etc.

In both these accounts these managers are critiqued from an exterior position which privileged the critical account over the account given by knowledge workers of their own desires. Either way, the managers are made wrong – either by being sucked in and therefore not *really* enjoying themselves, or by really enjoying themselves at the expense of others (for whom it is assumed they have no concern, and of whose position they have no valid analysis).

What if these statements were put in the mouths of academics, say, or artists or activists? Would spending long hours in the service of work they said they loved be seen in the same way? Many critical academics love their work and are committed to it; they work long hours with permeable boundaries between home and work, they have (relatively) secure jobs as university-employed academics. How many readers also work this way?

Of course, I am not being as disingenuous as to suggest that it doesn't matter who makes a certain statement, i.e. how a statement is embodied. In Foucauldian terms, the position of enunciation of any given discursive statement is inseparable from what it does politically. However, I do think it is important to inquire into the ways that we authorise ourselves to make critical interpretations, and the relationship between that authority and our reflexive accounts of our own contexts. What, if any, are the continuities between our interpretations of others' narratives of work practices and our own? There are many practices identified with knowledge work into which we might inquire reflexively. For instance, what could we learn about 'concertive control' from academic culture (Barker, 1993)?

There are inevitably continuities between our (tacit) assumptions about our own practices as knowledge workers and the ways that we frame knowledge work in our own scholarly practices. For instance, Roy Jacques argues that gendered assumptions about knowledge have 'blinkered' scholars in their assignment of types of work into the knowledge work category, so that work carried out by traditionally female occupational groups is less likely to be designated as knowledge work (Jacques, 1996b). Further, as Ann Game's account of organising in academia suggests, the organising practices of knowledge work are split off from knowledge work itself. This split is very familiar in the literature of women's unrecognised work, and reinforces the paradox that the 'relational activity' that is required to produce knowledge work is both necessary and largely invisible (Jacques, 1996b). I think it is of great interest that techniques for managing knowledge workers are ubiquitous in the managerial knowledge work literature, but that academics seem very uncomfortable and unskilled in explicitly addressing *in their own practice* issues of collaboration, group work, and the kinds of communicative and discursive competencies that these involve. Rather, difficulties with these issues circulate on the level of personal complaints. For me this situation reinforces Game's suggestion that intellectual identity is organised *against* the mess of the non-intellectual – where the interpersonal is relegated.

In looking critically at the work of practitioners, feminist writers have been skilful in invoking forms of reflexivity which *both* acknowledge the critical work done by practitioners themselves, *and* require a discursive reflexivity on the part of the scholar/researcher. For instance, here Anna Yeatman discusses the job of the policy analyst:

> The participant who wants to discursively contest policies as texts must come to understand how discursive practices operate, how they distribute power and constitute power, and how discursive interventions are possible. This will apply no less to *their own discursive practices*, including their own policy recommendations, as to those of others (Yeatman, 1990, p. 160, my italics).

Finding ways to 'understand how discursive practices operate' is an important element of the work of the specific intellectual, and work that we as critical management academics are well-placed to facilitate. If we want to be able to talk about 'how they distribute power and constitute power' in given specific contexts, and – more difficult – how discursive interventions are possible, I suggest that we will have to work collaboratively with practitioners to engage with the 'field' in critiquing 'our own discursive practices'.

Redefining 'Intellectuals'

In discussing the need to 'redefine intellectuals' in a post-modern public sphere, Douglas Kellner has protested that:

> One of the scandals of the past decades is that at the very moment when the economy, polity, society, and culture were undergoing momentous upheavals – on both the global and local level – many academic intellectuals took refuge in the most arcane theoretical discourse.... The responsibility of intellectuals today is to speak out in a language accessible to ordinary citizens (Kellner, undated).

While Kellner's call begs many questions – about communication, ordinariness, citizens, and so on – I believe his argument has force. My own experience is that post-structuralist theory, rather than functioning only as an arcane discourse, can be used and discussed in ways that make sense to non-academic practitioners. Attention to discourse, to communication and its constraints, is a familiar topic for practitioners. Looking at language also offers a useful basis for reflective practices, and bypasses the grandiose truth claims of organisation science. It is ironic that Foucauldian theory – which problematises the relationship between language and action, and shows how discourses are written onto specific bodies – has been appropriated to create a kind of flight from practice. The same theoretical resources could be drawn on to argue, as feminist Patti Lather does, that when grand narrative is dead, praxis is privileged, and reflexivity is a 'new canon' (Lather, 1991). Feminist writers have argued that it is only a critical reflexivity that allows for new epistemological positions, new subjectivities:

> My position is mine to the extent that 'I'... replay and resignify the theoretical possibilities that have constituted me, working the possibilities of their convergence, and trying to take account of the possibilities that they systematically exclude (Butler, 1995, p. 42).

Butler's replaying and resignifying depend on the possibilities of reflecting on discursive practice in action, in order to intentionally disrupt it. These are possibilities that could best be addressed, I suggest, through forms of action inquiry carried out through developing collaborations with practitioners which problematise identities, power relations, and knowledges, 'at the precise points where their own conditions of life and work situate them' (Foucault, 1980, p.

126). In this kind of inquiry into *our own* knowledge work practices we can draw on the methods developed in various forms of action learning to problematise praxis from inside as well as outside, and to create a 'productive... dialogue' on ways of thinking about the 'specific nature of the political, intellectual and administrative ground that has to be negotiated to produce useful points of connection' (Bennett, 1998, pp. 7–8) between specific practitioners and specific intellectuals.

Knowledge matters – and in this moment it matters in new ways. As academics, knowledge is our commodity, our product, our stock in trade. While academics throughout the West are protesting that we do not want our knowledges to be commodified like that of other knowledge workers – how do we say that we are different? How do we collaborate with other knowledge workers to confront new knowledge/power relationships? In this context, reflexivity, by some definitions, could become – is already – a form of harvesting tacit knowledge. 'Danger', in Foucault's terms, is all around, as 'the ethico-polit-ical choice we have to make every day... to determine which is the main danger' (Foucault, 1984a, p. 343). These choices constitute our teaching, writing and research practices, our embodiment as knowledge workers, and our modes of interaction with colleagues, students, co-researchers. They constitute how we organise ourselves in our current crises.

The idea of the 'specific intellectual' does useful things. It pushes us to locate ourselves and specify our discursive contexts. It draws attention to regimes of truth and ways of engaging with them from within. It is a reminder that there is no essential purity in academic work. It confronts us with the processes of exclusion that allow us to be defined as academics. It invites us to consider when and how we want to own or disown the designation of knowledge workers.

References

Barker, J. (1993) 'Tightening the Iron Cage: Concertive Control in Self-managing Teams', *Administrative Science Quarterly*, 38, 408–37.

Bennett, T. (1998) *Culture: A Reformer's Science*, Sydney: Allen & Unwin.

Blackler, F. (1995) 'Knowledge, Knowledge Work and Organisations: an Overview and Interpretation', *Organisation Studies*, 16: 6, 1021–46.

Butler, J. (1990) *Gender Trouble: Feminism and the Subversion of Identity*, London: Routledge.

Butler, J. (1995) 'Contingent Foundations', in S. Benhabib *et al.* (eds.), *Feminist Contentions: a Philosophical Exchange*, New York: Routledge, pp. 35–58.

Calás, M. and Smircich, L. (1992) 'Re-writing Gender Into Organisational Theorizing: Direc-tions From Feminist Perspectives', in M. Reed and M. Hughes (eds.), *Rethinking Organisa-tion: New Directions in Organisation Theory and Analysis*, London: Sage, pp. 227–53.

Code, L. (1996) 'Taking Subjectivity Into Account', in A. Garry and M. Pearsall (eds.), *Women, Knowledge and Reality: Explorations in Feminist Philosophy*, 2nd edn, New York: Routledge, pp. 191–221.

Cortada, J. (ed.) (1998) *Rise of the Knowledge Worker*, Boston: Butterworth-Heinemann.

Education Amendment Act (1990). Wellington: New Zealand Parliament.

Fisher, K. and Fisher, M. (1997) *The Distributed Mind: Achieving High Performance Through the Collective Intelligence of Knowledge Work Teams*, New York: AMACOM.

Foucault, M. (1972) *The Archaeology of Knowledge.* London: Routledge.

Foucault, M. (1980) 'Truth and Power' (interview), in C. Gordon (ed.), *Power/Knowledge: Selected Interviews and Other Writings 1972–1977 Michel Foucault*, New York: Pantheon, pp. 109–33.

Foucault, M. (1984a) 'On the Genealogy of Ethics: Overview of Work in Progress', in P. Rabinow (ed.), *The Foucault Reader*, New York: Pantheon Books, pp. 340–72.

Foucault, M. (1984b) 'What is Enlightenment?', in P. Rabinow (ed.), *The Foucault Reader*, New York: Pantheon Books, pp. 32–50.

Foucault, M. (1986) *The Care of the Self* (History of sexuality, Vol. 3), London: Penguin.

Foucault, M. (1988) 'Technologies of the Self', in L. Martin, H. Gutman, and P. Hutton (eds.), *Technologies of the Self: A Seminar with Michel Foucault*, Amhurst, MA: University of Massachusetts Press, pp. 16–49.

Foucault, M. (1991a) 'Governmentality', in G. Burchell *et al.* (eds.), *The Foucault Effect: Studies in Governmentality*, Harvester/Wheatsheaf, pp. 87–104).

Foucault, M. (1991b) 'Questions of Method', in G. Burchell *et al.* (eds.), *The Foucault Effect: Studies in Governmentality*, Harvester/Wheatsheaf, pp. 73–86.

Foucault, M. (1992) *The Use of Pleasure* (History of Sexuality, Vol. 2), London: Penguin.

Fournier. V. and Grey, C. (1998) 'At the Critical Moment: Conditions and Prospects for Critical Management Studies', paper presented to the *1998 International Labour Process Conference*, 7–9 April.

Game, A. (1994) '"Matter out of place": The management of academic work", *Organization*, 1: 1, 47–50.

Gordon, C. (1991) 'Government Rationality: An Introduction', in G. Burchell *et al.* (eds.), *The Foucault Effect: Studies in Governmentality*, Chicago: University of Chicago Press, pp. 1–51.

Jacques, R. (1996a) 'Manufacturing the Employee: Management Knowledge From the 19th to 21st Centuries', Thousand Oaks, CA: Sage Publications.

Jacques, R. (1996b) 'Hidden in Plain Sight: The Post-Industrial Knowledge Work "Subculture" and our (Pre)Industrial Blinders', *Proceedings of the Standing Conference on Organisational Symbolism (SCOS) Annual Conference 'Exploring the Post-Industrial Subculture'*, Los Angeles, July. Available at: http://www.anderson.ucla.edu/research/conferences/scos/abstract/jacques.htm.

Kellner, D. (undated) *Intellectuals and New Technologies.* Available at: http://www.gseis.ucla.edu/courses/ed253a/dk/int.htm.

Kelsey, J. (1993) *Rolling Back the State: Privatisation of Power in Aotearoa/New Zealand*, Wellington: Bridget Williams Books.

Kelsey, J. (1997) *The New Zealand Experiment: A World Model for Structural Adjustment?*, 2nd edn, Auckland: Auckland University Press/Bridget Williams Books.

Kemmis, S. and Wilkinson, M. (1998) 'Participatory action research and the study of practice', in B. Atweh, S. Kemmis and P. Weeks (eds.), *Action Research in Practice: Partnerships for Social Justice*, London: Routledge, pp. 21–36.

Lather, P. (1991) *Getting Smart: Feminist Research and Pedagogy With/in the Postmodern*, New York: Routledge.

Lilley, S. (1997) 'Stuck in the middle with you?', *British Journal of Management*, 8, 51–9.

Marsick, V. and O'Neil, J. (1999) 'The Many Faces of Action Learning', *Management Learning*, 30: 2, 159–76.

McKinlay, A. and Starkey, K. (1998) in A. McKinlay and K. Starkey (eds.), *Managing Foucault*, London: Sage, pp. 230–41.

Minson, J. P. (1997) 'What is an expert?', in C. O'Farrell (ed.), *Foucault: The Legacy*, Kelvin Grove, Queensland: Queensland University of Technology, pp. 406–17.

Morris, M. (1988) *The Pirate's Fiancee: Feminism Reading Postmodernism*, London: Verso.

Peters, M. (ed.) (1997) *Cultural Politics and the University in Aotearoa/New Zealand,*, Palmerston North: Dunmore Press.

Probyn, E. (1993) *Sexing the Self: Gendered Positions in Cultural Studies*, London: Routledge.

Riley, D. (1988) *Am I That Name?: Feminism and the Category of 'Women' in History*, London: Macmillan.

Sawicki, J. (1991) *Disciplining Foucault: Feminism, Power and the Body*, New York: Routledge.

Schon, D. (1987) 'The art of managing: reflection-in-action within an organisational learning system', in P. Rabinow and W. Sullivan (eds.), *Interpretive Social Science: A Second Look*, revised and updated, Berkeley, CA: University of California Press, pp. 304–26.

Schon, D. (1994) 'Teaching Artistry Through Reflection-in-action', in H. Tsoukas (ed.), *New Thinking in Organisational Behaviour*, Oxford: Butterworth-Heinemann, pp. 234–49.

Shildrick, M. and Price, J. (1999) 'Openings on the Body: A Critical Introduction', in J. Price and M. Shildrick (eds.), *Feminist Theory and the Body: A Reader*, Edinburgh: Edinburgh University Press, pp. 1–14.

Sotirin, P. and Tyrell, S. (1998) 'Wondering About Critical Management Studies: A Review and Commentary on Selected Texts', *Management Communication Quarterly*, 12: 2, 303–36.

Townley, B. (1995) '"Know Thyself": Self-awareness, Self-formation and Managing', *Organization*, 2: 2, 24–8.

Trinh, Minh-ha (1994) 'Strategies of Displacement for Women, Natives and Their Others: Intra-views with Trinh T. Minh-ha', *Women's Studies Journal*, 10: 1, 5–25.

Yeatman, A. (1990) *Bureaucrats, Femocrats, Technocrats: Essays on the Contemporary Australian State*, Sydney: Allen & Unwin.

Zuboff, S. (1998) 'The White-collar Body in History', in J. Cortada (ed.), *Rise of the Knowledge Worker*, Boston: Butterworth-Heinemann, pp. 199–219.

11 Know, Learn and Share! The Knowledge Phenomena and the Construction of a Consumptive-Communicative Body

Craig Prichard

In Shoshana Zuboff's book, *In the Age of the Smart Machine* (1988), the author traces relations between the embodiment of paid work and the rationalizing practices of 20th century management. She argues that during this century management science's practices of work study, re-composition and 'reprogramming' have radically altered the character of labour power. With computer technology this process is both extended and re-orientated. While demand for (principally men's) physical labour and embodied craft work has been destroyed, management's rationalizing processes have intensified and extended demand for communicative labour (see Chapter 8). In place of bodies which act directly on materials and machines, Zuboff identifies demand for bodies which share, learn and can manage the intricate relationship work needed to accomplish and extend intellective and analytical skills. Zuboff (1988, p. 401) argues that

> the demands of managing intricate relationships reintroduce the importance of the sentient body and so provide a counterpoint to the threat of hyperrationalism and impersonalisation that is posed by computer mediation.

One effect of this is to challenge traditional military-style bureaucratic management.

> In a traditional approach to work organisation, employees could be treated as objectively measurable bodies and in return, they could give of their labour without giving of their selves... but when work involves a collective effort to create and communicate meaning, the dynamics of human feeling cannot be relegated to the periphery of an organisation's concerns. How people feel about themselves, each other, and the organisation's purpose is closely linked to their capacity to maintain high levels of internal commitment and motivation that are demanded by the abstraction of work and the new division of learning (Zuboff, 1988, p. 401).

In the case studies reported in her book Zuboff offers a vivid picture of how workers and managers 'reached and stumbled' as they attempted to shift the logic of their relations to one 'governed by the necessities of learning and performance rather than rules of an older faith – rules that sort, rank and separate' (Zuboff, 1988). Zuboff's 'new division of learning' refers to a developing division in computerised, informated organisations where learning is repositioned as a core aspect of work, alongside and challenging of traditional divisions of labour between management, workers and professionals.

If, as Zuboff argues, learning has become a core aspect of work, then it might be expected that management science's interests would extend to 'social technologies' which attempt to manage learning, knowledge generation and knowledge transfer. This chapter critically addresses this broad field of 'technologies'. 'Knowledge management', for instance can be read as one aspect of such a field and might also include research and prescription around 'knowledge work' (Cortada, 1998), 'organisational learning' (Easterby-Smith, 1996; Crossan *et al.*, 1999;) and the economics of so-called 'knowledge economies' (OECD, 1996). Knowledge management, for instance, includes attempts to intensify the collection, classification, sharing and application of organisational knowledge either through computer-based technologies or more embodied conversational practices (O'Dell and Grayson, 1998; Leibowitz and Beckman, 1998). Such practices and prescriptions can be said to call on workers to refine and develop highly communicative embodied selves which are also emotionally literate, discursively flexible, interpersonally skilled, and instilled with a desire for lifelong learning.

Conceptually this chapter draws on both Marxian and Foucauldian resources. These are briefly outlined in the first section of the chapter. The developing discursive formation around knowledge and knowledge management is then mapped in the chapter's second section before the chapter turns to address links between 'knowledge management' and the work of philosopher Michael Polanyi (1969), whose distinction between tacit and explicit knowledge provides this formation with a key discursive 'pivot'. The chapter concludes by drawing on recent research in tertiary education (Prichard, forthcoming, in press) to explore how the reconstruction of this particular sector can be read as part of this much broader reconstruction of the conduct and the embodiment of work.

Bodily Knowing, Discursive Formations and 'Knowledge'

Labour, language and *power* are historically the three key themes of critical social science (Habermas, 1979). 'Labour' can be read, as in the case of Zuboff's work, as *embodied practices and embodied knowing*. Language can be understood as the texts and discursive practices through which we communicate and which are drawn from and can be said to form part of broad, *'discursive formations'* (Foucault, 1972). While power can be regarded as relations of domination or exploitation between subjects (be they individuals, or organisations, or states), it might also be read as a variably unstable and dispersed force/energy which has the effect of forming assemblages of practices (practices of seeing, of labour, of force and oppression). This is not to suggest that exploitation and domination are not prevalent and ongoing features of contemporary organisational life, nor is it to deny the very powerful way in which political economic analysis of the 'crisis' in the interactions between the forces and relations of production can aid our understanding. But it is to assume that power operates most efficiently and pervasively at a 'micro-level', that is, in the formation of practices and ways of knowing ourselves. Of course, for Marx it was the relations of production, not the forces of production, which distinguished the dominance of one mode of production or relations between different modes. While the current mode might be distinguished by its forms of technological production (petrochemical and computer chip-based technologies), the salient feature from this point of explanation, for both Marx and Foucault (in Foucault's terms), is the *relations of production:* the politics that surround the formation of knowledge-able labour, its access to and combination with these forces of production.

While Foucault recommended political economic argument as one way of explaining the transformation and dispersal of discursive formations (1977, 1991), what was important is *how* the formation works on and provides productive forms of self-knowledge and discipline. Writers influenced by Foucault's cartographies (1983, Deleuze, 1988, Knights and Willmott, 1989; McKinlay and Starkey, 1998; Butler, 1997) suggest that in the current era relations of exploitation and domination are less important than the power relations embedded in relations to oneself and one's body. Power relations work in the first instance to establish us as subjects with particular responsibilities for a body, a self, or as *individuals* with particular tastes, biographies and dispositions. Power in this view is the production and constitution of forms of embodied conduct and reflexivity through various knowledges (for example knowledges of management and organisation). In our relations with the world these work to focus, enhance, empower or enliven our responsibility for our 'selves', and thus in the process constrain or pattern our forms of conduct or dispositions. It is these knowledges and practices of enhanced self-responsibility, as Foucault argued (1977, 1983), which underpin relations of exploitation (our disassociation from the products of our labour), and domination (relations of violence and force). As a result the questions become: what 'new' forms of self and new ways of working on the body are put to work, and what power-knowledge practices are engaged in such production? Analysis based on such a questions might address, for instance, how the knowledges and practices of the so-called 'knowledge economy/society', intensify and constitute 'learning' or 'innovative' or 'creative' body-subjects.

Using these assumptions, the power-induced relations between labour and language can be said to live through the body, on its surface, in its depths, in what Burrell identifies as 'visceral morphological flows' (Burrell, 1996, p. 657). In relation to employment and particularly the highly interactive service and knowledge jobs of the current era, McDowell and Court (1994, p. 773) argue that

> power relations in the workplace are based not solely on bureaucratic domination from above but also through the manipulation of patterns of desire, fantasy, pleasure, and self image, in which gendered notions of appropriate behaviour and expressions of sexuality in this widest sense are important mechanisms in the establishment of particular norms of acceptable workplace behaviour.

'Knowledge's' Discursive Formation

Like McDowell (1997), I am concerned here with the way power works in the so-called 'knowledge-based economies' (Neef, 1997a,b) on bodies and attempts to (re)construct patterns of desire, pleasure and self-image. The term 'body' is used here to reference a conceptualisation of corporeality which links both the 'surface' features of physical performance and the 'depth' features of emotion, desire, anxiety (see Prichard (in press) for a fuller outline of this conceptualisation). Of course, this move to explore the embodiment of so-called 'knowledge economies' would need to include the family – particularly – and the school, as institutional sites where particular dispositions are variably recommended, prescribed, invested with desire and enacted. While below the focus will be on the workplace and tertiary education, these other institutional terrains are of equal salience.

In broad terms though it is clear that the 'knowledge era/economy' has as its target two key forms of conduct: an 'innovative' or 'creative' disposition, and the inculcation of a 'desire to share' (Moran, 1999; Dhawan, 1999). In order to address these forms of conduct I shall briefly outline what can be regarded as the key features of the discursive formation around 'knowledge'.

For Foucault, a 'discursive formation' is a group of statements, linked together by a whole range of discursive practices. These allow particular objects and subjects to be identified and articulated. More specifically, discursive practices delimit a field of objects, provide a legitimate perspective for the agent of knowledge, fix norms for the elaboration of concepts and more generally provide a 'play of prescriptions that designate its exclusions and choices' (Foucault, 1977, p. 199). To illustrate it is helpful to take a statement and draw out some of these points. The following is from Max Boisot's *Knowledge Assets, Securing Advantage in the Information Economy* (1998, p. 2).

> Promoted by the rapid spread of the information economy, we are only beginning to think of knowledge assets as economic goods in their own right.

The statement can be read as a microcosm of the discursive practices of the 'knowledge' formation. It assumes for instance the 'information economy' as an object and agent, i.e. something that 'spreads'. The 'information/knowledge economy', also known as the 'knowledge era', might be regarded as the meta-object/agent around which this formation 'orbits'. Most publications, authorities and practices reference this object/agent drawing on various authorities from different disciplines for veracity: from sociology (Bell, 1974; Castells, 1994), from economics (Machlup, 1982; OECD, 1996; Nelson and Winter, 1982; Nelson, 1996; Howitt, 1996; Chandler *et al.*, 1998) and from management (Drucker, 1988, 1993; Stewart, 1997; Nonaka and Takeuchi, 1995).

As Foucault outlined, discursive practices frequently assemble a number of diverse disciplines and sciences and 'regroup[s] many of their individual characteristics into a new and an occasionally unexpected unity' (Foucault, 1977, p. 200). For example, various statements from these disciplines mentioned are linked by the sets of the publishing, publicity and consultancy practices of governments, international policy authorities (OECD) and the management consultancy industry (the 'big four' global accountancy/consultancy firms are key players here). This industry, particularly, provides a raft of established relations, clients, databases and marketing practices which speed up and intensify the distribution of this formation.

The distinctive aspect of this 'age', 'era', 'economy', as Boisot's phrase suggests, is that the industrial economy of goods, is being replaced with the 'weightless', 'less tangible' but highly concentrated post-industry economy of knowledge. Here earlier work is drawn on. Fritz Machlup's categorisation (1980), for instance, asserts that the primary areas of such an economy are in education, communications media, information machines and information services. Extensions of this categorisation suggest a primary 'information market' and a secondary sector, usually industrial, where knowledge-intensive production is replacing capital or labour-intensive work. The OECD and DTI use a categorisation which slides from high-technology knowledge-based industries and knowledge-based services such as telecommunications, computer and information services, finance, insurance, through medium and low-technology industries (DTI, 1998).

The general point, though, is that such statements as that made by Boisot fail to discuss their own textuality as they work to establish the objects and subjects of discursive formation around 'knowledge' which they describe. If this form of analysis was addressed, then statements such as Boisot's would not be understood as emanating from and establishing a 'we' which is 'beginning to think of knowledge assets as economic goods in their own right', that is as emanating from thinking subjects, but critically, as providing *subject positions* through which a person may come to speak and act, in relation to and thus re-confirming the meta-object/s, i.e. the information economy.

Professor Boisot 'himself', meanwhile becomes identified as an authority and source of value in relation to the 'knowledge economy' for the consultancy industry, the academic discipline, the conference, the seminar and the publishing industry. These then reinforce a subject position which can speak on behalf of the formation's 'object' – e.g. the knowledge economy/era/society/age or 'knowledge assets'.

The Play of Prescriptions

In terms of the formation's 'play of prescriptions', the 'worker' and 'manager' and 'professional' are construed as knowledge workers and 'knowledge managers' whose desire should be to increase the depth, sharing and intensity of knowledge-ability in institutions. To achieve this information and communication technologies are frequently identified along with more mundane practices. Murray argues for instance that 'knowledge management is primarily a people and process issue and only partly a technology issue' (*Insurance Today*, 1999). Just to underline this, in a roundtable discussion on knowledge management published in the US computer trade paper *Information Week*, one chemical company executive claimed that:

> Until you can get *very comfortable sharing*, you have a real problem accelerating the creative process (Buckman in *Information Week*, 1999; emphasis added).

And his colleague in the greeting card company suggested that:

> There is an inherent tension between efficiency and innovation. Current organisations have been designed for efficiency. What we're looking for in the future is innovation (Bailsford in *Information Week*, 1999).

And this is not simply an issue for white collar workers. The British Government's Knowledge Economy white paper argued that 'success in the knowledge driven economy requires entrepreneurship from *everybody* in a position to innovate' (DTI, 1998, sect. 41.4; emphasis added).

> Important knowledge may reside as much in the deliveryman (sic) who takes the product to the customer as it does in the highest paid scientist in the organisation (DTI, 1998, sect. 5.3).

This raises, of course, the question of who benefits and how best to 'capture' and 'share' this knowledge. One approach to this latter problem of extracting knowledge from such 'communities of practice' is for researchers to study and codify innovation and knowledge-sharing practices. John Seely Brown, director of Xerox's Palo Alto Research Center, for example, outlines in a *Harvard Business Review* article (1996) on 'knowledge management' how Xerox, in what has become a much copied practice (Nardi and O'Day, 1999), employed anthropologists to 'harvest local innovation' (Seely Brown, 1996, p. 162) from its own office workers. They 'found' that

> *clerks were constantly improvising*, inventing new methods to deal with unexpected difficulties and to solve immediate problems.... These informal activities remain mostly invisible since they do not fall within the normal specified procedures that employees are expected to follow or managers are expected to see... such informal insights rarely spread beyond the local work group (Seely Brown, 1996, p. 163; emphasis added).

'Knowledge management' then involves 'harvesting' (from the female locale in this case), codifying and distributing these innovations in computer software and copying techniques to Xerox's clients. The key point is that it is the tacit knowing produced by improvising female bodies engaged in seeking some control over the conditions of their daily working lives which becomes the 'fruit' for Xerox's innovations in document management. The target is the tacit, momentary, process-based knowledge which may or may not be spoken about (that is rendered explicit) by those whom enact this knowing.

Meanwhile, alongside this modern-day work study programme, there is a 'play of prescriptions' which include combinations of computer based communications, data technologies and enhanced formal or informal gatherings (Davenport and Prusak, 1998; Liebowitz and Beckman, 1998; O'Dell and Grayson, 1998; Stamp, 1995; Allee, 1997; Willmott and Snowden, 1998; Willmott, 1998). Liebowitz and Beckman (1998), for instance, prescribe, a typology of practices: collecting, selecting, storing, sharing, applying, creating and selling knowledge with each stage demanding different processes and technologies. 'Identifying' might involve for instance the traditional training processes of 'skills assessment' and the filling of knowledge gaps with training activity. In this formation, however, such practices are recast as appropriate for 'learning officers' who might also be assigned the tasks of 'collecting' or acquiring knowledge to fill gaps in an organisation's knowledge domain.

Alongside these research programmes and consultant prescriptions, the formations might also be said to link to media and advertising campaigns particularly for the new 'products' of the knowledge era – computers and telecommunications. These frequently feature innovative, creative body-subjects. Microsoft's 'pianist' in its Office 2000 promotion (Figure 11.1), who is at the keyboard of a computer decked with candles and who hold one hand in the air in a musician's flourish, is a good example here. The image shows how the body is confirmed as the site where the demands of the knowledge economy – for innovative practice – are literally played out. It also indicates how these power relations are often identified with men. Of course there is an incongruity here in that the first two occupational groups identified in the advertisement's caption are those most associated with women.

The caption reads:

> Creativity belongs to artists and musicians... and typists and administrators and managers. The impact that Microsoft Office 2000 has on personal productivity is dramatic. By automating processes and providing seamless communications, you can now spend less time on head-down menial jobs and more on the lively, creative aspects of business.

Of course I am not assuming here that anthropologists at Xerox, or advertisers working for Microsoft, or knowledge management officers or the plethora of consultants and computer sales people involved in the selling of 'knowledge

Figure 11.1

work/management' are succeeding in enlivening and producing an innovative sharing, creative body-subject who will act as seed-head for the harvesting and distribution of lucrative tacit knowledge. Most research-based accounts of knowledge management highlight that the politics of knowledge and expertise continue to be sites of struggle in workplaces (see Chapters 5–7 and Huysman *et al.* (1999). I am suggesting, however, that the political activities engaged in the formation of knowledge-able labour are played out in numerous sites, and that these operate in and through our learned dispositions and forms of conduct demanded *of bodies*. It is the 'body' – its discursive practices, surface covering and affectivity – and how we learn through it which is a target, not just in training schemes, media promotions, new work practices and the competence-orientated pedagogical practices of tertiary education but also in the micro-practices of memos, demands for action and meetings. Rather than being discarded as unnecessary in a world of information and communication technologies, the body remains a crucial site for economic relations. Of course, this is not Marx's 'body' of industrial capitalism – a body subject to 'the uniform motion of the instruments of labour' which worked to form 'the peculiar composition of the body of working people' (from *Capital* in Elster, 1986, p. 161). I refer here rather to the body whose innovative performance, desire to share and tacit knowledge is the target and site of the political activity.

Inevitably though this 'body' presents as a problem for firms seeking for instance to retain valuable knowledge, and countries seeking to maintain stocks of human capital. In relation to this the traditional 'problems' of labour mobility, of hierarchy, of divisional structures, of professional group closure have been intensified. As the DTI notes:

> Where the employees in the company *embody* the firm's assets, new types of incentive structure are required to ensure they are motivated and retained.... Investment in skills also need to be supported by a culture in the workplace that allows knowledge, creativity and commitment of the workforce to be fully exploited (DTI, 1998, sect. 1.18; emphasis added).

Unsurprisingly it is the 'sharing' of valuable knowledge which is most frequently identified as the core problem to which knowledge management addresses itself. The official KPMG report of 'lessons learned' at the consultancy's Knowledge Management Conference in London in 1998 noted that most participants were concerned with turning

> Individual knowledge into organisational knowledge (by means of connecting them or have them share experiences to a database or stimulating their innovativeness) rather than finding creative ways of retaining their professionals (KPMG, 1999).

Knowledge management, the report says, 'embodies the dream that when one person learns something, everybody else in the company knows it' (KPMG, 1999). Yet, as KPMG's Daniel Andriessen argues (1998), this dream has meets the harsh lessons learned by workers during years of corporate downsizing. They are said to be simply unwilling to

> trust the company for which they work. They ask themselves: 'Why should I share my knowledge with the company and risk getting the axe once they have all I know?' Companies are faced with a seemingly insoluble problem: How to gain the trust of employees to share knowledge against an on-going background of downsizing and re-engineering programs. The situation becomes even more severe when there is a drive to use IT (e.g., Lotus Notes) to share knowledge. The problem with systems like these is that: everyone wants to get knowledge out, but nobody wants to put knowledge in (Andriessen, 1998).

These comments are echoed in a recent *Computer Weekly* column:

> Two options exist: manage the knowledge (it's an object), or manage the people with the knowledge (it's a process). IT prefers the former because it puts knowledge into databases and squirts it around networks. The latter approach accepts irritating realities, like the fact that employees are chary of yielding up their knowledge, as it's their own personal 'unique selling point/value proposition' (*Computer Weekly*, 1999).

It is perhaps little wonder then that prescriptions for 'sharing' or 'knowledge transfer' (Davenport and Prusak, 1998) prescribe 'talk' as the key site and method. '"Start talking and get to work" is better advice in an economy driven by knowledge', advise Davenport and Prusak (1998, p. 91). Of course, this can involve any number of formal and informal settings and practices: water cooler chat, debriefings, fairs, conferences and forums with direct face-to-face contact identified as the most effective.

It is tempting to suggest that if business people need to turn to a book on 'working knowledge' to discover that 'talk' is the key to sharing knowledge, and 'a major factor in the success of any knowledge transfer project is the common language of the participants' (Davenport and Prusak, 1998, p. 98), then a broad crisis in the relations of production, to take this form of analysis for a moment, is under way. But I want to suggest that the presence of such prescriptions, shrouded often as 'research', suggests that the formation is also at work *on the body*. The emphasis on physicality, on breaking down barriers, on speaking in a common language, on sharing through face-to-face communication, suggests an enhanced 'communicative body', which carries a desire to share, teach and learn, and forgets, or puts aside, its positioning as a commodity by individuating economic relations.

Putting the Body Back in – the Special Place of 'Tacit' Knowing

At the core of this emerging discursive formation around 'knowledge', however, is Michael Polanyi's treatment (1958, 1969) of the distinction between explicit and tacit knowing (Machlup, 1980, p. 45–6; Nonaka, 1996; Nonaka and Takeuchi, 1995; Davenport and Prusak, 1998; Boisot, 1998; DTI, 1998, sects. 5.6, 5.9). Polanyi's oft-quoted remark – 'we know more than we can say', is spread widely across this discursive surface and provides a crucial discursive pivot for the formation. While key aspects of his work are frequently left out of its reproduction in these works (for example his opposition to positivism and his broad phenomenological reflections on knowledge, the body and meaning) his work serves as a touchstone. Why?

Despite Polanyi's credentials as a scientist, his concern with the basis of scientific discovery and his anti-communism, it is, I would argue, *the functional and instrumental character of tacit knowledge*, as he describes it, and to a lesser extent the promise of revealing to the 'knower' the whole, the true and the real, which is the *most* seductive aspect of Polanyi's work for this discursive formation. Polanyi's understanding of 'knowing' is based on what he calls the *integration* performed by a person as embedded knowledge (*subsidiary* understanding) bears on a *focal object* (Polanyi, 1969, p. 182). It is this process of integration which turns us into 'knowers' who create meaningful knowledge. As Polanyi argues:

> Meaning arises either by integrating clues in our own body or by integrating clues outside, and all meaning known outside is due to our subsidiary treatment of explicit things as we treat our body. We may be said to interiorise these things *or to pour ourselves into them*. It is by dwelling in them that we make them mean something on which we focus our attention (Polanyi, 1969, p. 183; emphasis added)

In essence, knowing is a result of pouring ourselves into or folding the outside into ourselves – interiorising an outside. Given this, Polanyi argues that all knowledge, including mathematics and sciences, is *'either tacit or rooted in tacit knowledge'* (Polanyi, 1969, p. 195).

> The ideal of a strictly explicit knowledge is indeed self-contradictory. Deprived of their *tacit co-efficients*, all spoken words, all formulae, all maps and graphs are strictly mean-ingless (Polanyi, 1969, p. 195; emphasis added)

The discursive formation on 'knowledge' meanwhile takes aspects of this but ignores Polanyi's more general position. Nonaka (1996), co-author of the much referenced *The Knowledge-Creating Company* (Nonaka and Takeuchi, 1995), for instance suggests that

> tacit knowledge is highly personal. It is hard to formalise and, therefore, difficult to communicate to others. Or in the words of philosopher Michael Polanyi, 'We can know more than we can tell'. Tacit knowledge is also deeply rooted in action and an individual's commitment to a specific context (Nonaka, 1996, p. 28).

Having said that, Nonaka then goes on to identify four 'basic ways of creating knowledge in the organisation'. One involves the translation of tacit knowledge into explicit knowledge. While Polanyi's phenomenological musings might attract some to his framework, it is as a means of addressing the largely unspoken, action-based, situated and shared character of much knowledge (and possibly through this helps challenge simplistic and exploitative reading of 'knowledge management') which proves highly useful. At the same time, though, it is Polanyi's understanding of the body which is crucial to the inclu-sion of his framework in this formation.

Polanyi's body is, in all the experiments and practices he cites, a masculine, instrumental ideal. As Polanyi summarised: 'In all our transactions with the world around us, we use our body as our instrument', (Polanyi, 1969, p. 183). Polanyi's sense-giving and sense-reading body is found, in his texts, at work on experiments, reading, swimming, and learning to read X-ray and stereoscopic images of other bodies. The body at work is, in short the body of a masculine, 'knowledge-worker', who in the course of its egocentric marvelling at its own abilities, lacks a broader imagination of its positioning in social relations. Unlike for instance the philosophical treatments of meaning and knowledge in the social world presented by the critical theorists, or the radical relations of meaning to embodiment presented by the post-structuralists (Deleuze and Guattari, 1988; Kristeva, 1997), Polanyi's body is an idealised agent which performs instrumental actions and skills, and is thoroughly versed, although this is not explored, in the encultured knowledges of the professional/manage-rial middle class. The body of which Polanyi speaks (frequently his own) is the standardised body of 'man the knower' (Grene, 1969, p. xvi). This body, as Acker so clearly articulates, is understood as physically-able, disengaged from reproduction, emotionally under-control, lacking desire, and broadly isolated in its own performance (1990). While Polanyi's phenomenological challenge to positivism is clear, his 'experience' of his body, from which he tends to theorise, has a purity, a detachment and an idealised universalism. It is this which proves highly seductive for the discursive formation around 'knowledge'. It is this which helps to secure Polanyi's body of tacit knowing as the discursive pivot from which knowledge management is read.

Of course Spender (1998), Spender and Grant (1996) and others of a more critical persuasion (Tsoukas, 1996) regard 'tacit knowledge' as a polite and reasonably unproblematic label for what is a raft of forms of knowing, e.g. erotic, intuitive, spiritual, carnal and psychic. In the pluralist epistemology suggested by Spender these might be legitimate ways of knowing. The discursive formation itself tends, however, not to speak of these. In place of these, Polanyi's rational-instrumental body provides a sanitised and safe source of inspiration. While Polanyi's work provides a means of challenging a cognitivist epistemology, 'tacit' knowing is positioned as instrumental and broadly rationalist. In short, recourse to Polanyi's 'body' secures a sense of control, rationality and certainty to proceedings. To draw on 'tacit' knowledge is not to speak, as others have recently, of:

- an erotic body engaged in pedagogic or organisational work (McWilliams, 1996; Burrell, 1984)

- a seductive body of leadership (Calás and Smirich, 1992; Hearn and Parkin, 1995; Hearn *et al.*, 1992)

- homosocial desire embedded in a manager's body (Roper, 1996; Moss Kanter, 1977)

- or the oppressive seemingly unconscious body engaged in discrimination and harassment of women by men in non-traditional work (Collinson and Collinson, 1996; Cockburn 1991; McDowell, 1997).

'Tacit' knowing then is political, but political in a way Polanyi did not recognise. When he did explore the political character of 'tacit' knowing – in his critique of Stalinism in the context of the Cold War (Polanyi, 1958) – his position is so centred in his revulsion for the un-freedoms of the Soviet Bloc that it lacks, as the Frankfurt School critical theorists outlined, a critique of western indoctrination and privilege. Yet it is Polanyi's lack of a critical or critically self-reflexive position which has meant that his frameowrk has proved useful for the discursive formation around 'knowledge', the target of which is an instrumental, physically able, reproductively disengaged body. A critical reading, however, upsets this linkage. By challenging Polanyi's politically neutralised notion of interiorisation, and replacing it with an understanding of how power relations are interiorised in the micro-morphological flows of desire, perception and action, a critically engaged reading of the embodiment of a 'knowledge society' is possible. To illustrate this I now want to turn to a brief account of tertiary education in the current era.

Knowledge Business – Tertiary Education in the Knowledge Economy – a Case of 'Find a Knowledge Market, Suck It, Satisfy it and Move On?'

The above suggests, via a brief critical reading of Polanyi's work, the importance of the 'body' to relations of production or forms of power embedded in the so-called 'knowledge economy'. The body, but more precisely the structuring of its desires, the inscribing of its surfaces and its forms of practices, must be regarded as a key site for the encounter between forces and relations of production (Prichard, in press; Morse, 1994; Hetrick and Boje, 1992; Jackson and Carter, 1998). As noted, the discursive formation around 'knowledge' takes a keen interest in *learning* – identified as a desire to know, to share, to become innovative/creative.

> In the knowledge corporation, though, the push of training is converted into the pull of learning. Instead of waiting to be trained, its employees *seek out knowledge on their own*.... The focus of responsibility has shifted to being taught to wanting to share (Dhawan, 1999; emphasis added).

This same issue of course has become a core aspect of the reconstruction of pedagogical practice in formal sites of 'learning'. The discursive formation around 'knowledge' locates these sites as central to the extension of the 'knowledge economy/society'. International policy advice, 'guru'-style management publications and the education research literature have begun to re-position post-compulsory education as a core site in the emergence of the 'knowledge economy' (Bayliss and Vandevelde 1996; David, 1997; DTI, 1998; Eisenstadt and Vincent, 1998; Hamel and Prahalad, 1996; Organisation for Economic Co-operation and Development, 1997; Robertson, 1998; Stewart, 1997; Machlup, 1980; Slaughter and Leslie, 1997). Universities, for example, become the incubators of the digital age (Aley, 1997) as students and educators become knowledge workers or knowledge capitalists while the interests of corporations and universities converge (Gibbons *et al.*, 1994) to produce a mutually supporting 'knowledge infrastructure' (Etzkowitz and Leydesdorff, 1997). As the sociologist Manuel Castells observes:

> If knowledge is the electricity of the new informational-international economy, then the institutions of higher education are the power sources on which the new development process must rely (Castells, 1994, p. 16).

Knowledge, however, is broadly reconstructed. From a complicated set of reading and writing practices and relations between student and teacher, it tends to be construed as a commodified good or service packaged and sold either directly to a variety of markets or supplied on contract to firms and agencies, including State funding agencies. In Canada, Australia, New Zealand and the UK this reconstruction has been aided by the Neo-Liberal shift in public policy, the increasing participation in post-compulsory education, the redistribution of the costs of tuition to immediate consumers, and the progressive managerial reconstruction of these public service organisations. The result is a more highly corporatised and commercially focused tertiary education. While 'knowledge' and learning have always been valuable positional goods, in the current setting they have become market goods, to be sold through advertising and consumer marketing practices (Marginson, 1996; 1997).

But if we draw a Foucauldian line of analysis, the emphasis is not on the way in which education practices are commodified, but on the way the new practices work on and through the body – how we become saturated consumers of knowledge, willing collaborators or helpful formalisers of tacit knowing. Commodification then is a broad term under which a more materialist reading of power (that is, the way power works on the body), might be provided. Foucault suggests that in order to understand the productivity of power, 'One needs to study what kind of body the current society needs (Foucault, 1980). If, as has been argued above, it is the communicative, sharing, knowledge-able body which the developing order 'needs', then tertiary education has a distinctive position and part to play. Tertiary education's role is not simply as a source of exploitable knowledge, but more broadly an institutionalised space where bodies can be inscribed as 'learners', preferably with lifelong consumptive habits/desires for knowledge goods.

To put this in some context, Foucault argued that power would be weak if it worked simply by repression – by constraining the body, forcing it to undergo rigorous disciplinary practices. Repression invited a 'revolt' of the body (Foucault, 1980, p. 56). Like Daniel Bell, Michel Foucault regarded the student protests of the 1960s as just such a 'revolt of the body'. Bell noted that:

> In post-industrial society, the chief problem is the organisation of science, and the primary institution the university or the research institute... in greater measure the student revolt (of the late 1960s) was a reaction to the 'organisational harnesses' a post-industrial society inevitably drops on intellectual work (Bell, 1974, p. 116–18).

Foucault, in developing his ideas around this, argued that power's response to this 'revolt of the body' has been an 'economic (and perhaps almost ideological) exploitation of eroticisation, from sun-tan products to pornographic films' (Foucault, 1980, p. 57).

> We find a new mode of investment which presents itself no longer in the form of control by repression, but that of control by stimulation: 'Get undressed – but be slim, good looking tanned' (Foucault, 1980, p. 57).

What might this suggest for education? The 'knowledge economy' demands lifelong knowledge users and producers. Tertiary education is regarded as a significant site on both counts. Power works in both the formal and informal curricula not to repress and control the 'student body', but to enliven it, stimulate it, and engage and focus its desire on itself, on different forms of pleasures, lifestyles, modes of consumption and communication (Burrell, 1993). The effect is to accentuate the university not as a generator of knowledge goods, but as a site of consumption, much like a shopping mall, where knowledge is consumed[1] (Thompson, 1998; Ritzer, 1996).

Consider, for instance, the way 'education' is positioned in a recent advertisement from the Australian-owned ANZ Bank (Figure 11.2). The advertisement's caption reads: 'How ANZ can help you have a home and a life'. The advertisement uses acupuncture's theory of body lines to display what the bank regards as the typical consumption items on people's life line. The advertisement clearly links the body, consumption and education.

Consider also the following advertising copy from Britain's newest University:

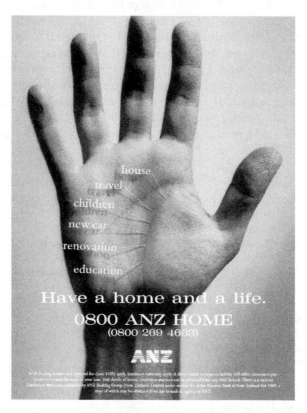

Figure 11.2

Vibrant, vivacious, and very exciting – that's life at the UK's first new purpose-built University campus in 25 years. Enjoy the very best of student life in a unique water-front setting surrounded by a wealth of bars, night-clubs, cafes, cinema and sport amenities in the heart of the fast growing and changing city of Lincoln. The University of Lincoln campus experience – *study it live it love it.*

Here the more formal aspects of learning and teaching have become sidelined to the consumptive aspects of higher education (see also Fairclough, 1993). Ritzer meanwhile observes that:

Making themselves more like shopping malls is a positive step that universities can take. However in order to attract and please student-consumers, universities will also need to eliminate as much negativity as possible. After all, shopping malls have few if any negatives; the emphasis is on the positives. Thus we can expect universities to continue the trend toward grade inflation... steps will be taken to reduce the number of students who drop out or flunk out... (and) a process of 'dumbing down of higher education' (Ritzer, 1996, p. 15).

Thus the more formal curriculum is likewise being reconstructed ostensibly in the interests of graduate employability, but also on the basis of consumer choice and satisfaction (Trowler, 1998). Customer surveys and audits have followed which demand the demonstration of 'satisfaction' and quality of 'services'. In the process, though, a new kind of student is evoked – the communicative, consumptive, performative student-body for whom stimulation, satisfaction and knowledge consumptive dispositions and desires are to be enhanced – particularly via information and communication technologies (Shore and Selwyn, 1998; Edwards, 1998). Yet this may not be enough. Cultural theorist and self-proclaimed cyber-feminist Sadie Plant suggests that the new knowledge consumption patterns will leave the universities in their wake. She locates this desire to learn with the students themselves.

It has become increasingly obvious to students that specialist knowledge is increasingly unhelpful in a parallel world which favours versatility, adaptability and breadth.... This generation needs neither training for careers, nor simply 'education for its own sake'. But rather the confidence and the ability to learn, survive and communicate in a world increasingly geared to the new discontinuities and contingencies which lie in wait on graduation day. Twentieth Century students are in any case learning to learn for themselves, becoming detectives, hunting for contacts and data on the Net... these developments themselves have significant intellectual and institutional effects (Plant, 1995, p. 46).

The quote highlights, astonishingly perhaps, how closely aligned this cultural theorist's work is with that of international policy advisers, corporations and various vice-chancellors of the new economy (Eisenstadt and Vincent, 1998). It also illustrates how desire for the consumptive aspects of learning is being enhanced and dispersed away from the established disciplines and into electronic networks. Of course the 'oral logic' (Morse, 1994) of this desire is the focus here – bodies first and then minds and ideas. What is induced is the production of 'tacit' structures for the information economy; that is, the consuming, stimulated body which seeks out its intensities in knowledge goods and a desire to communicate, innovate and share.

Performing the Manager's Body in the New Tertiary Education

But perhaps in relation to tertiary education this work on the body is most pronounced in those sites where the new commercial economy of stimulation is most focused: on the bodies of the senior post-holders, in the management teams and in the micro-spaces of managerial offices where the bodies of these 'managers' are orientated to these new 'realities' of 'knowing'. While mainstream academics might, as Plant writes, be 'traumatised' or be nostalgically re-emphasising a golden age where classes were small and jobs were for life (Plant, 1995, p. 44), it is among the newly suited managerial elite of tertiary education that the body is most radically being worked on (Prichard, in press).

To illustrate this I shall draw on a short piece of text from a much wider study (Prichard, forthcoming) of 'managers' in post-compulsory education. Here, the head of an engineering department in an East Midlands Further Education College (equivalent to a community college in the USA or a Polytechnic in New Zealand) described his work practices in the newly established tertiary education 'market':

> There is a market out there, get in there, suck it, satisfy it, and then move on. The only way you can do that is by staying light on your feet, and we are being slowed down a little (by course accreditation processes and the funding authority).

This demonstrates in a few highly evocative terms the newly marketised character of post-compulsory education in the UK. What is unusual about this quote is the way this head of department articulates his positioning, and links the practices demanded by the new environment *with a new kind of body*. This entrepreneurial body-subject needs to be 'light on its feet', alert to demand/desire/fashion for educational consumption – to 'gaps in the market' – and performs its commitment by satisfying this demand/desire/fashion.

Of course, such a 'body' is also an effect of reductions in public funding, the shift to an recruitment-based funding regime, and what Whitehead (1996) describes as the re-masculinisation of senior management. But again analysis here is not simply of broad political economic relations. It is on how these inscribe our body surfaces in different cloth and garment (Trethewey, 1999) (e.g. as managers), enact our bodies in new spaces (e.g. the management team), and reconstruct our desires toward the marketised consumption of knowledge.

Conclusion

By taking up resources from critical social science, this chapter makes two broad points. It argues that the centrality of education and higher or tertiary education to the 'knowledge economy' is not due simply to the sector's functional or developing commercial position as a source of marketable ideas or intellectual property revenues. It is due to its positioning as a site for the production of the dispositions demanded by the new economy: bodies disposed to the consumption of knowledge goods and to intricate communicative relations. While much of the discursive formation around 'knowledge' provides a play of prescriptions to enhance and extract knowledge for codification, application and distribution, tertiary education is evoked as a source for the development of knowledge-able bodies disposed to lifelong learning in the service of these extractive processes. The chapter also more broadly addresses the way that the discursive formation around knowledge understands the body. The chapter has challenged the narrow, instrumental, masculine and extractive assumptions which found the current business and government policy advice in relation to knowledge management and the knowledge economy. While the inclusion of Polanyi's phenomenological position is a clear departure from highly rationalised and positivist understanding of knowledge, 'tacitness' must be read fully by including forms of knowing beyond the instrumental: erotic, consumptive, somatic, seductive and affective ways of knowing. The instrumental sanitised masculine body ideal, exemplified and reproduced through Polanyi's work, limits both the potential for exploring the full nature of our humanity in social relations, and, analytically, limits our understanding of how power works in the development of these relations.

References

Acker, J. (1990) 'Hierarchies, Jobs, Bodies: a Theory of Gendered Organisations', *Gender and Society*, 4: 2, 139–58.

Aley, J. (1997) 'The Heart of Silicon Valley', *Fortune*, 136: 1 (7 July), 66–7.

Allee, V. (1997) *The Knowledge Evolution; Expanding Organisational Intelligence*, Boston, MA: Butterworth-Heinemann.

Andriessen, D. (1998) 'You can lead a professional to knowledge...', *IT Chapter News*, 22: 4–5 (Institute of Chartered Accountants in Australia) available at http://icaa.org.au/.

Bayliss, B. and Vandevelde, H. (1996) 'Headhunting the Knowledge worker', *FE Now!*, issue 45, p. 20.

Bell, D. (1974) *The Coming of Post-industrial Society: A Venture in Social Forecasting*, London: Heinemann.

Blackler, F. (1997) 'Knowledge, Knowledge Work and Organisation, An Overview and Interpretation, *Organisation Studies*, 16: 6.

Boisot, M. (1998) *Knowledge Assets, Securing Advantage in the Information Economy*, Oxford: Oxford University Press.

Burrell, G. (1984) 'Sex and the Organisation', *Organisation Studies* 5: 2, 97–118.

Burrell, G. (1992) 'The Organisation of Pleasure', in M. Alvesson and H. Willmott (eds.), *Critical Management Studies*, London: Sage, pp. 66–89.

Burrell, G. (1993) 'Eco and the Bunnymen', in J. Hassard and M. Parker (eds.), *Postmodernism and Organisations*, London: Sage, pp. 71–82.

Burrell, G. (1996) 'Paradigms, Metaphors, Discourses, Genealogies', in Clegg *et al.* (eds.) *Handbook of Organisation Studies*, London: Sage.

Butler, J. (1997) *The Psychic Life of Power, Theories of Subjection*, Stanford: University of Stanford.

Calás, M. and Smircich, L. (1991) 'Voicing Seduction to Silence Leadership', *Organisation Studies*, 12: 4, 567–602.

Castells, M. (1994) 'The University System: Engine of Development in the New World Economy', in J. Salmi and A. Verspoor (eds.), *Revitalizing Higher Education*, London: Pergamon.

Chandler, A. D., Hagstrom, P. and Solvell, O. (eds.) (1998) *The Dynamic Firm, The Role of Technology, Strategy, Organisation and Regions*, Oxford: Oxford University Press.

Cockburn, C. (1991) *In the Way of Women: Men's Resistance to Sex Equality in Organisations*, Basingstoke: Macmillan.

Cortada, J. W. (ed.) (1998) *Rise of the Knowledge Worker*, Boston: Heinemann.

Curry, J. (1997) 'The Dialectic of Knowledge-in-Production: Value Creation in Late Capitalism and The Rise of Knowledge-Centered Production', *Electronic Journal of Sociology*, 2: 3.

Computer Weekly (1999) 'If it Quacks and it Waddles… It's a Duck, How to Ask the Right Questions of Your Knowledge Management System, *Computer Weekly*, 10 June, p. 62.

Collinson, M. and Collinson, D. (1996) 'It's Only Dick: the Sexual Harassment of Women Managers in Insurance Sales', *Work, Employment and Society*, 10: 1, 29–56.

Crossan, M., Lane, H. and White, R. (1999) 'An Organisational Learning Framework: From intuition to institution', *Academy of Management Review*, 24: 3, 522–37.

David, P. (1997) 'The Knowledge Factory': A Survey of Universities, *The Economist*, 4 October.

Davenport, T. and Prusak, L. (1998) *Working Knowledge, How Organisations Manage What they Know*, Boston, MA: Harvard Business School Press.

Deleuze, G. and Guattari, F. (1988), *A Thousand Plateaux*, London: Athlone.

Deleuze, G. (1988) *Foucault*, London: Athlone.

Department of Trade and Inustry (DTI) (1998) *Competitive futures: Building the Knowledge Driven Economy*, London: DTI.

Dhawan, R. (1999) 'The Knowledge Corporation', *Business Wire, Living Media*, India, 7 May (accessed through Reuters Business Briefing).

Drucker, P. (1988) The coming of the new organisation, *Harvard Business Review*, January–February.

Drucker, P. (1993) *Post-Capitalist Society*, Oxford: Butterworth-Heinemann.

Edwards, M. (1998) 'Commodification and Control in Mass Higher Education', in D. Jary and M. Parker (eds.), *The New Higher Education*, Stafford: Staffordshire University Press, pp. 253–72.

Easterby-Smith, M. (1996) 'Disciplines of Organisational Learning: Contributions and Critiques', *Human Relations*, 50: 9, 1085–113.

Eisenstadt, M. and Vincent, T. (1998) *The Knowledge Web, Learning and Collaborating on the Net*, London: Kogan Page.

Elster, J. (ed.) (1986) *Karl Marx, A Reader*, Cambridge: The Press Syndicate.

Etzkowitz, H. and Leydesdorff, L. (eds.) (1997) *Universities in the Global Knowledge Economy*, London: Pinter Press.

Fairclough, N. (1993) 'Critical Discourse Analysis and the Marketisation of Public Discourse: the Universities', *Discourse and Society* 4: 2, 133–68.

Foucault, M. (1972) *The Archaeology of Knowledge*, London: Routledge.

Foucault, M. (1977) 'Intellectual and Power', in D. Bouchard (ed.), *Language, Counter-member, Practice*, Oxford: Blackwell.

Foucault, M. (1980) *Power/Knowledge: Selected Interviews and Other Writings by Michel Foucault, 1972–77* (ed. C. Gordon), Brighton: Harvester.

Foucault, M. (1983) 'The Subject and Power', in H. L. Dreyfus and R. Rabinow (eds.), *Michel Foucault: Beyond Structuralism and Hermeneutics*, Chicago: Chicago University Press, pp. 208–66.

Foucault, M. (1984) 'The Order of Discourse', in M. Shapiro (ed.), *Language and Politics*, Oxford: Blackwell, pp. 108–38.

Foucault, M. (1991) *Discipline and Punish, The Birth of the Prison*, London: Penguin.

Gibbons, M., Limoges, C., Nowotny, H., Schwartzman, S., Scott, P. and Trow, M. (1994) *The New Production of Knowledge, the Dynamics of Science and Research in Contemporary Societies*, London: Sage.

Grant, R. M. (1996) 'Toward a Knowledge-Based Theory of the Firm', *Strategic Management Journal*, 17 (Winter special issue), 109–22.

Grene, M. (1969) 'Introduction' to *Knowing and Being, Essays by Michael Polanyi*, London: Routledge.

Habermas, J. (1979) *Communication and the Evolution of Society*, Boston, MA: Beacon Press.

Hamel, G. and Prahalad, C. K. (1993) *Competing for the Future*, Boston, MA: Harvard Business School Press.

Hamel, G. and Prahalad, C. K. (1996) Competing in the New Economy, Managing out of Bounds, *Strategic Management Journal*, 17, 237–42.

Hearn, J. and Parkin, W. (1995) *'Sex at Work': The Power and Paradox of Organisational Sexuality*, 2nd edn, Hemel Hempstead: Harvester.

Hearn, J., Sheppard, D. L., Tancred-Sheriff, P. and Burrell, G. (eds.) (1992) *The Sexuality of Organisations*, London: Sage.

Hetrick, W. and Boje, D. (1992) 'Organisation and the Body: Post-Fordist Dimensions', *Journal of Organisational Change Management*, 5: 1, 18–57.

Howitt, P. (ed.) (1996) *The Implications of Knowledge-Based Growth for Micro-Economic Policies*, Alberta, CA: University of Calgary Press.

Huysman, M., de Wit, D. and Andriessen, E. (1999) 'A Critical Evaluation of the Practice of Knowledge Management', paper presented to *The 6th European Conference on Computer Supported Cooperative Work*, Copenhagen, Denmark, 12–16 September. Available at: http://www.cs.uni-bonn.de/~prosec/ECSCW-XMWS/.

Information Week (1999) 'Knowledge Sharing Roundtable', *Information Week*, 26 April (accessed through Reuter Business Briefing).

Insurance Today (1999) '"Making the Most of Knowledge": report on Open University Knowledge Management Seminar', *Insurance Today*, 24 March (accessed through Reuter Business Briefing).

Jackson, N. and Carter, P. (1998) 'Labour as dressage', in A. McKinlay and K. Starkey (eds.), *Foucault, Management and Organisation Theory*, London: Sage, pp. 49–64.

Knights, D. and Willmott, H. (1989) 'Power and Subjectivity in Work', *Sociology*, 23: 4, 537–55.

KPMG (1999) 'IKON Conference Report', Available at http://kpmg.interact.nl/new/confer_IKON.html.

Kristeva, J. (1997) in K. Oliver (ed.), *The Portable Kristeva*, New York: Columbia University Press.

Liebowitz, J. and Beckman, T. (1998) *Knowledge Organisations, What Every Managers Should Know*, Boca Raton, FL: St Lucie Press.

Marginson, S. (1996) 'University Organisation in the Age of Perpetual Motion', *Journal of Higher Education Policy and Management*, 18: 2, 117–23.

Marginson, S. (1997) *Markets in Education*, Sydney: Allen & Unwin.

Machlup, F. (1980) *Knowledge: its creation, distribution and economic significance: Volume 1, 'Knowledge and Knowledge Production*, Princeton: Princeton University Press.

Machlup, F. (1982) *The Branches of Learning*, Vol. 2 of *Knowledge, its Creation, Distribution, and Economic Significance*, Princeton, NJ: Princeton University Press.

McDowell, L. (1997) *Capital Culture, Gender at Work in the City*, Oxford: Blackwell.

McDowell, L. and Court, G. (1994) 'Performing Work: Bodily Representations in Merchant Banks', *Environment and Planning D: Society and Space*, 12, 727–50.

McKinlay, A. (1999) 'The Bearable Lightness of Control', paper presented at the *International Labour Process Conference*, Royal Holloway College, University of London, March.

McKinlay, A. and Starkey, K. (1998) *Foucault, Management and Organisation Theory, From Panopticon to Technologies of the Self*, London: Sage.

McWilliams, E. (1996) 'Touchy Subjects: a Risky Inquiry Into Pedagogical Pleasure', *British Journal of Sociology of Education*, 22: 3, 305–17.

Moran, N. (1999) 'Knowledge is the Key Whatever the Sector', *Financial Times*, World Survey – Knowledge Management, 28 April, p. 1.

Morse, M. (1994) 'What Do Cyborgs Eat? Oral Logic in an Information Age', *Discourse*, Spring, 86–123.

Moss-Kanter, R. (1977) *Men and Women of the Corporation*, New York: Basic Books.

Nardi, B. and O'Day, V. (1999) *Information Ecologies, Using Technology with Heart*, Cambridge, MA: MIT Press.

Neef, D. (ed.) (1997a) *The Knowledge Economy, Resources for the Knowledge-Based Economy*, Butterworth-Heinemann.

Neef, D. (1997b) *Making a Case for Knowledge Management: The Bigger Picture*, Centre for Business Innovations, Ernst and Young, available at: http://www.businessinnovation.ey.com/mko/html/making.html.

Nelson, R. (1996) *The Sources of Economic Growth*, Cambridge MA: Harvard University Press.

Nelson, R. and Winter, S. (1982) *An Evolutionary Theory of Economic Change*, Harvard: Belkrap Press.

Nonaka, I. (1996) 'The Knowledge Creating Company', in *Harvard Business Review on Knowledge Management*, Boston, MA: Harvard Business School Press, pp. 21–45.

Nonaka, I. and Takeuchi, H. (1995) *The Knowledge-Creating Company*, Oxford: Oxford University Press.

O'Dell, C. and Grayson, C. (1998) *If Only We Knew What We Know; the Transfer of Internal Knowledge and Best Practice*, New York: Free Press.

Organisation for Economic Cooperation and Development (OECD) (1996) *Employment and Growth in the Knowlege-based Economy*, Paris: OECD.

Prichard, C. (forthcoming) *Making Managers in Universities and Colleges*, Open University Press and SRHE.

Prichard, C. (in press) 'The Body Topography of Education Management', in J. Hassard, R. Holliday and H. Willmott (eds.), The *Body and Organisation*, London: Sage.

Plant, S. (1995) 'Crash Course, as Old Certainties Crumble, What Sort of Education Will Take Us Into the Future?', *Wired*, April, pp. 44–7.

Polanyi, M. (1958) *Personal Knowledge: Towards A Post-critical Philosophy*', London: Routledge.

Polanyi, M. (1969) *Knowing and Being, Essays by Michael Polanyi*, London: Routledge.

Prusak, L. (ed.) (1997) *Knowledge in Organisations*, London: Butterworth-Heineman.

Ritzer, G. (1996) 'McUniversity in the Postmodern Consumer Society', Plenary address to the *Dilemmas in Mass Higher Education Conference*, Staffordshire University, April.

Robertson, D. (1998) 'The Emerging Political Economy of Higher Education', *Studies in Higher Education*, 23: 2, 221–8.

Roper, M. (1996) 'Seduction and Succession': Circuits of Homosocial Desire in Management, in J. Hearn and D. Collinson (eds.) *Men as Managers, Managers as Men: Critical Perspectives on Men, Masculinities and Managements*, London: Sage.

Schement, J. R. and Curtis, T. (1998) 'The New Industrial Society' in J. W. Cortada (ed.) *Rise of the Knowledge Worker*, London: Heineman.

Seely-Brown, J. (1996) 'Research that Re-invents the Corporation', in *Harvard Business Review on Knowledge Management*, Boston, MA: Harvard Business School Press, pp. 153–80.

Senge, P. (1990) *The Fifth Dimension: the Art and Practice of the Learning Organisation*, New York: Doubleday.

Shore, C. and Selwyn, T. (1998) 'The Marketisation of Higher Education: Management Discourse and the Politics of Performance', in D. Jary and M. Parker (eds.) *The New Higher Education*, Stafford: Staffordshire University Press, pp. 153–71.

Slack, J. and Fejes, F. (eds.) (1987) *The Ideology of the Information Age*, Norwood, NJ: Ablex Publishing.

Slaughter, S. and Leslie, L. (1997) *Academic Capitalism: Politics, Policies and the Entrepreneurial University*, Baltimore, MD: Johns Hopkins University Press.

Spender, J.-C. (1996) 'Knowledge and the Firm: Overview', *Strategic Management Journal*, 17 (Special Issue), 5–9.

Spender, J.-C. (1998) 'Pluralist Epistemology and the Knowledge-based Theory of the Firm', *Organisation*, 5: 2, 233–56.

Spender, J.-C. and Grant, R. M. (1996) 'Knowledge and the Firm: Overview', *Strategic Management Journal*, 17(Special Issue), 5–9.

Stamp, D. (1995) *The Invisible Assembly Line, Boosting White-Collar Productivity in the New Economy*, New York: AMACOM.

Stewart, D. (1997) *Intellectual Capital: the New Wealth of Organisations*, London: Doubleday.

Trethewey, A. (1999) 'Disciplined Bodies: Women's Embodied Identities at Work, *Organisation Studies*, 20: 3, 423–50.

Thompson, G. (1998) 'Does Higher Necessarily Mean Better? Reinvigorating the Humanities and Social Sciences', in D. Jary and M. Parker (eds.), *The New Higher Education*, Stafford: Staffordshire University Press, pp. 288–302.

Trowler, P. (1998) *Academics Responding to Change, New Higher Education Frameworks and Academic Cultures*, Society for Research in Higher Education and Open University Press.

Tsoukas, H. (1996) 'The Firm as a Distributed Knowledge System: a Constructivist Approach', *Strategic Management Journal*, 17 (Special Issue), 11–25.

Whitehead, S. (1996) 'Men/Managers and the Shifting Discourses of Post-Compulsory Education', *Research in Post-Compulsory Education*, 1, 151–68.

Willmott, H. (1998) *Knowledge Management – A Real Business Guide*, London: Caspian Publishing.

Willmott, H. and Snowden, D. (1998) *Managing Knowledge: Promises and Pitfalls*, London: FT Mastering Management.

Zuboff, S. (1988) In *the Age of the Smart Machine; The Future of Work and Power*, New York: Basic Books.

Note

1   Massey University is situated in Palmerston North – a provincial city some 140 miles from New Zealand's capital, Wellington. The city's main 'industry' is often regarded as education and 'knowledge'. In the early 1990s the city was 're-branded' by marketing and communications consultants hired by the city council as *The Knowledge City*. Massey University, various Crown Research Institutes (AgResearch, Crop and Food Research, Hort Research, Landcare, and the NZ Dairy Research Institute), a Japanese-owned private university, International Pacific College, and a polytechnic make up the core of this sector. Economic impact studies argue that about 40% of the city's working population are employed directly in the sector, while every 100 full-time students add $2.6 million to the economy, generate 17 direct jobs and 18 indirect jobs, and fill 17 four-bedroom housing units. There are more than 6000 student rental properties in the city.

Conclusion
Theorising Knowledge as Work: the Need for a 'Knowledge Theory of Value'

Roy Jacques

Introduction: What Creates Value? Who Has a Right to It?

When I give food to the poor they call me a Saint.
When I ask why the poor have no food, they call me a Communist.
(Dom Helder Camara)[1]

It is a curious paradox. Within managerialist writing (that is, not writing about management and organizing, but the dominant business school discourse which treats the goals and interests of management and investors as the goals of 'the organization', *per se*), the most commonly stated purpose of management is that of maximising shareholder value. One might expect, then, that the central question guiding managerialist research would be 'what creates value?'. A corollary question implied in the goal of channelling organisational wealth to investors is 'Who has a right to what part of the value created?'. Yet the question of values is discussed only in the hermetically sealed domain of 'business ethics', which is peripheral to any significant relations of power as they relate to the theories or practices of organising. Meanwhile, prescriptive practices of strategy formulation, organisational structuring, training, development and human 'resource' policymaking proceed with the question of value presumed. Based on my historical studies of the development of managerialist discourse, it seems that *despite having defined its role as value maximisation, at no point in its history has managerialist writing inquired into what value is or how it is created.* If I might be forgiven an anthropomorphic comparison, we might attribute this illogic to the troubled historical context into which management was born. As psychologists know well, a cardinal virtue espoused in dysfunctional families where the parental generation are abusers or the products of abuse is silence. One does not talk about certain things for fear of shattering the 'we're OK, we're good people, we're normal' myth that the family system constructs. If we look at the record (Jacques, 1996), we find that management was not produced spontaneously at the birth of the large organisation. It was produced considerably later *as those who controlled large organisations began to successfully cover up the bloody beginnings of the industrial order, to naturalize them as social 'evolution' and to legitimate the self-interest of investors as the general interest of all.* This is not to say simplistically (e.g. Marglin, 1974) that management was produced only as a system of expropriation. It is to say (and in this, we can find much insight in Marglin (1974)) that the expropriative role has distorted the development of managerialist thought from its inception by axiomatically imposing that those speaking of management accept that, 'The principal object of Management should be to secure the maximum prosperity for the employer, coupled with the maximum prosperity for the employé' (Taylor, 1911, p. 9). Oh, and we must also remember that 'without doubt the greatest gain through this change has come to the whole people – the consumer' (Taylor, 1911, 136). Thus, the interests of employers are presumed congruent with the interests of all.

It is difficult to imagine what questions could have pierced this insulating bubble more effectively than 'What creates value?' and 'Who has a right to it?'. Any curiosity in this direction is squelched with the legitimating myth we inherit which states that such questions were invented by Marx; Marx was a bad man; [and more recently] because the Soviet Union failed, we know that everything Marx believed must have been wrong. Critical theorists of many stripes have, of course, long recognised that the legitimating story covered up other quite different stories, and they have sought to give voice to these marginalized perspectives of the workers and consumers who did not feel that industrialisation and consumer society had been unalloyed benefits to humanity.

Classical economists had also sought to explain value and its equitable distribution, but neoclassical utility theory has given business interests a vehicle for leaving the relatively hard reality of differing interests at precisely the point where this reality became an encumbrance. As managerialist discourse has rocketed into the tautological stratosphere of value defined as a function of utility (which is defined as what is valued), the 'bottom line' types ironically cast off untethered into the ether of antiessentialism decades before the first postmodernists straggled in to join them. This, no doubt, is linked to the labour theory of value having come to be seen popularly as inherently Marxist, which further insulates mainstream discourse against the need to entertain dialogue about value creation.

Value, Values and 'Knowledge Work'

It is an important part of [my] duties to find out what [the workers'] ideas and opinions are... and thus to make capital out of their originality and their suggestions (Thomas Alva Edison, 1917, p. 81).

While critical and managerialist interests are, overall, as irreconcilable as ever, there is an emerging point at which they are congruent. The signifier marking the site of this limited congruence is that of 'knowledge work'. For finance capital, little has changed in the post-industrial world. As Paddy Chayefsky so succinctly expressed it through the words of the Chairman of the conglomerate CCS in the movie *Network*:

> There is only one holistic system of systems. One vast and amazing, interwoven, inter-acting, multivariate, multinational dominion of dollars.... It is the international system of currency which determines the vitality of life on this planet. That is the natural order... the atomic and subatomic and galactic structure of things today.

Even in this rarified atmosphere where all life is comparable in terms of international currency exchange rates, problems are arising such as how to value technology stocks. Distant as this world is from the production of goods and services, when knowledge is the critical factor to be valued, it, too, is beginning to worry that its ability to survive is tied to outdated reifying processes of financial accounting which depend on concepts of labour and capital without adequately accounting for the valuation of knowledge.

For *production* management, however, this crisis is far more immediate. For instance, a couple of years ago I was involved in an action research project which gave me access to several sites within a major Silicon Valley computer manufacturer employing about 9,000 people. In one case, I remember sitting in a meeting with the Vice-President of Finance and his Senior VP, discussing issues of 'face time' (time actually working in the office as opposed to time working elsewhere), job sharing and the possibility of evening out cyclical rushes of work that employees had said were making it hard to balance their work and family commitments. These were neither naïve nor callous people. The VP was a Harvard MBA with twenty years experience and an African-American with an apparently genuine interest in social equity. But, as the discussion proceeded, it became apparent that these intelligent, successful people had only the vaguest idea what was actually important at the task level and how it related to the completion of the general processes of the department. In order to make basic, operational decisions – what jobs could effectively be job-shared, when people had to be physically present in the office, how to tell who was doing the most valuable work for job assignment, compensation and promotion – these managers were being led toward the uncomfortable question 'what creates value?'. To the extent that this was linked to compensation, they were also in a limited way asking 'who has a right to it?'

In another unit of the same company, we interviewed a sales team who were, at that point, having difficulty 'making their numbers'. As they described their work, the members of this team showed us that they were aware their work depended on the maintenance of a complex web of interpersonal relationships between the sales team and the technical support people in their organisation and comparable technical support and purchasing groups on the client's side. What the corporate decision-makers were doing at this time was severing these relationships, not deliberately, but indirectly as a result of good 'bottom line' decisions related to downsizing, the substitution of technology for human contact, limiting travel budgets and so forth. As a result of their 'efficient' management, the sales unit was in a vicious cycle. They were making fewer sales because selling had become more difficult. Because they had less revenue, their budgets were cut, further eviscerating their network of connections. This made sales even harder to make and the cycle continued. What we see again is a situation where, even from a managerialist perspective, failure to see how value is produced leads to ineffective decisions. Corporate decisions were being made on presumptions about value that were incongruent with the relationships to which the decisions applied. These assumptions were not the result of mere ignorance. They were a form of learned ignorance, reflecting industrial and managerialist 'common sense' about reality. Management coalesced within a context where worker knowledge was relatively unimportant. Bear in mind that management began to emerge *after* the deskilling of craftspersons into an industrial proletariat was highly advanced (Jacques, 1996), although it has been an ongoing force for deskilling. If we wish to understand Taylor's Schmidt, it is relatively adequate for industrial engineering purposes to view him merely as a 'human motor' (Rabinbach, 1990) because he was used as little more than a power source. Even Taylor did not overlook the importance of worker knowledge and attitude, as he is sometimes represented as having done, but from his time until recently it has remained possible to keep worker knowledge and attitudes from impinging seriously on top-down norms of managing. Only in recent years has the importance of work sites where worker knowledge and discretion are critical to effective organisational performance become a critical issue for managers. As this problem has grown into a central issue (one can, for instance, find a regular discussion of it in the last 15 years of *Fortune* magazine, one of the most articulate voices of managerialism) it has placed managerialist and critical students of organising in the ironic position of having a shared interest in asking a question hitherto raised only by critical management studies: who produces value?

'Knowledge Work' and Value

Admittedly, discussion to date of 'knowledge work', 'knowledge-intensive firms', and 'learning organisations' has seldom been explicitly connected to questions of value. In it's more popular forms (*e.g.*, Senge, 1990; Argyris, 1992) it has had to do with little more than individual or small group learning *within* organisations. Like the question of value itself, the question of what we mean by knowledge has been largely presumed. Rather than creating a dialogue about the meaning of knowledge in organisations, this literature has – predictably – skimmed over substantive issues, going immediately to prescriptive tomes on building a 'knowledge organisation.' Before dismissing this stream of theory and practice as simply a tool of the *status quo* (which I do believe it to have been), I urge us to consider these knowledge-related signifiers as possible hooks for connecting a critical dialogue to managerialist interests. Within the investigation of knowledge as a factor of production, I believe four objects of investigation have been produced:

- *'The' knowledge worker*: Individuals who presumably differ in their relationships to employing organisations from the traditional characters of management inquiry: the generic employee and the manager.

- *Knowledge work*: As an intersubjective phenomenon this is not simply the work that knowledge workers do. Knowledge work may be an element of work done by those not defined as knowledge workers and vice versa.

- *The knowledge organisation*: Organisations whose competitive advantage is lodged more critically in forms of knowledge than in forms of capital and labour.

- *The knowledge econom(y/ies)*: Sociopolitical entities whose most critical economic factor is related to knowledge rather than to land, labour or (working) capital. Or perhaps we might say economies whose capital is derived more from knowledge than from land, labour or machine production. Alternatively, we might speak of *the* knowledge economy as an international force, relationships with which shape the destiny of all sociopolitical entities, regardless of their internal constitution.

I doubt that these terms are even approximately adequate to describe the objects and/or relationships they are presently being used to signify. As some feminist writer, the reference to whose work I have unfortunately lost, once wrote, it would be like asking a Florentine of 1600 what they think of 'the Renaissance'. It is perhaps more useful to think of these terms (along with so many other terms in our 'post-' condition) as place markers, flags indicating sites where complex and exciting things we only vaguely perceive are occurring.

There is a fifth object of inquiry on which we might concentrate. I would like to suggest that it is a prerequisite for better understanding the four above. That would be:

- *Knowledge as a 'root metaphor' for understanding work*: This has been less discussed in the literature. Understanding of emergent phenomena in post-industrial systems of production requires that we treat knowledge as a metaphor for understanding work, rather than as a mere element of the work relationship.

In a frequently cited review of organisational culture, Smircich (1983) distinguished between those who studied culture as a variable and those for whom it was a root metaphor. To date, academic writing about knowledge work has predominantly treated knowledge work, the knowledge worker, the knowledge organisation and the knowledge economy (the 'knowledge _____ terms') as new categories to understand within the existing interpretive frameworks of organisation studies. This project is probably futile. The very idea that it may make sense to talk of 'post-industrial' work suggests that work relationships are shifting sufficiently to have achieved a new centre of gravity. While this has been a factor in discussions of postmodernity and, to a lesser extent, the post-industrial, it has had very little impact on discussions of knowledge work.

Historicising the Discourse of Work

Over time, profound remappings of what is considered 'real' work – that is, work about which formal knowledge is required – occur. 'Virtually the whole range of industrial employments', Veblen long ago reminded us, 'is an outgrowth of what is classed as *women's work* in the primitive barbarian community' (Veblen, 1899/ 1979, p. 5; emphasis added). In the warrior culture of late Medieval society, 'real' knights scorned the elevation to nobility (and thus to public power) of the emerging *noblesse de la robe*, the relatively effeminate (but male) 'knowledge workers' who assisted the king with a pen rather than a sword (Tuchman, 1978; Duby *et al.*, 1988). In Thomas Munn, we find a 17th century discourse of work and wealth governed by mercantile nation states, whose central metaphor of wealth was *hard currency*. In Smith, Ricardo and the French Physiocrats, we find an agrarian, aristocratic reality reflected in a political economy centred on *land* and *rents*. But also emerging in Smith is an analysis of exchange between equal-status *producers*, reflecting the emerging power in Smith's 'land of shopkeepers', of the wide swath of society ('the butcher, the brewer, or the baker') who could attain the knowledge and capital to pursue most occupations. More or less contemporaneously, in Colbert's France we find a shift reflecting the increasing centrality of *production* (Braudel, 1982, p. 140). As reality becomes increasingly industrial, we find work interpreted as a function of *capital* and *labour*, most prominently in Marx. Later industrialisation saw another shift from a discourse of production to one of *productivity*, a managerialist and finance capitalist 'ratio-nalisation' [*sic*] of reality (Jacques, 1996).

As Kuhn (1970) noted, a new paradigmatic system cannot merely explain new problems; it must also explain old data and phenomena. Each of these interpretations forms a lens through which one can view all prior work relationships. Within managerialist histories, this succession of metaphors is understood as a path of progressive enlightenment, each emerging system being a bit closer to the truth than its predecessors. I am more sympathetic to Foucault's (1973) explanation emphasising that each reality is adapted to understanding the central problems of a time as defined by the dominant power–knowledge relationships of that time. In this sense, the terms are kaleidoscopic; as Gintis and

Bowles (1981, p. 19) argue, 'Any basic commodity is a consistent basis for value theory'. The issue is not what things really are, but what view of things will make problems most amenable to solution.

This is an important time to remind ourselves that, by design, what is represented in our body of knowledge is not the world *per se*, but a small portion of that world which has been central to problems defined as important by a particular era[2] and particular interest groups – 'the totality of our so-called knowledge... is a man-made [*sic*] fabric which impinges on experience only along the edges' (Quine, 1953, p. 42). Theories are extreme simplifications of reality, useful only if the simplification highlights important phenomena relative to the object of analysis. Since our present theoretical frameworks have taken the shape of the past century's dominant problems, if the phenomena we wish to study are emergent, their critical elements probably exist in the areas of experience between the isolated islands of theoretical knowledge created by industrial organisational theorizing. What organisation studies have mapped is only the small portion of lived experience relating to the key problems of industrialists or industrial workers. For instance, there is still a great deal of discussion regarding ways for managers to motivate and lead workers to greater levels of efficiency and productivity. Such discussion fails to consider that management, motivation, leadership, efficiency and productivity emerged as topics to research in response to specific industrial problems. For instance, the question 'How does one motivate knowledge workers?' presumes an industrial context in which motivation is a central problem (which it was not prior to industrial times and is not in many emergent contexts).

In Marx's England, knowledge flowed relatively freely, but the capital necessary to apply knowledge was difficult to attain. Today, the effect of knowledge on capital is replacing the effect of capital on production as the focal point of analysis. Understanding the capitalisation of knowledge is emerging as an analogous metaphorical (epistemological, discursive) problem for the understanding of work. What, then, are the processes through which knowledge is turned into value? What are the 'relationships of knowledge'[3] through which one receives a larger or smaller share of the value produced? Treating the 'knowledge _____ terms' as flags indicating changing paradigmatic boundaries might lead to more usefully reflective questions in this regard.

Learning, not Knowledge, is the Problem

An unlikely source, Naisbitt (1982), begins a section entitled 'We Need to Create a Knowledge Theory of Value to replace Marx's Obsolete Labor Theory of Value', writing

In an information economy, then, value is increased, not by labor, but by knowledge. Marx's 'labor theory of value,' born at the beginning of the industrial economy, must be replaced with a new *knowledge theory of value*. In an information society, value is increased by knowledge, a different kind of labor than Marx had in mind (Naisbitt, 1982, p. 17; emphasis in the original).

Important as Naisbitt's observation is, he does not pursue it, leaving the project of writing the post-industrial *Das Kapital* – or, for that matter, the post-industrial *Wealth of Nations* – to others. In the spirit of moving in this direction, I would like to suggest that the central problem signified by the 'Knowledge ____' terms is one of *capitalisation*.

What might make organisational learning processes distinct from the processes of a traditional Weberian bureaucracy? Starbuck (1992), almost in passing, suggests a more promising conceptual foundation than the pop concept of organisational learning.

> Besides knowledge held in individual people, one can find knowledge in: (a) capital such as plant, equipment, or financial instruments; (b) firms' routines and cultures; and (c) professional cultures. People convert their knowledge to physical forms when they write books or computer programs, design buildings or machines.... People also translate their knowledge into firms' routines, job descriptions, plans, strategies and cultures (Starbuck, 1992, pp. 718-19).

As Marx so clearly saw (on his better days!), industrialisation did not simply increase the pace of business, or merely magnify the degradation of the labourer. It did these things as a byproduct of the role it played in the social construction of a new reality, one which, over several centuries, replaced the institutions and power relations of feudal Europe with new ones. That is, through changing relationships of commodification, capital produced new objects and relationships of wealth. Imperfect as he inevitably was, Marx has not been surpassed to this day as a theorist of these relationships, the processes of their social production, and their changing modes over time. But, by having the shortsightedness to die in 1883, Marx limited his perspective on capitalist relations to the period where machine production was the primary channel for capitalisation of value. By 1920, an industrial order was in place in the most-industrialized countries within which the capitalizing force of machine production was already yielding to managerialism and professionalism as the key relationships of capitalisation, as was reasonably well-understood at the time.

The constitutive problem of the [industrial] employee has, from the beginning, been that of knowledge. During the clashes between capital and labour in the late 1800s, employers had fought to obtain a work environment in which knowledge was built into technical systems. The ideal employee [to them] was unskilled and interchangeable. But the second industrial revolution around 1920 was founded on the recognition that even in the most regimented environment only limited success could be achieved without workers possessing several forms of special knowledge. The least skilled worker was more valuable when retained over a long period and educated in the practices of a good employee. Hays (1917) tells a story more commonly associated today with 'high' tech companies of the 1980s, of a company bankrupted when an employee quit, selling proprietary technical knowledge to competitors. Rights to capital in machines could be established in court or, if need be, by Pinkerton guns. Rights to human capital could not be so coerced. Thus, a discourse emerges emphasising kinder, gentler industrial relations designed to induce workers to voluntarily, 'give us the very finest products of their heads and hearts, and, therefore, of their hands' (Blackford and Newcomb, 1914, p. 9, cited in Jacques, 1996, p. 143).

The Edison leitmotif used earlier on shows that the 'wizard of Menlo Park' was quite self-conscious about his processes for capitalizing knowledge nearly a century ago. A century later, the company Edison founded, General Electric, is one of the world's largest companies 'with an unrivaled reputation for getting maximum returns on its money' (Koenig, 1996:114) – selling industrial-era products such as turbines, light bulbs and plastics. Capitalizing knowledge, it would seem, is a problem that is anything but emergent for this industrial exemplar. The phenomena signified by the 'knowledge _____ terms' apparently do not mark the emergence of difficulties in capitalizing knowledge. But they may mark a difficulty in capitalizing *learning*. Similarly, the industrial profession acts analogously to the industrial organisation as an institutional storehouse for capitalized *knowledge*, but offers us little as a model for capitalizing *learning*. Returning again to Taylor, we find recognition long ago that 'the training of the surgeon has been almost identical in type with the teaching and training which is given to the workman under scientific management' (Taylor, 1911, p. 126). If we contrast a group of heart surgeons with a group of software developers, one difference we find is that, beyond narrowly prescribed limits, creativity is a serious liability in heart surgery, but it is the 'heart' of software development. The surgeon's primary occupational responsibility is to *know*; the software team's primary responsibility is to *learn*. Surgery as an institution learns, of course, but ideally the learning comes from those doing medical research, a distinctly specialised occupational role. The individual surgeon does not learn to create new knowledge, but to apply the knowledge proprietary to the profession. Mintzberg (1979) has useful comments about surgery in this vein. In the structuring of the profession of surgery, we can find a close analogy in detail to the structuring of the industrial organisation and a functional analogy to the pre-industrial guild. In this sense, while the body of surgical knowledge is complex, the practices for capitalizing it are well developed. In contrast, for the software team, the work itself is a form of learning. In this sense, the very search for the *knowledge* worker is a red herring; it is the *learning* worker whose work is puzzling us.

Capitalizing Learning

If 'learning work' is an emergent problem, it is largely because the problems of capitalizing learning are quite different from those of capitalizing knowledge. In

Capital, Marx is often at pains to distinguish between labour and labour power. One distinction is that labour can quite easily be reified into machines and tools, while labour power is inalienably a possession of the worker. Similarly, machines, standard operating procedures and stored media such as books and electronic data bases are all adequate to store knowledge. Learning, on the other hand, threatens the entire structure of industrial relations, which, as the term implies, are relations shaped within industrial organisations. Whether tangible or intangible, knowledge is a discrete entity. It can be accumulated, stored, leveraged, applied and contested within the structures of managerial organising and labour relations that have been coalescing since the 19th century or earlier. Taylor, Follett, the Gilbreths, Gantt and their colleagues were not merely offering new solutions to problems; they were important participants in the replacement of a sensory organisational reality with an abstracted, numeric one, a 'world ruled by number' (Schabas, 1990) which capitalized knowledge in then-new ways. Four generations later, this reality, in its decline, still dominates managerial discourse. In order to better understand these phenomena, yet another organisational reality will have to be produced. In this regard, the practitioners have gotten out of the starting gate before we theorists.[4]

For instance, it is difficult to remember how epistemologically and politically radical such a now-routine practice as cost accounting was just a century ago. Through it, an entire constellation of abstractions were 'manufactured' into a hard reality (e.g. Hoskin and Macve, 1988 and since). Learning is no more impossible to capitalize than allocated fixed cost. The point is that *as the process is being undertaken now, where and how is it happening? Who will influence it?* These are questions of great import. Industrialisation required new 'disciplinary' technologies for capitalizing[5] knowledge. It dramatically and painfully altered relationships between owners and workers. It 'manufactured' the employee and the manager (Jacques, 1996). Today, the importance of learning may indicate a comparable watershed. Unlike knowledge, which is now easily capitalized, learning is the property of the worker or the workgroup until it is applied. Once applied, it becomes knowledge and can be capitalized, but if every situation is unique, it is the learning and not the knowledge that is the primary source of value. As the shelf life of an item of knowledge approaches zero, knowledge ceases to be power; the ability to *change* knowledge – to learn – becomes the source of power.

The mandate to be able to change knowledge destabilizes the ability of today's firm to capitalize static knowledge. Like labour power, knowledge vested in workers rather than company-owned assets is mobile. It can quit or be hit by a bus and disappear. Worse yet, it can walk to the competition, the police or regulatory bodies. Even if retained within the organisation, its mobilisation is fragile. Its application is subject to worker attitude, to communication problems and innumerable 'soft' obstacles to the smooth flow of knowledge. Early in this century, employers began to realise and actively discuss the need to retain worker-embodied knowledge. Although such knowledge was not directly controllable by the organisation, it was effectively stabilized through development of the long-term employment relationship. Documents from the time show this to have been a quite deliberate strategy. As employers today announce this relationship a nullity, replaced by a 'new employment contract' of mobile relationships, the now-traditional containers of worker-embodied knowledge are shattered.

Toward a 'Knowledge Theory of Value'

In sum, then, the central problematic is this: *Organisations perform complex tasks. Within organisations, people with differing interests and perspectives must collectively determine* **what** *tasks to perform and* **how** *to perform them effectively. They must then* **distribute** *the value produced among those involved in the production.*[6] Knowledge is not value, but, under certain conditions which are becoming more widespread, knowledge may be the most critical factor in the creation and distribution of value. On this basis, I am interested in being able to understand value in terms of knowledge.

As long as people have worked in groups the basic problematic that I summarise above has been applicable, but only in times of significant rupture in the relationships governing work and wealth do they emerge from our social 'common sense' to become theoretical and practical challenges. At such times, there are often dramatic shifts in the ways in which the questions are formulated. The emergence of the 'knowledge ____' terms is associated with significant shifts in the centres of gravity of relationships governing markets, work processes, the environment and techno structure of work. Given the profound changes produced in the last decade or two by these changes or by responses to them, it makes sense to ask whether the present world of production and exchange can be better understood through new root metaphors. So what are our starting points?

Utility theory

Neoclassical economics is of very little help to us, since it has abandoned the idea of value altogether, except in the tautological sense that if people exert effort or spend money for something, they are assumed to value it because they place this value on it. The distinction from classical economics between exchange value and use value has disappeared by definition. If Bill Gates's net worth is equal to the total worth of the lowest-income 45% of American families, this cannot, by definition, be inequitable, since his worth is used to measure the value he has created. Similarly, if CEOs in 1990 made 50% more in real terms than they did in 1980, while other workers made about the same amount, that is what CEOs and other workers are worth. What the market will pay determines value.

If our goal is to market products, utility theory may be a useful metaphor, since it is a model of the consumer. If 'economic [wo]man' finds more utility in Budweiser than in Kirin, s/he will purchase it. If my advertising campaign leads to more purchases of Bud/Kirin, I have increased its utility. We need not understand at a deeper level for these purposes. If, however, my goal is to better understand work processes – for reasons of organisational effectiveness *or* reasons of social equity, or both – utility tells me nothing. The phenomenal reality[7] of personal preference has no connection to the material[7] relationship between the actions of a person and the value produced through the processes in which they participate.

Perhaps, before we disregard neoclassical economics entirely, we can take one insight from it. Campbell Jones, a colleague of mine from the University of Adage, has in the past observed that I may be seeking too scientistic, too objective, a theory of value, and he may be right. We cannot follow utility theory into the radical phenomenology of consumerism, but we might use this flight as a reminder that the hope for a mechanistic, objective theory of value may be a form of positivist nostalgia.

Labour theory

If we do not draw on utility theory, our remaining candidate is labour theory. And since such theorizing has been dead for a century outside of critical circles, labour theory more or less means the Marxian tradition. Throughout the century, we have seen noble efforts to update and expand Marx's framework to remove contradiction, omissions and crude materialism. Nonetheless, both the brilliance and limitation of Marx's vision remains the skeleton on which subsequent work has been hung. Having recently re-read *Capital, Volume 1* for a discussion group at the University of Adage,[8] I believe several basic assumptions about the theory make it unusable for a knowledge-based root metaphor of value. I know this discussion fails to include a good deal of relevant theorizing since Marx. My justification in going back to 1867 is that I believe these are root problems embedded in the basic formulation of the theory. In brief:

- The criteria of 'necessary' and 'surplus' labour are too relativistically conceptualized.

- While a distinction is made between labour power and knowledge, this distinction is not – cannot be? – developed.

- Knowledge power apart from labour has no legitimacy within this model.

- Marx's definition of the value of the machine as being equal to the labour power reified in the machine defines away the central problem of value in a technology-intensive society.

- While Marx recognised that capitalist relations were different from the relationships of machine production, the problems of his time led to inordinate emphasis on the latter in Marxian labour theory.

Definition of 'necessary' and 'surplus' labour
This goes to the question of who has a right to value produced. In Marxian labour theory, this is formulated as a question of who has a right to surplus value, which is the value left over after the 'necessary' labour needed to reproduce the worker has been accounted for. The trouble is, Marx is relativistic about what is necessary, permitting it to vary from culture to culture. I would suggest that the history of industrial capitalism suggests necessary labour to be relatively specific – the bare food and shelter needs necessary for abject survival. As a result of this conflation, the question of what is surplus and what is necessary has not been answered. This, in turn, interferes with the subsequent question of who has a right to what portion of surplus value.

Labour power and labour knowledge
As with the classical economics of Smith and Ricardo which influenced it, Marxian theory embodies a humanist assumption, reflected from Hobbes to Locke to the US Bill of Rights, that every individual, given the opportunity, has more or less the skill and knowledge to do anything (a view Hofstadter (1963) has termed 'the omnicompetence of the common man [sic]'). The careful reader can find Marx occasionally distinguishing between labour as a generic, unskilled motive force and the knowledge which directs this force, but the two remain theoretically bundled. Labour power implicitly presumes the *savoir faire* to direct the power. For instance, if a half-hour of labour power is required to grind a smooth face on a valve seat, both the ability to expend energy (power) and the ability to grind (skill) are represented as a generic entity, 'labour power'.

The simplistic corollary that the value of one's labour power is increased by the value of the time put into developing one's skills changes things little. I call this simplistic because there is no reason to believe that the time spent in learning skills is in any way correlated with either the price that one's enriched labour will command or the value that one will be able to produce. In the time it took me to become a professor, I could have become an MD, but the average MD makes several times the salary of the average professor. Better still, my market price after six years of doctoral study was *decreased* from my prior market price as an MBA! Both the price and the value of knowledge seem to be determined by factors other than time invested in developing it – but what are they and where do they fit into a theory of value?

Knowledge power apart from labour
Similarly, Marx accords no portion of the value of a product to functions such as management, marketing, product development and accounting. Admittedly, it is reasonable to ask how much these functions contribute to value creation and

how much they contribute to value expropriation (from labour to capital). Certainly, as they have been constituted within a capitalist society, these functions are imbued with relationships of expropriation. At the same time, were it somehow possible to magically recreate the world in a non-capitalist form, complex organisations would require specialised planning and coordinating tasks whose contribution to value is not adequately measured by the labour power (in terms of direct labour) expended. How are we to account for these in a society where the bulk of the knowledge embedded in a product is *not* a function of the direct labour expended on that product's production?

Productive value of the machine

To my mind, this is the foremost limitation of labour theory. For Marx, the tool or the machine is nothing but dead labour. If a thousand hours were required to produce it, then it is assumed to transfer the value of one thousand hours' labour into the products it is used to produce over its lifetime. Were this true, the idea of a 'labour-saving device' would be an oxymoron. But who says that, for instance, a front-end loader built with a thousand hours of labour cannot replace ten thousand hours of hand shovelling? There is no necessary relationship between the labour required to produce a machine and the labour it replaces in the production process.

The Marxian argument merely treats the machine as an alternative form of labour power. What about the increasing ability of machines to exert knowledge power? What is the value to a fishing trawler of a radar system that senses fish that unaided humans would not know was there? How is the knowledge component of that machine's work to be valued? We are talking about two major failings here. One is that Marx misses the productive power of the machine entirely. The second is that even if we accounted for the productive power of machine labour, we would still not be accounting for the knowledge contribution of machine 'intelligence' (a word we might choose to avoid, given the hyper-inflated rhetoric associated with artificial intelligence since its inception).

This formulation may have served well in a time when the oppression of workers by machine production was the central economic, ethical and political problem to address, as it was for Marx. We cannot extrapolate a system built on this formulation into the present, however, because the centre of the problem has changed. Imagine a factory assembling a computer. How much of that computer's market price is represented by the direct labour of the factory worker and how much is embodied in the 'dead labour' of the circuit boards, the microchips, the management, accounting and marketing processes? We *can* look at this process through Marxian eyes; it is not incorrect to do so. But what we will be able to explain accounts for only a few pennies out of every dollar of market (exchange) value. We need a system that can weigh the productive value of the largest portion of value, which Marx consigned to the unproductive category of dead labour.

Capitalism as other-than-industrial

It would be grossly unfair to accuse Marx of confusing capitalism with machine production, as he was a major figure in helping to conceptualize capitalism as a set of relations of production independent of any specific mode of production. Nonetheless. It is also fair to say of Marx (as Engels said of others, excepting Marx), that none can 'go beyond the limits imposed upon them by their epoch' (Engels, 1883/1978, p. 684). This caveat applies to us as well, but just as labour theory was an appropriate metaphor for the epoch of machine production which produced it, perhaps a knowledge theory is needed for understanding the emerging epoch.

Marx's formulation of capitalism as a mode of relationships not inherently tied to industrialism provides a still-useful framework. For instance, Fernand Braudel's study of pre-industrial capitalism, *Civilisation and Capitalism*, elaborates on relationships less detailed in Marx, but still fitting into the Marxian framework. As we ask how the emerging world fits into this framework, however, the specific examples and relationships we are given to work with deploy the metaphor of labour within an environment of machine production. Where work is knowledge-intensive and highly discretionary, the metaphor is of extremely limited usefulness.

What Would a Knowledge Theory of Value Have to Include?

There is much that we might salvage from Marx conceptually, if we do so in a piecemeal fashion, but we need a new *gestalt* into which to fit the old pieces. In some cases, we need new pieces that perform the function of the old ones, so that we must replace Marx to continue in his spirit – that of determining the sources and distributions of value and working for equity in these relationships.

But as concrete formulations, we are left largely with utility theory and equity theory. In various ways, both systems reflect the values and problems of industrializing economies. Knowledge is an integral contributor to value in these theories, but it is either treated as commonly distributed or as subordinate to other factors. Neither permits adequate representation of the relationships structuring work in a society where the ability to change one's knowledge base is a competitive advantage overriding both the ability to deploy labour and the ability to deploy capital.

To outline a knowledge theory of value and apply it to present issues in organising and managing goes well beyond the scope of this chapter. I open this can of worms to indicate the scope of the project we must undertake if we truly believe we are attempting to understand fundamental changes in work relationships. Where do we turn for a foundation on which to build? That question is still open. Actor-Network theory (e.g. Law and Hassard, 1999; Callon, 1998; Law, 1992) may prove rich as a resource, since it offers the central metaphor of a dispersed network of knowledge which (nominally, at least) privileges neither material nor human elements of the network. The Actor-Network metaphor has also been constituted as a very loose system embodying most of the main currents in post-essentialist social thought of the last several decades. But the prize for the post-industrial *Das Kapital* has not yet been awarded. Perhaps other theoretical bases will proves still more promising. Perhaps having *a* theory of work is, itself, a bit of humanist nostalgia. To do more than transform these emergent phenomena (the 'knowledge _____ terms') into old problems and old solutions from a declining industrial reality, it will be necessary to follow the long path toward formulating work in terms of a knowledge-based reality. We cannot, in other words, add knowledge to our understanding of work. We must learn to understand work as a form of 'doing knowledge'. To do this, we must return to the questions long buried in management discourse: *'What adds value?'* and *'Who has a right to it?'*.

References

Argyris, C. (1992) *On Organisational Learning*, Oxford: Blackwell.

Braudel, F. (1982) *Civilisation & Capitalism 15th–18th Century: Vol. 2 The Wheels of Commerce*, New York: Harper & Row.

Callon, M. (1998) (ed.) *The Laws of the Markets*, Oxford: Blackwell.

Duby, G., Barthélemy, D. and de la Roncière, C. (1988) 'Portraits', G. Duby (ed.), in *A History of Private Life: Revelations of the Medieval World*, Vol. 2, Cambridge, MA: Harvard University Press, pp. 33–310.

Edison, T. A. (1917) Aphorism cited in A. W. Shaw Co. (ed.), *Handling Men*, Chicago: A. W. Shaw, p. 81.

Engels, F. (1883/1978) 'Socialism: Utopian and scientific', in R. C. Tucker (ed.), *The Marx–Engels Reader*, 2nd edn, New York: W. W. Norton, pp. 683–717.

Foucault, M. (1973) *The Order of Things: An Archaeology of the Human Sciences*, New York: Random House.

Gintis, H. and Bowles, S. (1981) 'Structure and Practice in the Labor Theory of Value', *Review of Radical Political Economics*, 12: 4, 1–26.

Hays, J. W. (1917) 'Your right in your employees' inventions', in A. W. Shaw Co. (ed.), *Handling Men*, Chicago, IL: A. W. Shaw Co., pp. 193–200.

Hofstadter, R. (1963) *Anti-Intellectualism in American Life*, New York: Vintage.

Hoskin, K. W. and Macve, R. H. (1988) 'The Genesis of Accountability: the West Point Connection', *Accounting, Organisations and Society*, 13: 1, 1–24.

Jacques, R. (1996) *Manufacturing the Employee: Management Knowledge from the 19th to 21st Centuries*, London: Sage.

Koenig, P. (1996) 'If Europe's Dead, Why is GE Investing Billions There?', *Fortune*, 9 September, pp. 114–18.

Kuhn, T. S. (1970) *The Structure of Scientific Revolutions*, 2nd edn, Chicago: University of Chicago Press.

Law, J. (1992) 'Notes on the Theory of the Actor-Network: Ordering, Strategy, and Heterogeneity', *Systems Practice*, 5: 4, 379–93.

Law, J. and Hassard, J. (1999) *Actor Network Theory and After*, Oxford: Blackwell.

Marglin, S. (1974) 'What Do Bosses Do? The Origins and Functions of Hierarchy in Capitalist Production', *Radical Review of Political Economics*, Summer.

Mintzberg, H. (1979) *The Structuring of Organisations*, Englewood Cliffs, NJ: Prentice Hall.
Naisbitt, J. (1982) *Megatrends*, New York: Warner.
Quine, W. V. O. (1953) *From a Logical Point of View*, Cambridge, MA: Harvard University Press.
Rabinbach, A. (1990) *The Human Motor: Energy, Fatigue, and the Origins of Modernity*, New York: Basic Books.
Schabas, M. (1990) *A World Ruled by Number: William Stanley Jevons and the Rise of Mathematical Economics*, Princeton, NJ: Princeton University Press.
Senge, P. M. (1990) *The Fifth Discipline*, NY: Doubleday.
Smircich, L. (1983) 'Concepts of Culture and Organisational Analysis', *Administrative Science Quarterly*, 28: 3, 339–58.
Starbuck, W. H. (1992) 'Learning by Knowledge-Intensive Firms', *Journal of Management Studies*, 29: 6, 713–40.
Taylor, F. W. (1911) *The Principles of Scientific Management*, New York: Norton.
Tuchman, B. W. (1978) *A Distant Mirror: The Calamitous 14th Century*, New York: Knopf.
Veblen, T. (1899/1979) *The Theory of the Leisure Class*, New York:

Notes

1   I do not know the provenance of this quote. It is taken from a poster decorating my office.
2   This definition is political, because it influences who shall have voice and who shall benefit, but that is not my central point at the moment. Whatever our values may be regarding emerging work relationships, conservative, liberal and radical share a common need to map out what those relationships are within which we contest voice and value.
3   These may indeed be 'power-knowledge' relationships in a Foucauldian sense. I wish, however, to emphasize the 'knowledge' pole of the relationship in this instance.
4   To establish this assertion would require another chapter. I suggest the sceptic compare the last five years of *Fortune* magazine features with the content of any textbook on Organizational Behaviour, Organization Theory or Human Resource Management.
5   Let us remember that capitalism is not inherently industrial. While highly successful in a symbiotic relationship with industrialism, agrarian and mercantile capitalism preceded industrialism and knowledge-based capitalism may well succeed it. Whatever else has changed since *Das Kapital*, the Marxian dictum to distinguish between modes of production and relations of production remains important.
6   A legitimate complication that I wish, however, to bypass here, is that the organization as a whole receives a certain amount of (primarily) financial wealth from society which is a proxy for value, but which is only loosely correlated with actual value produced. The alignment of wealth with value is a topic in its own right.
7   Cut me a little slack here. I mean 'material' in a post-analytic, discursive sense. We need some new terms!
8   I thank Campbell Jones, Shane Grice, Peter Fleming and Bobby van de Kuilen for stimulating my thinking – although they should be held blameless for the consequences!

From Knowledge to Learning

Hugh Willmott

Introduction

I'm not sure that I can agree with Roy Jacques' opening gambit that the most common stated purpose of management – by which he means the purpose identified by 'dominant business school discourse – is that of maximising shareholder value. My perception is that maximising the wealth of shareholders is the *hidden* rather than the overt agenda of such discourse. I would say that the purpose of management is more generally couched in universalistic terminology, such as improving efficiency or effectiveness, seemingly as ends in themselves.[1]

This is no accident, I think. It is part of what has been termed the 'legitimatory function' of modern management and its apologists. That is to say, management discourse is concerned with gaining cooperation by representing the specialist work of managers as a neutral activity that is of benefit to everyone – 'maximum prosperity' for both employee and employer. Within the terms of this discourse, the *ethical* issue of how value is distributed – Jacques question of 'Who has a right to that part of the value created? – is silenced by the exclusive focus upon identifying and developing the most *technically* efficient/effective means of producing value.[2] Or, at least, it is a way of representing current and innovative practices as the most technically superior, and therefore unproblematically, 'best practice'.

It seems that the veiling of management's agenda within a discourse of technical supremacy is now changing, by degrees at least. The discourse of efficiency etc. is being complemented, and to a degree displaced, by a discourse that emphasises shareholder value. Increasingly, senior managers, aided by consultants and perhaps not a little induced by their acquisition of stock options, are becoming less guarded (and perhaps less self-deluded) about the positioning of managers within capitalist relations of production and the 'purpose' that is forged within these relations. Seemingly, it is now more acceptable, and maybe even commendable, for managers to present themselves, even when addressing their employees, as pursuers and defenders of shareholder value. What was once a veiled, somewhat embarrassing and even shameful objective, is now openly allowed, and even celebrated.

It is no coincidence, perhaps, that a less inhibited celebration of shareholder value has surfaced in an era that has seen 'the fall of Communism', legislation and intervention that has weakened organised labour, a widespread shift to the centre right of politics and a broadening, though very uneven, distribution of share ownership. A discourse that was once restricted to the private spaces, board rooms and pages of the financial press has become widely disseminated and even embraced as the acid test of managerial virility. If this is the case, then one interesting question to be explored is: what are the effects of this new 'truth'? Is capitalism now more or less secure as a consequence of its champions' confident discarding of the legitimatory fig-leaf of technical rationality? Is the class war over, as Prime Minister Blair declared at the Labour Party conference in 1999?[3] If this is the case, then there is no longer any need to be so cautious in saying what capitalism and its management is for. Or are contradictions in capitalism unresolved, so that the discarding of legitimatory discourse heightens vulnerabilities to future crises?

Shareholder Value

What value means in the brave new context of 'shareholder value' is quite straightforward. It means: whatever it takes to increase the value of stocks and shares. For management, it means producing and releasing knowledge-cum-information to major players in the financial markets (e.g. fund managers) who make assessments of its credibility and significance for the share price. If their calculations indicate that the share price will rise within a relevant time horizon – which is more likely to be minutes, days or weeks than months or years – then stock is bought. If the calculation turns out to be correct, there is an increase in value. Or, conversely, there is a fall in value. In producing and releasing information, numerous developments can increase a stock's value – such as plans to slash costs, making acquisitions or divestments, or postponing new investments, as well as calculations about expected growth in particular markets. For the most part, the big players in the stock markets – the market makers – are concerned with corporate performance in the short run. They are unconcerned by the sustainability of a company's performance, as they will be the first to switch their holdings to an alternative supplier of shareholder value at the first sign of weakening in present or projected performance.

Who, then, creates *shareholder* value? The value ascribed to shares (as contrasted with the goods or services produced by companies) is determined by everyone who contributes to the process of making assessments about a company's present and projected performance. They are amongst the employees to whom the title 'knowledge worker' is often attributed.[4] They are, in Reich's (1993) terminology, symbolic analysts who develop and articulate specialist forms of knowledge that result in a (changing) value being placed upon companies. This is an example, I take it, of what Jacques describes as 'the effect of knowledge on capital' which, he contends, is 'replacing the effect of capital on production' (p. 215).

What Jacques means by this is not entirely clear, to me at least. What I understand him to be suggesting is that, in emerging industrial societies, a central problem was the design and development of work organisations (i.e. companies) that could accomplish the profitable production of goods and services. In this context, the (craft or everyday) knowledge required to produce ordinary goods and services 'flowed relatively freely' (p. 205). What was more problematic, Jacques suggests, was the availability of specialist expertise – eventually distilled in the theory and practice of management – that would appropriate, marshal and recast this everyday knowledge in ways that could secure and maintain a profitable margin when sold in the market-place. Fordism is perhaps the most notorious example of 'the effect of capital on production' in which 'machine production was the primary channel for capitalisation of value' (p. 206).

From Knowledge to Learning

What, then, of 'the effect of knowledge on capital' and 'the capitalisation of knowledge' (p. 205) that are considered by Jacques to be key distinguishing features of the contemporary era? In this era, capital is understood to be increasingly dependent upon the *recurrent generation* of knowledge that requires *continuous learning* and 'reskilling'. No longer can capital simply appropriate *existing* skills (as Taylorism aspired to do) or substitute machinery for many of these skills. The capitalisation of knowledge presents new challenges to management. It is no longer 'simply' a matter of capturing knowledge and/or disembodying it. It is more a question of how to foster it and diffuse it.

The difference between these – past and present – orientations to knowledge is evident in their different conceptions of its 'management'. For many, and especially those with an IT background, 'knowledge management' is about the storage and retrieval of information – as exemplified in data warehousing. For others, who are in a minority, 'knowledge management' is about discovering and developing ('new') organising processes that value and cultivate a dynamic process of learning that is *collectively shared and irreducible to information*. As Jacques persuasively points out, the current challenge for 'capital' and its managerial agents is much less the capitalisation of *knowledge as information* than it is the capitalisation of *knowledge as learning*. This, for me, is the nub of Jacques' chapter, which is somewhat camouflaged by its title and associated demand for 'a knowledge theory of value'.[5] What he writes about learning is worth quoting at some length:

> ...it is learning and not knowledge that is the primary source of value. As the shelf life of an item of knowledge approaches zero, knowledge ceases to be power; the ability to *change* knowledge – to learn – becomes the source of power (p. 208)

I agree that learning – the ability to change knowledge or make it redundant – is of increasing importance in contemporary work organisations. Competitive advantage is being sought through *continuous* innovation as well as in other ways (e.g. brand building). But I am personally not persuaded that 'the central problematic' in contemporary capitalist work organisations is concerned with the distribut(ion) of value produced among '*those involved in production*' (p. 209)'. Rather, as I see it, the central problematic continues to revolve around the issue of how to establish, maintain and develop organisations in which value is transferred to those who are *not* involved in production.

Continuities as Well as Change

Changes there may be – characterised by Jacques as a move from 'the effect of capital on production' to 'the effect of knowledge on capital' – in how value, in the form of wealth, is extracted. But there remains *a dependence upon potentially recalcitrant labour* to design and assemble the source of value – the machines, circuit boards, services, brand images etc. Without seeking to defend Marx's Labour Theory of Value,[6] which is the target of Jacques's critique, it is relevant to challenge what he takes to be 'the foremost limitation of labour theory' (p. 212).

Jacques claims that Marx's theory is incapable of appreciating or incorporating a new scenario where 'machines exert knowledge power' rather than simply acting as substitutes for labour power. What Jacques seems to confuse or conflate here is the meaning of *labour* as a physical activity that produces goods or services, and *labour power* which is the creative capacity or potential to be productive. As a consequence, Jacques equates machines with the 'dead labour' that substitutes for physical activity. In turn, this association leads him to claim that Marx's analysis is incapable of dealing with the 'dead labour' that is, he argues, a fundamental element of value. Let us examine this more closely.

To support his argument, Jacques takes the example of a fishing trawler with a radar system that is able to 'sense fish unaided' and thereby to identify fish that would otherwise remain undetected. 'How', he asks rhetorically, 'is the knowledge component of that machine's [i.e. the radar system] work to be valued?' This example is used to attribute two failings to Marx's theory. First, it is claimed that Marx 'misses the productive power of the machine'. Second, it is argued that the labour theory of value has no way of accounting for 'the knowledge contribution of machine 'intelligence', such as the radar system on the trawler.

Here Jacques seems to overlook two key elements in Marx's thinking. First, from a Marxian standpoint, machines are assemblies of parts fabricated by the labour power of human beings who also use machines (e.g. radar systems or robots) to design, build or identify other machines, goods and services. The fact that the labour hired to assemble the radar system comprises a tiny fraction of the value of its component parts, or even the machinery used to assemble the parts (if the assembly operations are largely automated), is irrelevant. Jacques overlooks how productive activity has become highly specialised. To overcome his objection, it is necessary only to conduct a thought experiment. Imagine that instead of being distributed around many sites across the world, *all* the activities that went into the production of the radar system – from mining the minerals, to making the metal parts to printing its operating manuals – are gathered together in one place. One then gets a sense of the labour power embodied in the radar system. Second, the radar system is no different in principle from any other device – such as a (low-tech) length or cotton or a strand of hair stretched across a portal to provide an unobtrusive measure of movements into a room – that records what would otherwise be unseen.

The Recurrent Problem

Largely unacknowledged and certainly unresolved by the contemporary preoccupation with the capitalisation of knowledge as learning is the endemic problem of capitalist work organisations – namely that the efforts (or 'strategies') by shareholders, mediated by senior management, to secure an acceptable transfer of value to themselves recurrently encounter demands by those upon whom they depend for the production of this value. Despite employers' best efforts to convince employees otherwise (Willmott, 1993), the employees' priorities are to improve their income and conditions of work, including opportunities for confirming or developing their sense of identity and control. In practice, the competing priorities of capital and labour are accommodated through a negotiated settlement.

The negotiated process of converting labour power into productive labour is generally easier in benign trading conditions when sufficient values are being generated to ensure a transfer of values to shareholders without seemingly disadvantaging employees. In less favourable conditions, however, or when increasing shareholder value is commended and pursued irrespective of the conditions, the precariousness of the accommodations becomes evident – with the consequence that, for example, labour threatens to withdraw its productive capacity or productive activity risks being exported to more benign locales.

One difficulty currently facing employers, as Jacques usefully points out, is how to foster (and not just retain) 'worker-embodied knowledge' (p. 208). This challenge is heightened in conditions where employers have been inclined to minimise the costs and risks that are associated with the cultivation of long-term employment relationships; and where, conversely, the flattening of hierarchies has contributed to rapid career advancement being achieved through frequent employment changes. Where the production of exchange and surplus value is conditional upon the *recurrent generation* of knowledge that requires *continuous learning*, managers are obliged to develop alternative strategies for fostering and facilitating the translation of labour power into the productive and profitable generation of goods and services. Among these strategies are teamworking, where, in principle, knowledge is pooled and collectively shared as a means of minimising unproductive time (Ezzamel and Willmott, 1998); stock options that tie people into companies and give them an inducement to cooperate with each other by working more flexibly and intensively (Ezzamel *et al.*, 1999); and diverse efforts to exploit untapped sources of value – for example, learning practices that are officially unacknowledged or formally invisible, yet are discovered to be critical for hitting key performance targets, are being disclosed and appropriated as sources of knowledge capitalisation (Contu and Willmott, 1999). Each of these areas offers itself for further consideration in future investigations of how knowledge and knowledge workers are managed in (post)modern organisations.

References

Alvesson, M. and Willmott, H. (1996) *Making Sense of Management*, London: Sage.

Contu, A. and Willmott, H. (1999) 'Learning and Practice: Focussing on Power Relations', Paper presented at the *Society for Organisational Learning Conference*, Cambridge, MA.

Ezzamel, M. and Willmott, H. (1988) 'Accounting for Teamwork: A Critical Study of Group-Based Systems of Organisational Control', *Administrative Science Quarterly*, 43: 2, 358–96.

Ezzamel, M., Willmott, H. and Worthington, F. (1999) 'Accounting, Organisational Transformation and Work Organisation', *Accounting, Organisations and Society Conference*, Marshall School of Business, University of Southern California, Los Angeles.

Reich, R. (1993) *The Work of Nations*, London: Simon & Schuster.

Willmott, H. (1990) 'The Dialectics of Praxis: Opening Up the Core of Labour Process Analysis' in D. Knights and H. Willmott (eds.), *Labour Process Theory*, London: Macmillan.

Willmott, H. (1993) 'Strength is Ignorance; Slavery is Freedom: Managing Culture in Modern Organisations', *Journal of Management Studies*, 30: 4, 515–52.

Notes

1 Jacques himself cites Taylor who emphasised that management should seek to secure the maximum prosperity for employer and employee. For a more developed statement of my conception of management, see Alvesson and Willmott (1996) and Willmott (1997).

2 I am aware that use of the term 'value' is sprinkled through this commentary in a promiscuous way. Unless preceded by some other term, such as 'stockholder', what I mean by value is something (a good or service) that is considered to be useful to the person who ascribes value to it. An artefact, for example, may be worthless in terms of what can be exchanged for it, but it is nonetheless valued because it has use (e.g. for recognising or preserving deep sentiments) to an individual or group. Precisely what is considered to be 'useful' is situationally and culturally specific. In the contemporary context, *use value* is ascribed to employees who are deemed to be capable of learning (or innovating). Such capabilities (or 'competencies') are also ascribed an *exchange value* in terms of the reward they receive in the labour market. But, in the context of capitalist organizations, this reward is offered only because it is calculated (rightly or wrongly) that a learning capability will yield *surplus value*, in the form of wealth for shareholders. Although I am using Marx's terminology to identify different kinds of

'value' (shareholder value being equivalent to surplus value), I have major reservations about Marx's labour theory of value and his analysis of the labour process, which have been aired elsewhere (e.g. Willmott, 1990).

3   As one wag wanted to know, if the class war is over, who was it that won?

4   This is a classic example of 'the labour of division', which, at a stroke, denies or devalues the presence of knowledge within *all* forms of labour. 'Knowledge work', the 'knowledge worker' and the 'knowledge economy' are most plausibly treated as elements of a particular 'regime of truth' that invites us to perceive and participate in the world in a particular way. I am not denying that work in advanced capitalist economies is becoming 'deindustrialized' (in the sense that the balance of productive or value-generating activity is shifting towards service work). I just believe that it is more plausible to view ideas about 'knowledge work' etc. as a hegemonic way of making sense championed by businessmen, consultants, politicians and associated symbolic analysts who seek to 'manufacture' a different kind of employee and citizen, themselves included, who takes individual responsibility for acquiring and applying knowledge.

5   As Jacques acknowledges in the final paragraphs of his contribution, 'To outline a knowledge theory of value and apply it to present issues in organizing and managing goes well beyond the scope of this chapter' (p. 213).

6   This is not the place to review the complex and persuasive arguments that have been marshalled against Marx's labour theory of value. Suffice it to say that it is difficult to sustain the claim that labour alone is the source of value.

Responding to Jacques' 'Theorising Knowledge as Work: the Need for a Knowledge Theory of Value'

Richard Hull

Jacques' provocative and interesting argument essentially seeks for a radical critical development of theories of organisation, management, and the labour process, and the products and commodities that are their 'outputs'. There are for me two quite distinct ways of responding to this, at the meta-theoretical and pragmatic levels. The first would question whether it is feasible and desirable to utilise *knowledge*, on its own, as a unit of analysis within any such radical critical development, and elsewhere in this book I have sketched the contours of such an argument. Further, I would add in this context that Jacques perpetuates a common mis-reading of *Capital* which 'naturalises' labour-power, treating it as a timeless entity and possession of the labourer which has merely been expropriated. Jacques deploys this naturalistic argument in order to demonstrate that labour-power always includes and presumes the *'savoir faire'*, the knowledge required to direct that power, and that contemporary conditions have drastically raised the relative importance of that knowledge in relation to the 'power', the ' brute force of labour', and should hence be treated separately. Marx is in fact quite clear (see especially Marx, 1961, pp. 714–15) that labourers only come to 'own' this peculiar entity of labour-power *after* they have been robbed of all other means of production, so that the only way they can subsist is to sell the only 'thing' they have left – it is in these conditions that the entity labour-power was created as a thing, a 'peculiar commodity' (p. 170). But, and this is the important point, that 'peculiar commodity' was always a *misrecognition* of labour, work and value; it hid the real relations, it obliterated that original theft, it caused labourers to misunderstand their 'self' and their subjectivity, and it caused both labourers and employers to understand labour-power *only* in terms of its immediate utility, its value to the employer (see also Rose, 1984, p. 3). Consequently, any 'knowledge element' of labour-power must also be a misrecognition of labour, work and value. We cannot merely identify that knowledge element as a natural, timeless entity, and then argue that its importance to capital has increased in this century, without perpetuating the original violence that was done to labourers in robbing them of all other means of production and

223

assigning them only their labour-power to sell. Jacques is quite right to call for modifications of Marxist thought in the light of our current conditions, but for me this requires retaining elements of Marx (and indeed Hegel) that Jacques would seem to discard.

However, I want to develop here a more pragmatic response, which moves towards amending Jacques' formulation, in the form of a *speculative* 'knowledge and power theory of value'. Firstly, one of the key insights from both Marx and Hegel that is worth retaining is the speculative element of the 'theory of commodity fetishism', as Gillian Rose has argued (1984, p. 30ff; 1995, Chapter 3). The master–slave relation and its concomitant in property law together result in the misrecognition of not only labour but also the very categories of Subject and Object. This is a speculative proposition because it must also mean (*contra* some other more 'scientistic' elements of Marx's thought) the radical inability to strictly distinguish theory and praxis, because we continue to misrecognise the Subject who theorises and labours and the Objects (material and ideal) with which they work. This is thus further confirmation of the dangers of separating out 'knowledge' as a unit of analysis. Secondly, one way of moving around this difficulty is to acknowledge, with Foucault, that one cannot speak about knowledge without also speaking about power. But *contra* some interpretations of Foucault, this does not mean they are the same or equivalent; what it does mean is that there always complex and shifting relations between them.

To illustrate these first two assertions consider how we might determine the 'value' of genetically modified (GM) soya. Initially, one route might be through distinguishing use-value from exchange-value, and asserting that the latter has clearly been drastically affected by attempts to prevent the separation of modified and non-modified beans, and hence prevent the separate labelling of products containing each. However, this quickly leads us to realise that these attempts, and the reactions to them, have also had significant effects upon common understandings of the use-value: where once we had a situation where the 'public', and especially US consumers, were generally unconcerned about GM soya, the resistance in Europe has now begun to provoke a questioning among those consumers. Clearly then, use-value is more complex than merely the evaluations and assessments of the scientists, engineers and other 'knowledge workers' engaged in producing GM soya; clearly, both use-value and exchange-value are related to the complex and shifting relations between knowledge and power in this specific case. Indeed, Busch and Juska (1997) have further demonstrated, in an analogous example, how the evaluations and assessments of the value of modified rape-seed or 'canola' (though not genetically modified) entailed reconfiguring the complex 'actor-network' of scientists, regulators, professional and commercial associations, R&D managers, growers, seed suppliers and potential customers. By doing this what they also illustrate is that the 'object', the commodity of canola cannot be properly understood outside of that complex actor-network, and similarly for the 'subjects' within that network. They are, in other words, moving towards rectifying the misrecognitions resulting from commodity fetishism.

This leads me to the third element of the argument. As Jacques correctly notes, an additional intellectual resource which we can draw upon is the (diverse group) of Actor-Network approaches, which precisely recognise the problems with hard and fast distinctions between Subject and Object, and between Nature and Society. In addition, however, some of the empirical and theoretical work within this broad approach argues that the process of 'framing' the characteristics and attributes of any specific commodity – what it is, what it does, who might want it – involves complex interactions between producers, regulators and consumers, or in more traditional economic terms, between supply and demand (Callon, 1999). So, if the very attributes of any commodity are thus configured, this must also apply to the value, in whatever terms, whether we are talking about use-value (need, demand) or exchange-value. This thus means that any 'theory of value' that we begin to formulate must pay attention to *both* production and consumption, whereas Jacques' current formulation is totally production-oriented; it focuses only on 'value-added' processes within production.

Indeed, a similar recognition of the importance of reconfigurations in both production and consumption has been at the heart of some developments within Marxist Political Economy since the late 1970s, especially in the example of Regulation Theory. Here, the interest is in examining deep shifts in the long-running regimes of capital accumulation, and the argument in essence is that there are periodically major shifts in the patterns of both production and consumption, corresponding to shifts in the generic underlying techno-economic arrangements underpinning both production and consumption. The notable example, of course, is the shift from 'Fordism' to 'post-Fordism', which is currently characterised, in part, by the increased 'knowledge-intensity' of 'flexible production methods' (interestingly, there are currently a number of attempts to bring together Regulation Theory and Actor-Network approaches – see Wilkinson, 1997). However, if the increased 'knowledge-intensity' of work is merely a secondary phenomenon albeit an important one, if it is merely a side-effect of broader shifts in the techno-economic arrangements for both production and consumption, then that lends further support to the argument for augmenting Jacques' proposals.

This illustrates that we have now come full circle, and with a triple difficulty. Firstly, the chief merit of the labour theory of value as originally proposed was that it enabled the identification of the hidden dynamics arising from the inherent contradictions of capital accumulation, and especially how those dynamics play out in production, in the field of work and organisations. But we have seen that we can no longer rely on that theory for that purpose. Consequently, we clearly require new forms for understanding contemporary changes within work and organisations, and this project proceeds apace in various formats – Critical Management Studies, Labour Process Theory and

Organisation Studies. Secondly then, there is also a requirement for new forms of understanding of the consequences and effects of capital accumulation – or 'wealth' as Mike Chumer has eloquently put it – and current developments within Political Economy and Regulation Theory may provide some possibilities. Finally, however, we cannot throw out the baby with the bath water. We cannot abandon any attempts to 'value' products and labour, goods and services (and the example of GM soya provides a stark illustration of this). It is not sufficient merely to describe the complex processes entailed in the shifting evaluations of GM soya. We also require means of establishing our own radical critical evaluations that will enable us to come to some form of judgement, however tentative, on its 'value', rather than abandoning such judgements to either genetic scientists or popular movements. In other words, any new 'theory of value' is precisely about replacing Marx's original and unfortunate reliance on theories of 'natural' needs, wants and desires, his overly scientific and naturalistic understanding of use-value. Consequently, if we can no longer rely on scientistic and naturalistic theories of needs, wants and desires, any theory of value must be 'speculative', posing questions and tentative answers in a 'reversible' manner that 'recognises the intrinsic and contingent limitations in its exercise' (Rose, 1995).

I suggested above the concept of a speculative 'knowledge and power theory of value'. Now that we are clearer on its purpose – as a form of evaluation, rather than an explanatory device to apply to work and organisations – we can also be clearer on its parameters. Firstly, or rather in parentheses, any such theory can clearly be also used to *evaluate* current changes within work and organisations, but this must proceed alongside the various developing forms of understanding those changes. Secondly, given Foucault's emphasis on the specificity of relations between knowledge and power, the quite different ways in which those relations are configured and reconfigured in specific instances, there is a requirement to remain open-minded about the particular configurations one might find for the particular 'objects' (or rather object-assemblages) or formats (forms of work organisation) one wishes to evaluate. This requires detailed empirical work, whether ethnographic or historical, and careful attention to method. Thirdly, any form of evaluation requires categories. The 'deconstructive' work of Derrida and before him Nietzsche showed clearly how existing categories shape our understanding of the world, but that does not provide much help in devising improved categories for the necessary task of judgement. We have a number of available categories for power relations – sovereign, disciplinary, mediated, consensual – and we may need to expand these. Categories of knowledge abound, unfortunately, and this means considerable work ahead in deconstructing these (especially the horrendous and inherently contradictory notion of tacit and explicit) and developing new ones, for instance that pay attention to ownership, format, power-effects, and what Foucault called 'truth-effects'. In other words, and finally, such a theory must also be part and parcel of attempts to renew our capacity for critical reasoning.

References

Rose, G. (1984) *Dialectic of Nihilism: Post-Structuralism and Law*, Oxford: Blackwell.
Rose, G. (1995) [1997, Vintage Edition], *Love's Work*, London: Chatto & Windus.
Busch, L. and Juska (1997) 'Beyond Political Economy: Actor Networks and the Global-ization of Agriculture', *Review of International Political Economy*, 4: 4, 688–708.
Callon, M. (1999) 'An Essay on Framing and Overflowing: Economic Externalities Revisited by Sociology', in Callon, M. (ed.) *The Laws of the Markets*, Oxford: Blackwell.
Marx, K. (1961) [1886] *Capital: a Critical Analysis of Capitalist Production*, Vol. 1, (transl. S. Moore and E. Aveling; ed. F. Engels); 1961 Edition: London: Lawrence & Wishart Ltd, for Foreign Languages Publishing House, Moscow.
Wilkinson, J. (1997) 'A New Paradigm for Economic Analysis?', *Economy and Society*, 26: 3, 305–39.

Response to Jacques

Mike Chumer

Roy Jacques makes the point, with which I agree, that the knowledge management discourse should permit space for constructing a knowledge theory of value. He sums up the central problematic by stating, 'Organisations perform complex tasks. Within organisations, people with differing interests and perspectives must collectively determine what tasks to perform and how to perform them effectively. They must then distribute the value produced among those involved in the production' (p. 209). He then exits to a note (note 6) which states, 'A legitimate complication that I wish, however, to by pass here, is that the organisation as a whole receives a certain amount of (primarily) financial wealth from society which is a proxy for value, but which is loosely correlated with actual value produced. The alignment of wealth with value is a topic in its own right' (p. 215).

I think that the strength of a knowledge theory of value resides in tackling (not bypassing) the central issue of that footnote, researching and explicating the correlation between societal value, organisational value, and the influence of both on knowledge management. In order to fully understand the relationship between societal and organisational value and value creation, a basic understanding of the assumptions underlying that relationship must be surfaced and critically reviewed. The key is to separate the knowledge impact on value construction from the point of view of the owners of capital and the knowledge impact on value construction from the point of view of the controllers of the organisation, the management of capital production. In the modern day organisation (except for entrepreneurial organisations) the ownership of capital is separate from the control (management) of the organisation. However the owners of capital, primarily stockholders, may construct value differently than the controllers of capital production (the 'techno-structure of work' as referred to by Jacques).

The dichotomy between the owners of capital and controllers of capital and its production is referenced and explained by John Kenneth Galbraith (Galbraith, 1985). Galbraith states, ' With the rise of the modern corporation, the emergence of the organisation required by modern technology and planning and the divorce of the owner of the capital from control of the enterprise, the entrepreneur no longer exists as an individual person in the mature industrial enterprise'. (Galbraith, 1985, p. 64). Galbraith introduces the term techno-structure, used by Jacques, as a way of defining the organisational entity involved, as controllers, in capital production by being major contributors to information within group decision making. Galbraith, in further defining the techno-structure, states that, '...it extends from the most senior officials of the corporation to where it meets, at the outer perimeter, the white and blue collar workers whose function is to conform more or less mechanically to instruction or routine. It embraces all who bring specialised knowledge, talent or experience, to group decision making. This, not the narrow management group, is the guiding intelligence-the brain-of the enterprise. There is no name for all who participate in group decision making or the organisation which they form. I [Galbraith] propose to call this organisation the techno-structure.' (Galbraith, 1985, p. 65). This organisational sub-entity, this techno-structure, whose size and shape differs from one organisation to another, is characterised by Galbraith as the decision-making body. It assimilates information and through the knowledge of its resources processes that information resulting in organisational action that has value. This value may result in new products or services, or in streamlining production processes, or in organisational concerted action in response to changing market conditions.

The problematic with constructing a knowledge theory of value is formed at the intersection, the nexus, between the owners of capital and the techno-structure. To what extent does the value created by the owners of capital, upon investment, influence the knowledge, resulting in value, created by the techno-structure? The reverse must also be researched, that being the influence of techno-structure knowledge and its value creation on the flow of capital into the organisation by prospective owners.

It is the flow of capital into and out of organisations, at least in the USA, that is influenced to a large degree by the financial community, mainly Wall Street, as it interprets various indices and data surfacing from the workplace. Though far from being a scholarly source of information, the US media report upon the reaction of Wall Street to certain forms of data released by the US Government as workplace indicators. Recently one of these indicators, the average wage of all workers, was released. It was reported that the average wage increased since the last reporting period. On the surface this would appear to be good news, reflecting a positive direction in the economy. A rise in wages should be a good thing for the employee. However, the collective wisdom of the financial community was different. The rise in wages was viewed as a bad thing for organisations. The overall reaction of Wall Street as influencers of capital flow was negative. The reason was that increases in salary indicate a deterioration of organisational profits. To Wall Street this was not a good thing. The rationalisation of the financial community was that increases in salary had a negative effect on the bottom line. Holding down salary, as an expense affecting the 'bottom line', was a better organisational course of action. By doing so profits would not deteriorate and organisations would position themselves more attractively as recipients of capital. Because of this news the market took a downturn which meant that some capital flowed out of organisation coffers.

What would be the reaction of the organisational techno-structure to the reason behind the outflow of capital, i.e. higher average wages being reported? Perhaps nothing initially, but the financial community mind-set can begin a chain reaction that will affect organisational cognition in some rather subtle ways. This chain reaction begins with the financial community and influences the owner's flow of capital, affecting organisational cognition and action. A form of cognitive creep finds its way into decision making which might affect the knowledge creation processes of the techno-structure. I can speculate as well as the next person and in so doing suggest that organisational decisions about salary increases as well as starting salaries would be negotiated downward. Perhaps the knowledge contribution by existing employees during decision making, which may result in some form of value to the organisation, might not result in a monetary reward. Such could be the subtle effects by capital owners on the controllers of the enterprise as they move forward in their decision making.

I feel very strongly that a knowledge theory of value must address head-on the 'legitimate complication' that Jacques seeks to avoid in his footnote. The complication explained as being '...the organisation as a whole receives a certain amount of (primarily) financial wealth from society which is only loosely correlated with actual value produced' is indeed ripe fodder for scholarly investigation. I do not believe that a knowledge theory of value can exclude or treat as a separate topic 'the alignment of wealth with value'. Both are linked and both form pillars that will hold up theory in this case.

Knowledge management as a discourse is presently being formed from the techno-structure point of view, the role that knowledge plays in group decision-making scenarios, and the ultimate creation of value. However, as a discursive function it did not give birth to itself but relied upon something else, another discursive function within which it grew and took shape. In the space residing above a management but just beneath a total societal discourse lies wealth creation. It is formed at the intersection of the organisation and society as a separate and distinct function in its own right. Wealth creation assumes that the flow of capital has a net positive effect and this is of value to the owners of capital. Attracting and producing capital are important roles of the organisational techno-structure. This duality in role structure has the potential of causing dissonance in the group decision-making processes underlying organisational action. As knowledge becomes positioned as vital contributor to organisational product, service, and process; its value becomes dependent upon its organisation and management. Now is knowledge managed for the sake of attracting and keeping capital, producing capital, or some mixture of both? If knowledge is managed for attracting and keeping capital then the wealth creation discourse would seem to influence the management of organisational knowledge. However, it is this formulation that Jacques suggests is a topic in its own right. If knowledge is managed for the sake of capital production then the present knowledge management discourse would influence the management of organisational knowledge. Researching this latter formulation seems to be the focus of Jacques' suggested knowledge theory of value. I tend to feel that the theory formulation must take into account both wealth creation and capital production, the assumptions of each, and the nature of mutual discursive influences. If scholarly investigation is directed into the heart of this discourse on duality influence, then I feel we will get close to a rich knowledge theory of value.

Reference

Galbraith, J. K. (1985) *The New Industrial State*, Boston, MA: Houghton Mifflin.

'A Theory in Search of a Problem?': a Response to Roy Jacques' 'Theorising Knowledge as Work, the Need for a Knowledge Theory of Value'

Craig Prichard

Just recently I heard that a technology research lab working for financial service companies was developing 'relationship technologies' to be embedded in 'intelligent furniture' – I kid you not! It seems that banks, building societies and financial salespeople want to use home appliances to deepen their relationships with us (for details, see `http://www.knowledgelab.com/`). They need to learn more about us, and we need, such initiatives suggest, to learn more about them. In this scenario, bits of high-tech 'furniture' like microwaves double as conduits for more intimate 'conversations'. What this suggests, of course, is that the companies have identified learning as crucial to building long-term commercial relationships. How people learn about a company, and how a company can intensify that learning and in the process make itself more indispensable (and us more dependent?) have become crucial 'problems' to which technological solutions might be found. While designers and engineers working these projects might regard their efforts as 'helping people learn how they can make better use of their money', such developments have a Brave New World-ly feel.

Now, I'm not about to suggest that Roy Jacques and the furniture scientists share the same post-industrial dream, or are working on the same problem. But I have a similar kind of problem with the scientists' work, as I do with Jacques' engaging, provocative and thoroughly plausible work on the need for a knowledge theory of value. What the 'intelligent furniture' scientists might be said to have forgotten is the commodity status of the relations they are involved in attempting to secure, maintain and extend via technology. What has been put aside (but definitely not forgotten) at crucial points in Jacques' writing is, likewise, the *commodity status* of labour power. Let's just clear up this issue of labour power first. Jacques' core argument, if I can paraphrase it mercilessly, is that Marx's definition of labour power is insufficient to understand today's circumstances. Marx describes labour power as 'the aggregate of those mental and physical capabilities existing in a human being, which he (sic) exercises

232

whenever he produces a use-value of any description' (Marx, [Capital, Vol. 1 Ch. 6], 1978, p. 336). This is certainly a broad definition. But it is nevertheless possible to accept Jacques' point on this (that Marx's definition related to his era and society and thus has less purchase on our own) *and* challenge Jacques' move to replace 'labour' with 'knowledge' in Marx's labour theory of value. To do this we need to agree that for Marx labour was not the crucial issue. For Marx it was the *commodity status* of labour, and not the theory of labour in and of itself which was of utmost import. Issues such as the character of the labour, where it is located, how it can be divided up and reorganised, whether it is about learning or knowledge or professional, white, blue, or pink collar activities are important but inevitably secondary problems.

What is crucial is that knowledgeable activity *must* be sold like other commodities to be of value. It is this which must be foregrounded, and it is this which many chapters in this collection of critical essays argue has the greatest bearing on the character of so-called knowledge-work, knowledge management and the knowledge economy.

The problem for me with Jacques' engaging writing is that the work tends to address capitalism's organisations and management, and not its commodity relations. If we foreground this latter field then we do not necessarily need to raise, in the first instance at least, questions surrounding the capitalisation of learning or knowledge. Of course Jacques is not setting out to undermine this part of Marx's formulations. But there is nevertheless a sense that this issue has been passed over. While not central to his discussion, Jacques notes however that, 'Marx's formulation of capitalism as a mode of relationships not inherently tied to industrialism provides a still-useful framework' (p. 213).

In short, then, Jacques' call for a 'knowledge theory of value' ought to begin with the assumption that it is the commodified character of activities and things which is at the core of Marx's labour theory of value. But there is another issue in this relating to *the reason* a labour theory of value was written in the first instance and the character of critique.

Capital was written by a man who dipped his pen in molten anger, as Darendorf once wrote. The target of Marx's anger was of course the wage–labour relation. It was this that dehumanized, he argued. When the tip of Marx's pen scorched a fiery path across his manuscripts it was propelled by his utter rage at how so-called civil society, supported by bourgeois economic theory, could justify such theft as that which constituted the wage–labour relation. And more than this, Marx railed against the oppression that a society based on such theft wrought upon the bodies and minds of people whose submission was gained through their utter human need to carry on living. Of course, Jacques does reference equity and a fairer distribution of value as a core rationale for evoking the need for a knowledge theory of value. But how might we get to questions of equity and the distribution of value from a 'knowledge theory of value'? How might such a theory do justice to the moral and political imperative that comes with the term, ' a labour theory of value'?

For me, such an imperative provokes a questioning of terms like: 'knowledge economy' (who could be against knowledge?). It provokes a questioning of furniture scientists and their desires that we develop more intimate relations with the banks. It provokes a questioning of the shift from dull monotonous labour to utopian continuous learning environments?

Now, I'm not suggesting that commodity relations explain everything! But the point is that these relations gather together other practices and processes to support their realisation. It is around this issue that a knowledge theory of value potentially provides an exciting conceptual incision. Commodity relations themselves might be regarded as blunt instruments. Faster and more intense consumption and production seems to demand that a huge range of 'other' practices and processes be drawn in. For example, psychic anxiety, intensified individuation, existential angst and eroticism are among those employed at different phases (including at work) in realising economic value. A knowledge theory of value potentially opens up discussion of the way these 'other' knowledges – particularly these highly embodied ways of knowing – are drawn into and become part of processes for realising value, be this at work, at play or embedded deeply in familial and intimate relations with ourselves and significant others.

On this the practitioners – the furniture scientists in this case – seem to be one step ahead of us 'theorists'. While we argue about where to place knowledge in our theories of value, they are promoting themselves as: 'pioneering innovative techniques for extracting valuable knowledge from customer data, in order to build richer and more sustained relationships between financial services companies and their customers' (KnowledgeLab, 1999). It is patently clear to them that knowledge and value go together, and they go together best in the commodity form. As we read on we learn that 'sustained relationships' are based solely on profit. The introduction of 'relationship technologies' is set against the calculation of 'lifetime value'. This is 'the profit a business expects to make with a customer from the present time until the customer either dies or ends the relationship'. No prizes for guessing then that it will be the rich whose relationships the banks are courting, and whose kitchen microwaves might well sport donated e-commerce-able ATMs, or whose clothes include wearable computers.

References

KnowledgeLab (1999) Financial Services Knowledge Lab, http://www.knowledgelab.com/top.htm.

Marx, K. (1978) *The Marx Engels Reader*, 2nd edn, (ed. R. Tucker), New York: Norton and Co.

Roy Jacques writes back

Roy Jacques

I have enjoyed reading these responses to my comments. In general, they leave me with three thoughts we might pursue were we able to continue corresponding. These are (a) the points with which I disagree, (b) the points which highlight the shortcomings of my initial thoughts and (c) the points which underscore paradigmatic differences between us.

On the first point, there is very little with which I disagree completely in these responses. I am surprised, however, to see that in Richard's view I naturalize labour-power. I must become clearer on this point as it seems to me that he and I are in substantial agreement that labour-power has a historical and cultural locus. The central issue I wish to question is attachment to this way of thinking about work while relationships of production change. Just as labour was a metaphor that aided understanding of industrial relations of production, other metaphors may be useful for understanding the world into which we are heading. I think the remainder of Richard's comments deserve careful consideration.

Ultimately, both returning to the roots of Marxian thinking and attempting to sever our thinking from those roots are important exercises for trying to shake the dust off of our habitual assumptions about life and work.

On the second point, I think it can be seen from all three responses that there are substantial issues for us to work through merely in order to have a sketchy outline of the relationships structuring the emerging world of work. I plead guilty as charged to most of the sins of both commission and omission raised by these commentators. All I demand is that we continue to debate the points without reverence for now-traditional assumptions about what it is we are trying to understand. Let us continue to try to generate ideas and to judge them by what we can do with them, rather than by their correspondence to a canon.

Finally, I am again reminded that while my colleagues who are responding to this are primarily interested in understanding from a radical perspective – that is, a willingness to return to the roots of knowledge and conceive of the good society *de novo* – I am less bold. Perhaps it is because I write from the USA, where alternatives to conservatism – let alone capitalism – are extremely marginal. Perhaps it is for other reasons. Nonetheless, I think it would be fair to say that my goals are more liberal than radical and, as a consequence, my assumptions incorporate certain capitalist relationships because I do not imagine any likely future outside of them. I am ambivalent about this compromise, but my primary interest is to formulate knowledge that I can take into a work reality that I expect to remain capitalist. Rather than wasting time asking which view is 'right', I see it as more useful to incorporate dialogue about these trade-offs and assumptions into our dialogue so that we may better understand the sources of our differences and work, not to resolve them, which is unlikely and perhaps undesirable, but to build bridges of understanding and connection between them.

Index